WORDS
APART

WORDS APART

THE LANGUAGE OF PREJUDICE

JONATHON GREEN

KYLE CATHIE LTD

For Kyle

First Published in Great Britain in 1996 by
Kyle Cathie Limited
20 Vauxhall Bridge Road
London SW1V 2SA

ISBN 1 85626 216 2

A CIP catalogue record for this title is available from the British Library.

Designed by Libanus Press Ltd, Marlborough
Printed and bound in Great Britain by WBC Book Manufacturers Limited, Bridgend, Mid Glamorgan

CONTENTS

CONTENTS

AUTHOR'S NOTES

TO COMPILE a book of this nature, as should be apparent, is to walk blindfold into a minefield. It is impossible, and I have never believed otherwise, that someone, somewhere, will not be offended. That has never been my intention, although I trust that my own anti-racist feelings are made unequivocally clear. At least everyone, as readers will soon discover, gets as equal as possible coverage. And of one thing I remain utterly unrepentant. To anyone who believes, for whatever reason, however sincerely felt, that such words and feelings should be swept beneath the carpet I can only quote the opinion of the late Lenny Bruce: 'Everyone wants what should be, but what should be doesn't exist. There's no such thing as "what should be", there is only what is.' These words and phrases, might I suggest, represent all too grimly what is. None of us should be proud, but equally so, none should be fearful either.

In designing the text, I have made ample use of both **bold** and *italics*. As far as possible the bold type indicates a 'word apart' – the essential vocabulary that forms the meat of the book – while the italic indicates either a source, a synonym (often a slang term) or a foreign, slang or standard term that, while pertinent to the material under consideration, does not actually have a direct racial or national meaning. Languages such as Russian, Greek and Chinese have been transliterated. Given the volume of material I have attempted to maintain consistency; if there are any errors, they are all mine.

As ever I owe thanks to a number of people, especially those individuals who have offered me words and phrases; I am duly grateful. Two people, however, stand pre-eminent. Kyle Cathie, who as my editor and now publisher has been letting me explore the more exotic by-ways of the language for more than fifteen years; and Kate Oldfield, whose wit and intelligence, not to mention patience, make her a truly wonderful editor.

INTRODUCTION

W ORDS APART is a study of the language of nationalism and race. Not simply racism, but any words, whether from the standard, the colloquial or the slang vocabularies, that have been influenced by the differences between one 'tribal' grouping and another. Primarily taken from English, whether of the UK or USA, there are a number of foreign terms, proving, if nothing else, that xenophobia is by no means an anglophone monopoly. There are upwards of four thousand such words and phrases included here – I have chosen to omit several hundred proverbs and allied national and racial *donnés* – and before turning to any ancillary topic one must ask: what makes a 'word apart', what qualities assure entry to this controversial, all too wide-ranging lexicon? In the first place, as one might expect, we are dealing with the hardcore of racist terminology: the *niggers* and *kikes*, the *dagoes* and *honkies*, the *micks* and *spicks*. These are the essentials, the debasing currency that underpins the rest, and they alone will certainly make this a challenging read. But there is more to *Words Apart* than that.

The core vocabulary of abuse may be simple enough, but beyond it lies a more complex world, that of the racial and national stereotype, and while stereotyping may be of its nature unappealing, it exists and, as the terminology will make clear, takes race-related linguistics into an area far greyer and more subtle than the black-and-white certainties of gut-level malevolence. This wider vocabulary includes *Jewish typewriters*, *Irish hurricanes*, *Mexican credit-cards*, *French letters* and much more. Further still from the hate-motivated centre, comes what one might call racism by default. *German measles*, the *luck of the Irish* and *going Dutch* are all part of the everyday vocabulary – none but the obsessively politically correct would equate them with rougher terms – but nonetheless they too have their roots in nationalist imagery. This is the world, one might suggest, of teasing rather than torment. Indeed, this is the greyest of areas, with time serving to erode the negative imagery of a word's origin. In so many cases the users of these dusty old terms quite literally 'don't know what they're talking about'. Finally, at the furthest distance from the centre come words that, whatever their etymology, have no racial overtone, simply a link to a given country, place or person. For instance *Doolally*, meaning mad, refers ultimately to the Indian town of Deolali; it has no overt racist inference, but its geographical background has won it a place. All these themes, and more, are covered in the pages that follow.

The overall nature of the language ranges from standard to slang. Like the vocabulary of obscenity, many of the hardest-edged race terms are not really slang as such, but find themselves in a no-man's land, part embarrassment, part taboo, that has set them beyond the bounds of the mainstream lexicon. Thus, like the obscenities, they have been absorbed into slang. But, as the text will make clear, race-related terms cut right across the linguistic spectrum, from the coded, mandarin pontifications of the leader columns to the barely literate grunts of the gutter. The aim of *Words Apart* is to look at every aspect. To do this I have chosen to distinguish my researches not on simple race-lines – the Jews, the Irish, the Blacks, the Poles – but to look at the way the vocabulary can be seen as falling into certain identifiable clusters. These clusters in turn reflect the various patterns into which racism and nationalism fall. Race obviously imposes certain structures – like it or not the stereotypes mean that there is, for instance, an excess of 'Jew' words in 'Money' and 'Mexican' ones under 'The Poor' – but things are fortunately not that simplistic. Starting with the most fundamental of differences – colour and language – I have moved onto the words based on national and personal (i.e. obviously race-related) names, thence to a collection of negative characteristics – branding people as arrogant, as cheats or liars – and onwards to the ways in which certain groups are linked to certain foods, drinks and even drugs. Other groupings are linked to differences in the body, sex and clothing. The roles of religion, of anthropomorphism (linking animals and racial types), of work, politics, intelligence (or more usually the lack of it) and other predominant categories (see *Contents*) are all represented. The aim has been to show how the bigger picture – race and nation – can be broken into such groupings and, with as many foreign equivalents as possible, to show the universality of such characterizations.

To state the limits of the language to be considered is relatively easy.

To assess its causes is harder. Why does it exist? And in suchprofusion? Optimistic pieties aside, we do not very much like one other. The much-vaunted 'family of man' is not a happy assembly, at best it resembles a grumpy Christmas get-together, at worst humanity divides into an infinity of face-offs, pitted one-on-one in innumerable civil wars. The natural state of man, as Thomas Hobbes put it in *Leviathan* (1651), is war. While self-interest or external authority may modify or even suspend that state, it remains at the heart of human relations. Never more so than as evinced by the subject of this book, racism, or more properly by the linguistic terms that racism, across the world, has thrown up. It is all very simple. We don't like 'the other'. For all the cheery nostrums promoting 'variety' as the 'spice of life' what most of us seem to want is what we know, the easy comfort of certainty. And when we get something else, up rise the hackles, the mailed fist protrudes from the velvet glove, and sadly, but inevitably, we go, in nuclear bunker terms, to DefCon One.

Xenophobia can be seen to work on two levels. As the lexicologist Geoffrey Hughes has pointed out, 'The basic conceptual division in the field is between general terms, such as *alien* and *intruder*, and the more specific words of insult, such as *frog*, *hun* and *gook*.' To put it another way, the first reflects the act of intrusion by an alien into one's own culture; the second stems from the stereotype of the intruder. The concept of invasion tends to provide the chronologically earlier terms: thus such generalities as *heathen*, *paynim* and *infidel* were all established prior to the earliest recorded 'specifics', such as *Bugger* (from Bulgaria), *Turk*, *Greek* and *Coolie*. And while the coinage of general terms gradually dried up, references to specific stereotypes hugely expanded. Thus with the exception of the general term *native*, first recorded *c.*1800, such mainstays as *savage*, *alien*, *intruder*, *interloper*, *barbarian* and *foreigner* had all been coined by 1600; while conversely the specific terminology, still relatively limited in 1600, began its wide expansion in the 18th century. This expansion seems have peaked around 1900, with the great migrations from Europe to America, and has yet to abate.

Words Apart concentrates primarily on the latter forms, the vocabulary that accrues to given races, rather than more general terms, although some of these will be found. These are not pretty words. To steal once more from Hobbes, it is not just human lives, but humans' words that can be 'nasty, brutish and short'. And in many ways and for many people, especially in the decades since World War II, the exposure of these words represents the breaking of a new form of taboo. The cheerful, thoughtless racism of forty or fifty years ago, and of even more recent eras, has been largely marginalized. That said, this awareness of its negative force is relatively new. The word racism itself was only coined in 1936, significantly in a study of American fascism. This does not mean, of course, that this vocabulary is not used, and widely used as well, but that the words, once voiced almost unconsciously (so inbred and so defended were our assumptions) now create their own frisson. Eurocentricity is no longer taken as read; open anti-semitism, whether highbrow – see T.S. Eliot – or populist – see Agatha Christie and many of her best-selling peers – has at least become somewhat quieter (or neatly repackaged as 'anti-Zionism' – see sections of the broadsheet press). The throwaway references to 'niggers' or 'chinks' that were second nature to Kipling, and many more recent users, not all of them so overtly jingoistic, cannot be used so blithely now.

Yet the vocabulary, however pernicious, does exist, and it is my purpose to explore it as closely as one would the subjects of any lexicographical study. That these are words that come with baggage far greater than most, that people have been shot, hanged, gassed on the basis of such terminology – and will undoubtedly continue so to suffer – cannot detract from the need for analysis. Many of these words are deeply offensive,but this is not a racists' handbook. As when considering the terminology of political correctness, one may safely assume that those who most require such admonition are least likely to note it. Racism, especially in a declining country such as Britain, where the pervasive culture lends itself to the empty reiteration of fantasies of 'our' superiority, is not merely aggressive; for many, fearing to face the new, depressing realities, it is a form of last-ditch, desperate self-defence. If 'we' persist in perpetuating the tired old stereotypes of 'them' as 'bad', then there's always a chance that 'they', swamped by such propaganda, will believe so too, especially in those lines that say that 'we' are not merely 'good' but in every way 'the best'. Decline and self-defence, however, hold no copyright on racism. American parochialism may render the remainder of the globe nigh-on invisible but such insularity hardly makes for domestic tolerance. With grim irony a land of immigrants and of 'aliens', tops the abusers' league, each racial group apparently loathing its peers and subjecting every new wave of arrivals to the litany of dislike. American coinages are responsible for an overwhelming proportion of this book.

The word *xenophobia*, the fear of strangers, is a 20th-century invention, but the emotion is as old as humanity. The idea of simply hating foreigners is basic: they're foreigners – and for many people that's good enough. Though how many, for example, of Britain's Little Englanders or France's *poujadistes* have ever left their suburban fastnesses to check the validity of their isolationist whinging? But when those same foreigners start impinging on one's own territory, whether as invaders or immigrants (or even tourists), then the emotional temperature really rises. What might have been no more than unfocussed fear – they're not like me, there must be something wrong with them – becomes totally pointed loathing.

Yet, if this knee-jerk dislike does underpin all racist terminology, then there is a definite pattern in its development. Once again one can see an analogy with swearing. In the Medieval or Renaissance world, when religion truly mattered, oaths, based on 'God' or 'Christ' and thus *de facto* blasphemous, had a powerful resonance. Today's obscenities, based mainly on sex and excreta, may shock, but the moral subtext is missing. To quote Geoffrey Hughes once more, 'The categories change from those of strong moral stereotyping (with religious connotations) in earlier times to comparatively superficial characteristics of diet and appearance in modern times.' The images of savagery, cruelty and wanton destruction that underpin *Vandal, Goth*, and *Hun* or of primitive backwardness implied in *Hottentot* or *bog-trotter* are much more virulent than the comparatively 'jokey' ones that, based for instance on food, give *macaroni, frog, limey* and *kraut*. In addition one sees the way a basic fear of 'the other' can be refined into the various forms those others take. Forgetting political or religious differences, there is the not unreasonable dislike of the invader, who offers only fire and the sword but demands one's land and stability. Beyond this comes the fear of immigration: now 'they' displace 'us' from jobs and, with those vestiges of their culture that they have imported, 'pervert' or ruin ours. As our 'justifications' for racism expand, the terms, it would seem, become more general, or at least more willing to grasp at linguistic straws. If the Germanic tribe of Vandals lent their name to the xenophobe's vocabulary (*c*.1700) it was for their razing of cities and destruction of empires; when the Italians became *spags* two centuries later it was through no more than their appetite for pasta. Hardly the same thing, although the end-product and indeed the stimulus, mutual loathing, are identical.

Race is based on stereotypes; without them the majority of these terms would not exist. And while stereotypes, by their very nature, are rarely accurate, there is a fundamental desire to create these pared-down characterizations. In this world of aggression, what matters is not the ingredients, but the brand-name. Like the Goths or the Tartars, who gained their image from their role as invaders, the Vikings, whose invasion broke the Anglo-Saxon hold on Britain, were universally loathed. While still debatable, the linguistic root of Viking is seen as either the Old English *wic*: a camp or settlement, or the Old Norse *vik*: a creek. Such niceties were irrelevant to those who labelled them. The lexicographer Abbot Aelfric, compiling his *Dictionarium Saxonico-Lat-ino-Anglicum* soon after 1000, defined the word as 'pirata', i.e. a pirate. The *Anglo-Saxon Chronicle* (*c*.891-1164), a continuing 'diary' of national events, uses for *its* definition the unadorned 'heathen'. Neither creeks nor camps entered the argument.

This primacy of propaganda over accuracy persists across the racial and chronological spectrum. Not every one of these words has the same effect, nor have all been as deadly as the sedulous preaching against the Jewish 'Christ-killers' which led inexorably to Auschwitz and Tre-blinka, or the doctrine of Black inferiority which helped fill the slave-barracoons of the West African coastline and justify the horrors of the 'Middle Passage' – but the general effect is all too simple: brand a people long enough and anything is possible. The most obvious example may be the 'softly-softly' approach of Germany's Nazi rulers, gradually piling one racist law upon the last, until the 'final solution' no doubt seemed a logical step. But whatever the context the drip-drip-drip effect of these words is to numb their users (and hearers) to their full

14

import. It is only recently that, for most people, *nigger in the woodpile* has become unacceptable, while the yachting fraternity still use the phrase *boat nigger* to describe the least important member of the crew. The generalized equation of black as 'bad' and white as 'good' will probably never vanish. And so it goes on.

Rejecting stereotypes is hard. Even the great dictionaries have only relatively recently begun to modify what were once unchallenged entries for terms such as the verbal use of *Jew* (long since a source of bitter controversy) or one definition of *Hottentot*: 'a person of inferior intellect or culture; one degraded in the scale of civilization, or ignorant of the usages of civilized society.' This last is now modified by a parenthesis: '(This derogatory sense, which was based on a failure to understand an alien culture, appears now to be very rare.)' However this not a crusading book, but a lexicological one, and if these words exist, then like any other they are deserving of study. One should not be too pious. The line between a stereotype and a national characteristic is razor-blade thin, but there is a line. Certain peoples have certain characteristics; to deprive them of those social identifiers is to deprive them of an essential part of their identity; the mistake, of course, is to use those characteristics either as bludgeons to attack, or as props to support our own insecurities.

In verbal wars as well as physical ones, truth is the first casualty. To focus on one's own backyard one need only glance at the grubby editorializing of the British tabloid press, with its endless railing at the wicked Frogs or Krauts, to see the persistence of the old evils. Not that the tabloids are the sole repository of British, or rather English racism. It is surely no coincidence that the Nazi-oriented National Front, so popular during the 1970s, an era of predominantly Labour govern-ment, found itself redundant once Margaret Thatcher's Tories came to power. Thatcher herself led the way, with her fears of immigrants 'swamping' the country, but her successors proved equally amenable. The spectacle, at the time of writing, of an immigrant, Jewish-born Home Secretary dedicatedly proclaiming values and policies that would have delighted those same racists whose ideology drove his father to seek refuge in the UK, is particularly sickening.

Writing against the cacophony of 'Europhobia' it is ever-more clear that England remains, perhaps more than any other similar country, imbued with the stuff; and that social grouping known as 'Middle England' is as dedicatedly xenophobic as the proles. There is only a tiny space between the patrons of the golf club's 'nineteenth hole' and of the public bar, or the baying back-benches of the House of Commons and the football terraces. Were it not so intrinsically vile, such hollow self-aggrandisement would be the most pitiable of conceits.

In the end these words are here to stay. Indeed some of them have gained a remarkable longevity – but then again, so too have the stereotypes to which they respond. The outlawing of such terms, while in essence a positive move, is unlikely to abolish their use. We wish, if liberal, that such vilification should not exist; we know, as observers and listeners, that it does. The last decade has seen a substantial rebirth of nationalism – and racist terminology feeds most assiduously on nationalism, at the same time as it sustains the whole apparatus of prejudice: the love of 'us' and hatred of 'them'. That process is likely to intensify, rather than fade.

Lexicology is, ideally, a neutral discipline. Whatever the words, one notes, analyzes and lays out the relevant findings. Reality, of course, is not so chilly. The lexicologist is not a robot and he or she will always be hard put to exclude every vestige of emotion. Never more so than in a work such as this, where the the language is so unremittingly negative. But if the definitions are almost unreservedly distasteful, the words themselves, like those of any language, are infinitely fascinating. It is the illumination of these areas of communication, however murky, that is my overall aim.

A Note On The Text: the dating of slang (and much of what follows is slang or at least colloquialism) is notoriously difficult. The dating (and indeed spelling) of foreign-language slang is even harder. No polylinguist, I have relied on my sources. Thus I can only apologise to those who find archaisms, mis-transcriptions, and other errors. I trust that, however distracting, they do not diminish the overall value of the book.

COLOUR

L ET'S LOOK at it this way. In a book primarily concerned with
words, how better can one begin than to consider at once at a
couple of fundamental examples. Here, then, are some of the non-racial
uses of 'black' and 'White', as listed in the *Oxford English Dictionary*.
The bracketed dates indicate of first use.

Black: foul, iniquitous, atrocious, horribly wicked (1581); having
dark or deadly purposes, malignant; pertaining to or involving death,
deadly; baneful, disastrous, sinister (1583); clouded with sorrow or
melancholy; indicating disgrace, censure, liability to punishment
(1612); dismal, gloomy, sad (1659); of the countenance...clouded with
anger, frowning; threatening, boding ill; the opposite of bright and
hopeful (1709); to look black: to frown, to look angrily (at or upon a
person) (1814). And for White: orally or spiritually pure or stainless;
spotless, unstained, innocent (971); fair-seeming, plausible (1374);
highly prized, precious; dear, beloved, favourite, pet, darling. Often as
a vague term of endearment (1425); free from malignity or evil intent;
beneficent, innocent, harmless (1651); propitious, favourable; auspi-
cious, fortunate, happy (1629); honourable; square-dealing (1877).

There is, undoubtedly, a degree of 'chicken-and-egg' here, but the majority of these definitions predated the racist terms that follow, and it is asking a great deal, with so embedded a range of assumptions, to expect that the Black/White divide, in racial terms, would be the source either of sweetness or light. Colour is the most obvious of all racial differences. Even more than the trumped-up outrage and medical quackery based on physical differences – thick lips, large noses, slanted eyes – it demonstrates difference in the most literal of 'in your face' ways. It has justified untold massacres, enslavements, crusades and pious missions. Few have turned out to be of benefit, other perhaps than in giving profits to the slavers and pious self-satisfaction to the missionaries. In linguistic terms it has generated, probably to no-one's great surprise, more slurs than any other category of vilification.

Wash the Ethiopian White

The first term to identify the alien Black man, as opposed to the familiar White, is **Ethiopian**, or rather **Ethiop**. And it may not be mere coincidence that the first citation of its use comes in Wyclif's then revolutionary vernacular edition of the Bible, published amid much controversy in 1382, where he translates *Jeremiah* xiii. 23 as 'Yf chaunge mai an Ethiope his skyn.' The full quote, as written in the Authorized Version of 1611, runs 'Can the Ethiopian change his skin, or the leopard his spots? *then* may ye also do good, that are accustomed to do evil.' Already, Black is bad. Indeed, retreating into the classics one finds the image popular in Rome, where the everyday saying declared **Ethiops non dealbavit**: 'the Ethiopian cannot be washed White'. Ethiop was never a simple description nor a neutral image. In 1490 Caxton places these strange individuals in 'the last part of the earth' and twenty years later Stephen Hawes writes in *The Pastime of Pleasure* that, 'Out there flew, ryght blacke and tedyous, A foule Ethyope.' In 1600 Shakespeare, in *As You Like It*, turns person into character with 'Ethiop words, blacker in their effect | Than in their countenance.' And at the same time one way of delineating an attempt at the impossible was to **wash the Ethiop White**. This image persists throughout Europe and over several centuries. A popular illustration in early 16th-century Italy was captioned 'You wash an Ethiopian. Why the vain labour? Desist. No-one can lighten the darkness of black night'; in France the saying went 'Wanting to bleach a Negro, the barber loses his soap', while in 18th-century Holland, as in England, the equation of such a vain enterprise with searching for the impossible was a widely accepted pronouncement.

This 'washing' motif is remarkably old and has maintained a frightening longevity. As early as 711, when a Black man was taken prisoner by the Goths at the siege of Cordoba, a chronicler reports that, having 'never seen a Black man before', they set about washing off his colour. As Jan Nederveen Pieterse has pointed out (*White on Black*, 1992) this was not merely ignorance: it laid down a pattern that has yet to disappear, the inability of Whites to accept Blacks for what they are. This determination to transform the Black and eliminate any differences underpins so much of what has followed. The impossibility of so doing, laid out in the line from *Jeremiah*, is equally frustrating. And apart from any other considerations – that Black equalled bad, inferior, unassimilable – was perhaps the most frustrating of all concepts: that the hapless Blacks didn't actually *want* to change their colour. 'Cleanliness is indeed next to godliness', urged John Wesley, sermonizing on dress in 1791, but it is unlikely that he would have realized that as well as coining a cliché that would serve for generations of earnest moralists, he was also offering soap manufacturers a whole new slant on merchandising their product. Well into the 20th century such companies would take the image of the poor darky, desperate to bleach his skin, as an apparently acceptable advertising image. And sometimes, with the artistic licence of such creations, he might even succeed. He would not, however, be admired: the term **washed**, coined recently by America's Black community, refers to one who has been absorbed into White culture and assimilated by the mainstream both to the detriment of one's Black sensibility.

Hay Moros en la Costa

The **Moors** were originally defined as natives of Mauretania, a region of Northern Africa corresponding to parts of modern Morocco and

Algeria. Latterly the word referred to people of mixed Berber and Arab race, Muslim in religion, and making up the bulk of the population of North-western Africa. It was these Moors who in the 8th century conquered Spain and engendered, among other things, the Spanish warning **hay moros en la costa**: 'there are Moors on the coast', i.e. look out! As aliens, and Africans too, Moors – who would today be seen as Arabs from the Maghreb (Arabic for 'western') – were generally assumed to be black, or certainly very swarthy, and by the 16th century the nationality was duly synonymous with the colour.

By the end of that century, for all that Shakespeare's Othello 'the Moor of Venice', was a celebrated general, the average European's experience of the Moor was as a servant. Brought home as trophies by early traders and explorers, Moorish servants, usually boys or teenagers, became popular status symbols and one can see their images in a number of contemporary paintings, especially as waiting on their rich White mistresses. By the 18th century the black servant, whether in England, in Holland, in France or Prussia, was as common an artefact as the family pet – and often held approximately the same position in the domestic hierarchy. Unlike the pet, however, he had a secondary function, at least in the visual arts, where his appearance, for instance in Hogarth's *Rake's Progress* or *Harlot's Progress* (as well as less 'satirical' works) was to add an element of sexuality to the scene. Like the Ethiop and soap, the Moor has also appeared in advertising, but in a far more positive context, the image promoted being more 'exotic foreigner' or 'King of the Moors' than 'servile/alien Black'. Nonetheless Coleridge, writing in 1795, used the adjective **moorish**, to mean barbarous and cruel; this use, however, would seem to have been a one-off. Today the Moor, other than in archaic use, has largely vanished, although the French term **être pris comme le More**: 'to be taken in like the Moor' means to be outwitted when least expecting it. The Moor in this context lives in Morocco.

Black a Moors

Ethiop did not survive the 17th century, other than in literary use, but it would not lack for successors. For a while **Blackamoor**, originally

Black Moor, defined as 'a black-skinned African, an Ethiopian, a Negro; any very dark-skinned person' ran in parallel to Ethiop, appearing in its Black Moor form in Andrew Boorde's *Introduction to Knowledge* in 1547. Blackamoor, actually spelt Black a Moor, arrives in 1581 (as another example of the impossibility of 'washing' such a figure) and by the 17th century it is in regular use, by Dekker, Pepys and many others. Occasionally it could even mean the devil. Blackamoor, once again other than in literary use, had faded by the mid-18th century, but linguistically, as well as chronologically it provides the perfect bridge between the relatively antique Moor and the modern Black.

Negromania

Writing up the letter N for the *OED* in 1906 the lexicographer William Craigie defined **Negro** as 'an individual (esp. a male) belonging to the African race of mankind, which is distinguished by a black skin, black woolly hair, flat nose and thick protruding lips'. Its etymology lay in the Spanish or Portuguese *negro* and before that the Latin *nigrum*, both meaning black. It was cognate with the French *nègre* and for a short period, roughly 1540-1620, was occasionally spelt **nigro**. Readers were recommended, without comment, to look also at Neger and Nigger.

Much of Craigie's definition remains today, although the second half, bowing to contemporary standards (although the cynical might see little more than euphemism) now reads 'black tightly-curled hair, and a nose flatter and lips thicker and more protruding than is common amongst White Europeans'. The signpost to 'nigger' remains. On either count the term itself is in general disrepute and when encountered has, at best, a somewhat musty air, as if disinterred from the back of a rarely opened cupboard. That said, it remained perfectly respectable for nearly half a millennium and only began to lose that image when the vicissitudes of Black self-determination and the struggle for civil rights began putting Black self-description, at least in America, through the series of changes of nomenclature that has currently paused at *African American* and *person of color,* but is unlikely to stay there permanently.

Negro entered English in 1555, when it was apostrophized alongside a reference to Ethiopians. Fifty years later Middleton and Dekker's *Roaring Girl* (the story of the real-life pickpocket Moll Cutpurse) uses it for yet another version of the 'washing' metaphor. The term, however, does not properly come on stream until the 19th century. And even then, given its relative respectability, if 'negro' usages are at all insulting, it is more often by default rather than deliberation. (In offering such a generalization, one is of course entering dangerous ground but if one is to give the genuinely racist terms their full import, then to be sidetracked by these 'throwaway' references would surely be a mistake. One must also, like it or not, note the period in which such casual labels were thus bandied.)

They often refer to flora or fauna, and just as similar references to Jews drag in such 'typical' attributes as a long nose, equate the plant or creature with either the blackness of negro skin or the 'wooliness' of negro hair. Among them one finds **negro ant**: a common black ant; **negro hair**: western sedge and **negro vine**: an herbaceous vine with hairy foliage and purple flowers. Similar terms include **negro bat**, a European and Asiatic bat (*Vesperugo maurus*) of a black or sooty-brown colour; **negro coffee**, the seeds of *Cassia occidentalis*; **negro monkey**, a black monkey of the Malay Peninsula or Java, the **negro tamarin**, a tamarin monkey (*Midas ursulas*) of the lower Amazon; and the **negro yam**, the West India yam (*Dioscorea sativa*). None of these is *de facto* offensive; the negro yam, for instance, is in recognized use in Jamaica.

Others, often rooted in American slavery, are far less neutral. A **negro dog** is a dog used in hunting runaway negro slaves; **negro cloth** or **negro felt** is a form of tough, coarse grey cloth purpose-woven to be worn by Black slaves, while **negro cachexy** (lit. 'the depraved habits of Blacks') described a propensity for eating dirt (known properly as geophagy), peculiar to the natives of the West Indies and Africa. A variety of standard suffixes also provide for a further group, not negative in linguistic terms, but, given the racial backdrop against which they appeared, bearing an undoubted air of pejoration; all stem from the 19th century. Among them are **Negroism**, either a Negro peculiarity of speech or a support of Black civil rights; **Negrocide**, the killing of a Negro; **Negrodom,** the region or community of Negroes; **Negrofy**, to make into, or as black as, a Negro; **Negrohood**, the Negro

22

race or stock. Some terms were used of Whites: **Negroite** or **Negro-phile**: one who professed affection for Blacks and their interests, **Negrolatry**, excessive admiration of the Negro; **Negromania**, extravagant **Negrophilism** and thus **Negromaniac**.

And some are unequivocal. The 19th century's **negro-fellow** was defined as 'an opprobrious term for a Black man, supposed to carry intensive contempt with it'; the French **negrillon**, literally a 'pickaninny' described a child with a dirty face and the Spanish **boda de negros**, a 'Negro wedding', described any boisterous, noisy occasion. **Negress**, while no more than a female Negro, has, like the cognate Jewess, a slightly negative inference. However the apparently 'colour-coded' French expression **c'est le nègre**: that's a knockout, a wow, the thing, may well have nothing to do with **nègre** at all. The roots of this piece of student slang appear to lie in the Latin *ne plus ultra*: the ultimate, the supreme.

Nigger Pot

If Negro veers towards respectability, its slangy derivative **nigger** leaves one in no doubt as to its intention and with it one meets gut-level racism. Alongside such race-related terms as **kike**, **wop**, **mick** and **spick**, nigger is one of the most opprobrious of all such words. Like Negro it comes from the French *nègre*, and Spanish *negro* and was initially spelt **Neger**, a spelling that is still found in Holland, Germany, Denmark and Sweden. As the current edition of the *OED* puts it, the term is 'colloquial and usually contemptuous...[it is] now virtually restricted to contexts of deliberate and contemptuous ethnic abuse'. Only, as the *Dictionary* notes, within the context of Black English vernacular, i.e. one Black person talking to another, does it shed (and then only in terms of deepest irony) its negative connotations. The term appears in English around 1785, used by, among others, Robert Burns (recounting the legend of Noah's son Ham – the supposed progenitor of all Black races) and shortly after him Lord Byron. For them, and for a number of British writers, the term was general: it covered any Black, as much as did those otherwise characterized as 'fuzzy-wuzzies' and similar dismissives. Kipling's 'Soldiers Three' talked blithely of 'naygurs' and they were not alone. The readers of such jingoistic journals as the *Sporting Times* (better known as *The Pink 'Un* – from the colour of its stock – and professing racial and nationalist attitudes that would seem utterly familiar to the readers of today's *Sun* newspaper) knew a nigger when they saw one – and certainly didn't demur in saying so. It was in 1901 in the pages of the *Pink 'Un*, after all, that the highly respected illustrator Phil May (1864-1903) offered his drawing of 'The Complacent Coon'. There were no complaints.

Like Negro, nigger has been used in a variety of combinations since the 19th century and both *Webster III* and the *OED* list a number of these, usually referring to birds, animals and crops, without comment – the assumption being that, for better or worse, they are an accepted (if local) usage; and while they, like the parallel uses of negro, are also based on stereotypes, it is more those of colour than of primarily racist assumptions. Thus, to take examples at random, **nigger daisy**, the 'black-eyed Susan', **nigger fish,** a small grouper (*Cephalopholis fulvus*), found in the West Indies and off the coast of Florida; **nigger lice,** informal name of the prickly awns (bristles) of various species of plants, esp. of the genus *Desmodium*, **nigger pea,** a species of coarse black bean and **nigger toe,** a Brazil nut; **niggerweed**, queen-of-the-meadow and **niggerwool**, western sedge. At the same time another stereotype, the traditional role of the Black man as an unskilled labourer, taking on a variety of strenuous tasks, gives a number of other terms. To take just a few, culled from the jargons of various occupations a **nigger** can be a cotton spinner (the machine not the human), dark ore, a machine used to position logs for cutting in a sawmill, the turnip sawfly, a steamboat hoist, a motor which runs the capstan on a ship and a fault in the insulated covering on an electrical conductor. Used without the article it can denote a patois of English and African words.

That, however, is as far as equanimity goes. And even that is limited: the word rankles, however it appears. Nigger is in the end a pejorative term that means Black man or woman (and is used similarly in Australia, where it has referred to the Aborigine or Native Australian since the 1840s). Classically pronounced 'nigra' (among the comedian Lenny Bruce's best-known 'bits' was that in which the southern-born president Lyndon Johnson – paradoxically a champion of Black civil rights

– fought to master the respectable 'northern' word 'Negro'), it is most commonly found in the southern states of America. Occasionally one also finds the equally hostile abbreviations 'gar or nig.

Thus one finds **niggerdom**, the world of Blacks; **nigger-gal**, a Black woman or girl; **nigger-boy**, a Black boy; **niggerkin** or **nigger-ling**, a Black child. A **nigger baby**, other than its obvious use, can also mean a sanicle (*Heuchera villosa*), a plant with purple flowers, a large cannon ball, (as used during the American Civil War; the gun from which they were fired being known as a *swamp angel*) or a form of sweet or candy, this last found as recently as 1948. A **nigger killer** means both a hard taskmaster (1856) or a revolver (1944). A **nigger-shooter** is a slingshot, a **nigger-trigger** a gun, a **nigger-stick** a baton as used by prison warders and a **nigger chaser** (1883) a small firework that scurries about on the ground (Britain's jumping-jack). A **nigger catcher**, as well as meaning a man who captured escaped slaves and returned them to their masters, also described a small, slotted leather flap on a saddle: once caught the slave would be bound and then attached to the saddle via a rope tied through this flap.

The **nigger heaven** (otherwise known as the **Ethiopian paradise**, **Ethiopian heaven** or the **peanut heaven**) was the upper circle or 'gods' in a theatre. Only here were seats cheap enough for Black wages. Its best-known popular use came in 1926, as the title of a best-selling look at 1920s Harlem – then a favourite centre of rich, White slumming – by the socialite Carl van Vechten. The use of nigger heaven to mean the roof of a freight car refers to the time when Blacks joined the ranks of tramps 'riding the rods' across Depression-era America. The synonymous **nigger gallery** referred, in the mid-19th century, to those seats, also up in the 'gods', set aside for Black patrons. The poker games of **big** and **little nigger** are those in which, respectively, the hand with the high or low spade splits the pot; Damon Runyon's 'Big Nig' was a crap shooter, but presumably there was some reference to the other popular gambling game. The exclamation **niggers!** is used as a mild oath. **Nigger pot**, however, as recounted by Terry Southern in *Red-Dirt Marijuana* (1973) is not in fact cannabis (as the slang word *pot*) but a form of *moonshine*, illicitly distilled whisky. **Niggero**, blending the 'respectable' and the pejorative terms, merely underlines the antipathy.

The entire vocabulary, is perhaps best summed up in the mid-19th-century Americanism **humble as a dead nigger**, meaning utterly subservient and laying out, consciously or otherwise, the preferred role, as seen by many of their fellow-citizens, of the American Black.

Nor is nigger exclusively an American phenomenon. In one notorious British by-election campaign of the 1960s Conservative supporters suggested that the local electorate should 'Vote Labour if you want a nigger for your neighbour'. Like earlier uses of the word in Britain, the reference was not to American slaves or their descendants but to West Indian and African immigrants (the former of which groups had, of course, been slaves in their own right). The less discriminating racist includes Indians and Pakistanis (and indeed anyone else with a dark skin) in the term, but 'properly' it applies to Blacks only. The British also enjoy **nig-nog** (which actually began life meaning a foolish person; hence, a raw and unskilled recruit) and the term has been exported to Australia, where **nog** and **noggy** both mean a Vietnamese (originally the north Vietnamese soldiers and iregulars against whom Australians fought in the late 1960s).

Like America, Australia boasts a number of 'nigger' combinations, typically **nigger-country**, land inhabited by Aborigines; **nigger farming**, farming that is underwritten by a government grant to Aborgine farmers; **nigger-twist**, a form of cheap, rough tobacco 'which would knock a White man into a coma' and which was often used instead of cash to pay wages to Aborigine labourers, and **nigger-hunting**, the 19th-century hunting of Aborigines for 'sport'.

A **nigger ball**, in South Africa, is a large sweet – the main effect of which was to turn one's teeth black – known in the UK as gob-stopper and presumably 'related' to America's nigger baby; its use in the international hit single 'Ag Plees Daddy' (1962) caused ne'er a ripple in the English consciousness. West Indians themelves have a variety if 'nigger' terms, which may be acceptable between Black people, but are considered highly offensvive if used by Whites. Among them are **nigger-man** and **nigger-woman**, **niggergram** or **nigger-mouth**, a malicious, groundless rumour, and **nigger ten**, the mark 'X' made by an illiterate.

I'm Black and I'm Proud

The first recorded use of **Black** comes in 1625, when the clergyman-author Samuel Purchas (1575?-1626), in *Pilgrimes* (a study of various early voyages, very loosely based on the work of Richard Hakluyt), referred to 'The mouth of the Riuer [Gambra], where dwell the Blackes, called Mandingos'. Thereafter it appeared in a variety of works, but was by no means the major description of Black people. Not until the mid-1960s, with the advent of the Black civil rights movement in America, with its calls for 'Black Power' and slogans such as 'Black is Beautiful' and 'Say It Loud, I'm Black and I'm Proud' did the term enter mainstream use. It is grimly paradoxical then, that despite the 'pride' that underpins these uses of Black (currently supplanted by African-American) that so many terms prefixed by the word Black are used in so derogatory a manner.

Starting with **blacky**, which appears in 1815, the list of names includes **black nigger** (usually found as an insulting term of address by one Black man to another), **black dust** (an extremely black-skinned person), **blackhead, blackamuffin** (a blend of blackamoor and raga-muffin, a term that began life as the proper name of a 14th-century demon, but went on to mean one who is dirty or disreputable) and a **black indian**. (A **faggamuffin**, punning on the 'straight' use, is a Black gay man.) **Black-out, black-rascal, black-teapot** (from the colour of the fire-blackened utensil) and **black-tulip** (presumably from the celebrated variety of plant) all mean the same. **Black-cattle** (1819) equated the boatloads of slaves with those of dumb animals, while **black-jack**, used for both male and female genitals as well as simply for a Black man, has a range of other meanings running from a large leather jug, coated externally with tar, to a synonym for the pirate's skull and crossbones, to a weighted bludgeon. **Black-fellow**, coined in early 19th century Australia, refers to Aboriginals in general, as well as to the **black-tracker**, an Aborigine employed to help the police in tracking down fugitives or persons lost in the bush.

Black women are dismissed in similar combinations. **Black cunt** is perhaps the least compromising, but **black-doll, black-mama** and **black-skirt** are hardly congratulatory. **Black diamond** is usually a synonym for **coal**, which itself can mean a Black woman. Other coal-related terms include **charcoal, coal-shutes-blackie, load-of-coal** (a gathering of Blacks of either gender), **hod, scuttle** (an abbreviation of coal scuttle) and **scuttle-sault**, which means a woman and the sexual intercourse one has with her. Sault possibly refers to the French *sauter*: to jump, itself a synonym for copulation. Only **black beauty**, a reference either to the title of Anna Sewell's equine bestseller of 1877 or to the Black Power slogan, lifts the general tone. Finally a trio of geographical terms: a **black joint** was a Black nightclub catering specifically to the White 'tourists' who flocked to such ghetto areas as Harlem, while **Black Belt** and **Black Bottom** (also **Coon Bottom, Buttermilk Bottom** and sometimes simply **bottom**) both refer to the Black section of an American town or city. The former works on the model of the Jewish **Borscht belt** (with its reference to the traditional Polish/Russian beetroot soup *borshch*), while the various forms of bottom refer to the *bottom land*, that land sited near a river and which (while prized for its fertility in the country) tends to refer to the poorer areas of a town.

Alongside direct references to black, come those to dark, with all its sinister overtones. Thus **darky, darkee, darkey** or **darkie** (1775) (which has also meant a blind person), the **dark-brethren**, a **dark-cloud** (1900, a group of Blacks), and a **dusky** or **dusky-dame**. (The Australian term **choke a darkie** means to defecate). Those with notably black complexions can be an **ink, ink-face, ink-spitter, inky-dink(y)** as well as **J.B.** (for jet black). **Black ivory** referred to those unfortunates imported to America via the lucrative African slave trade while **ebony**, or **(little) bit of ebony** or **God's-image-cut-in-ebony** all meant a Black person. (**Bleached ebony** describes a half-caste.) More recently **eightball**, the black ball in pool (and originally made of ivory) also means Black. (It can also stand for Old English 800, a popular beer among rap fans, or for drug users an eighth of an ounce.) **Ned** also implies a notably dark complexion. **Scobe** (possibly from the dialect *scob*: a dark hole), **mud flap** and **gombay** all refer to Black people. Gombay, a West Indian term, implies a particularly dark skin and comes either from the dialect word *gombay*: a drum or drummer and figuratively the African-ness that goes with such drums (which includes the possession of a dark skin); an alternative etymology, the Kongo *nboma*: a drum, points in a similar direction.

It would be a mistake, however, to hypothesize that only in America are Blacks subject to so many demeaning nicknames. Similar coinages, based on the word Black, can be found very far from the old plantations or the newer ghettoes. Among the best-known is **spade** or **ace-of-spades** (from which it derives). Used at one time by American Blacks to indicate a person with very dark skin, it became popular in the UK in the 1960s, thanks to among others the author Colin MacInnes in his novels *Absolute Beginners* (1959) and *City of Spades* (1961); MacInnes also coined the nonce word **spadelet** to describe a Black infant. **Club**, another black suit, means the same. The rhyming slang **razor blade**, generally abbreviated to **razor**, or **luke** (from **Lucozade**, otherwise a soft drink) equals spade. **Super-spade**, an American coinage of the 1960s, was a Black person who was noticeably self-conscious about his/her race. It also punned on the comic hero Superman. Yiddish offers **schwarze** (with its variations **schwarz, swatzy, schwerze, swartzy, schvartza, schvartze, schvartzeh, schwartze, schvartzer, sehwartzer, schvugie**) as well as **shokher**, the Hebrew word for black which by itself or as **schocherer** means just that. The Portuguese **preto**: 'black' means a black-skinned Brazilian and in Papua New Guinea **blakskin** means a Black American (as well as a native New Guinean) as does the somewhat paradoxical **blakpela waitman** (literally 'black-fellow Whiteman').

Similarly the PNG use of **blakman** can mean both an uncivilized person and a Black American; the two terms are coincident, and not meant synonymously. South Africa's **munt**, from the Bantu *umuntu*: a Black person, a servant, is a widely used but wholly derogatory name for a Black South African. In Russia **cernomázyj**: 'black grease', means a Black man while **cernozádnij** or **cernozópye**, literally 'black arse', refers not to Black people but to the various Soviet Turkic Nationalities such as Tadzhiks, Uzbeks, Azerbaijanis and Turkomen. Such nationalities are also known as **cucméx**, which is linked to the Kazan Tatar *cuci*: 'to be frightened, to shake' a word that in turn, with a slight shift of stress gives *cuca*, or cunt. Australia's **sable** (a synonym for black, especially in heraldry) means Aboriginal.

One last variation on black is when applied to the Gypsies or Romanies. According to one theory the original gypsies were followers of the Hindu mother-goddess Kali, a terrifying figure usually appearing black-skinned, blood-stained and engirdled with snakes and skulls. Her name comes from the Sanskrit *kala*: black, and it is on this basis that Spanish gypsies are known as **kaló** (male) and **kalí** (female), literally the Black man and Black woman. Their language is *Romanó-Kaló*. A similar image can found in Finland, where the **mustaleinan** or 'blackies' are gypsies.

Tar Babies & Blue Skins

Tar, a sticky, pitch-black substance, is responsible for several terms. The **tar-baby** or **niggertar-baby** or **tar-pot** all mean the same thing: a Black child. The original tar-baby was created by Joel Chandler Harris in 1881, when in one of his *Uncle Remus* tales the scheming Brer Fox, determined to catch Harris' lapine hero Brer Rabbit, 'got im some tar, en mix it wid some turkentime, en fix up a contrapshun what he call a Tar-Baby', and Rudyard Kipling disinters it in *Debits and Credits* (1924) when *his* heroes, Stalky and Co., 'were toiling inspiredly at a Tar Baby made up of Beetle's sweater, and half-a-dozen lavatory towels... and most of Richards weekly blacking allowance for Prout's House's boots.' At the same time the phrase came to mean variously an object of censure; a 'sticky' problem, in other words one which is only aggravated by attempts to solve it. By the 1940s such variations had largely vanished (other than as found occasionally in the US) and the racial element predominated, both in America and in New Zealand where the term was used of a Maori.

A **tar-heel**, usually a nickname for a (White) North Carolinian (where the production of tar is a central industry) has also meant a Black, as has **tarbrushed folk**, a description that comes from the phrase a **lick** or **touch of the tar brush**, and which means have mixed Black (or Indian – whether American or sub-continental) and White blood. The phrase is first cited in Grose's *Dictionary of the Vulgar Tongue* (3rd. edn. 1796) where it is part of the definition for another once-popular term, **Blue-skin**, 'a person begotten on a Black woman by a White man...any one having a cross of the black breed...'. Grose also defines it punningly as one 'of the blue squadron' (at the time one of the three divisions of the British navy: the others, patriotically, were red and White; an *admiral of the blue* was a publican). The term, however, was somewhat older, since Joseph Blake, an accomplice of one of the 18th century's best-known villains, Jack Sheppard, used it as his 'street name' around 1720. Blueskin makes a second appearance, this time fictional, in James Fennimore Cooper's *The Spy* (1821). Other 'blue' equals 'black' names include **blue**, used according to the American philologist H.L. Mencken for Black servants by German residents of Baltimore in the 1880s; they changed it to **die Schwarze**: 'the black', when their employees caught on (the term is still found among older American Jewish homes that employ Black charwomen), and Australia's **blue-gum**, properly the blue gum tree or *Eucalyptus globulus*, but effectively an Aborigine. When used in America the same term means an African American who is seen by the (White) speaker as especially malevolent; the belief was that his or her bite is supposedly poisonous.

Casper the Friendly Ghost

Aside from the Chinese, whose pigment will be dealt with below, and the Jews, for whom the colour had different associations than with skin-tone, **yellow** is most commonly found as a description of light-skinned Blacks, especially girls. Although almost invariably relating to America these days, its first use appears to have been in the late 18th century, when a writer noted that 'the Turks have any just reason for holding the coast of Yemen to be a part of India, and called its inhabitants Yellow Indians'. Within thirty years the term had relocated to America and **high yaller** or **high yellow** (meaning light-skinned, possibly mixed-race Black girl) appears in the early 19th century, while **yellow ass**, a light-coloured Black girl, comes slightly later. A **lemon**, for men or women, is an earlier coinage, while another 'foodie' reference, **cheese**, flourished in the 1970s. **Yeloskin**, similarly formed, is used in Papua New Guinea to describe a light-skinned Black person, especially someone from Milne Bay Province.

Other terms include **pinkie** (a pale Black girl; **pinktongue** means any Black, as does **White palms**), **brownskin** and **brownskin baby** and **bright**, which means light-skinned and may well have been transferred from the earlier use of bright on the plantations to describe light-coloured tobacco. (It may also be linked to **shine**, a Black person, although that is generally seen as a work-related term.) **Headlight** (1930s/40s) is similarly 'shiny', as is **spotlight**, an African American term of the 1960s that means both a light-skinned Black woman and a person of mixed ancestry. **Tush**, more usually found as a Yiddishism for the posterior or buttocks, can also be used of a wealthy, light-skinned Black person. **Casper,** as used by African Americans, pays tribute to the popular cartoon character, Casper the Friendly Ghost. A **mustard seed** is a light-skinned Black person, and the West Indies use **brasshead** to describe one who has a reddish tint to their hair (the result of a diet lacking sufficient protein) and **chaben, chabin** or **shabeen** to characterize a person of mixed African/European descent; such people have pale brown skin, coarse reddish hair and sometimes freckles and greyish eyes. The name comes from the French word *chabins*: sheep bred in Berry, with thick, long hair; such sheep were once seen as a sheep/goat cross and the term, exported to Dominica, was used as a synonym, now aimed at humans not sheep, for 'half-breed'. **Half-scald**, another West Indian usage, applies in Guyana to a mulatto whose light skin is slightly red; the term was often used of a Portuguese. Another racial mix, that of a Chinese person with either a Black or Indian one, gives more West Indian terms: **chinee-creole, dougla** (from the Hindi *dogalaa*: a 'cross-breed', or mongrel) and **royal** (which seems to come from the old Spanish coin, a *real*, which was worth only one quarter of a peseta and thus, figuratively, implied the lowest social status; royal also, with much the same etymology, means the backside or, since the term is slang, the *arse*).

A Lick of the Tar-brush

Aside from terms that link the word black with the Black person, there are a number of cognates that play on dirt, darkness, smoke and similar concepts. Thus **midnight** refers to a particularly dark Black person, and **smoke, smokey, smokey-joe** and **smokestack** have all been popular since the 1920s. The Bono people of Ghana, admirers of light skin tones, revile the very black as **wo ho tuntum se tren wisie**: 'your skin is as black as train-smoke'. Harlem slang of the 1940s used **smit** (presumably from *smart*) **smoke** to mean a highly intelligent Black person. **Moke** (mid-19th century) may well be an abbreviation of smoke, although it might relate to **mocha**, itself meaning Black, although the colour is usually defined as dark brown. **Mochalie** is a Chinese person. The female version is **femmoke**. **Smudge, speck, sooty, smutt-butt** and **smidget** all carry an implication of dirt and grubbiness, as perhaps does **snuff,** with its implication of sneezing the brown powder into an unwashed handkerchief. **Dinge,** favoured by Raymond Chandler, is a straight lift from *dingy*: 'a (disagreeably) dark and dull colour or appearance;... usually implying a dirty colour or aspect due to smoke, grime, dust, weathering...'; **dink**, more usually associated with Orientals, is also found for Blacks and may be a version of dinge. Properly found as a description of a half-caste is the 18th-century **dingey Christian**: a mulatto or anyone with a degree of mixed blood and whom the slang lexicographer Francis Grose terms 'anyone who has, as the West Indian term is, a lick of the tar-brush'. **Boogie** (or **bo, bu** and **boo-boo**), which means Black, has been used since the 1920s (giving **boogie-box** as a synonym for the outsize radio-cum-tape-decks otherwise known as **ghetto-blasters** or **wog-boxes**); the abbreviation **boog** and the extension **booger** (more commonly found in Afro-American use meaning something unpleasant and as **booger bear** someone notably ugly) is sometimes found. **Shit-skin,** as found in modern Scotland, is depressingly self-explanatory. Today's *person of color* is one of the acceptable terms for Black and brown Americans, but **colored** or **the coloured**, often spelt **cullud** and appearing in such deliberately 'black' pronunciations as **cullud-gemman** (coloured gentleman) or **cullud-gal** (coloured girl), was used as a euphemism in America from early in the 19th century. More recently that same 'gal' has been known as a **raven beauty** (a pun on raving beauty and raven black) or an **Indian princess**; a **Zulu princess** is a gay term, meaning a young, handsome Black man. Another girl's name is **seal,** reflecting on the smoothness of sealskin, while **suede,** reflective more of colour than texture, will serve for any Black person.

A less common term, also taken as it were from the wardrobe, is **domino**, which originally referred to a form of hood or habit for the head, thence a veil used by mourning women and then the small black mask used at masquerades or masked balls. The domino, which must be linked to the Latin *dominus*: lord, and thus God or Christ, presumably began life referring to the covering of one's hair (at least when in church) out of respect. All that said, the racial use may equally well be based on the game of dominoes, with its predominantly black pieces.

The supposed 'humour' of racial terminology is rarely that funny. A variety of terms, making heavy-handed jokes on the basis of calling Blacks White, fail to break the mould. **Snowball** (1780) pushed this deliberate paradox, as did **lily-white** and the 18th-century **chimney chops** (referring to the blackness of chimney sweeps). In the case of this latter it is interesting, given the continuing arguments vis-à-vis the inclusion of racial abuse in dictionaries and the general insouciance of his era as regards racial abuse, to note that Francis Grose (in 1785) defines this term as 'a jeering appellation for a negro'. Of these terms snowball would be reclaimed by African Americans in the 20th century when it meant, logically a White, and, as the abbreviation snow gave such combinations as **Lady Snow** (a well-heeled White woman, as well as cocaine), **snow bunny** (a White girl), **snow queen** (a Black homosexual who prefers White lovers) and the phrase **put some snow in one's game** (for a Black hustler to profit from catering to the wants – usually sexual – of a White acquaintance).

The last of these 'coloured' terms refers usually not so much to Blacks, but to browns. **Wog** was defined originally as a 'vulgarly offensive name for a foreigner, especially one of Arab extraction'; this may have been true then, but it is Indians and Pakistanis who, in Britain at least, are more likely to meet the term. That said, wog is an all-purpose term for foreigner, a true representation of the dearly-held British belief that 'wogs begin at Calais'. Kindred non-British uses have included a name for the Vietnamese and, rather more surprisingly, for the Irish (as found in America). Wherever its use, wog is a coinage of the 1920s and is first cited by F. C. Bowen in *Sea Slang* (1929) who includes 'Wogs, lower class Babu shipping clerks on the Indian coast', but provides no further detail. Popular belief has always chosen the

acronym *WOG*: *w*esternized *o*riental *g*entleman or *w*ily *o*riental gentleman, but this has no real basis. Perhaps the most likely etymology, and
that backed by Eric Partridge, accepts what may well be the simplest
and most obvious root: an abbreviation of the standard English word
golliwog. Thus the Papua New Guinea term **olly**, which is used on the
island by Whites when talking of the local people, may well be another
abbreviation of golliwog, although it may come from the PNG dialect
Tok Pisin 'ol i': 'they'.

The golliwog itself – possibly a combination of the interjection *golly!*
and the word *polliwog*: a tadpole (though quite why it is harder to say –
it would appear that the etymology is in fact an invention of Robertson's, the jam-maker, in an attempt to offset attacks on their logo) –
appeared in 1895 as the title of the American author Bertha Upton's
book: *The adventures of two Dutch Dolls and a Golliwogg*. The object in
question was a crude representation of a Black man, typified by garish
clothes (a version of the popular 'minstrel style: frock coat, bow tie) and
a shock of fuzzy hair. He smiled broadly (once more in the minstrel
way) and while Black, was seen as a variation on two other characters
in the game, the 'Black Servant' and the 'African'. The image became
a popular one, found throughout British life – in other books, at the
theatre and the circus – and perhaps most vitally, was picked up in 1930
as a brand image by the Scottish firm of Robertson's for their range of
best-selling jams and marmalades. It had already been used by such
products as Tuck postcards and Riley toffee, but the Robertson's
identification made the golliwog very big business. By 1980, when
Robertson's celebrated the centenary of their 'gollies', they flooded the
country with 'Golly'-related merchandising, some 20 million items in
all, and coincidentally, found themselves facing off against the race
relations lobby, specifically the National Committee on Racism in
Children's Books, who wished to remove this offensive symbol from
books, toys and other forms of merchandise. Robertson's fought back,
saying that the golly represented an intrinsic part of Britain's national
culture. These days, although Robertson's have dropped the 'wog' and
talk only of golly, as in 'Golly! It's good!', this once-popular doll, with
its caricatured 'black' features that both the *OED* and *Webster* define as
'grotesque', has generally been marginalized as politically incorrect.

Red Devils

For the purposes of race **red** almost invariably means a Native American. France has the phrase *roux comme un Allemand*: red as a German, referring to the Germans' ruddy complexions; **redbone** can mean an Afro-American woman while in Papua New Guinea the Highlanders, whose complexions can be slightly reddish, are known as **redskins**, or just **skins**. But the 'red Indian' remains the dominant nation here. Native Americans were called Indians almost as soon as White Europeans began landing on America's eastern shoreline, and the 'red' image begins in 1699 when a writer talked of 'ye wicked onsaults of ye Red Skins'. **Red man** followed in 1725, and thereafter came the **red-race**, a **red brother** (1832), **red-devil** (1834), and simple **red** (1878). **Red indian** itself is a relatively late arrival, appearing in 1878. The link, loosely based on the natives' skin-tone, in reality no more 'red' than the Europeans' was 'white', seems to have come from the extinct Beothuk people of Newfoundland, supposedly seven-foot giants, whose use of red ochre as body paint apparently made them the first 'red men', thus spreading the term across the continent.

Little Brown Brothers

Compared to black, **brown** has a relatively limited currency. Its uses to mean light-skinned have already been noted. Otherwise Filipinos are **brownies**, as are the Japanese and the Pacific Islanders, or **(little) brown brothers** (which can also mean Chinese). Mexicans too are brown, but America reserves somewhat more pungent epithets for its 'neighbor to the south'. A more suprising link is to Italy, in the term **guinea** which, long-used for America's Italian immigrants, seems to refer to the brown skins, originally of those who arrived from West Africa's Guinea coast, and latterly to anyone seen as more swarthy than the 'White' American majority. The first use appears to be both as **guinea** (1789) and soon afterwards in the combination **guinea-negro**, both of which referred to the importation of Black slaves from West Africa, specifically the coast that runs from Sierra Leone to Benin. West Indian Creoles, who were born in the West Indies, referred to African-born Black people, imported across the Atlantic, as guinea-birds. Once settled in America the guinea-negro described a mixed-race group native to Maryland, Virginia and W. Virginia, who call themselves *Our People* or *Melungeons*. An alternative etymology, for what it is worth, suggests that the term stems from the willingness of impoverished Italians to work for English pennies (known facetiously as guineas) which were still circulating in the US. It seems very unlikely. Guinea has a variety of synonyms: **ginzo, guinzo, gingo** (1920), **guin, ghin** or **gin**. **Ginny** or **ghinny** seem to be the most popular, at least as judged by the spelling used in many books of 'hard-boiled' fiction. It provides such combinations as the **guinea football** (also an **Italian** or **dago** football), more commonly known as a bomb. Guinea also provides a couple of mongrel terms: **spaginzy**, meaning an Italian, blends **spag** or **spaghetti**, a term in its own right, with guinzo, while the Afro-American **ofaginzy**, a term for Whites, mixes the Italian identification with **ofay**, itself a derogatory term for a White person, used by modern American Blacks.

Yellow Perils

The equation of the colour **yellow** with negative terminology, be it of people, emotions or ideas, begins early: the Jacobean plawrights of the 1600s (Dekker, Massinger, Middleton and others) all used the word in the context of jealousy (Shakespeare's Malvolio, in *Twelfth Night*, has significantly yellow cross-gartering) and the concept lasted until the mid-19th century. At this point, perhaps coincidentally, it took on a new, if equally negative meaning: that of cowardice. *Yellow streak*, its reification, arrives around 1896. For the purposes of this study, the term of greatest import is **yellow peril**, a phrase that was coined in approximately 1900, but which reflected on an unease, both in America and in Britain, that had been growing for the last fifty years. The synonymous, but relatively short-lived **yellow agony**, as used in Australia, appeared at around the same time.

Ever since the early 19th century, Chinese immigrants had gradually been moving east, whether to America, spreading out from the Californian ports, or to England, where they tended to settle in London. In

England they remained, as their descendants do today, a closed community, in those days centred on the East End area of Limehouse, not far from the docks where they would have disembarked. In America they were an equally tight-knit society, but as 'coolies' working on the expanding railroads, or as the ubiquitous face to be found in every local laundry, they had a more noticeable image. And thus, inevitably, a more negative one. As the century progressed the Chinese, who shared barely any of their characteristics, other than a similar role of playing foreigner to America's mainstream, found themselves equated with the Blacks. The calumnies that created so many false characterizations of the Black community, were transferred wholesale to the Chinese. They were heathens, they lacked morals, they were at the same time infantile and sexually rampant, they were savages and, most bizarre of all, they apparently looked like the hated Blacks.

The image of the **yellow peril,** of the essentially sinister 'Chinee', is very much a fictional construct, although the real-life Boxer Rebellion of 1900 had undoubtedly urged the process on. It grew from novels such as Dickens' *Edwin Drood*, where the opium den run by Princess Puffer lies in deepest Limehouse; in the short stories of Conan Doyle, e.g. Sherlock Holmes' tussle with 'the Yellow Face' (nothing remotely Chinese but where perhaps interestingly the problem is solved when a hideous yellow mask is torn aside to reveal the face of a small, supposedly mixed-race Black girl, whose White mother wishes to hide her antecedents), and most of all in the series of thrillers 'starring' that epitome of Chinese devilry: Dr Fu Manchu. Fu Manchu was created by Sax Rohmer (1883-1959) in *The Mystery of Dr Fu Manchu* (1913), who would later claim that, on asking an ouija board where his fortune might lie, received the answer C-H-I-N-A-M-A-N. Rohmer continued writing the tales until his death, and his creation continued on screen until the 1970s. A journalist and adept of the Order of the Golden Dawn (an occultist group whose members included the poet W.B. Yeats and the self-styled 'Great Beast' Aleister Crowley, and which propounded what were at best highly right-wing views on race), Rohmer had been on assignment in Limehouse. Apparently there, amidst its teeming alleys, lurked a mysterious Oriental 'godfather' a Chinese super-villain named 'Mr King'. Rohmer searched in vain. There was no King, but he returned with the inspiration for a fictional Chinaman, more villain-ous by far than any supposed East Ender. The image of Fu Manchu, with his slit eyes, his drugs, his henchmen, his languorous girls (both Chinese, and far worse, White) became the image of China for much of the Western public. Not until Chairman Mao gave the whole picture a new twist in 1949 would it gain any real counterbalance and even then, with the image of Pearl Harbor fresh in many minds, for all that this was a Japanese not a Chinese attack, the East remained a dubious environment. And it has yet fully to vanish. Michael Creighton's 1992 best-seller *Rising Sun*, with its fearful images of a Japan hells-bent on America's destruction tapped on the old fantasies. Fu Manchu may have swapped his opium pipe for a laptop, but for fearful xenophobes the visceral terrors remain.

If the Chinese were cruel, larcenous, drug-addicted White slavers, then even more were they yellow. Skin tone, that useful denominator of social and moral type, came swiftly into play. America offered a range of synonyms: **yellow back, yellow belly** (coincidentally the self-de-scription of natives of the English county of Lincolnshire), **yellow bastard, yellow cur, yellow dog, yellowguts, yellow heel** and **yellow pup**. The underworld term **mustard** meant a Chinese person. **Yellow man** played the same role for the Chinese as 'red man' did for Native Americans (although **yellow man** in the West Indies refers to an albino as does **yellow fellow** in Australia, and **red-skinned** in the West Indies). A **yellow goodsman** was one who smuggled Chinese workers (**yellow goods**) into America. Yellow might have meant cow-ardly several decades prior to the Chinese 'invasion', but the old use served perfectly to underpin one more negative aspect of the new one. Terms such as **little yellow men**, which come World War II would serve muster to describe a new yellow peril – the Japanese – left no-one in doubt as to the prevailing mood. Nor did one have to speak English; the word **zeltokózie**: 'yellow-skin' meant Chinese to any Russian.

The Colour of Money

A less well-known linkage of the colour yellow and race is that between it and the Jews. The Jews may, according to the race propagandists, sport among other distinguishing marks horns, outsize noses, and a distinctive, unpleasant smell, but in case the wandering peasant failed even then to cotton on, it was made compulsory for all Jews to sport a variety of physical symbols – usually some form of patch affixed to their clothing – to make sure that no-one failed to notice. The colour, of course, reflected the inevitable link between the Jews and money or gold. As the German saying had it, **the favourite Jewish colour is yellow**. Such badges were the ultimate in 'no-win' adornments: if one wore the badge one was open to persecution; if one refused it, one faced prosecution. The first of such laws was passed, on the orders of Pope Innocent III, in 1215, and it was quickly followed by others. A similar ruling was made in France in 1227 (demanding that all Jews wear a circular patch on the chest of all garments), and there were variations throughout Europe. In Provence, where the town of Carpentras held a substantial Jewish community (so large that during the 18th century even the town's Christians were nicknamed 'Jews' – **li jusiou de Carpentras**: the Jews of Carpentras – by the local farm people), Jews had to wear a distinctive yellow cap, known as a 'Jew's ear' because of the yellow bow-like patch which hung down from it. This cap was worn in a number of countries and Jew's ear is also a nickname for *Hirneola Auricula Judae*: a tough fungus that grows on decaying elder trees and resembles, at least to peasant imaginations, the same badge.

Jew became a synonym for 'snake' and from time to time the church articles were examined to see whether they had become yellowed – as a result of Jewish influence. Given the standards of contemporary paper-making, the odds were that they had, and another excuse for a pogrom was conveniently provided. At the same time the term **judiouva**, literally a Jewess, came to mean yellow. Although such practices gradually vanished, they were not forgotten. At the start of the 19th century Christian Friedrich Ruhs (1781-1820), then Professor of History at the University of Berlin, suggested that given increasing Jewish assimilation, they should, for the security of the German people, be forced back to the identifying yellow badge. The idea was rejected, but not for ever. As the Nazis came to power first in Germany and gradually extended that power across Europe, they were swift to bring back this antique form of humiliation – Jews once again found themselves condemned to wear a badge, this time a yellow star of David. Only irony makes palatable a later recommendation for such 'badges of shame', that proposed in 1996 by Britain's Jewish-born Home Secretary who, it was reported, wished to see those expiating their crimes with community service thus marked.

The Wearing of the Green

Emerald green... the wearing of the green... the Orange and Green... that **green** is Ireland's emblematic colour should surprise no-one. The link had been made in the late 18th century when in 1797 the Irish song *The Shan van vocht* asked 'What colour should be seen | Where our fathers' homes have been, | But our own immortal Green?' and around a year later another song, *The Wearing of the Green*, recounted that 'They are hanging men and women | for the wearing of the green.' Green became the colour of southern, nationalist, republican Ireland, just as **Orange** (memorializing William III – victor of the Battle of the Boyne) represented the protestant, British north. Racial terminology, naturally, did not overlook the fact, although the 'green' terms are, with one exception, relatively mild. **Emeralder** (1845) (from the *Emerald Isle*) would hardly open any wounds, nor would the use of **Irish favourite** (1920s) to mean the precious stone. **Green nigger** is, however, a different matter, reflecting perfectly the way in racial terms, the characteristics (and nomenclature) of one despized race can easily be passed on to another (however much the facts argue against it). In turn Afro-Americans have been called **sunburned** or **smoked Irishmen**, showing that the process cuts both ways. (The 1820s briefly offered **smoked Yankee**, referring to newly freed Black slaves.) Other terms include **shamrock** or **sham**, from Ireland's national plant. But colour is never that vital to a White race, and the Irish, barely grazed in this context, are more severely savaged elsewhere.

Little Black Sambo

The half-caste, the mulatto, the mestizo – racial blends are never universally popular. Caste, after all comes from the Latin *casta* meaning pure: 'semi-purity' is an unsatisfactory state; *mulatto* means literally a young mule, another form of cross-breed and hardly a congratulatory term when applied to a human, while *mestizo*, the Spanish/Portuguese synonym means dismissively 'mixed'. The racist's fantasies of 'tainting' and 'swamping' are made all too living flesh in these offspring of different races.

Among the oldest of such terms is **Sambo**, generally used to mean a Black man but probably based in the Spanish *zambo*, used to describe those of mixed Negro and Indian or European blood; that the term also described a breed of yellow monkey and may have been the same word as that meaning bandy-legged merely underlines the gut racism that informs such language. The American use, however, which emerged during the era of slavery, may have a different root: the Foulah *sambo*: uncle or the Hausa homonym meaning second son, or name of the spirit; the suggestion by the slang collectors Farmer & Henley of a third root, an African tribe the *Samboses* (for whom they claim an appearance in a text of 1558) has no validity. *Sambo* began as a neutral term, but as slavery fell into increasing disrepute, so did its terminology; the word was widely popularized by Helen Bannerman's best-selling children's book *The Story of Little Black Sambo* (1923) but the term, and that book, have long since been considered unacceptable. As **dark sambo** it recurs in West Indian use as a person of mixed race, with one quarter White to three quarters Black; in Australia, where the racist use is undoubtedly in use, it also means a sandwich. The Brazilian dance, the *samba*, which has no ostensible racial edge, is simply the feminine version of the word.

The West Indies also see **sambo backra**, used for a person who is three quarters Black. The phrase mixes the Black 'sambo' with the term **buckra**, which means a master, a boss; and thus a White man. The term comes from the patois of Surinam where *bakra* means master; this in turn was based on the Efik (the language of the Calabar coast) *mba*: everything plus *kara* to encompass, get round, to master (a subject); thus *mbakara, makara*: a White man, a European, with a parallel meaning of a demon, a powerful and superior being. Other combinations of buckra include **buckra-nigger**: a 'White man's negro' or subservient Black or a despized mulatto; **buckra-bittle**: buckra victuals or White man's food; and **backra-betters** those who, while Black, move in White society and see themselves as the White man's equal. **Backra-johnny** is a poor White. Other West Indian terms for poor Whites include **Dorsetshire-Hill Bajan**: a poor White Bajan (Dorsetshire-Hill is near Kingston, St Vincent, where a community of poor-White immigrants from Barbados have lived since the 1860s); **Mount Moritz Bajan** (also known as a **mong-mong**, Mount Saint Moritz is an estate in Grenada on which many impoverished Bajans worked as market gardeners from the 1870s), and **ecky-becky**, another word for poor White Bajans, in this case apparently derived from the Ijo *beke*: a European or from a mix of Igbo *Ekee*: God plus *beke*. In either case it is considered the most derogatory of all anti-Bajan terms. **Mustee**, used in Barbados and Guyana for the offspring of a White and a mulatto parent comes from the local pronunciation of *mestizo*. **Payol** comes from the Spanish *espanol* and means in Trinidad a mixed-race person who retains traces of Spanish ancestry and culture and in Grenada a Spanish-speaking person, especially a Venezuelan. The term is rated as nearly as offensive as either nigger or coolie and those designated 'payol' call themselves either 'Spanish' (in English) or 'venezolanos' (Venezuelans) in Spanish.

The contemporary role of **woman** or **man of colour** has been noted above. In 18th-century West Indies it seems to have been a euphemism, denoting a person of mixed race. Other West Indian terms include **red nigger**: a person both of whose parents are of mixed-African/White descent, and **rial** or **royal** (1940s). Meaning the offspring of an East Indian woman and a Black man they are based on the 19th-century *real*: a coin of low value; other race blends include the **Chiney-rial, Indian-rial**. Finally there is **dominicker** which can also mean a coward and which refers to the *dominicker* or *Dominique fowl*, which has mottled or barred plumage; the dominicker rooster was believed to back down when challenged by another rooster. A similar term, also meaning half-caste and also based on a species of fowl, is America's **black ankle**.

More terms for the Black/White mix include **ginger-cake** (from the ginger-toned shade of the person's skin), **tan** (thus **black and tan joint** or **black and tan resort**: a place where the races can mix freely) **sepia** and **sepe**. **Half-and-half** means a half-caste; for African Americans it can also mean mixed gender as well as mixed race, i.e. an hermaphrodite. **Spill** and **spookerican** (a blend of *spook* and *Puerto Rican*) describe a Puerto Rican/Black mix, while a **blue gum** is a person of mixed Indian, White and Black ancestry. (It can also refer to bootleg whisky.) **Spic and span** are a mixed Puerto Rican and Black couple. Another complex mix is the Afro-American **bone**: a combination of English, Irish and Black ancestry. A **kelt** or **keltch** (apparently from the Scots *kelt*: a homespun cloth, usually of black and White wool) is more complex still, a quadroon or octoroon, who could pass for White and thus used for a Black person setting out to do just that. In other contexts it means simply White. **Boogerlee** (using **booger**: a Black person and punning on the popular tale of the doomed Black hero *Stagolee*) is another term for half-caste; it also means a Cajun (a person of French descent born in Louisiana) and a Frenchman.

A food motif is found in **chop suey**, which despite its overt Chinese feel actually refers to any mixed race person: the focus is on the mixture rather than the race. Chop suey, from the Chinese *shap suì*, means 'mixed bits' a dish of stir-fried meat and vegetables, created by Chinese chefs for their Western customers; not part of Oriental cuisine, it was seen as adequate for the Western palate. A **fly-in-the-milk** is a child of mixed Black-and-White parentage, and gives the image of the black fly in White milk. In the 1970s **salt and pepper queens** were a mixed-race gay couple.

Mexico, where the basic term is **mestizo**: the offspring of Indian and White parents, irrespective of sex, also gives the rarer **albarazado** (feminine **albarazada**), a mixture of Mexican and Chinese parents; the literal translation, far from flattering, is 'afflicted with White leprosy'. **Cholo**, a Mexican either of lower social class or of mixed race comes from *Cholollán*, now *Cholula*, a district of Mexico while a **canisa** (a mongrel) is the offspring of a mestizo or half-caste father and an Indian mother. Over the border a **coyote**, literally a prairie dog, is a half-breed (like the animal, such half-breeds lead a nomadic life) as is a **hound dog**, once more suggesting the mongrel image. The plain and simple term **half-breed** has also been used to mean Mexican. The Japanese word *hampa*, meaning half, underpins both **happa**, a contemporary US campus term meaning half White/half Asian and the

Papuan **hapkas**: variously a half-caste, a Eurasian, an adoptee from another clan, or a dark-skinned European. In Australia a **piebald** or **piebald pony** (1920s) was a half-caste White/Aborigine and a **halfie** (1940s/60s) a plain half-caste. A **magpie**, reflecting the black and White bird, meant a convict in the 19th century – the reference is to the parti-coloured yellow and black clothes such men had to wear – while more recently it too has meant mixed-race.

White Negroes

An albino is 'a human being distinguished by the congenital absence (partial or total) of colouring pigment in the skin, hair and eyes, so that the former are abnormally White, and the latter of a pink colour, and unable to bear the ordinary light' (*OED*). The word was coined in the late 18th century by Portuguese explorers (from Portuguese *albo*: White), who encountered 'White Negroes' on the coast of Africa. Given the 'peculiarity' of such individuals, albinos have attracted a number of terms, the bulk of them found in the West Indies. In the main they tend to emphasize one or another of the albino's defining characteristics: the skin colour (or lack of it) and the poor eyesight.

Thus, to take eyesight first, one finds **glimpse, parrot-eye, patu-eye** (the *patu* – an owl or a nightjar – prefers the darkness to light), **puss-eye** (cats apparently squint) and **periin** (from the standard English *peering*). **Mongoose** refers to the animal, which has a light-brown coat and reddish eyes. The skin tone is found in **freckle-nature, speckle** (1950s), **ripe banana** and **side-pork** (referring respectively to what is seen as the 'yellow' or 'pink' skin tone) and **gray-nayga** (lit. 'grey nigger'), **grey-bo** ('grey boy'), **grey-owl** (a version of patu-eye) and **grey puss**. **Grey** here reflects the Afro-American use in which the word is used for a White person. Some other terms make the equation even more basic: **White-man, White-nayga, Whitey-Whitey, White labour** and **White cockroach**. **Norwegian** echoes that nation's stereotypical pale complexion and White-blonde hair. Finally there are three oddities: **cedar** (based on a Jamaican riddle: 'Cheap cherry bears cedar': the Jamaican cedar has a fruit that looks like a plum but is inedible), **quaw**, from the Twi *kwaw*: a boy who is born on a

Thursday, and which can also mean a peasant or country bumpkin, and Papua's **wel masta**, a pidgin term that translates as a 'wild European'.

Mr Charlie and Miss Ann

If the iconography of White racism has set out a list of Black stereotypes (apostrophized in 1973 by American film critic Donald Bogle as 'toms, coons, mulattos, mammies and bucks') and provides a vocabulary to match, then the Black rejoinder, at least in terms of language, divides Whites into three main groups: pigmentation, ignorant peasants or 'White trash' and oppressors (including businessmen).

Pigmentation provides the majority of these terms, although few of them are simple descriptions and most carry some form of hostility. While Whites rarely define Blacks in terms of their being 'not White', Blacks have a number of words and phrases that depict Whites as 'not Black' or at best a 'washed out Black', i.e. grey. And, utterly unequivocally, there is **White nigger** (used in the US and Sierra Leone, which can also be extended to light-skinned Blacks). Typical are **fade**, and its synonym **fagingy-fagade** (its opposite is **spagingy-spagade**: a Black person; both come from 'pig-Latin', an invented language based on reordering consonants) and **gray** or **grey** (with the combinations **grey-boy, gray-dude, gray-skin, gray-cat** and the female **grey-broad**), both of which imply not just colour (or its absence), but a comment on what Blacks perceive as the unexciting, 'colourless' behaviour and character of Whites, especially the middle classes. Thus one finds **anemic** (literally 'bloodless'), **pale, paleface** and **paleface nigger** (an especially hostile term which once more can also be aimed at a light-skinned Black, especially one who is attempting, successfully or not, to ape White behaviour). Less common is **pale-sault**, a White woman, in which *sault* may come from *sauter*: to jump, which in slang means to have sexual intercourse.

Whiteness pure and simple is found in **blanco** (from the Spanish), **chalk** (1970s/80s), **lily** (more commonly found as a reference to effeminacy), **lilywhite, milk, vanilla** (used in other contexts to mean run-of-the-mill, predictable), **White eyes, White meat** (usually of women, and in an overtly sexual context), **snowball, flake** and **frosty** (all carrying intimations of a 'White Christmas') while **pink, pinkie** (sometimes a light-coloured Black) and **pink whoogie** (and **whoogie**) all refer to the 'real' skin-tone of a 'White' person. A **pink-chaser**, therefore, is a Black person who purses the company and friendship of Whites. **Pinktoes** means a White girl, as do **blondie, bale of straw** (**hay-eater**, coincidentally, means a White rustic) and **golden-girl** – which trio refer not to skin, but to hair-colour. **Bright-skin** (1920s) is essentially another version of bright, used of a light-skinned Black.

Like **buckra**, a White man or master in the West Indies, the roots of which lie in a synonymous word meaning 'demon', **ofay** (sometimes abbreviated as **fay**), an Afro-American term for White since the late 19th century, comes from a similar image. In Yoruba *ofe* is 'a charm that lets one jump so high as to disappear'; by extension this becomes the cause of such a disappearance, thus trouble and thus a White man (the essence of trouble). An alternative etymology suggests the French phrase *au fait*: sophisticated, aware. A mix of ofay and guinea or guinzo, two popular terms for Italian, gives **ofaginzy**.

Long before the arrival of such popular 1980s socio-acronyms as *yuppie, buppie* or *dinky*, the vocabulary of race relations had **WASP**: White Anglo-Saxon Protestant or, less commonly White Appalachian Southern Protestant, a term that was used to refer to migrants from the poor Appalachians to Chicago and other midwestern industrial cities. **SAM** is a Southern Appalachian Migrant, although there may be an added reference to *Uncle Sam*, the embodiment of White America (coined in 1813 and possibly taken from the nickname given to Samuel Wilson, a government official during the War of 1812). Variations on that theme include **WASC**, White Anglo-Saxon Catholic, and used for the early English Catholic settlements in America; and Canada's **QWASP**: Quebec White Anglo-Saxon Protestant. **Anglo** (1941), while an abbreviation rather than an acronym, has been used by Mexicans and, increasingly, others for Americans of Anglo-Saxon descent, tends to be specific to Protestants. **PIGS**, Poles, Italians, Greeks and Slavs, are what America calls 'ethnics' (a term that in Greek originally meant heathen). A parallel shorthand can be found in **hyphenates** a term that embraces such formations as Polish-American, Mexican-American, Irish-American and the like.

Other generic terms for Whites include **face** (1940s) used especially for a stranger; **dem** and **dey**, ironic, self-mocking alterations of 'them' and 'they'; **dap**, which is probably backslang from **Paddy**, properly an Irishman but good for any White, and **faggit**, presumably from the slang term *faggot*: a male homosexual, but in this context carrying no reference to gender or sexual preference. A **faggamuffin**, punning on faggot and ragamuffin, is used for a homosexual Black person, usually a male. Two last terms are **hoople**, perhaps from the cartoon character *Major Hoople* (an incompetent White officer) and **pig**, more usually used to describe policemen but used, as is Babylon, to describe the White power structure and those who benefit from it.

In the absence of any opportunity to develop a Black middle class the African-American's peer in socio-economic terms was for decades the poor White, usually as found living in the same rural areas as did the Blacks themselves and eking out much the same living. The difference, of course, was skin colour and racial hatreds are rarely so acute as between two disadvantaged groups who, other than their colour, know that their lives are all too similar. The majority of anti-Black vocabulary (at least that found in relatively open use) would come from poor Whites, and the Blacks responded in kind. The phrase **White trash** (literally White rubbish) or its extension **poor White trash** was coined in the late 18th century (although Shakespeare had used *trash*, without racial overtones – albeit in *Othello* – to refer to a person in 1604) and by the early 19th century was a part of mainstream American speech. More ironic was **plain folks**, a wicked twist on the cheerful self-description of many White farmers, and a rebuttal of those same farmers' euphemistic **coloured** or **coloured folks**. The hail-fellow complacency of **Good ol' boy** hides the less savoury aspects of the term. Embraced by those it describes, it is used with grim irony by those outside their circles, and refers once more to the Southern White male, not necessarily poor, but a happy upholder of 'traditional values', among which segregation, or at least Black inferiority, is more than likely a component. Less affectionate is **peckerwood** (1920s) a term which opposed the red woodpecker, a symbol of Whites, to the black crow, that of Blacks. Peckerwood gives the abbreviations **peck** and **pack**, **wood** and **wood hick** (from *hick*: a peasant). The Black disdain for such figures is echoed in the phrase **mean enough to steal acorns from a blind hog**, i.e. possessing all the characteristics of 'poor White trash': stupid, rustic and unsophisticated. Similarly antagonistic is **cracker**, with its cognates **Mr Cracker** (a variation on the synonymous **Mr Charlie**), **cordwood cracker, soda-cracker** and **cracker-ass** (which can also mean a thin person). Although it only entered Black use in the 1920s, cracker is among the oldest of such terms, dating back to before the American Revolution, when in a letter of 27 June 1766 a correspondent, one G. Cochrane, wrote to his patron in London, 'I should explain to your Lordship what is meant by crackers; a name they have got from being great boasters; they are a lawless set of rascalls on the frontiers of Virginia, Maryland, the Carolinas and Georgia, who often change their places of abode'. Cochrane may not have been correct: cracker is more likely to be an abbreviation of *corn-cracker* (later a native of Kentucky; Georgia is the cracker-state). Occasionally it was used to mean the light-skinned Black. A similar coinage is found in **ridgerunner,** the Arkansas version of Kentucky's crackers, defined as a Southern mountain farmer or a hill-billy and thus a variant on 'White trash'. The term appears to offer an image of such farmers moving over the ridges of soil in a ploughed field. **Stump-jumper, gully-jumper** and **stubble-jumper**, varying only as to the object leaped, all have much the same role.

Both cracker and ridgerunner began life as dialect terms indicating a native of a particular part of America, before in Afro-American use they expanded to define an entire racial type; the same is true of **hoosier**, which means a native of Indiana, thence a peasant or rustic simpleton and in Black use a White person, especially a racist. Its etymology is obscure – one idea suggests the slow-witted country people asking 'Who's here?', but it may more feasibly come from the old Cumbrian dialect *hoozer*: something large of its kind and as such reference to the size of the cornfed farm-boys. **Razor-back**, otherwise a native of Arkansas, has been used in the same way. Another 'geographical' term is **jeff**, a word that refers to Jefferson Davis (1808–89), president of the Confederate States during the US Civil War of 1861-5 and thus to the whole South. As well as indicating a White rustic and a dullard of any race, it has a variety of other uses, all of them

Afro-American. They include the verb to **jeff** or **jeff-davis**: either to use a given line of talk to deceive or seduce another person (thus the phrases *tight jeff*: well-rehearsed patter and *slack jeff*: spontaneous ad-libbed chatter) or to act subserviently to a White person (a synonym for **tom**). A **rabbit**, with rural rather than naming emphasis behind it, is yet another term for White. **Joey** meant White in the 1950s, especially as in **three-bullet Joey**: the White police.

Charlie, charles or **chuck** (a nickname for Charles), another name, all mean White, although more usually a White in authority. Thus the variations **Mr Charlie** (seen in James Baldwin's book *Blues for Mr Charlie*) and **Boss Charlie**, as well as the phrases **charlie goons** and **charlie nebs** (from *neb*: a beak and as such a term reminiscent of the 16th-century *harman beck* – the 'magistrate's beak' – perhaps the earliest recorded slang term for policeman) both meaning the police. **Sylvester**, a proper name and possibly taken from Mel Blanc's ridiculous black cartoon cat (the rival of the angelic bird Tweetie-Pie) is a synonym. A similar term, **Mr Gub** (in which gub refers either to garbage or government), means much the same for Native Australians. Other such Australian terms are **gunjie** and **balander** (a pidgin term based on Hollander, thus Dutchman). Unlike cracker or peckerwood, Charlie is not restricted to describing farmers and peasants. It is equally applicable to town-dwellers. So too is **honkie, honky, hunky, honkey** or **hunkamo**, all of which terms refer explicitly to the urban White working class. The term comes from **Bohunk** (also **bohak, bohick, bohink**); it means a Slav immigrant or an oafish prole, and is itself a combination of Bohemian, i.e. Czech, and Hungarian. From there it became **hunkie**, a term that began as a specific reference to the Poles who worked in the Chicago stockyards. The spelling was changed from hunkie to honkie during the 1960s, allegedly as part of the desire of the contemporary Black militants to distance themelves as far as possible from White culture. Honkie can also be found in **Honkie-Town**, the White working-class section of a town and **super-honkie**, an exceptionally authoritarian White person. **Hunkyland** is Hungary. **Tug**, presumably referring to the standard term *tug*: to drag or haul and meaning Slovene, also focusses on the Middle European's supposed propensity for hard labour. The older **bohawk** or **bohak** were coined for Lithuanians, and they too became all-purpose 'Slavic' words. Another 'urban' phrase is **feel a draught**. Coined by the jazz musician Lester Young it has twin meanings: to sense racial antagonism in one's conversation or dealings with Whites and to warn one's friends that a White person has entered the room.

White, as a synonym for ethical, honourable and generally admirable entered the language in the 1850s. Coined in Australia where, ironically, the first citation appears to refer to a Black farm worker as 'the Whitest man on the farm'. It was used without the slightest taint of irony and in the strangest combinations, e.g. John Buchan's fictional American entrepreneur Blenkiron who talks of 'the Whitest Jew since Jesus', casting, unconsciously, a light on the way that 'blackness' informed all sorts of racial sterotyping: Jews, Irish and others could be 'tarred', the palapable facts notwithstanding. It has become a grim joke in more recent years, when the Eurocentric view of imperialism and its effects has become, at least ostensibly, modified. No more would a White man be defined as 'a person of impeccable character'. Nowhere more so than in Black America where **White** now has a quite different meaning: anyone (irrespective of colour) who is seen as immoral or unethical. That said, the term has been used in South Africa for many years to mean cheeky or impudent, in other words, attempting to act the equal of a White person.

The imperial legacy has also lingered in Papua New Guinea where Tok Pisin gives a range of terms that recall the White 'masta': itself still meaning a European. Thus **liklik masta**: 'little master' means a White boy, **missis** is a White woman and **taim bilong masta**: 'time that belonged to the European' is the era of White or imperial rule. Imperialism also gave two early 19th-century terms, used by African-Americans for their White masters: **algereen** and **buccaneer**. Both mean a pirate (the first referring to the Algerian privateers and the second to the pirates of the Caribbean) and they equate the White captains and crews who ran slave ships from Africa with the equally villainous pirates. The effect that Whites have had on local environments is seen in the native American **White man's foot grass** (*c*.1800), meaning White clover and so called from the Indian's notion that it grows wherever a White man has walked

The White as hypocrite, as liar, above all oppressor can be seen in a number of allied terms. **Hack**, which in American cant otherwise means a prison officer, has become a generic term for any White person; **mickey mouse** (otherwise referring to something insignificant or second-rate) is used similarly, as is **maggot**, already a general term of abuse and which once itself meant **magpie**, a mixed race epithet. The spread of rap vocabulary has brought **caveboy**, a modern twist on the old 'down from the trees' canard. According to some Black anthropological theorists, while prehistoric Black Africans lived on the plains the Whites remained, terrified, in their caves. **Monkey**, another term that has been used for Blacks, has also been turned back on itself, now referring as much to Whites (although it can also be used of Chinese or West Indians, who are also known as **monkey-chasers**).

According to its founder Wallace D. Fard, the Nation of Islam, better known as the Black Muslims, holds that the Black man is locked in battle against the 'big-headed scientist' Yacub. Yacub preached against God and against his servants in Mecca. For this he was exiled, and in revenge he set about creating a new, hostile race: blond, pale-skinned, blue-eyed 'White devils', who have ruled the world for the past 6,000 years. As dubious as any religious myth, the concept has many adherents, and thus the abbreviation **yacoo** means White, as does devil itself; **beast** was also a Black Nationalist coinage; originated in the 1960s it has re-emerged in the last five years. The Islamic prohibition on eating pork gives **swine eater**. Another quasi-religous term is found in **ballhead**, meaning first a bald person and then a White one. Essentially a Rastafarian term, it implies not merely White people, but White society as lined up against the Rasta sensibility.

From political persecution to economic power: the role of the White businessman in Black neighbourhoods – less common today, but once ubiquitous – has brought down a good deal of hostility. Known generically as the **other man** (perhaps an acknowledgement of *the Man*: slang for the police) the prominence of Jews amongst such businessmen (especially in New York's Harlem) has created **Goldberg**, using the typical Jewish surname to stand for an entire breed; **jew**, a boss, irrespective of his actual religion, and **fast talking Charlie**, adding the Jew's sales patter to the general term Charlie. **Three balls**, usually a pawnbroker, is also a Jew; pawnbrokers (as in the 1964 movie *The Pawnbroker*, where Rod Steiger plays just such a figure) in Black areas were often Jews. The image of the three balls supposedly comes from the arms of the Italian Medici family (although they originally boasted six red balls, rather than the three gold ones of pawnbroking) and were imported to London by the Italian bankers of Lombardy; from there they arrived in America. The link between Jews and pawnbroking can be seen again in the old German student phrase **My coat is studying Hebrew**, i.e. my coat is in pawn.

This last category of name-calling covers those 'wannabe' Whites, desperate to abandon their own culture and take on the Black lifestyle. Thus the **faded boogie** means both a Black informer, and a White who imitates Black fashions (see also *Politics*). More recently the hip-hop world has generated the **wigga** or **wigger** (i.e. 'White nigger'); not satisfied with buying the music and attending the concert, or even dressing à la gangsta, these Whites want to take on the whole Black lifestyle. The term is invariably derogatory, used by Blacks to sneer at those who ape their culture; it is also used by racist Whites, as a synonym for the age-old **nigger-lover**. Another, older term is **jig-chaser**, using the older term **jigaboo**: an Afro-American. One last term reverses the process. **Hincty**, which otherwise means a snob or an arrogant, self-opinionated person, can also be used to describe any Black abandoning racial pride for attempts to ape White manners and styles. Nor need one be Black to loathe Whites; the Chinese term **teh** means a rascal, and by extension any European.

LANGUAGE

A ND THE Lord said, Behold, the people is one, and they have all one language...and now nothing will be restrained from them, which they have imagined to do. Go to, let us go down, and there confound their language, that they may not understand one another's speech. So the Lord scattered them abroad from thence upon the face of the earth...Therefore is the name of it called Babel, because the Lord did there confound the language of all the earth...' (*Genesis xi*: 6-9). Thus the Babel myth, as recounted in the King James version of the Bible. A unified language means maximized knowledge and such universality, according to the Church, is not to be tolerated. There must be no 'towers', figurative or otherwise, via which the masses can access their rulers.

Unfortunately the myth is etymological as well as religious: a marginal note translates *Babel* as 'confusion' but there is no linguistic basis for the theory; Babel more probably stems, as does Babylon, from the Assyrian *bab-ilu*: the gate of God. Not that such quibbling matters; the bigger picture holds sway. Ignorance, especially as ordained for others, is indeed bliss. A mere nine chapters into *Genesis*, just after Noah, half a page of 'begats' prior to Abraham, the inference is that not only is

54

linguistic difference good, but it is vital. A situation where 'the whole earth was of one language and of one speech' (*Genesis* xi:1) was unacceptable to God and, it would appear, a variety of Esperantos not withstanding, shall be so ever more.

Babel is, of course, no more than a myth, the real foundations of language are somewhat more prosaic, but the lack of a unified tongue is hugely influential on human relations. Colour aside, language is one of the simplest ways of establishing 'otherness' and is thus the source of a variety of ethnic slurs. If 'they' can't talk 'like we do' then they're suspect. And their ignorance confers an extra pleasure in our unity: the simple fact that we understand and they do not reinforces our own togetherness, and pushes them even farther into the outer darkness.

It's all Greek to Me

The basic slur, of course, is mutual incomprehensibility. However subtle, however sophisticated, the simple fact that the language is not one's own, renders it nonsense, gibberish. For once there seems to be no specific stereotype. Any language qualifies, as long as it isn't one's own. Ignorance, on these grounds, is indeed bliss.

The idea is lodged deep in history, with the Hebrew word **b'laaz**, meaning 'in the stammering (or jabbering) language', in other words, in any language other than Hebrew or Aramaic. It happens too that the word *laaz* contains the initials of *loshon avodah zorah*, 'the language of strange worship', but this may be coincidence rather than design. Either way, the concept is undiminished and, typically, the Biblical and Talmudic commentator, Rashi, used b'laaz to describe French, his own vernacular, in the French glosses of his celebrated work. The Yiddish term **targum-losim**, literally 'translation-language' is used to delineate a language as unintelligible or nonsensical. Effectively it means 'not Yiddish or Hebrew' and was initially directed at the translation of the Hebrew text of the Bible into Aramaic. Nonetheless, Aramaic would in time serve as a source of many colloquialisms in Yiddish. Similarly the ancient language of Syriac (spoken in Syria) offered **loz**, to speak barbarously, to stammer, and was used in practice to refer to speaking Egyptian. And still in the Middle East the Spanish word **algarabia**, properly 'Arabic' and doubtless referring to the Arabic occupation of Granada, means gabble or jargon (a word literally and originally translated as 'the twittering of birds', although still prefiguring the modern definitions as both obfuscation and 'professional slang').

More recently the Spanish have looked nearer home, to the Basques, for their attacks on 'nonsensical' language. **Vascuence** means 'the Basque tongue', i.e. nonsense; the Portuguese **vasconcear**: 'to talk Basque' means to talk nonsense, while France's **parler français comme un basque espagnol** can be translated as 'to murder the French language'. The alternative **parler français comme une vache espagnole**: 'to speak French like a Spanish cow' is equally uncomplimentary but while apparently acceptable as a phrase in its own right the *vache* (cow) may in fact be no more than a mis-spelling of Basque. But if Basque discomfits its neighbours, so does Spanish itself have its critics. The Czech phrase **To jest mu španělská ves**: 'it's all Spanish to me' is a euphemistic version of 'what a load of nonsense'.

Much the same feeling is found in the Danish/Norwegian **det kommer mig noget spansk** for 'That strikes me as rather odd'. **Das kommt mir spanisch vor**: 'This sounds Spanish to me', say the Germans, and translate it as 'Sounds like rubbish to me'. The Spanish apparently hit back with **germania**: 'gypsy cant', but in this case the 'German' may in fact refer not to the country but to the earlier use of the word, meaning kinship or relationship (e.g. cousin-german) – although such an image would surely run contrary to the 'alien-ness' that lies behind all these usages.

France, like Spain, uses one of its own minority languages as a target. **Bretonner**, literally 'to Breton' (from Brittany, in north-west France) means both to stammer and to speak unintelligibly or barbarously; natives of Provence, in southern France, use **bretonejar** in an identical way. Indeed France, traditionally jealous of its own linguistic purity, launches a scattershot assault on a variety of unacceptable languages. Une **espèce de flamingue**: a Fleming type, means either an insincere person or one who speaks French badly; **flaminguer**: to speak Flemish, means to lie, or at least to speak insincerely. **Latin**: Latin, is just a synonym for argot or slang. **Hacher de la paille**: 'to chop straw' means to talk German and thus to jabber unintelligibly; **c'est du haut alle-**

mand pour moi: 'it's High German to me' means I can't make head nor tail of it. High German or *Hochdeutsch*, originally confined to High or southern Germany, is in fact the 'literary' language of the whole country. Its opposite Low German or *Plattdeutsch*, covers the nation's dialects and indeed is applied by philologists to all the West Germanic dialects except High German (thus including English, Dutch and Frisian). **C'est de l'hébreu pour moi**: it's Hebrew for me, is best translated as 'it's all Greek to me', although France also has the more literal **c'est du grec** and in any case 'Hebrew', in 17th century England, was synonymous with 'Greek' when it came to metaphorical unintelligibility. The French also offer **chinoiser**: 'to Chinese', an underworld term that, like its peers, means to jabber, talk gibberish, cant or slang. Other countries stigamtize China too, although with no criminal overtones. In Hungary there is **ez nekem kínai**: 'that's Chinese to me', that's Greek to me; while in Russia **eto dila menya kitaiskaya azbuka** means 'this is the Chinese alphabet to me'; **kitaiskaya gramota**, or 'Chinese writing' denotes anything deemed unintelligible.

Across the Channel however, the French, as ever, find something of a fight-back. **Pedlar's French** is one of the terms cited in the earliest of slang 'dictionaries', the fifty-odd terms of cant or criminal slang included in the London printer Robert Copland's *Hye Waye to the Spyttell House* (*c*.1530). It translates as both underworld slang and as gibberish in general. It has been suggested that Chaucer's reference to the 'French' of Stratford-atte-Bow is an even earlier use of this slang-related term, but it seems unlikely that the Prioress, to whose imperfect bilingualism Chaucer is referring, would have been versed in the world of the 'counterfeit cranke' or 'mort wap-apace'. (She was, on the other hand, well aware of some racial stereotyping: it is in her tale that the blood libel of Hugh of Lincoln, a child supposedly sacrificed by the city's Jews, is recounted). More likely, as suggested by Baugh and Cable (*A History of the English Language*, 4th edn 1993) he is reflecting on the generally 'provincial' character of the French spoken in England (heavily influenced, unsurprisingly, by the Norman dialect), for as Chaucer says 'Frensh of Paris was to hir unknowe'. For further remarks on this and other nationally-based criminal jargons (including Lingua Franca: 'the French – Frankish – language') see *Crime* below. In dialect

Frenchy and **Frenchman** both refer to one who cannot speak English, and thus to any foreigner, irrespective of origin. On this model one could have 'French Frenchys', but equally well 'Swedish' or 'German Frenchys'. **French** is also an all-purpose term of contempt and an adjective meaning very bad or in serious trouble. In Italy **francesume**: a 'Frenchism', rather than the more respectable 'Gallicism', refers to the use of French for no reason other than showing off.

Although no one language has a monopoly on unintelligibility, and mere proximity is often sufficient justification for a sneer, the phrase 'it's all Greek to me' is undoubtedly one of the best known. The English use is first found in *Patient Grissil*, a play co-written in 1603 by Thomas Middleton and Thomas Dekker (himself a devoted exponent of criminal cant). Apart from the French use, above, the Spanish **hablar en griego**: 'to speak Greek' means to say something unintelligible, and a variety of cognate terms, while not always citing 'Greek' as such, are translated into English by this single phrase. Sometimes, typically in Ben Jonson's *Alchemist* (1610) the term is amplified as **heathen Greek**.

And after Greece, the Netherlands. Like Greek **Dutch**, or more usually **double Dutch** (coined *c*.1789) is a synonym for unintelligible talk, gibberish, or just foreign speech. Earlier phrases, with an identical meaning include to **talk High Dutch** (the earlier name of what would become High German and thus, to be accurate, not in fact 'Dutch' Dutch); while **Dutch jawbreakers** are words that are very difficult to pronounce, a problem that stems from the common duplication of vowels and semi-vowels. Even earlier (*c*.1590) is **talk Dutch fustian**. Fustian, which usually refers to a kind of coarse cloth made of cotton and flax, was used in this sense to mean inflated, turgid, or inappropriately lofty language as well as jargon and gibberish. The development of its synonym, *bombast*, shows the way such terms develop and change. Bombast was, like fustian, a material, in this case a sort of cotton-wool used as padding or stuffing for clothes. From there the meaning grew to encompass that same cotton-wool, stuffed into one's ear as a prophylactic against noise; and from there to describe the noise itself. Fustian has followed a similar path. Bombast, it has to be added, does not, alas, come as has been regularly proclaimed, from the proper name of the wonderfully baptised Philippus Aureolus Theophrastus Bombastus von Hohenheim, a Swiss physician and alchemist better known as Paracelsus. English dialect offers **talk as Dutch as Daimport's bitch** (literally *Davenport's* – the background of this Cheshire worthy is sadly lost – *bitch*) and a reverse of the usual use in **talk Dutch**: to talk in standard English rather than in one's local dialect; likewise the adjective **Dutch**, as applied to language, can mean 'stuck-up' or affected. The 'foreign-ness', in both cases, being in the idea of any world outside the local one and the same feeling underpins the Provençal **franchiman-deja**: to affect a northern accent. Far away, but absolutely similar is Japan's **gairaigo**, literally 'from outside words', and typifiying any imported European loanwords.

Perhaps due to distance, or more probably to the (subsconscious) knowledge that their two languages share many long-established similarities, the British seem to have excluded German from the list of 'nonsensical' languages. Such consideration does not extend to Germany's neighbours (nor indeed to somewhat farther-off countries). Thus in Poland German is **barani język**: literally the 'wether language' (a wether being a castrated ram) because to Polish ears it sounds like bleating. Germany reciprocates with another farmyard idiom, calling Polish the 'quack language' from its use of '*tak, tak*', meaning 'Yes, yes.' The Poles hit back with **szwargota po niemiecku**: 'to jabber in German.' Other German terms, in the dialects respectively of Saxony and Silesia offer **palatschen** and **palatschkern**: these also meaning to jabber (in this case in Polish). **Pallebratsch reden**: to speak over-familiarly, as the Poles are supposed to do, comes from the Polish **panie bracie**: 'sir brother' and **polnisches Geschnatter** translates as 'Polish cackling'. **Pan** itself, meaning 'sir', has been used sarcastically by Germans as a generic for all Poles, the implication is of the grovelling Polish peasant. Nearby Lithuania adds **vacieja**: the 'unintelligible ones', in other words, the Germans, while in Scandinavia the Norwegians use **tydska** and the Danes **tyske**, both meaning literally 'to German' and as such to gabble or jabber. In Russia **nyemets**: a German, means both one who cannot make himself understood and a linguistic incompetent, while the Icelandic **djflaka**: 'the devil's German' refers variously to gibberish, to any badly-spoken language and to foreign speech. Russia also equates the Latvians with nonsense: 'I can't under stand a word – he might as well be a Lett'.

The Jews, despite lacking their own country until 1948, did have an indigenous vernacular. This was not Hebrew, the language of the Scriptures and in its modern form, of the Jewish state of Israel, but Yiddish. This is an Anglicized version of the German *jüdisch:* 'Jewish' and itself an abbreviation of *jüdisch deutsch*: 'Jewish-German'. (The English word has been taken back into German as *jiddisch*.) Yiddish, used traditionally if less and less frequently by Ashkenazim (a Hebrew word that means literally 'German' but covers all the Jews of Europe and of Russia – but not Spain and North Africa where they are known as sephardim: 'Spanish') in Europe and America, is based mainly on German, especially that of the Middle Rhine area, plus a certain number of Balto-Slavic or Hebrew words; it is printed in Hebrew characters. This strong link to German has not precluded Yiddish (which Goethe termed 'baroque') being branded, in Germany and elsewhere, as an outlandish tongue. Thus **Judendeutsch**: 'Jew German', means gibberish as does **Jargonsprache**, literally 'jargon language' but generally recognized as meaning Yiddish. In Holland **Smousentael** means both Yiddish and gibberish. It is obviously linked to **smous** or **Schmouss** (pronounced 'schmoos') which originally referred to a German Jew, but was broadened to cover Jews as a whole. The term itself seems to come from the Yiddish *shmuess*: 'chat', and in turn from Hebrew *shmuah*: news. In a parallel usage the Polish **jamroty**: to jabber, is another word for Jew, although it can also mean a German. Yiddish itself has **terkish**: Turkish, while Italy's **parlare turco**: 'to speak Turkish' means to say something that makes no sense. **To talk turkey**: to speak frankly, to get down to business, however, has a different background, being based on the bird rather than the country (although the bird, of course, does have links to Turkey – it gained its name through being imported from its native Guinea, through countries which were under Turkish rule).

A few more examples exist. **Ruotsi**, which in Swedish means 'inarticulate' is a synonym for Finnish; **choctaw**, properly describing a Muskogean North American Indian people, originally inhabiting Mississippi and Alabama, and thus their language, has been used since the mid-19th century to describe an unknown, difficult or simply nonsensical language. It has also been used, in the American West, to mean Spanish (the language of nearby Mexico and at one time Texas and California too). The Yiddish word **deitshuk**, literally Chinook, another tribe, can be used to mean German. For some Americans nonsense can also be **Mexican oats**. Finally comes **gibberish** itself, originally a cant term and defined in the *OED* as 'unintelligible speech belonging to no known language, and supposed to be of arbitrary invention; inarticulate chatter, jargon. Often applied contemptuously to blundering or ungrammatical language, to obscure and pretentious verbiage.' Its etymology remains a challenge but may possibly stem from a conflation of *Gypsy* and *jabber*, itself generally acknowledged as onomatopoeic. Another, highly feasible source may be in the Romany *chib* (the tongue).

The Frankish Tongue

The 'otherness' of foreign languages is also reflected in the use of such tongues – French, Greek, Welsh – as synonyms for criminal jargon or cant. One of the first slang collections, published in Germany in 1510, was the *Liber Vagatorum* (the Book of Vagabonds). This was enormously popular, with editions in High and Low German, Low Rhenish and Dutch. The Protestant reformer Martin Luther even contributed a foreword to that of 1528, admitting that 'I have myself of late years been cheated and befooled by such tramps and liars more than I wish to confess'. A pioneer of the 'beggar-books' that would launch an unbroken succession of slang dictionaries that reaches forward to the present day), it offered a detailed list of 28 varieties of villain, a 'dramatis personae' that would be seen again in many successors. Among the terms listed are *barlen*: to speak (from French *parler*); *fetzen*: to work (from German *fetzen*: tatters, the 'uniform' that beggars used); *kabas*: the head (from Latin *caput*); *bosshart*: meat (from Hebrew *basar*), and *zwicker*: the hangman (from German *zwicken*: to pinch). The language in which all these were written was known as **rottwelshe** or beggar's patter. This German word comes from the Middle High German *rot*: a beggar and *welsch* or *wälsch*, which, cognate with one use of the English word *Welsh* means a 'strange, outlandish language'.

61

Welsh itself was not the target; the word could equally well, and often did apply to Italian. The terms **rotvalska** (Swedish) and **Kauder-welsch**: corrupt Welsh (German) mean much the same.

And while Welsh came to be the name of the Britons who had fled West away from the Anglo-Saxon invaders, its root *Wälsche* meant barbarian. This in turn came from the Anglo-Saxon *wealh*, used by the invaders to describe those who fled before them. Like the *barbar* in barbarian, *wealh* was basically a mocking sound, implying that the speech of these terrified peasants was meaningless and incomprehensible. Ironically, in this construction, it was the indigenous 'Welsh' and not the invading Anglo-Saxons, who thus became the foreigners – strangers, as it were, in their own land. Over time the word became increasingly pejorative: as the Celtic world became increasingly devalued, *wealh* began to mean a slave or servant (equating, like *slav*, the people and their status) and from thence a 'wanton' or 'shameless person'. *Wealh word* meant a 'wanton word' while *wealian* was 'to be impudent, bold or wanton'. *Wealh* may also be linked to Sanskrit *mlekkha*: a person who talks indistinctly. This in turns becomes the possible root of the Beluchi (natives of Beluchistan), who at one time were considered mumblers. *Wälsche* itself is found in a very different context, but with exactly the same meaning, as the root of the word walnut, in other words *Wälsche nuss:* a foreign nut. Another example of 'Welsh' as meaning alien or incomprehensible comes in the 18th-century nickname for the Jabbering Crow, a bird native to Jamaica. This was 'the Welshman', a name chosen because, as Edward Long's *History of Jamaica* (1774) explains, 'with their strange noisy gabble of gutteral sounds...[they] are thought to have much the confused vociferation of a party of Welsh folks exercising their lungs and tongues at a grand scolding match'.

Two further criminal terms are **Lingua Franca** and **St Giles' Greek**. The first, Italian for 'the Frankish tongue', began life as a form of pidgin used in the Levant, consisting mainly of Italian words deprived of their inflexions. From there it came to mean a mixed language created and used between people speaking different languages (this too being a form of pidgin). Typical of such terms, in English, are *madza caroon*: half a crown (from *mezzo*: a half), *nantee*: nothing (from *niente*) and *cattivo cazza*, translated as *kertever cartzo*: a 'bad cock', and thus venereal disease. St Giles' Greek, a later creation, refers to the criminal rookery (an underworld slum) centred on the parish of St Giles in central London, and destroyed when New Oxford Street was cut through the slums in 1847. The **greek** takes on its usual role as a 'foreign' or 'outlandish' tongue.

Ballyhoo at the Blarney Stone

Foreign-ness and even criminality aside, further national slurs can be taken from the use of language-related terms to describe those who are boastful, insincere and who tend to bragging and flattery. And once more, while there are no stereotypes as such, there is no denying that two of the best-known such words, **ballyhoo** and **blarney**, are indelibly associated with Ireland.

The first of these, ballyhoo, is defined both as rubbish, nonsense and empty praise, and a form of excessive, grandiose publicity, often used when the product cannot live up to the manufactured image. The term comes from carnival and fairground jargon and means a barker's speech, touting a given attraction. Its precise etymology remains obscure, but the theories are these (as cited in H.L. Mencken's *American Language*). From the Gaelic *bailinghadh* (pronounced *ballyhoo*): collect; the predominantly Irish fairground touts of the mid-19th century shouted '*Bailinghadh anois!*' ('Collection now!') when they passed the hat for payment. Alternatively the cod-Arabic cry *b'Allah hoo*: 'through God it is', used by the 'dervishes' in the Oriental Village sited at the Chicago World's Fair of 1893. Much less likely is a putative combination of the standard English *ballet* and *whoop*.

The second, blarney, has an incontrovertible link with Ireland, its derivation from the village of Blarney, sited near the southern city of Cork, which has a castle in which lies an inscribed stone. The stone is hard to approach and the popular belief is that anyone who kisses this 'Blarney stone' will ever after be gifted with a persuasive, plausible tongue. Originally defined as boasting and bluff, especially as in the phrase 'tip the blarney', it later acquired the sense of flattery, nonsense and charming but empty chatter. Similar, but geographically separate, is another phrase, the 19th-century **dipped in the Shannon**, meaning shameless or devoid of shyness. Like Achilles, whose immersion in the Styx gave him almost total invincibility, those who are dipped in the Shannon, Ireland's main river, are supposedly rendered free of any self-restraint.

Nor are the Irish in sole possession of such terms. The French, keen to damn half Europe as purveyors of gobbledygook, and whose highest intellectual conclave, the *Académie Française*, has been fighting vainly for a purified French since the 17th century, are skewered with the Dutch **een Fransch kompliment maken**: 'to pay a French compliment' which can mean to run off ('to take French leave') but also means to flatter, to 'soft-soap' and **Fransch praten** (also Dutch) which uses the literal translation 'to talk French' to mean to boast, to 'talk big'. Similarly **Franscmans**: a Frenchman, is a braggart. Undaunted, as one might expect, the French use Spain's **habler**: 'to speak (Spanish)' to mean to boast or show off; and **venir de Cracovie** or **avoir ses lettres de Cracovie** (to come from Cracow or have letters patent from Cracow) to mean to 'play the braggart'. The term comes from the French **craquer:** to bluff, and the image of Poland, of which Cracow was once the capital, as a home of self-aggrandizing pomposity. Back with Spain the English terms **Spanish money** and **Spanish coin** were similarly defined in the 18th century as 'fine words that cost little', i.e. flattery or smooth talk. In Spain itself to speak **portuguesada**: 'in a Portuguese manner', is to make vain, empty boasts. More blatantly racist is America's **nigger talk**, a mid-19th-century term for irresponsible, exaggerated gossip, plus the patronizing **negro nomenclature**, laid down in Bartlett's *Americanisms* (1861) as any 'high-sounding but ridiculous term for Negro religious and political organizations'. The French term **parler petit nègre**, literally 'to talk a little nigger', has the same implication.

Two questions conclude this section. The punning **how high is a Chinaman?** (from the 'Chinese' name *How Hi*) is used as the answer to a statement or question which the speaker considers to be absurd or unanswerable and in Spain the indignant cry **Somos chinos?**: 'Are we Chinamen? is the popular reaction to long-winded explanations of simple matters.

Excuse my French

If language, alien language, is de facto 'bad', then bona fide 'bad language' is always good for a racial nudge. The English, the most self-censored and, for all the glories of their own language, the most linguistically squeamish of nations, are keen to brand others with the use of such terminology. Unsurprisingly, given the identification of France with 'dirtiness' of body and mind, it is the French who are similarly loaded with a supposed 'dirtiness' of tongue. Aside from the **French novel,** assumed to be a respository of filthy thoughts and deeds, the simple word **French** means, as a writer as recently as 1959 stated without any apparent blush, 'perverted' and thus obscene and thus, finally, obscenity. Hence the coy phrase, redolent of purse-lipped, fearful lower-middle-class rectitude: **Excuse my French**, a phrase used to sidestep what are presumed to be the horrid consequences of swearing in public. It can also appear as **pardon my French**. To **loose French**, around 1900, meant to swear or, as the slang lexicographer J. Redding Ware put it, to indulge in 'violent language'. The Germans too have the foul-mouthed French in their sights with **fluchen wie ein Franzose**, to swear like a Frenchman, although both Italy – **bestemmiare come un turco** – and Denmark – **bande som en tyrk** – lay their plaints at Turkish feet. The French themselves turn back on the English and suggest that to swear properly one must **jurer comme un Anglais**: swear like an Englishman.

English swearing is unique insofar as a number of phrases exist which play on its frequency to equate the obscenity itself with the pure fact of being British. Thus in Japan the British are **damuraisu h'to**: the 'damn your eyes people', in France **les fuckoffs** or **les goddams** (and thus Britain is **Godamland**); in late-19th-century Canada a **goddam** was an Englishman. Nor are such usages invariably obscene. They can simply reflect the tricks and verbal 'hiccups' that characterize English speech. The Chinese and French both use **I-say** to mean Englishman, Oregon Indians, first meeting English colonists, referred to them as **kinchotsch**: King George. A number of Pacific Islanders use **oleboi** (old boy) or **oleman** (old man) to mean an English person, while in Papua New Guinea a cry of **olaboi**! means Wow! Most recently it is reported that the Falkland Islanders distinguish between officers and 'other ranks' in the British Army by the way they start their sentences. Thus an officer is a **whenwun**: when one... while the other ranks are **wheneye**: when I...

Parleyvoo, Paisan?

In some cases the links between a nation and its language are defined by a negative use of the actual language itself. The words that are used, or the way in which they are pronounced define the term. Deliberate mispronunciation adds to the list, thus **ay-rab** means Arab, **orsetraylian** Australian and **Eyetalian, eyetie** (or **Itie**) Italian. Australia also suffers **arsey, aussie,** and **arsetralian.** The word-into-slur formation is somewhat more extensive. **Bootchkey,** an American slang term for Czech, supposedly comes from a cry of *pockej:* hold on!, which immigrant Czech children once shouted as they played; **goo-goo** or **gu-gu,** another Americanism, means a Filipino, originally a soldier fighting in the Spanish-American War, 1899-1902, but more recently any Filipino. It supposedly mimics of Filipino speech. Another term for Filipino, **chico,** comes from Spanish *chico:* a boy, while **kac,** which in Georgian means man, is used by Russians to typify the entire Georgian population. The uncommon **walliyo** or **walho,** both meaning Italian probably comes from the Tuscan *guaglione:* a boy. In America the Spanish words **ese**: a man, a guy, and **hombre**: a man, have been adopted to mean any Mexican. **Paisan** or **pizon,** meaning fellow-countryman, can be extended to mean Italian-Americans in general. In Australia **pong,** mocking the 'ong' sound of Chinese speech, means a Chinese person.

The mid-19th-century **slawmineyeux** was used to mean a Dutchman by British sailors; it was a corruption of the Dutch phrase *ja mijnheer*: 'yes, sir'. Affirmation also gives **wi-wi,** from *oui-oui* meaning yes, thus a Frenchman, though given the on-going animosity between Britain and France, the nursery term for urination, *wee-wee,* should not be overlooked. French also gives the late-19th-century **parleyvoo,** from *parlez-vous*: do you speak?, **mounseer, mossoo** or **mosso,** all from *Monsieur* (the most celebrated Mossoo was Billy Bunter's unfortunate French teacher), and **dee-donk,** which comes from the French *dis-donc*: so tell me. Dee-donk, a British usage, dates from World War I, but it has antecedents in the synonymous **didones** (used in Spain after the Peninsular War, a century earlier), **dido** (as used in Lingua Franca) as well as, somewhat later, the Javanese **orang deedonc**: 'the dis donc people'.

Everyday German phrases, often transmitted through the agency of war or occupation, have the same effect on the naming process. **Dasti-cotter**: to use or speak German, comes from the German imprecation *das dich Gott*, while the Dutch **yah-for-yes folk** stems from the German *ja*: yes. The Poles, never any great friends of their Western neighbour, talk of the **derdydasy**: Germans, from versions of the definite article: *der, die, das*, and further categorize them as **fadry-mu-tri**, from *Vater*: father and *Mutter*: mother, and **farfiuk**, from the German *verflucht*: damned (a usage that echoes the various terms, listed above, in which as far as the British are concerned the oath makes the man). The Poles themselves have been known in Russia as **prsem pana**, from the Polish phrase meaning 'excuse me, sir', and in America as **yaks**. Some see this as an abbreviation of the Polish phrase *Jak sie masz*: How are you?, but it may be no more than an extension of the general slang term *yak* or *yack*: a fool.

Keeping up this formation, White Americans were known, in the early 19th century, as **guessers**, at least by the Black population, from their continued use of the phrase *I guess* (a linguistic tic that, for all its modern identification with the most stereotypical American, actually dates back to 14th-century English), and in French slang a Swiss is a **lifrelofe**: because his speech seems to consist of such sounds. The Swiss German term **Schweize**, which in dialect means a spiced butter sauce, is used in the phrase **eine lange Schweize** to mean a long-winded, tedious explanation or a rigmarole, often without rhyme or reason. In the provincial Swiss dialect, **mache shwai(t)zi** means 'to lay it on thick.'

Speaking of Sea-Slugs

Pidgins are hybrid, artificial languages concocted primarily to create a way of communication between, initially, Western buyers and Eastern or Southern sellers, and as exploration and trade expanded, to facilitate all forms of communication between two mutually incomprehensible cultures. The term, also pidjin, pidjun and pidgeon and known synonymously in the Pacific as **bêche-de-mer** (the word originally meant a sea-slug), is classically pidgin itself: a corruption in Chinese mouths of the English word *business*. Coined around 1820 it described the language that grew up between the European traders and the merchants with whom they dealt at Chinese sea ports, the Straits Settlements and other centres of commerce. Pidgins are not racist in themselves. Nor are such blends as *Franglais, Yinglish, Yidgin-English* and *Finnglish* (respectively French/English, Yiddish/English and Finnish/English) or the Scandinavian term *kineserengelsk*, literally Chinese English. But as noted by Nigel Lewis (*The Book of Babel*, 1994) the Chinese etymology is not the only one, and other potential sources, typically Portuguese *pequeno*: a 'little' or 'child' bring a patronizing, racist edge to the concept. The supposedly unsophisticated native is, as it were, a child, and the language one uses to communicate with him is in effect a form of 'baby-talk'. This idea is carried further in some of the names given to a variety of pidgins. French is **petit nègre**, Dutch **baby hollands** and Malay **baba Malay**. Pequeno, in addition, gives **picanniny**, a small Black child.

Turks, Greeks & Joosh-Pipples

While much of this section, indeed much of this book, might be defined as 'speaking badly', the inability of the 'other' to speak 'our' (or indeed their own) language properly adds more fuel to the nationalist fire. Perhaps the most obvious and widely used of such slurs, is **spic, spik** or **spick**, a term coined around the beginning of the 20th century, and which refers to Spaniards, Italians, Mexicans, Filipinos, Pacific Islanders and Latin Americans and Mediterraneans in general. There are various theories as to its etymology, but the best attested appears to be the phrase 'no spicka da English', or variations on that less than literate theme. Other versions include **speck** (with its added implication of a worthless, tiny speck of matter), **spig**, and **spiggoty**, which give rise to additional theories that the term might be linked to *spaghetti*, the stereotypical Italian food. Writing in 1936 Mencken, among others, suggests that it originated as a description of Italians, but the *OED*, which ignores Italians altogether, links it specifically to 'a Spanish-speaking native of Central or South America or the Caribbean' and adds that the term also refers to the Spanish language.

A similar play on bad pronunciation, **joosh-pipples**, i.e. Jewish people, mocks the 'Mittel-European' accent of America's newly arrived Jews. **Mauscheln** is a German term defined in Paul's *Deutsches Wörterbuch* (1921) as 'the presence in language of unique Jewish elements'. Used colloquially this is transmuted to spell out those elements, typically to gesticulate, to mutter, and ultimately to speak Yiddish. In Wagner's view it proved that however assimilated a Jew might be and however long they have lived in a land, the specifically 'Jewish' use of a national language will invariably proclaim their essential alien-ness. They cannot (and unspoken, they must not) fit in. It is related to America's **Mouchey**: a Jew; they both stem from the Hebrew *Moishe*: Moses. (Moses may also lie behind the term *mosey*: to slink away, to move off, with its negative imagery of a Jewish pedlar trudging the streets, but its American orgins make the Spanish term *vamos*: let's go – which gives the derivative *vamoose!*: go away! – a more potent contender.) The use of one's hands to intensify one's speech is hardly a Jewish monopoly, but the Czechs, like the Germans attribute it thus, and underpin their distaste with **jednati po židovsku**: 'to talk or gesticulate like a yid'.

Linguistic incompetence inspires a wide variety of terms. **Böhmakeln,** in German, means to speak with a Czech accent or intonation, and thus to speak German badly; in Poland **Czerkieska odpowiedź** means a rude answer and the phrase **Po czerkiesku co zbyć** translates as to dismiss one in short order; to deal summarily with one. In France **parler français comme un Iroquois** is to talk French appallingly, while French colonialists called the Vietnamese **mangeurs de syllables**: syllable-eaters, and this solicitude for Francophonia extends elsewhere: badly spoken French, in Holland, is **Fransch met haar op**: 'French with the hair up', while in Portugal it becomes **francesear**: 'to speak a poor French'. The idea of dumbness, of simply being unable to speak a language informs another group. It starts early: the classical

Greek **aglossoi:** the speechless, was a synonym for barbarian – the one version defining the outsider by the incomprehensibility of their speech, the other by its absence. If an accent is placed on the Polish word **niemiec**, usually meaning German, it becomes a verb meaning 'to become speechless' or 'to turn mute'; there are similar terms, all meaning German, in Russian, Bulgarian, Slovenian and Serbo-Croat. For instance the Russian **nyemchura**: 'Germanry', means a group of Germans, usually keeping to themselves. The Latvians term Germans **vociete**: 'the dumb people', while in Macedonia the neighbouring Slavs are known as **dilszi**: 'the tongueless' and Turks use the same word to characterize Austrians.

The use of Greek to mean alien emerges again in a **Grecian accent**: an Irish brogue, although Irish immigrants have more usually been known as **Turks**. This identification of Ireland with a nation that would otherwise have been seen as far from its normal purlieus emerges again in the term **Milesian** based on the name of *Milesius* or *Miledh*, a legendary (if fictional) Spanish king whose sons are reputed to have conquered and reorganized the kingdom of Ireland *c*.1300BC. Thus Thomas Carlyle's tirade against 'the wild Milesian... the sorest evil this country has to contend with. In his rags and laughing savagery, he is there to undertake all work that can be done by mere strength of hand and back; for wages that will purchase his potatoes. He needs only salt for his condiment; he lodges...in any pighutch or doghutch, roosts in outhouses...There he abides, in his squalor and unreason, in his falsity and drunken violence, as the ready-made nucleaus of degradation and disorder.' (*Chartism*, 1839)

Other Irish terms include **broganeer, broganier** or **brogueneer**, all meaning one who speaks with a brogue (a word that means both Irish accent and a kind of rough shoe, originally made of hides – the former, it is thought, may well stem from the latter and refer to 'those who wear brogues' and as such a parallel term to Russia's synonym for a peasant, **lápotnik**: 'one who wears bast shoes'). The phrase **broguen speech** mixes the brogue and a pun on 'broken speech'. A more general term is **Irish**, which can be used by itself to mean contradictory statements, a concept found similarly in **Irish bull**: a statement in which the first part negates the second. (Despite temptation, this **bull** cannot be equated with an abbreviation of *bullshit*: nonsense – the chronology is wrong – nor with the papal *bull* or theological edict; and more likely stems from Old French *boul*: fraud or deceit, modern Icelandic *bull*: nonsense or Middle English *bul*: falsehood). Actual Greeks term a Rumanian **koutsoblachos**: 'a lame Wallachian', Wallachia ('the country of the Vlachs') being a precursor of Rumania; their impediment is verbal rather than physical.

Chee-chee, used by the British in India since the late 18th century to mean a half-caste, may come from the South Indian exclamation *chhi-chhi!* (dirt, filth), which was supposedly a common one amongst the Eurasian community, but it may equally come from half-caste speech patterns. The dictionary of Raj slang, *Hobson-Jobson* (1886), suggests that 'the term is a kind of onomatopoeia, indicating the mincing pronunciation attributed to the class and cites a similar suggestion in *Fraser's Magazine* for October 1873. The 'Chee Chee twang', remarks another citation 'becomes so objectionable to every Englishman before he has been long in East' and attributes it to 'the convent and the [Christian] Brothers' school'.

Flannel in the Chinese Church

Some nations, it would appear, are born to chatter. **Flannel-mouth** and **chawmouth** mean both a gossip as well as an Irishman in America; in both cases the word alludes to the 'thickness' of the brogue, and, nudgingly, to the blurred syllables of one who, in the way of another Irish stereotype, is too drunk to speak clearly. The German term *Quatsch*: nonsense, is used to create the slang term **Quatschkowski**: 'a Polish chatterbox'. Nearer home is **schwabeln**: 'to talk like the Swabians', Germany's equivalent to Britain's Irish, and thus to engage in silly chatter. The Yiddish-American term **buttinski**: one who interferes or 'butts in' uses a similar formation. Also German is **Tatarennachricht**: a Tartar report, i.e. a rumour. **Tartar** in this case actually means gypsy, and the phrase was coined during the Crimean War, when in 1854 the gypsies spread the specious news that the Russian fortress of Malakoff had been taken by the Allies. Spain uses **parlar**, a play on the French *parler*, to mean 'prattle' or 'chew the rag.' The last term for a rumour is the Dutch **Chineesche kerk**, literally a Chinese church, a centre, it must be assumed, for community gossip in a pre-Communist world.

Parliamentary Language

The casting of other nations as more than usually noisy is one of the less well-known of racial slurs, but it has nonetheless generated a number of terms. The idea that this noise should come from a notional national assembly (so unlike, we must assume, the measured elegance of our own 'Mother of Parliaments') is especially alluring, giving the British nautical slang a **Portuguese parliament**: a situation in which many people are speaking at once, and hardly anyone is listening. The **Polish parliament** is seen as equally indisciplined and the phrase, meaning generally bedlam and confusion, occurs as **polsk rigsdag** (Swedish, Danish and Norwegian), **polnischer Reichstag** (German), and **Poolsche landdag** (Dutch). The German use seems to have been the first and is based on the endless arguments, and the lack of actual legislation in the 19th-century Polish assembly.

Similar terms, albeit undignified by any association with a parliament, are the **Dutch concert**: any performance in which each musician plays a different tune; thus a general pejorative for a bad performance, musical or metaphorical; synonymous terms are a **Dutch tune** (18th century) and a **Dutch medley** (19th century). **Chinese fire drill** is bedlam or chaos; the same name as given to a US campus game whereby a car stops at the traffic lights and all those inside would jump out, run round and round the car and then jump in again before driving away. Slightly more dignified, although only in allusion, are various terms hingeing on the Jews. The Czech **židovská škola**: 'a Jewish school', means pandemonium; Germany's equivalent is **ein Larm wie in der Judenschule**: 'a commotion like in a synagogue' (here *schule* indicates the Yiddish word *shul*: a synagogue); the Dutch use **Jodenkerk**, literally a 'Jewish church' and the Russians **kagál**: a meeting of Jewish elders. All are equally uncomplimentary.

Other terms include **Indianergeheul**, a German term meaning 'Indian cries', colloquially infernal howling or pandemonium; an **Indian pow-wow**: a noisy frolic or discussion and a **nigger hoedown**:

general revelry. Of the last two, the former actually comes from an Algonquin word meaning a priest, sorcerer, or medicine-man, and thus a meeting presided over by such a shaman, while the latter is the equivalent of a *breakdown*, a noisy, riotous dance 'in the peculiar style of the negroes' (Bartlett: *Americanisms*). In Spain **suiza**: a Swiss woman means a commotion or 'all hell broke loose' while in Sweden **leva som en ryss**: to live like a Russian means to 'make whoopee'.

Nobody

ALIENS

O F ALL the characteristics that makes 'them' repellent to 'us' the sheer fact of 'their' being different – culturally, psychologically, physically, verbally – is perhaps the most potent of all the factors that those seeking to analyze this problem must encounter. For a myriad of psychological reasons we veer away from the other, and have created as a reflection of this emotion a wide-ranging lexicon of terms that refer not so much to any specific colour, race or religion, but to the simple fact of this otherness and difference. Nor is it simply veering away, not only do we withdraw, we also push the other as far as possible from our side. None of which is that surprising: in some ways, of course, the whole apparatus of racist terminology not only emerges from this difference, but depends on it.

Such terms are a constant, irrespective of circumstance, but they are never so apparent as in war-time when the enemy has to be dehuman-ised thorough propaganda, often of the crudest sort, so that he or she (and even their children) become that much easier to kill. Here language is used as the bluntest of weapons, facilitating and perhaps more important justifying what for most people is still an instinctively repug-nant act and one which, in a peacetime context, would be murder. Such dehumanizing can work in peacetime, but it is best pursued against the background of a military band, thus Hitler's desire to extirpate the Jews, enunciated plainly in *Mein Kampf*, some 16 years before he would declare a war for real, was underpinned by the deliberate fostering of this image of a war against them. That the Jews themselves were involuntary combatants, indeed to all intents non-combatants, merely helped the process. That the propagandizing found such fertile ground will be considered at *Religion*. But the demonization works in any context, whether 'they' are Jews or Palestinians, Tutsi or Hutu, communists, capitalists or whatever. Otherness is all.

Savage, Rude, Viciously Cruel

Of all the words that imply both fear and loathing of the different and alien the Greek *barbaros*: **barbarian** is the oldest. It meant variously foreign, strange or rude, and came from a root which actually meant to stammer; above all it meant 'not Greek'. As the Latin hegemony succeeded that of Greece, the term became *barbarus*, meaning much the same and was linked to *balbus*: stammering. As explained in the *OED* the senses developed from foreign, non-Hellenic or non-Roman, to outlandish, rude, brutal; thence to pertaining to those outside the Roman empire; hence uncivilized, uncultured, and later, with the advent of Christianity non-Christian, and beyond that Saracen, heathen; then generally savage, rude, viciously cruel and finally, inhuman. It is this last group of definitions that dominate today.

The alienness has given rise to other meanings, including not literary Greek or Latin, thus uncultured and even illiterate. To the lexicographer and critic Samuel Johnson 'illiterate', literally 'unlettered', meant unable to read Latin and Greek, and he thus excluded from 'literacy' the vast majority of his 18th-century contemporaries.. In the same way barbarians speak a foreign language and have outlandish 'foreign' customs. These, given the automatic fear of the 'other', are *de facto* uncultured, uncivilized, unpolished; rude, rough, wild and savage. In this context barbarian is one more synonym for uncivilized. Finally it has meant savage in the use of cruelty to others and, as regards speech, harsh-sounding, rudely or coarsely noisy.

Scandals in Bohemia

If the 'otherness' of barbarian can be seen as a breakdown in taste, then the fears that lie behind **Bohemian**, a word of much more recent coinage, are those of control, or to be more precise, the abandoning of control. Those who rail against the Bohemian represent those for whom control, of themselves and inevitably of others, is the grail that sustains life. This is the world of the censor, of both self and of others; it is, in Freudian terms, the super-ego's struggle to repel the libido.

The linkage of the geographical entity of Bohemia, the old name of what would become Czechoslovakia (now divided once again) to a certain lifestyle began in 15th-century France, where *bohème* and *bohèmien*, were applied to the gipsies. It was assumed, rightly or not, that they had come from Bohemia or at least crossed that country on their way to France. This was a contrast to England's term, *gypsy*, which comes from Egyptian and thus Egypt, the country that British theorists presumed to be the picturesque, and sometimes threatening nomads' first home. **Dark as Egypt**, at least in America, itself means strange and mysterious.

Modern French has dropped the direct link to the gypsies and defines *bohèmien* as vagabond, adventurer, person of irregular life or habits. It is this meaning that William Thackeray used in *Vanity Fair* (1848) when he described a character as being of a 'wild, roving nature, inherited from father and mother, who were both Bohemians, by taste and circumstances' and amplified it thirteen years later when in the *Cornhill Magazine* he spoke of 'Bohemia...A pleasant land, not fenced with drab stucco, like Tyburnia or Belgravia, etc.' As the *OED* defines it, the Bohemian is 'A gipsy of society; one who either cuts himself off, or is by his habits cut off, from society for which he is otherwise fitted; especially an artist, literary man, or actor, who leads a free, vagabond, or irregular life, not being particular as to the society he frequents, and despising conventionalities generally. (Used with considerable latitude, with or without reference to morals.)'

It is, of course, this last parenthesis, that renders the Bohemian suspect, especially in such a dedicatedly anti-intellectual society as that of Britain, where the general attitude to such figures is summed up in

Lord Montgomery's comment on being asked to sit for a portrait by that *echt*-Bohemian Augustus John: 'Who is this chap? He drinks, he's dirty, and I know there are women in the background'. Arthur Conan Doyle's Sherlock Holmes story 'A Scandal in Bohemia' uses both meanings of the term. For Holmes, Bohemia is the country of the atlas and of the mind. And Holmes himself, at least in Dr Watson's late-Victorian eyes, has Bohemian traits: the cocaine, the dressing-gown at all hours, the unbridled emotion. And it is in this story, of course, that Watson faces a major threat to his own controlled life. It is Holmes' one (possible) dalliance with 'the fair sex', in the person of Irene Adler, *the* woman (and with that surname perhaps even a Jewess too) whose appeal threatens not merely a crowned head of Europe, but the Watson-Holmes establishment in Baker Street, that happy ménage of sublimated homo-eroticism.

Apart from France, where a *Bohémien* thus implies an unconventional, erratic, and not too responsible person, with artistic pretensions, the term has a variety of allied uses around Europe. For Germany, **böhmische Dorfer**: 'Bohemian villages', the names of which sound so unpronounceable to a German, became a synonym for anything strange or impossible. Germany also uses the synonymous **spanische Dorfer**: 'Spanish villages'. **Böhmsche**: 'a Czech woman', meant a gaudily dressed, and thus presumably immoral, woman. **Bemsche**, literally a Czech, is a scallywag or scamp. This link between Bohemia and the Czechs and a poor image is found again in the Hungarian phrases **csehül áll**: 'he stands in a Czech way,' i.e. he is 'going to the dogs and **csehül van**: 'He is in a Czech way' or he is going from bad to worse. Germany's **Lause-Wenzel**, literally 'louse Wenceslaus' and a derogatory reverse of the name of the Czechs' patron saint, means a ragamuffin, a knave and a brand of especially foul tobacco.

The same construction can be found in the French **bohémienne** and in Poland's **cyganka**: 'a Gypsy woman.' This last, while not taken from Bohemia, uses the alternative term for gypsy, *tzigane*. Found variously as the French *tzigane*, Russian *tsýgan*, Ruthenian *tsýhan*, Slovenian *cigan*, Romanian *ţigan*, Lithuanian *cigonas*, Bulgarian *tsiganin*, and Croatian *ciganin*, every variation stems from the original Magyar *cigány*, meaning first a Hungarian gyspsy, and latterly any one of the tribe. Back in Bohemia, the Austrian exclamation **O, du Bõhm!** means 'Oh, you villain!', though the recipient of the attack need not be an actual gypsy. One last gypsy term is the Yiddish **totter**, which translates literally as tartar and means variously a queer bird, an outlandish person and a gypsy.

Damned Clever, these Chinese!

In George Orwell's ironic list of popular racial stereotypes (in his essay 'Boys' Weeklies' [1939]) a 'typical' Chinese is listed as 'sinister, treacherous, wears pigtail'. Setting aside the hairstyle, not to mention the slanted eyes – both of which are dealt with elsewhere – the image of the sinister Chinaman underpins a good deal of China-centred vocabulary.

The **heathen Chinee** (coined in 1870 by US writer Bret Harte [1836-1902] in his poem 'Plain Language from Truthful James', and better known, from this coinage, as 'The Heathen Chinee') is not just different, but wily, inscrutable and Oriental too. The **Chinaman** is not to be trusted, and the underlying implication is one of something slightly out of true, either physically, ethically, or otherwise. Typical of this attitude are the phrases **damned clever, these Chinese**, or **clever chaps these Chinese**, both of which are used when remarking on some particularly ingenious or incomprehensible invention; apparently coined in the services during World War II and then filtering into 'civvy street'; it is not skill, but cunning that is the real subject. Similarly the US phrase **harder than Chinese arithmetic** not only implies something overwhelmingly difficult, but adds the impression that in some way that difficulty is unfair. Still in America, the campus phrase to **get Chinese** is to succumb heavily to a given drug; the inference, as ever, is in the stereotype; it is the deviousness of the Chinese that underlies the term, rather than any reference to drugs as such, for all that opium, of course, has long been branded as a quintessential Chinese obsession.

As far as language goes, **China** has always been equated in one way or another with this sense of otherness. London's mid-19th-century Cockneys used it as a blanket term, meaning anywhere other than England (possibly even than London) or the place rich people went for holidays; a **Chinaman**, logically, was thus anyone, irrespective of origin, not wearing Western dress. Nor is the idea of the Chinese as an eccentric restricted to English. The Dutch **Chinees** and the Greek **Kinézos** both translate as an odd, erratic or unpredictable person. American's **Chinese arithmetic** is echoed in a pair of Russian phrases: **kitaiskaya gramota**: 'Chinese writing', meaning anything unintelligible, and **eto dlia menya kitaiskaya azbuka**: 'This is the Chinese alphabet to me', a synonym for the English phrase 'It's all Greek to me.'

The trickery implicit in 'Chinese' is not limited to language. Used in American politics the **Chinese hat trick** means, to repeat that great piece of electoral wisdom, 'vote early and vote often'. The belief was that since 'all Chinese look alike', one could obtain a few venal specimens, dress them in a succession of different hats, and send them back to the polling booth time after time. **Chinese boxes,** a set of boxes, each of which fits into the next, have become an image of complexity, inscrutability, and deliberate tricksiness. Similarly the **Chinese puzzle** has become synonymous with intricate, baffling complexity. These puzzles appeared in England around 1815, when a pamphlet announced the availability of 'A Grand Eastern Puzzle. The following Chinese puzzle is recommended to the Nobility, Gentry, and others, being superior to any hitherto invented for the amusement of the Juvenile World'. Such puzzles are properly known as *tangrams*, a word that, for all its apparent Chinese-ness, may in fact be an English or American invention. The Chinese name for these puzzles, which comprise a square dissected into five triangles, a square, and a rhomboid, all of which can be combined to make a variety of figures – houses, boats, bottles, glasses, urns, birds, beasts, men – is *Chi chiao tu*: 'seven ingenious plan'. (A **Greek puzzle** means much the same, although no such object exists – presumably it reflects the equation of Greek with incomprehensibility.) **Chinoiserie**, a French term meaning a Chinese knick-knack or curio, and imported as such into English, where it means a Chinese style of decoration, underlines this reputation for complexity. It can also mean a cruel trick.

The Great Wall of China also makes its contribution. In Russia **kitaiskaya steua**: a 'Chinese wall', means an inaccessible area or an insuperable barrier. And in banking or finance a **Chinese wall** is a variety of rules and safeguards – a Great Wall of China as it were – designed to prevent price-sensitive information, on which the unscrupulous can make profits, from passing between the dealing, fund management and corporate finance areas of the same financial conglomerate. In wider terms it can be no more than a self-imposed decision by colleagues to avoid talking about certain topics. Somewhat oblique, as is doubtless fitting, is the word **highbinder**, which in 19th-century America meant variously a prison inmate, a gangster, a thug, a corrupt politician and a swindler or fraud. Above all, however, to the contemporary authors (and readers) of penny-dreadfuls the word meant Chinese and all that that implied and was indeed drawn from the similarly named Chinese secret society that supposedly terrorised its fellow-Chinese throughout America. However, one must note also an early variety of high-binder, an early New York City gang, composed originally of butchers' boys and simultaneously known, in reference to their profession, as the Hide-binders.

But if the Chinese are strange to Western eyes, the West is simply evil to Chinese ones. The terms **fan kuai, yang kuei tse**, **yang weitz** and **gwei lo** (depending on which Chinese language one is speaking) all mean the same thing: foreign devil, in other words, anyone European. **Yáng-nú măi-bàn**, 'foreign slave and agent°, is a White merchant. Interestingly **gwei lo** has also been used of the Japanese, who in other contexts would be seen as equally Oriental. The Japanese themselves, whose own brand of inscrutability has been memorialized in America's **silent as a Japanese**, have their own take on the all too scrutable West. Although here too the initial impetus comes from less than amicable relations with China. The term **keto** means a White foreigner. It is derived from two syllables, **ke**: hairy and **to**: the Tung dynasty. The Chinese Tungs ruled Japan as colonizers and were duly loathed; thus *tung* came to mean 'abroad' in a general sense, and was duly incorporated in this term of opprobrium. Hairiness is equally unpopular in China itself where **dao máo-ze**, 'big hairy people' refers to White missionaries, a major force in pre-Maoist days, while their converts are dismissed as **èr máo-ze**, 'second-class hairy people'. In South Africa **mlungu**, from the Nguni *umlungu*: a White man, is used in the same, mocking way.

I'll be a Dutchman

The Dutch, whose image is usually one of stodgy normality, seem unlikely candidates for association with the strange and alien, yet a variety of terms declare the opposite. Here the over-riding implication is one of stark implausibility. The English phrase **that beats the Dutch** means roughly 'How amazing' and is a synonym for such slang exclamations as 'That takes the cake' and 'I'll be jiggered.' Similarly, **I'm a Dutchman** or **I'll be a Dutchman** means 'under no circumstances' or 'beyond possibility'. Thackeray, who introduced the concept of Bohemian to English also seems to have pioneered this phrase, when in 1837 he wrote in *Ravenswing* 'If there's a better-dressed man in Europe...I'm a Dutchman.' One might also mention another example of Dutch weirdness, the **Flying Dutchman**, characterized variously as a legendary Dutch mariner condemned for his crime to sail the seas until Doomsday; a phantom ship, considered a bad omen when seen (supposedly in the seas off the Cape of Good Hope); and, less mysteriously, as the nickname for an express train running on the old Great Western Railway between London and Bristol.

Bilyati Pani

The alien strain reaches out across the globe, taking in countries from France to Fiji. In Iceland, for instance, **finnagaidur**: 'Finnish witchery' implies anything odd and suspect; in Russia **tshukhonets**, literally a Finn, also means anything odd, strange or foreign, an allusion that come from the root *tshud*, connoting peculiarity. Croatians use the word **cudan** or **tsudan**: 'odd', to mean Spanish; Germany's **Fidschinsulaner**: 'Fiji Islander' translates as 'the wild man of Borneo', or anyone whose personality appears to inspire similar emotions. **Blighty**, meaning Britain and yearned for as such by generations of expatriates, comes from the Hindi *bilyati*: foreign and began life as a pejorative. Under the Raj *bilyati* was applied to a variety of nouns, typically *bilayati pani*: 'European water', used by Indians and Europeans alike for soda-water. During World War I a wound that brought a soldier his transfer back to Britain was a *Blighty*, or *Blighty one*.

The **Frenchman**, for English sailors, covered any foreigner, especially those of Mediterranean background, while **Frank**, a term of derision for Islam, especially in the period of the Crusades, meant the French in particular, but White Europeans in general. The favoured term in the East, or at least in the Indian subcontinent, is **feringee**: a foreigner or European, a term taken from the Arabic *faranji*: a Frank, and thus a European, and itself an adaptation of the Persian *farangi*. Frank itself, defined as a member of the Germanic nations that conquered France in the 6th century, and as such the origin of France, is generally believed to have come from the Old English *franca* or javelin, the Franks' preferred weapon. This transference of meaning echoes that behind another Germanic tribe, the Saxons, whose name is thought to have come from the Old English *seax* or knife. The idea that frank came from the adjective frank, meaning free, has been rejected; if anything the development proceeded in the opposite direction.

Across the Atlantic, the **Indian sign** means a spell or hex, a term that is based on a belief that Native Americans dabbled in the occult. As the lexicographer R. F. Adams explains in *Western Words* (1945) 'To put the Indian sign on someone meant to hex or curse him with some kind of witchcraft, also to get him where you want him'. Somewhat farther south one finds **gringo,** the Mexican term for foreigner, especially when an American or even Irishman, but not, given the links between the two nations, a Spaniard. A term of great disdain, and beloved of myriad movies, it may well come from *griego*, meaning Greek, in other words, as has been noted, strange and unfamiliar.

Moustache Pete

Despite the fact that many of the terms collected on these pages stem from the fact that Race A is already in situ while Race B has had the audacity to arrive sometime later, the immigrant as immigrant does not generate as many terms as might be expected.

The German worship of their nation's *kultur* – civilization as conceived on a German nationalist/militarist model and a source of much grim amusement (and not a little outrage) during World War I – led to Poland's mocking **kulturtregier:** 'bearer of culture' and thus a German settler (often far from cultured in fact) and linguistically a parody of the correct German term **kulturträger**. **Kulturnik** held the same meaning. Irish immigrants, both to Britain and the US were known as **Greeks** or **Grecians**, possibly through a heavy-handed comparison with the cultured subtleties of classical Greece and what were seen as the drunken, illiterate, bawlings of newly arrived Irish peasants. The comparison, however, may have been with an alternative meaning of **Grecian**: a roisterer, although that too concentrated more on Irish excess than anything that might, in Victorian England, have been judged more positive. As well as meaning a thug or muscleman, America's **jibone** meant a greenhorn, an innocent, a newly-arrived immigrant, usually from Italy, while a **moustache Pete** was one of the original Italian immigrants to New York, typified by their heavy moustaches; it also refers to original members of the American Mafia, who sprang from that same group of pioneers. A **South County Indian** is a Portuguese immigrant to America; South County, Rhode Island, has a notable Portuguese community. A **Latin from Manhattan**, taken from the title of a popular song, refers to a native New-Yorker, actually born of Central or South American parents, or posing as a genuine South American. Still on American soil, a **roundhead** is an immigrant from northern Europe, especially a Swede and a **forty-niner** an early immigrant to California, drawn there because of the gold rush of 1849.

Elsewhere one finds **Peruvian Jews**, a South African term for Jews, who having been unable to cope with conditions in South America come to settle in South Africa; **Kongkong** is a Malay or Chinese immigrant to Papua New Guinea. Australian slang offers **balt**, a term that covered a vast range of European immigrants, who arrived in the immediate aftermath of World War II; **ethno**: one of many immigrants to Australia, all of various ethnic persuasions and **reffo**: a derogatory reference to any immigrants during the 1930s; they were mainly Italian, Greek or Yugoslav. Finally , the Swiss dismiss undesirable outsiders with the curt **fetzel**, literally cunt.

Turks Head

NATIONAL NAMES

SOMETIMES THE slur is all too simple. All one needs is the name itself (with the occasional adjective or noun-combination) and there you are: the symbiosis of words and the pictures they conjure up is automatic; with language like this, the stereotype is self-explanatory.

In many ways, these are the most concrete of slurs. This is nothing to do with figurative differences, as seen in the idea of alienness, nor of the sensory differences detected by the eyes (see *Colour*) or the ears (see *Language*). These are the words that answer the question, when you think of Nation A, which images leap automatically into the mind?

At the same time, perhaps paradoxically, some of these words and phrases offer what can only be called racism 'by default' – Chinese this, Jewish that, Dutch the other. It is hard to feel that malice, aforethought or otherwise, is implicit in many of these terms, especially those plucked from nature, which seem common to every country and every ethnic group. We, all of us, throw around such phrases with barely a thought. So is their inclusion overly fastidious? It is only when one starts to deconstruct them, to tease out the stereotypes that prompted their coinage, darkening their ostensible innocence, that the problems begin.

Arab can also mean a Jew

Arab or occasionally **arabber**, in America and the UK, means any wild or excitable person, hence the phrase **wild Arabian**, a problem child or 'enfant terrible' (and indeed the synonymous **wild Indian**). It can also imply a degree of untrustworthiness, thus an **ashphalt arab** is a city person, as nicknamed by a country dweller, or a street urchin (originally an 'arab of the streets', reflecting on the nomadic Arabs of the Middle East) and an **arab**, in sporting slang, can be a street book-maker. (Synonymous is **street rat**, but the urchin this time has Irish parents.) The same goes for France where **arabe** means mixed-up and **fourbi arabe** translates as a 'sorry mess', and Russia where **Aràp**: Arab means either a 'blackamoor' or a thief. However the negatives are not invariable: **Arabier** in Dutch means Arab, and in turn a joke, a card or a comical fellow. As with a variety of terms for Italians and Scandinavians, mispronunciation can sometimes do the job. **Ay-rab** means arab in America, and was popularized in the 1962 chart hit 'Ahab the Ayrab' (the 'king of the burning sand') by Ray Stevens, a man whose repertoire included 'Bridget the Midget' and 'I Saw Elvis in a UFO'. Just to confuse matters, however, **arab** can also mean Jew, a usage coined in 1925 by Jack Conway, a writer for the 'showbiz Bible', *Variety*.

Aller en Flandre sans Couteau

As well as the condescending diminutives **belgie** or **belgy**, names for Belgium and its inhabitants include **belgeek** (a crude, phonetic spelling of French *Belgique*) and **blemish** (a blend of Belgian and Flemish, perhaps also reinforced by negative connotations of the standard English *blemish*). Another pun, **Flamingo**, is an inhabitant of Flanders, the older name for Belgium and once embracing an area now divided between Belgium, France and Holland; according to the philologist Ernest Weekley the bird was named for the country, but the *OED* has no truck with this: the deep pink flamingo, properly known as *Phoenicopterus* ('crimson wing'), comes from the Latin *flamma*: a flame. Flanders gives several other terms: **Flanderkin**: a very large man or horse; the 'joke' is that the suffix *-kin*, taken from the Middle Dutch

-*kijn* (there is no Anglo–Saxon equivalent) usually implies diminution rather than increase. A **Flanders piece** is a picture that looks much better at a distance than close to (a similar painting, no doubt, to the **Dutch dab**: a poorly executed landscape or still life); the French phrase **aller en Flandre sans couteau**: 'to go to Flanders without a knife' means to go somewhere or undertake anything without the necessary preparations. The saying stems from the fact that guests at the inns in Flanders were expected to bring their own knives.

The Middle Passage

Given the current role of 'African American' as the term of choice for describing America's Black community, it is interesting to note that **Afro** or **Afric** and its synonym **Congo** are among the earliest descriptions of that community, both in use around 1760. Even earlier (*c*.1730) are **cbo** (which some claim is an abbreviation of *ebony*: the colour black, but is far more likely to be a mis-spelling of *Ibo*, a tribe living near the lower Niger) and **hottentot**. This latter, which usually applies to a people found mainly in south-west Africa (their European-coined name comes from the Dutch *Hottentot*: 'stutterer' or 'stammerer', reflecting their 'clucking' speech) and thus immune to the slavers' depredations, was coined in the late 17th century; its use in America was less descriptive than figurative: by the early 18th century the term was synonymous with 'uncivilized'. Another 'geographical' name is the seemingly bizarre 19th-century **mollygosher**, which is a corruption of *Malagasy* and was coined to describe those Blacks who were thought to have come from Madagascar. Given the lack of choice when it came to being enslaved, the modern terms **African runner** or **African reject**, with their implication that somehow the slaves had wanted to make the grim Middle Passage to America, have a sad irony. **Nigerian** is used as an all-purpose description for any African (and in the UK, West Indian too). The **African Railroad** is a derogatory nickname for San Francisco's municipal bus line – principally used by Blacks (there may be some reference to the pre-Civil War 'underground railroad' an abolitionist organization that spirited slaves to freedom), and a **zulu** is either a Black person or, in railroad slang, a carriage taking immigrants and their chattels westward across America. **Russian** (1940s) is a pure pun: it means those southern rural Blacks who are 'rushing' towards the better jobs to be found (especially during wartime when manpower demands broke down – if only temporarily – workplace segregation) in the industrial cities of the north. A less complimentary 'translation' has them 'rushing' away from hard work.

Windcheater or Sheepskin Jacket

Insults to Canada tend to be internal coinages, echoing the rivalry between its English and French-speaking communities. Thus **anglo** has meant an Anglophone since 1800, with the added twist of **anglo-bluenose** (1845), a term that can mean any Anglo-Canadian but especially targets the Maritime coast (and thus mimics the use of bluenose for the inhabitants of America's New England states). Equally simple are **English** and **Englishman**, terms that deride an excessive dependence, as seen by French Canadians, of Anglo-Canadian culture on 'the mother country'. The English retaliate, equally unimaginatively, with **Frenchy** (a term that has also been used of the Cajuns of Louisiana) and **canajun**, a hybrid of cajun and Canadian. A **Newfie** or **Newf** is a native of Newfoundland. A **Canada pest**, despite its potential for vilification, attacks neither party; it is a herb of the gentian family. Equally inoffensive are **canadienne**, a windcheater or sheepskin jacket, and **carosserie canadienne**, a shooting brake.

From Greenland to Siberia

First named as early as the mid-16th century, the Eskimos, or more properly the Inuit, members of a widely spread people inhabiting the Arctic from Greenland to Eastern Siberia, have picked up a number of nicknames. **Esquaw** blends eskimo and squaw to mean a female Inuit (although the term may be a variant of the Algonquian *aqua*: a woman), as is **esquimuff**, which seems to mix Eskimo and *muff*, slang for the female pubic hair, although the slang term may be offering its alternative definition: a fool. The abbreviations **'skimo** and **skim** both emerged in the early 19th century while another set of alternatives suchemo, suckemo and seymo are products of the 1850s. Finally there is the best-known abbreviation of all, though hardly a direct reference: **Esky**, a portable, insulated container, used especially to keep food or drink cool, patented as such in 1962 by the Australian company Malleys, of New South Wales.

Middle Kingdom Men

The European/Latinized names of many countries are not those chosen or indeed still used by the countries themselves. China is such a case. Quite where it originated remains a matter for debate although the term *China* has been found in Sanskrit, a root-language for many European successors, around the time of Christ and starts appearing, typically in the writings of the Venetian explorer Marco Polo, in the mid-16th century. The first use in English is in 1555 when the translator Richard Eden (1521?-76) wrote in his collection of travel writing, *The Decades of the Newe Worlde, or West India* of 'The great China whose kyng is thought...the greatest prince in the world'. China reappeared a century later as a synonym for what the Portuguese, who began its import to Europe, had called porcelain (a word taken from the French *porcelaine*, which described the polished shell of a cowrie, which the glaze on 'china' was seen to emulate). First found, in 1634, as *china-ware*, it had been shortened to plain *china* by 1653.

Thus the first recorded use of **chinaman** is not as a native of China, but as a dealer in porcelain or 'china-ware', and it comes in 1772 when the *London Directory* listed 'Brown William, China-man, 1 Aldgate'. The chinaman had his female counterpart, the **china-woman** and they both conducted their business at a china-house, which was often alluded to as a 'house of assignation'. Given the rarified nature of the trade, the more exotic, i.e. foreign, term porcelain gradually came to dominate its vocabulary and the chinamen and women became 'dealers in porcelain'. But chinaman took on an new meaning in the 19th century: a native of China and, in the English and American context, an immigrant. Once again there were chinawomen as well as **chinaboys** and **chinagirls**. A more recent use stems from America, where it means 'one who has political influence'. The use of *chinaman* in cricketing jargon, to describe a left-arm bowler's off-break, is not ostensibly racist, but its origins are. The term was coined at Manchester, England in 1933 when the West Indian player Ellis 'Puss' Achong, bowled such a ball (apparently the first ever noted) and dismissed an English batsman. The batsman remarked, 'Fancy being bowled by a bloody Chinaman!' Inevitably, given the increasingly negative image of such immigrants (see *Colour*), a variety of nicknames, few of them congratulatory, developed. Among them were (and often still are) **chinee, chink, chinky** (and **chinky-chinaman**) and **chino**. China itself is **Chinkland**. 1940s America adds **coosie**, while Australia, another destination for Chinese immigrants, has **Mongolian**. **Chink**, an all-embracing term, has also been used, like dink or gook – both created for different targets – for the Vietnamese. **Tiddly wink**, a rhyming slang formation, means Chink.

The merchant and the immigrant are combined in a number of French terms. The slang verb **chiner** means variously to slander, to ridicule, to cadge, to work laboriously, to look out for a bargain, to buy and sell antique furniture (perhaps from *chinoiserie*) and to work as an old clothes man. A **chineur** performs many of these 'jobs' as well as specializing in touring the countryside and buying up the peasant girls' long hair. **Chinage** means selling plated objects as genuine silver. This element of trickery persists in the Dutch **chineezerij**: 'chinesery', a stupid prank. Likewise in Guyana the **Chinese Christmas Tree** (otherwise known as the *blindeye*) is a cactus-like shrub, covered in pencil-like twigs containing a milky sap; it looks appealing enough, but get the sap in one's eye and it can cause temporary blindness. **Kinesa**, 'to Chinese' in Swedish, means to stay overnight (perhaps a reference to these mendicant merchants seeking a place for the night) while in Denmark and Norway bureaucratic red tape is known as **Kineseri**: Chinese stuff. In France the term is **Chinoiserie de bureau**: 'office Chinesery'. In Russia the phrase **kitai podirnayetsya**: 'China is rising' means that something is brewing or something is up. Back in English **I'll be a Chinaman!** is a phrase that implies absolute surprise or unlikeliness, while the euphemism to **give a Chinaman a music lesson** means variously to visit the lavatory or to slip out for a drink. The punning **Chinese landing** refers to landing an aircraft with 'wun wing lo'. The pilot in such a case is a **Chinese ace**.

Ironically, although chinaman has been seen as an offensive term since the 1970s, and was officially proscribed by Britain's BBC in the early 1970s, its opponents are acting, however sincerely, in error. Unlike many racial terms this one quite fairly reflects the nation's own description. It is a literal translation of *djing-kuo run*: a Middle Kingdom man, using the same term, Middle Kingdom, as do the Chinese themselves. Given that China as such does not exist in China, the term 'chinaman' is as near as possible to the original.

Treacherous Contraptions

The basic term that seems to govern nearly all ethnic references to the Poles is **Polack**, a German word which has been adopted across Europe and in America. Aside from its basic meaning – a Pole – it can be a Polish horse, a kind of potato, a flogging on the posterior, the dregs of a glass or a pipe, a carved fowl and a kind of fish. In early 20th-century US police jargon polack means a vagabond. Germany, never a country to spare its eastern neighbour, uses a number of elaborations on the basic term. **Polackei**, which roughly equates to 'Polanderland' or 'Poledom', gives the phrase **Ein Pole aus Polackei**: a dyed-in-the-wool Pole; the 18th century talked of a **pralichter Polacke**: a swaggering Polack and **er schlägt Polack** refers to those seen beating their chests to keep out the cold. **Polacky**, a pejorative form of the usual *polsky*, performs the same function in Czech while **Polander**, another German word, takes the same form as **Hollander**: a Dutchman. The abbreviations **lekh** (Serbian), **ljak** (Russian) and **lyakh** (Russian) all carry the slightly contemptuous ring of the basic Polak. America too uses polack, as well as **polacker** and **polocker** (all dating from the late 19th century) and **poski**. Pole, in English, is sometimes found as synonymous with 'stupid'. Other German expressions include **polnische Brijcke**; a Polish bridge, used to mean a treacherous contraption hanging by a thread, while **poolsches Mosta**: a 'Polish pattern' is a Silesian dialect term for a loud, vulgar design. **Szkeber** or **Szkieber** is another neg-ative description.

A Hungarian Knifer

Bulgaria seems to attract puns: **burglar** is based on the slight similarity of spelling while **Vulgaria** (and thus Vulgarian) swaps the B for a V. Russia's **ruminskiy orkestr**: 'a Rumanian orchestra' describes the sort of third-rate music one finds in a restaurant and presumably targets the so-called gypsies, often from Rumania, who play it. Czechs are variously **cheskies** (from *czezski*) or **chessie** (both in America) and **Tschechuzen** in Germany's Sudeten dialect. The word **Magyar**, meaning Hungarian, gives the Carpathian dialect **Modjorbitschko** : a 'Hungarian knifer', or a short-tempered, impetuous person.

Scandihuvians, Skywegians and Scoovies

Scandinavian immigrants have been a staple of American society for many years and their presence there has engendered a variety of terms. They can be **Scandihoovians, Scandihuvians, Skywegians** and **Scandiwegians** and their country **Scowoogia,** all such terms blending forms of Norway, Sweden and Scandinavia. Swedes in particular are **swenskys, swenksers** and **swenskas, scoops** and **scoovies**. Other terms include the early 20th-century **sowegian** (a rough mix of Swede and Norwegian which also gives **scowegian** (also popular in Canada) or **scowwe(e)gian** and **scowoogian**. The precise target of all the terms, whether Swede, Dane or Norwegian varies as to the person apostrophized. **Silver-tip** (from their blond hair) is always a Swede (A *blond Swede* is a logger's term for an elderly man). **Scandie**, yet another variation, is also used to mean pornographic in the context of the sex industry, given the clichéd propensities of what the advertisers term those 'randy Scandies'. **Scans**, another abbreviation, is also a staple of sex ads although a **Swedish fiddle**, rejecting the slightest vestige of smut, is an accordian.

In Scandinavia itself the divisions are more obvious. In Sweden **Danskar** means a Dane, thus the children's game **skrämma danskar**: 'to frighten the Danes.' A **Norsker** is a Norwegian, the term becomes **norsky** in America. In Denmark **norsknorsk** describes an ultra-patriotic Norwegian while in Sweden it is **norsk norrmann från Norge**:

'a Norwegian Northman from Norway'. Swedish ultra-patriots are also mocked. **Storsvensker**: a 'big Swede' or ultra-patriotic Swede is translated as 'You think you're everything, don't you?'. In America **big Swede** or **swedie** means a large, clumsy person, as does **svejda**, a Czech term. The Swedes themselves are not blind to what they see as their own faults: **svensk avundsjuka** is 'Swedish envy.'

Nun ist Holland in Not

Setting aside the simple **Dutcher** and **Dutchie**, both of which may mean a Dutchman or a German in America (where the name *Dutch*, as in that of the gangster Arthur 'Dutch Schultz' Fliegenheimer, tends to mean German), terms involving the Dutch tend to a certain moral judgement. A **big Dutchman** is no compliment, rather it is used as a term of reproof, and a **Dutch uncle** (coined in the 1830s) is a paternal, not to mention patronizing individual who tends not so much to talk but to lecture, thus giving the phrase 'to talk to a person like a Dutch uncle', meaning 'to lecture one severely.' (A **Welsh uncle** is rather less dramatic: it means the first cousin of one's parent.) This same heavy-handedness is found in **Dutch comfort** and **Dutch consolation**, both nicknames for that style of comfort in which the speaker intones 'Thank God it is no worse'. To be **in Dutch** (an American term since 1912) is to be in trouble, to be 'on the carpet.'

Germany's phrase **nun ist Holland in Not**: 'now the Dutch are in distress' means much the same. It apparently refers to any situation where Holland deliberately breaks down its vital dykes in order to avert a threatened invasion. To maintain the negative mode a **Dutch brig** is a naval punishment cell (in American nautical slang). A **Dutch pump**, another piece of naval slang, is a form of punishment which requires the victim to do considerable pumping so as not to drown, and to offer a **Dutch defence** is to offer no defence whatsoever; indeed the implication is that one in fact betrays one's own side. The Dutch, whose own navy was once a major force, have also given such seafaring terms as **Dutchman's-breeches**: 'two streaks of blue in a cloudy sky' and a **Dutchman's cape**: a cloud on the horizon that is mistaken for land and thus any illusion that there is land in the far distance. Last of these nautical terms is the **dutch roll**, in fact a flying term but one that is based on the rolling gait of Dutch sailors. Such rolls, which begin with the left-right yawing of an aircraft's nose and which are caused by incorrect application of the rudder or by a lateral gust of wind, can force a pilot to lose control of the aircraft. A **Dutch row** is a faked quarrel, possibly to lure some victim into a confidence trick, while in boxing slang a **Dutch oven** was the mouth. Perhaps the most famous of all such blends of Dutchmen and sea is the legendary **Flying Dutchman**. This term is variously the Dutch version of the wandering Jew, i.e. a Dutch mariner condemned for his crime to sail the seas until Dooms-day, or a ghostly ship, supposed to be seen in the region of the Cape of Good Hope, which has been condemned to sail the seas for ever. Away from the sea the Flying Dutchman has been a particular express train on the Great Western Railway running between London and Bristol and more generally a fantasist, a wild-eyed individual or an eccentric.

Why the France!

Ignoring, for a moment, their supposed obsession with sex, and their dubious relationship with venereal disease, it is French manners, ap-parently, that enrage the world. Certainly a whole raft of phrases seem to pinpoint the phenomenon. The deliberately mispronounced **Fron-cery**, apparently mixing the French word *français* with a hint of the term *ponce*, meaning a pimp, refers to a French style, as does the synonymous **Frenchery**, which as early as 1593 meant French man-nerisms, clothing and general way of life. **Frenchy**, as an adjective means moody, flighty and capricious. Those who are seen as aping French manners, in the (mistaken) belief that such affectations connote sophisticated behaviour, are skewered across Europe: **franceseria** de-rides such mannerisms in Italy, as does **Französelei**: 'Frenchification' in Germany and in Holland **met den Franschen slag**: 'in the French manner' means superficially, perfunctorily; just to 'get by'. The term reappears in Greece, where **gallidzo** means to 'make oneself French'. In Holland one who worshipped France, warts and all, was known derisively as a **Franschelaar** and in Flanders as **fransquillon**. Finally England's **French fare**, which sounds as if it might be some form of gourmet food, was in fact elaborately polite behaviour in the 14th to 16th centuries.

It is not the manners, however, but the men who make them who are attacked in the Spanish **franchute**: a 'Frencher', a less than polite reference to the French, while the American **Frencher** (1826), more usually found in the world of sex, was coined by James Fennimore Cooper for *The Last of the Mohicans*. It means Frenchman. **Frenchy** or **Frenchie** was coined in 1883 making its most famous use, in Baroness Orczy's *Scarlet Pimpernel* ('We seek him here, we seek him there, | Those Frenchies seek him everywhere'), published in 1905 but set in 1790, some 115 years anachronistic. More recent uses of Frenchy can be found in the West Indies where in St Kitts the word refers to the original French settlers of the island, who were displaced when England took it over in 1690 and, as disenfranchized Catholics, were hugely reduced in status. The term also covers the descendants of an 18th-century settler group, who still live in a community in St Thomas. **Mooshay**, from *monsieur* and thus echoing such general terms as **mossoo** and *mounseer*, is a synonym.

The West Indies also give a unique euphemistic use of **France**, meaning to all other intents *fuck* or slightly less obscenely, *hell*. The basic use, **France!**, is as an oath, and refers to the horrors of World War I: many West Indians fought and died in the trenches of Flanders. Other uses, all of which can be parallelled by a use of fuck and/or hell, include such phrases as 'to France with that', 'get to France out of here', 'how/what/when/who/why/where the France...' and to 'give (someone) France'. The phrases may also have some background in the Dutch **Loop naar de Franschen**: 'run to the French', meaning 'Go to the devil.'

Various other denunciations of the French include America's punning **French heel**, defined as 'something of a cad' (the standard English *French heel*, from the late 18th century onwards, refers to a medium height, chunky heel, usually worn on women's shoes but once seen adorning those of a French dandy); **frautluzik**: a 'little Frenchman', a term used in Russian literature as belittling the lack of spirit in the French and the Yiddish **fun dem altn frantzoiz**: '(dating) from the old Frenchman', in other words out-of-date, antiquated, and very old fashioned. The 'old Frenchman' in question may well be Napoleon. The German term **altfrankisch**: 'Old Frankish' also means outdated. A **fransysk visit**: a 'French call' is in Sweden a flying visit, while a **French harp** is a harmonica in America.

Mercenaries

The Swiss, whose main sins appear to be their willingness (for the right price) to serve as mercenaries (see *Money*) and their supposedly habitual employment as hotel porters (see *Work*) have but two phrases that play on their name. Both are French: **fumer comme un Suisse** means to 'smoke like a chimney', while **penser à la suisse**: 'to think in a Swiss fashion' is to daydream or to be plunged in a 'brown study'.

Kadavergerhorsam

Alongside the basic terms for a German – the Czech **němec**, Danish and Norwegian **tydska**, America's **dutch** and **dutchy** (which date from the late 18th century), and the general use in Estonia of **Saksa**, literally a Saxon, to mean any German – there are a number of more pointed descriptions. **Raichy**, in Poland, referred to a citizen of the German Reich, while **niemkini** is a general term of distaste, giving the distinctly derogatory **niemra**: an ungainly, ugly German woman. Another Polish word, **Dajczmanek**: 'a little Dutchman', was also used to describe the national foe. Like their French equivalents, German, especially Prussian manners are not seen as an advantage. Thus in Italian **tedescheggiare** means to affect German mannerisms while **affetti di germanismo** refers to one who is 'imbued with the German doctrine'. The Dutch take on this is **mofferij**: the German manner of speech, German behaviour or policy.

And if the Germans are disdained in general, then the Prussians (a kingdom that lies to the east of Germany and since World War II has been divided between (then East) Germany, Poland and Russia) are of special interest. The original Prussians (spelt Pruzzi, Prutzci, Pruci, Prussi or Prusi) were conquered in the 12th century by the Knights of the Teutonic Order, and afterwards became a dukedom or duchy, in due course coming under the rule of the elector of Brandenburg, who in 1700 thence assumed the title of *König von Preuszen*, King of Prussia. **Prussian** itself is a pejorative, a synonym for **hun** when it comes to German wartime atrocities, but the image of the Prussian as a bully is found in the Scandinavian **være en riktig projser**: to be a real Prussian, i.e. to be a bully, and the German **preussich**: 'Prussian', aloof; not on speaking terms after a tiff, rude and irascible. The **junker**, literally *jung herr*: 'young sir' and thus a young German nobleman, became identified with the arrogant, militaristic Prussian aristocracy, desperate to maintain the exclusive social and political privileges of their class. The Dutch, never great lovers of Germany, say **het zal Pruisisch zijn**, literally 'It will be Prussian', when they mean that 'No good will come of it' and use **Pruisisch** to mean excitable or wrought up, quick to lose one's temper. Denmark also offers the adjective **projseri**: Prussianism, used to mean unflexing bureaucracy, pedantry and small-mindedness. Readers of Rudyard Kipling's *Stalky & Co.* (1899) will recall the ' "Prooshian" Bates', the boys' headmaster, a man quite capable of thrashing the entire school prior to sending them off on their holidays. In Germany **preussiche Zustände**: Prussian conditions, keep up the negative imagery, all in all a fitting tribute to a regime that, among other things, coined the term *Kadavergerhorsam*: 'discipline that would make a corpse stand to attention'. The French **je m'en moque comme du roi de Prusse**: 'I care about it as much as about the King of Prussia', i.e. 'I don't give a hang about it' refers less to the fearsome Prussian militarism, than to the ineffectuality of the King, whose powers had long been subsumed by a unified Germany. One term that appears 'Prussian', but for all its allure is in fact not, is the French **exhiber son prussien**: to turn tail or run off. Here *Prussien* comes from the Gypsy term **prusiatini**: a pistol and gives the punning 'breech' as in the pistol's 'breech-block' and the human's 'posterior' or 'seat of the pants'.

However they may regard themselves, the Germans, fairly or otherwise, have never been seen as witty. Practical jokers, perhaps, obsessed with bodily functions, undoubtedly, but witty, never. Thus Spain's sneer at **chistes alemanes**: German jokes, which are no jokes at all. Similarly the French term **le bonheur allemand**: 'German happiness' is at best happiness by default. Like Dutch comfort, it refers to a pleasure that exists only because 'things could have been worse.' The German who breaks his arm is happy – it could have been his neck. In something of the same tone, the Czech **německa růžička**: 'a German rose' is a thistle. America's **Dutch comedian**, while possibly funny, is no German (nor Dutchman), but a comic who takes the German immigrants as his butt. This ponderousness is further underlined in France's **querelle d'allemand**: a 'German quarrel' and as such a synonym for 'much ado about nothing' or a feud over trivialities. **Mof**, which means a 'sourpuss' and thus a German in Dutch, gives **Moffrika**, meaning Germany (the addition of *(A)frika* is presumably a slur on the way the Dutch see that continent's inhabitants), and **Zitten als ein mof**: 'to sit like a German', that is to sit stiffly and uncomfortably.

The Urinal of the Planets

Once a villain, always a villain. Of the many indignities heaped upon Ireland by her eastern neighbour – stupidity, poverty, political extremism – those that concern the weather might be considered the least important. But there they are, and if Ireland is not **England's umbrella** (foolish, but not that insulting) she is the **urinal of the planets,** a term that is made only marginally more palatable by its being, in dictionary terms, 'a literary usage that reflects the country's high rainfall'. In fact the term is first cited in B.E.'s *Dictionary of the Canting Crew* (*c*.1700), and is as such slang, but it stayed in use until the 19th century. More genuinely literary is **Hibernian**, which is only insulting if used in such a context, and which comes from the Greek *Ifernae*. A presumed Celtic root *Iveriu* leads to the Irish *Erui* and thus to *Erin*, the adjectival form of which *Eri*, gives Ireland. Still cultural is **harp**, and occasionally **harpy**, developed in America *c*.1900. It recalls the 'national instrument' (to be seen among other places on the Guinness bottle) but seems generally to have taken on a negative image, that of immigrant backwardness and the inability to cast off traditional ways. **Irisher** is another US coinage, appearing *c*.1800 and predating such terms as **Yiddisher**: Jewish. It remains in use.

Elsewhere it is back to the usual *canards*. **Irish draperies** are cobwebs, **Irish diamonds** rock crystal, an **Irish marathon** a relay race;

an **Irishman's fire** is one that never catches properly but burns only at the top; similarly, on sailing ships an **Irishman's reef** was a sail that was tied only at the top. The **Irish Railroad**, like its San Francisco cousin the **African Railroad** (the muncipal bus line, used primarily by African Americans), and the **Yiddish Highway** (US 301, running between New York and Miami – home to thousands of Jewish retirees from the northern cities), is the Chicago, Burlington and Quincy Railroad, catering to a mass of Irish-dominated suburbs. The **Irish(man's) sidewalk** is an avenue, possibly because, used to the rural lanes of the 'Ould Country', they haven't the sense to walk on the pavement. America's **Irish shift** or **Irish switch**, a political term meaning a more than routinely hypocritical action by a politician, refers to the supposed political flexibility, even hypocrisy of the Irish, whose allegiances are said to blow very much with the prevailing wind. Given that the word was coined in 1960, the 'Irish' in question may have been the Kennedys, whose scion John was elected President that year. Still political, but infinitely less subtle, is the British phrase **murderin' Irish**, which goes back to the Fenian dynamite campaign of the late 19th century, but was used as a general expletive denoting one's surprise at the outcome of given circumstances.

Laconic Helots

If one excludes the Italian **grechesco** and Rumanian **grecoteu**, both of which are pejorative forms meaning Greek, perhaps the most interesting word to come from a Greek name is **Helot**, usually translated as a serf or bondsman. Helots came from the town of Helos in Laconia, a part of Sparta, whose inhabitants had been enslaved. They formed a special class, between the ordinary slaves and the free Spartan citizens. A secondary phrase, a **drunken Helot** alludes to the fact that the Helots were on certain occasions forced to get humiliatingly drunk, so that the free Spartans might have living proof of how repugnant such excess might be. Laconia gives another term in its own right, **laconic**: brief and concise, whether in speech or writing. The image here is not of slavery, but of a Spartan distaste for unneccesary show.

In a very different context, that of the American educational system,

Greekdom refers to the world of fraternities and sororities, which designate themselves with a variety of Greek letters; thus a **Greek mother** is a housemother, looking after the various college clubs. Finally France has used **Athenien** or **Athenienne**: an Athenian (of either sex) to describe an elegant but all too often frivolous intellectual.

Mediterranean–Irish

As discrete from such synonyms as guinea or dago the basic **Italiano**, **Italyite** and **tally** (presumably an abbrevation) have been and are all used to mean Italian. So too is **Mediterranean-Irish**, the inference being more from the commonality of immigration rather than from any racial similarities. In the 1920s, with Italian-born gangsters rampaging through America's cities, **Siciliano**, Sicilian, became a newspaper code-word for all Italians.

Japs & Nips

Like a number of racial slurs, the best-known is based on nothing more threatening than an abbreviation. Thus **Jap**, which appeared in mid-19th-century America and soon made its way across the Atlantic. The *OED*, perhaps over-optimistically, suggests that due to its 'strong derogatory connotations' the term is now falling into disuse. The point seems to have been overlooked by Britain's tabloid press. The synonymous **nip**, from *Nippon*, Japan's own name for itself and meaning 'sun origin', is a coinage of World War II and is rarely used other than by veterans. Russia's **Japski**, a derogatory form of the standard adjective *japonskij*: Japanese, plays much the same role as Jap.

Just Jew–ish

Perhaps the simplest way to coin an insult is to do no more than deprive a noun of its article – 'a' or 'the'. Somehow this linguistic foreshortening renders an otherwise respectable word vulnerable. It works with nicknames – frog for French, wop for Italian – and it also works with otherwise standard English, no more so than with Jew. A Jew, the Jew, both terms may well be used in some negative way, but stripping off the article and talking of Jew this, and Jew that confer an extra sneer, especially when the combination stresses some accepted stereotype: Jew banker, Jew pedlar and the like. And the same thing goes for a modifier. Thus to reduce Jewish to Jew has the same unpleasant effect. As the polymathic Jonathan Miller noted, as part of 1961's satirical revue *Beyond the Fringe*, 'I'm not a Jew, just Jew-ish', although that makes no-one immune. A **Jewish compliment** or **Yiddisher kompliment**, for instance, has the same negative image as its Dutch relation. The phrase 'You're not looking so well', delivered when meeting a friend, is hardly guaranteed to make the other feel better. The **Jewish reply** describes the tic of answering one question with another. **Judenwitz**: a 'Jew joke', is Germany's term for biting sarcasm, while **Juderei**: literally 'Jewish manners' refers to usury.

In Italy **giudeaccio** is slang for a Jew, best translated as 'kike' or 'sheeny'; thus **giudesco**, literally Jewish, is effectively 'jewy'. **Noto in Guidea**: 'well-known in Judea', means notorious. The slang term **guino**: a Jew gives France's cant term **guinal**, which means variously a Jew, and thus a money-lender and as Barrère's *Argot and Slang* (1902) notes, is best translated as 'she[e]ney, Ikey or mouchey'. **Le Grand Guinal** was the *mont de Pieté*, or government pawnbroking establishment, while **un guinal** was a wholesale trader in rags. **Guinaliser**, another cant term, meant to lend money; in the 19th century it also meant circumcise. Other French terms for Jew are **youte**, **youtre**, **youdi** or **youpin**, all presumably from the German **Jude** (thus **jardin des youtres**: the Jewish cemetery), **frisé**, from *friser* to embroider (with gold), and **piedplat**: flatfoot, playing on the tradition that Jews suffer from fallen arches.

While **jewy** is an obvious pejorative, often applied to matters of taste, and America's 19th-century **jew-bastard** requires no translation, **jew-boy**, now an undeniable negative, was not always so. The term emerged in the late 18th century, when, ugly though it might sound to modern ears, it meant what it said: a boy who was a Jew. The mood shifted as the 19th century passed and by the 1920s, when D.H. Lawrence proclaimed his hatred for the 'moral Jew-boys', there was no doubt about the negative image of the term. Another term, one of the oddest, is **Jews' letters** (or **Jerusalem letters**) which refers to tattoos. Given the prohibition on tattooing ('You shall not make gashes in your flesh for the dead, or incise any marks on yourselves...' *Leviticus* 19:28) such a term seems utterly anomalous. Various theories have been put forward: that the symbols were Hebrew, that they were inscribed in memory of pious trips to Jerusalem, but the most likely surely draws on the use of the word *jew* in nautical slang, where it means a ship's tailor (irrespective of religion). The link between tattooed sailors, their tailor and his needles cannot be too distant. Slang gives a small subset of terms, all based on rhymes with 'Jew' or 'Yid'. They include **buckle my shoe, box of glue, fifteen-two, five to two, four by two, half past two, kangaroo, pot of glue, quarter to two, Sarah Soo, four-wheel skid** and **front-wheel skid**.

Like anti-semitism, 'Jew'-words flourish throughout Europe. Rumania has the contemptuous **jidan**: a Yid, and **jidovina**: a Jewess, also means a ravine or hollow, a term that must be cognate with the link between the Welsh *cwm*: a valley and the obscene synonym for the vagina, *cunt*. While *Jude* is the standard term in Germany, the abbreviated **Jud** is the slang one and **judeln** means to bargain like or to talk like one and **judenzen**: 'to judaize' means to act like a Jew. A **Judenbengel** is a Jewish youth, a 'mockie' or 'smouch', **Judenblatt** was any newspaper favouring or sympathizing with Jews. A **Judenfenster** or 'Jew-window' is the four in dice (perhaps the image comes from the simple four-square windows that would be found in the cottage of a poor Jew). **Judenpack**: 'Jew pack' and **Judengesind**: 'Jew rabble' both mean a crowd of Jews. The Spanish **judjo**: Jew is a word of contempt used by angry persons, while in Portugal **judiar**: 'to Judaize' is to mock or laugh at; Mexican Spanish uses **judiada**: 'Jewish manners', to mean any form of barbaric, inhuman act. Poland's equivalent to ikey is **judzki**, while Denmark and Norway use **jodesmaus** and **jodetamp** to mean much the same. A verb form of **kike** means to walk.

If Western Europe has Jew and Jude in a variety of forms, Eastern Europe and Russia prefer **Yid** or **Zhid**, and its variations. That said, the term Yid originated in Germany (geographically and culturally a mid-point in the pre-World War II Jewish community) where it comes from *Jude*, itself from Yehuda or Judah, one of the Biblical patriarch Jacob's sons. The term, as Leo Rosten, America's foremost expert on

Yiddish, has pointed out, is neutral if pronounced 'yeed' as it would be by Jews speaking the Judaeo-German language Yiddish, but unashamedly offensive if pronounced 'yid' with a short 'i'. It is this latter pronunication that, unsurprisingly, informs these English terms, which can be considered before passing to the East, where the 'y' is usually replaced by the Russian 'zh'. Yid appears in England sometime in the early 19th century and Hotten's *Slang Dictionary* (1860) cites 'Yid, or Yit, a Jew. Yidden, the Jewish people. The Jews use these terms very frequently'. So they do, but for the gentile community the term was at best neutral, and more often derisory. Its arrival in America is approximately contemporaneous, moving, as does the English use, from the immigrant Jews to the gentile world in which they lived. Variations, which appear between the late 19th century and World War II include **yiddie**, the plural **yidden** (1891), the adjective **yiddisher** and others. **Yiddle** (1941) which the slang lexicographer Eric Partridge claims is particularly applied to a Jewish boxer, is thus rather paradoxical: the original Yiddish word means a physically slight and otherwise insignificant Jew.

Partridge may still be right, but once one moves into Eastern Europe and beyond, **yid**, or more accurately **zhid** is uncompromisingly derogatory. Rather than the neutral **yevrey**: Hebrew, thus Jewish, zhid in Russian means a Jew, a miser and a greedy person; variations on this theme include **zhidyonok**: a Jew, **zhidedyonek**: 'a nasty little Jew', **zhidishka**: 'a contemptible little Jew', **zhidovin**: 'a damned Jew, a sheeny' plus **zhidovatyi**: 'Jew-like'. Similar terms can be found across central Europe: the Czech **židovec** is a Jew, viewed contemptuously (thus **židlati,**: to play music badly); Poland offers **Żydek**: 'a Jew-boy', as well as a cheap jack-knife in a wooden frame (Poland's **cyganek**: 'a gypsy boy', usually a peasant, can also mean jack-knife – such knives, presumably, were part of the stock-in-trade of Jewish peddlers), **Żydowica**: a Jewess (the standard term is **Żydowca**), and **żydziak**, another version of 'Jew-boy'.

Like nigger, Jew has been adopted for a variety of terms, often dealing with natural products, flowers, minerals and the like. The practice appears most common in English-speaking countries and in Germany and a sample, far from exhaustive, is included here. English, whether

American or English, has **jewbush**: a tropical American shrub possessing emetic qualities, **Jews' frankincense**: storax, a resin derived from trees of the genus styrax; **Jew's fish** (the halibut, a Jewish favourite), **Jews' lime**: asphalt (sometimes, deliberately elided as **Jew slime**) **Jew's mallow**: a potherb, **Jews' myrtle**: the 'butcher's-broom' or common myrtle, **Jews' stone** or **Jewstone**: a hard rock that is related to certain basalts and limestones and is used for road-mending, a **jew**: a black field beetle in Cornish dialect (it exudes a pink liquid and children, seeing this, would chant 'Jew, Jew, spit blood') and **jewing**: the wattles at the base of the beak of some pigeons (the reference is to the hooked 'Jewish' nose). Among the most interesting is **Jews' tin**, the tin found in old smelting houses in Devon and Cornwall, known as **Jew's houses** because once, around the late 11th century, the Jews mined for tin in those counties. (The black beetle reference above presumably refers to some ancient memory of these black-garbed exotics.) Germany is equally prolific. There one finds the **Judenbusch**: Jew-bush; **Judenbeifuss**: Judean wormwood, **Judenharz**: Jew-resin; **Judenkirsche**: 'Jew-cherry' or Winter-cherry, **Judenpfeffer**: 'Jew-pepper' or Jamaica pepper, and **Judenschwamm**: 'Jewish fungus'. So keen, it appears, were the Germans to brand everything 'Jew' that they included **Judhanf**, but that is Jute, not 'Jew-yarn'.

Castles in Spain

Although Latin Americans, typically Mexicans and Puerto Ricans, have regularly been termed **spic** (and Mexicans **mex** or **meskin**) the Spanish and Portuguese have been excluded from the term. Indeed the Portuguese have been left in relative peace on all fronts. **Portagee**, **Portergee** and **Portugee** were coined at the end of the 19th century, and can be found in America, Canada and the West Indies, otherwise there is little other than the French phrase **une entrée de portugal**: a poor horseman. – As with a number of other nationalities – **Britisher**, **Irisher** – the suffix *-er* serves to make a national adjective into a noun and in America **Spanisher** means a Spanish immigrant. For the Dutch **Spanjool** sneers at a 'Little Spaniard' while in France **courir comme un Basque**: 'to run like a Basque' denotes a speedy person. The

Basques, well-known for their athleticism, were at one time employed by the French nobility as couriers. The city of Castille gives, in French, a synonym for quarrelling, and thus **chercher castille à quelqu'un** means to pick a quarrel with someone and **être en castille** is to be at loggerheads. Perhaps the most famous 'Spanish' term is **castles in Spain**, another way of saying daydreams, visionary schemes or simply idle fancies. Occasionally varied as *castles in the skies* the term has been common in English since 1575. The French use, as **faire des châteaux en Espagne**, goes back to the 13th century, and French also offers **châteaux en Asie** and **châteaux en Albanie**. The image is thus linked less to Spain *per se*, but to any far-off land to which one has no concrete connection, let alone actual real-estate. In the case of Spain its mystery, at least prior to the 16th century, was its occupation by the distinctly exotic Moors.

As with many other nationalities, Spain has been used to describe various objects, with no real racial overtones. Thus **Spanish beard**, a form of moss, **Spanish pike**: a needle (which may bear a small hangover from the days of Anglo-Spanish rivalry), and **Spanish topaz**: a yellow rock crystal. **Spanish guitar**, meaning cigar, is simply rhyming slang, although **Spanish** by itself refers to the quality of flavour enjoyed in such a smoke.

Russian Roulette

Moscow, capital of Russia between the 15th and early 18th centuries, and again after the Revolution of 1917, seems to engender as fierce a dislike from outsiders as does the rest of Russia put together. However, in fairness, the references may be to the old kingdom of Muscovy, once the dominant power of the area. Thus every Polish term targets the city, even if the range of abuse is aimed somewhat more widely. **Moch** (an abbreviation that perhaps avenges Russia's dismissive **Lyakh**: a Polack), **Moskal** and **Moskwicin** (both of which latter terms were at one time forbidden in Poland by its Russian rulers) all imply Muscovite but can mean any Russian. Similar terms include the Ukrainian **Moskl** and Albanian **Muskof**. Only when they are actually talking of the Ruthenians, i.e. Ukrainians living in Galicia (East Poland), do the Poles talk of a **Rusak** (a term that can also mean a kitchen knife). **Russak** (using the negative suffix *-ak*) also means a Russian, viewed pejoratively by his fellow-Russians, as does **rus**, a negative use of *rus*: Russian. In Holland, however, **rus**, with the same meaning, denotes a plain-clothes policeman and the reference is presumably to Soviet Russia's KGB and similar 'organs of state security'. The phrase **slapen als een Rus**: 'to sleep like a Russian' means to be 'dead to the world' or to 'sleep like a log'. America, the Soviets' greatest enemy, usually talked of 'godless commies', but also used **russki** and **rooshkin**. The Poles indicate a lengthy, tedious period by the phrase **Ruski miesiac**: a Russian month, a term that is based on the ten-day difference between the Julian Calendar, still followed by Russia until the 1917 Revolution, and the new Gregorian version, which had been instituted in the late 15th century and gradually accepted throughout Europe in the decades that followed. In France **un Russe**: a Russian, was a trickster who posed as a spurious nobleman. Finally one has **Russian roulette,** in general terms any foolish, potentially self-destructive act and specifically the spinning of the chamber of a revolver which has been loaded with one bullet, pointing it at one's head, and then pulling the trigger.

'Me thocht a Turk of Tartary'

Although **Tartars** and **Turks** live at opposite ends of the Caspian Sea, it is acceptable to put them together as far as insults are concerned. They both started as tribes of Central Asia and certainly they seemed pretty much of a muchness to Europeans, typically the Scottish court poet William Dunbar (1465?-1530?) who in verses written between 1500-20 wrote 'Me thocht a Turk of Tartary | Come throw the boundis of Barbary | And lay for-loppin in Lumbardy'. Such a geographical confection – mixing the Eastern Mediterranean, Central Asia, North Africa and northern Italy – does not diminish the basic thrust: Turks were aliens, and Tartary an alien place. Tartars (the name seems to be Persian) first came to European notice as part of the armies of Jenghiz Khan (1162-1227) whose men overran and devastated much of Asia and Eastern Europe. It was the threat of further conquest that led to the celebrated quote, attributed to St Louis of France (*c*.1270), 'In the present danger of the Tartars either we shall push them back into the Tartarus whence they are come, or they will bring us all into heaven', a comment that coined **Tartarus** as a synonym for hell, and which was the first to use the Tartars as a term of abuse. This hellish mode can be seen in the Hungarian curse **vigyen el a tatár**: 'the Tartar take you!', the equivalent of the English 'The devil take you!', and **szegény tatár**, literally 'poor Tartar' and effectively 'poor devil'. The **Kutyafeju tatar**: 'dogheaded Tartar', merely underlines the contempt.

The tribe of whom Dunbar wrote was hardly so awe-inspiring, but the image stayed and with it have come a number of 'Tartar' terms. Tartar, meaning a military valet, is hardly abusive – the link is presumably to his riding of a horse – but the 16th to 17th century cant use meaning a strolling vagabond, thief or beggar, and as such cognate with Bohemian and Gypsy, certainly was. As was the contemporary use of **Tartar** as a general term of abuse. Those abused were seen as violent ruffians, irritable and intractable, and if a woman, a shrew and a termagant. Thus, presumably, the Russian reverse, the use of **bab**: an old woman, to mean a Tartar. The Russian term **axmétka**, based on the 'typical' Moslem proper name Axmet or Ahmed, also means a Tartar. Thus, still in the 17th century, the phrase **catch a Tartar**, meaning to get hold of someone or something that, whatever their or its outward appearance, proves 'too hot to handle'.

Americans, blithely vague as regards the world beyond their own shores, have called the Turks **arabs**, but a glance at the map will indicate certain differences. Like the Tartars, the Turks moved away from their base, and by 1300 had taken over the old Seljuk empire (based in Baghdad) and begun their expansion west and south. The word Turk appears around the time of the Third Crusade (1187-92), but it is actually used erroneously. The Seljuks were still in power, for all that their empire was crumbling, and the 'Turks' against whom Richard the Lionheart led his men were Seljuks, although his enemy Saladin was not in fact a Turk but a Kurd, then a tribe who fought as mercenaries for the Seljuks.

All of which is so much pedantry, as is so often the case, when it comes to using Turk as a negative. To quote the *OED*, the word is essentially 'applied to any one having qualities attributed to the Turks; a cruel, rigorous, or tyrannical man; any one behaving as a barbarian or savage; one who treats his wife hardly; a bad-tempered or unmanageable man...with alliterative qualification, terrible Turk; young or little Turk, an unmanageable or violent child or youth'. This reflection on children is echoed in Russia's **tatarskiy rebyenok**: a Tartar child, used to describe a moron or imbecile (and a term that echoes the latterday **mongol**). With that kind of build-up, everything that follows is almost anti-climactic. Aside from the American use of **Turk** to mean an Irish immigrant (which probably has a very different etymology), a Turk between the 16th and 17th century was both a 'human' figure at which to practise shooting and a hideous image to frighten children. More recent terms include a couple of phrases describing heavy smoking, the Italian **fumare come un turco**, and the Dutch **rooken als een Turk**, both meaning 'to smoke like a Turk'. The German term **Turkenkopf** refers to the 'Turk's head' that was carved on certain brands of pipe while the French **tête-de-Turc** (otherwise known as a **niggerhead**), a 'Turk's head' set up as a target (like the old military Turk) at fairs and amusement parks. The phrase also describes a shirker or a whipping boy, someone used as a butt for others' cruel humour. **Turc** ('Turk') itself meant, in 19th-century French cant, a native of Tours, and Touraine was known as **Turquie**. Finally the Hungarians use the phrase **törökot fogtam**: 'I caught a Turk' to denote an achievement of doubtful value.

The Tartar-Turkey mix also creates **horde**, a term that applied initially to the nomadic tribes who wandered across central Asia in search of pasturage, plunder or outright war. In the *Golden Horde* the term applied to that tribe which, from the 13th century to 1480, controlled the khanate of Kiptchak in eastern Russia and western and central Asia. The term arrived in English, when it described the Tartars, and came to mean a great collection of people – especially those considered savage, uncivilized, or uncultivated – in the early 17th century. The word comes from the Turkish *orda*, meaning camp and as adopted across Europe, though with an initial 'h', first grafted on by the Poles. Horde is also linked to *Urdu*, the language of north India and now of Pakistan, which comes, via the Persian *urdu*: camp, from the Turkish word and which in full is *zaban-i-urdu*: 'language of the camp'.

La Perfide Albion

Englisher and **Britisher**, both using the 'national' *-er* suffix, were apparently seen as derogatory in mid-19th-century America (and later in post-World War II comics, where the likes of 'Battler Brittain' slugged it out with Germans who called them *Englischer schweinhund*: Englisher pig-dog), and even **Briton**, in 18th-century Connecticut, served a similar purpose, but, as might be expected, it is non-Anglophones who find the English most repellent. **Albion** is primarily a literary term, first used in Bede's *History of the English Church and People* (*c.*900) and subsequently picked up by such as Chaucer, Shakespeare and many others, it refers (from the Latin *alba*: White) to the much-fêted 'White cliffs of Dover'; the classic phrase **la perfide Albion** is said to have been first used by the Spanish statesman the Marquis de Ximenés (1726-1817). The term points up England's allegedly treacherous foreign policies (and the Englishman's most besetting vice, at least in foreign eyes, hypocrisy). However a variation on the phrase appears earlier as **la perfide Angleterre**, coined by the French philosopher Bossuet in 1653. On either count the Russian word **Albión** has much the same implication. The French also offer **angliche**, a pejorative version of the usual *anglais*: English, and the phrases **damné comme un Anglais**: damned like an Englishman and, with cruel specificity, **être de Birmingham**: 'to be from Birmingham', i.e. to be bored to death.

Other countries are happy to follow suit. In the US **bimshah**, at least in Black use, means an Englishman; it appears to be a borrowing of an older term meaning a resident of Barbados, one of the most 'English' islands of the West Indies. In Poland **Anglik(a)** or **Anglelczyk**: 'an Englishman' means a phlegmatic person or a cold-blooded or indifferent person, and the phrase **Nic go nie zajmuje to Anglik!** explains that 'Nothing excites him. He's an Englishman'. Thus too the phrase **wygląda jak Angielska śmierć**: as pale as an English death scene', i.e. colourless, insipid, uninteresting. In Holland **een Engelschen brief schrijven**: 'to write an English letter' is to take a short nap, while in Sweden they talk of **engelsk spleen**: English glumness. The **English goodbye** (as used in Russian) is to leave without saying goodbye, and thus to leave rudely, and the English as a whole are known as **cpornye synov'j**, literally 'proper sons' or 'prim-and-proper boys'. The English en masse appear to worry South America where **inglesidad** (Argentina) and **inglezada** (Brazil) both mean an English mob.

Moving from England to Wales, **waler** gives America the opportunity yet again to pin the inevitable *–er* on another nation, and they add **welshie** for good measure. English itself, or at least its dialects, offers **Welsh ambassador**, meaning a cuckoo or owl, and by extension a fool who poses as wise, and the adjective **welsh** meaning mawkish or insipid (although this may also come from the nonce-word *wallowish*). In Yorkshire **Welch**, the alternative (and older) spelling, means a failure. In the West Indies the **welshman** is a fish that spends its days in hiding (reminiscent perhaps of the Welsh hiding from the Saxon invaders).

The Curse of Scotland

In the world of stereotyping, the Scots are generally linked to money, but as the terms that follow show, their tempers are apparently none too equable. The word **Scot** itself can describe an irascible individual, as well as meaning (like Ireland's **paddy**) a bad temper or fit of pique. **Scotty**, which in America is a simple diminutive, as defined in 1812 by Australia's first lexicographer, the transported convict James Vaux, is 'a person of irritable temper, who is easily put in a passion'. **Scotchy**, a Scotsman (1860) is generally used in a negative way. A **Scotch blessing** is a vehement scolding. In Holland **Schotschrift**: 'Scotch writing' is a libel, while the phrase **schotsch en scheef** means topsy-turvy. The term **Scotch cousin**, while meaning a distant relative and as such not especially abusive, is a punning antonym to the better known *cousin-german*, which in fact comes from the French *germain*: real, genuine, and usually means a first cousin. (A first cousin of one's father or mother is a *Welsh aunt* or *uncle*.) To answer **Scotch fashion** is to answer one question by asking another, a term that, like Jewish reply, shows that Jews and Scots are linked by more than merely pecuniary interests. Various dialect terms include the verb **to Scot**, to levy taxes (and to pay them); a **Scotch mark**: a defect, whether physical or moral, that serves to distinguish a given person; and **to Scotch**: to injure, to hinder or to get in someone's way (from *scotch*: to wedge or prevent from slipping).

As ever, the words Scots or Scotch have been tagged onto a number of terms, but none of these is especially abusive, even by default, other than the **Scotch attorney**, any plant of the genus *Clusia*, which has the property of 'squeezing the life out of' the tree that it envelops, and the West Indian creeper that is known as a **Scotchman hugging a Creole**. A **Scotch mist** is in fact a drizzling rain, and one that, as Francis Grose put it in 1785, 'will wet an Englishman to the skin'. Turning the tables, the **curse of Scotland** is the nine of diamonds. In the 'language' of cards diamonds imply royalty and according to legend every ninth king of Scotland was 'a tyrant, and a curse to that country' (Grose); a further suggestion is that the nine of diamonds resembles the arms of Duke of Argyll, who was one of the leading proponents of union with England, a move that was not wholly welcomed by his compatriots; another slang collector, John Camden Hotten, in 1860, suggests that this card was that on which 'Butcher' Cumberland wrote the orders for the mopping up of rebels after Culloden, that nine lozenges are the arms of Dalrymple, earl of Stair 'detested for his share in the Massacre of Glencoe', that the arrangement of diamonds resembles the St Andrew's Cross and adds 'the most probable explanation is that in the game of Pope Joan the nine of diamonds is the Pope, of whom the Scots have an especial horror'.

Turning Indian

While terms referring to America, at least by name, are generally complimentary – **americain** in French means shrewd, **avoir americain**: to take in a practical situation at a glance – those for the Native Americans, the 'Red Indians' of earlier terminology, are less charming. Starting with the early 19th century **abergoin** or **abrogan** (alternatives to the better-known *aborigine*) words have included **Injun** and **'jin**. **Indian** itself, coined in 1602, almost as soon as White men had set about colonizing the country, is, if not an insult, then certainly a misnomer. (For the combinations with 'red' see *Colour*.) **Papoose**, from the Algonquin for 'baby', came to be a general term for any non-White child, while **squaw**, based on a number of Algonquin dialect terms. all meaning woman, came to be used as a dismissive description of 'native' women. By extension the term, which the Indians themselves used for White women, came to mean one's wife, then any woman, 'red' or White, and thence an effeminate man. A **squaw-man**, however, was a White (or Black) man who married an Indian woman. Combinations with Indian or Injun give **Indian list**, a rancher's term for a blacklist, an **Indian orchard**: a group of wild fruit trees which settlers believed had been planted thus by the Indians, to **turn Indian**: the equivalent of the British Empire's 'go native', and **Indian side**: meaning the right side. This last is synonymous with the cowboy term **siwash side**, from **siwash**, a pejorative term for a Native American, and itself from the French *sauvage*: **savage**, another all-purpose name for the 'Indians'; such individuals, seen as bizarre by cowboys, mounted their horses from the right hand side, and wrestled down cows from the left – Whites preferred the left and right respectively.

The Bengal Scene

In this context Asia attracts relatively few terms, but worth mentioning are **Bengal scene**: a highly spectacular or sensational display on the stage or screen, **Paki** or **Pakki**, from Pakistan and used most notoriously in Britain's **Paki-bashing**: the beating up for no reason other than their colour of Britain's 'Pakistani' immigrants (few of whom are in fact Pakistani, the majority of Asians coming from East Africa, Sylhet or India). **Fip** or **Flip** means a Filipino, as does **goo-goo** or **gook**, a term that has been used for a succession of America's Asian bugbears, including the Koreans (1947), the Japanese (1951) and the Vietnamese (1968). Today's Germans term recent immigrants from Vietnam **Fijis**: Fijians. Finally the French phrase **rideaux de Perse** or Persian curtains refers to worn-out, 'holey' curtains. The pun on **Perse** and *percé*: pierced is obvious.

PERSONAL NAMES

METONYMY, THE substitution of a name for a quality, thus
making the one stand figuratively for the attributes of the other,
is common in racial abuse. It is the smart version of that
elbow-in-the-ribs knowingness epitomized by Monty Python's
'Nudge, nudge, wink, wink, know what I mean, say no more...'. Paddy
and Mick, Izzy and Abe, Hans and Fritz. Say no more indeed. There
may (or may not) have been a French procurer called *Alphonse*, but,
rhyming slang aside, this quintessential French name tells us all we
need to know. Thus it is across the terminological board.

Naming, whether positive or negative, is a selective process. While
the best-known of such names carry with them a weight of historical,
ideological and sociological baggage, some almost escape the net. Or if
caught, offer but a few sorry specimens. Only the countries and nations
with the longest and best-charted histories (justifiably or not) have
attracted a substantial lexicon. Thus one must lump together those
others for whom vilification has been less sizeable. That said perhaps
it is true, in this context if no other, that lucky indeed are the nations
that have no history.

Johnny Bono

Before passing to names taken from and thus attributed to specific nations, it is worth considering one of the most popular of English formations, the use of **Johnny**, combined with a given national name. Now confined largely to the ageing denizens of the golf club bar, such expressions have a lengthy pedigree. Its earliest use, ironically, was *of* rather than *by* Englishmen, and as noted by Lord Byron among others, was the term used around the Mediterranean by those who, bereft of any greater linguistic sophistication, attracted British attention by cries of 'Johnny!'. This version of the word gradually came to mean an idle and vacuous young aristocrat, and subsequent to that anyone seen as relatively ineffectual but well-meaning. Somewhat different meanings developed in such combinations as Australia's **Johnny Raw**: a new immigrant, and America's **Johnny Reb**, a supporter of the Confederacy during the Civil War. **Johnny**, an abbreviation of **Johnny Darby** in England (from the slang *darby*: a handcuff) and **John Hop** (rhyming slang for *cop*) in Australia, also meant a policeman.

As far as its application to foreigners is concerned, the earliest use of John or Johnny would appear to be the early 19th-century **John Chinaman**, a term that may have come from the use of the popular British name John as a catch-all name for the Chinese interpreters who dealt with the first merchants. The term spread throughout the empire, and was as popular in Australia as in England. It was still cited, without comment, in the 1970 edition of Brewer's *Dictionary of Phrase & Fable*, but seems to have been quietly excised since. Slightly nearer home **John Company** (an English translation of the earlier Dutch *Jan Kompanie*) had meant the East India Company; the idea, at least in Dutch eyes, was to personify the traders as the servants of one great overlord – Jan Kompanie. By the mid-19th century, native soldiers, otherwise known as Sepoys, who were enlisted in the British Army in India were known as **Johnnies**, as were the Ghurkas, the Nepalese troops of Hindu descent. **Johnny Turk**, perhaps the best known of all these expressions, and now used only as a joke, emerged during the Crimean War of 1854, while **Johnny Greek** and **Johnny Arab** (pronounced *a-rab*) are early 20th-century terms. A later engagement, Allenby's 1917 campaign in

Palestine, renamed the Turkish troops as **jackos**. The Arabs, like the Greeks, also used johnny to describe the British. Onion sellers from Brittany, rarely seen in contemporary Britain, though the traditional image of onion-bedecked bicycle, beret and striped Breton shirt lingers, if only in nostalgic advertising, were known as **johnnies** or **onion-johnnies** up to the 1960s. Last, and somewhat anomalous is **Johnny Bono** which, while sounding Italian, actually refers to an Englishman, and meant literally 'Johnny Good' (foreigners being naturally 'bad') in the late-19th-century East End of London, where it presumably sprang from the Italianate *lingua franca*.

Proud as Cuffy

Among the many names used as shorthand for a Black person, the oldest are probably a group taken from the African day-names – handed out according to the day on which one was born – that came from a range of West African languages (typically Twi and Fante, found on what is today's Ivory Coast) and that accompanied slaves on their trip west. The majority of these names imply a lack of sophistication, a rough and tough rural sensibility that seems naïve and gauche in town. Why this should be so is unknown, but may reflect the social gap, found in the West Indies, between the Creoles, those actually born in the islands, and the *saltwater negroes*, slaves who had been born before or during the voyage from Africa.

The foremost among these is **Cuffy**, which as *Kofi* was the Twi name for a boy born on a Friday. Adopted into English around 1710, the name lasted until the late 19th century, and developed the alternatives **cuff** and **cuddy**. Used among fellow-Blacks to denote an unsophisticated, tough peasant, its use in English tended to be patronizing, especially in the phrase **proud as cuffy**, meaning conceited and puffed up, and calling up what to White eyes was the ludicrous image of a Black man dressed up in his best clothes. Blacks had a different take on the name and perhaps the most famous of all Cuffys, the leader of the Guiana slave rebellion of 1763, is now a national hero of the renamed country, Guyana. **Kojo** refers to the Fante *Kodwo* and thus Ghanaian *Kodzo*: a male child born on a Monday, while **quashie** or **quashee** (1840s

114

onward) or **squasho** comes from the Twi *Kwasi*: a boy born on a Sunday. While making the usual connection with agrarian naïveté, quashie was also used by White sailors to mean any Black colleague. **Quashiba**, a foolish, uncultivated woman, comes from the Twi *akwasiba*: a girl born on a Sunday.

Not all of these terms are used in a White-to-Black context. The West Indies used **cubba**, from *Cuba*: the day-name of a woman born on a Wednesday, to mean a promiscuous woman or an effeminate man; **quaco**, another take on the countrified, ignorant person, is based on the Twi *kwam*: a boy who is born on a Saturday, while **quaw, quamin** or **quarmin**, all meaning much the same, but with the added meaning, in context, of an albino, is based on the Twi *kwaw*: a boy who is born on a Thursday.

Moving from Africa to America, one finds **Rastus**, a 'typical' Black name (presumably from the formal *Erastus*), especially as applied to the happy, dancing, servile Black as seen in so many early movies. Rastus' female companion was **Liza** or **Lize** and there was, at one time, a spate of 'Rastus and Liza' jokes, most of which turned on the couple's stereotypical stupidity. Lize, however, was by no means an exclusively Black metonym. Thanks to the hackery of one Edward Judson, a political fixer and bullyboy who as the author 'Ned Buntline' created virtually single-handedly the myths of what would become known as the 'Wild West', she also stood for the predominantly Irish 'Bowery g'hals' (the apostrophe denoting an 'Oirish' pronunciation), those tough denizens of downtown New York City whose fictional exploits, alongside her boyfriend the Bowery 'b'hoy' Mose, and their friend Syksey, delighted mid-19th century New Yorkers. Dressed to the nines (a multi-layered calico dress, a parasol and a poke bonnet) she, like her fireman paramour, smoked cigars and spent her days and nights in brawling and boozing.

Fiction, of an ostensibly higher class, was also responsible for another Black name: **Huck**, from *Huckleberry Finn*, the hero of Mark Twain's eponymous novel, published in 1885. **Jim** abbreviates Jim Crow (see *Animals*) while the much more recent **Jackie Robinson** (used in the 1940s/50s by Blacks of Blacks) referred first to any Black person who became the first to gain entry to a given profession and latterly to the penis. (Other Black pioneers have been termed *firsts*: the first person to break into an occupation, or *blockbusters*: the first Black family onto a hitherto all-White block; the term was reversed when the era of gentrification saw White families moving into the former all-Black ghettoes.) Given that the Jackie Robinson in question was the first Black star to break through the formerly segregated world of major league baseball, one must assume that the secondary meaning is a nod to the baseball bat. Other names include **James**, **Juba**, **Leroy**, **Mandy** (for women), **Willie** (also used in Australia by Native Australians to describe Whites) and **Marcus**, from the Black leader and 'back-to-Africa' advocate, *Marcus Garvey* (1887-1940). Female equivalents include **Sunshine**, **Summertime** and **Sapphire**, best known as a character in America's *Amos and Andy* radio show, a once-popular but now infinitely non-PC creation, which, with its White actors faking it as dumb but happy darkies, was one of the last interpretations of the old 'minstrel show'.

It is the minstrel show that inspired **Aunt Jemima**, a classic 'mammy' figure, whose image was popularized by the song 'Old Aunt Jemima,' published around 1876-7 and later reinforced by the 'Aunt Jemima' brand of pancake mix. Both **uncle**, **aunt** and **auntie** have all been used, usually for older men and women. **Uncle Remus**, the creation of writer Joel Chandler Harris, is another 'happy darky'.

Nic Frog

The most interesting of the Dutch names, which include **Nic Frog** (short for Nicholas and dating from an era when the Dutch, rather than the French, were 'frogs') is **Hogan** or **Hogan-Mogan**. This term, usually applied to rich and powerful figures, comes from the word *Hoogmogendheiden*, literally 'lord high mightinesses' and is, in the end, a simple mispronunciation. Coined in 17th-century England and thenceforth used contemptuously for the Dutch it came to mean any grandee or high and mighty person, used either humorously or contemptuously. It was also used as an adjective, to describe strong drink or as **hogan mogan rug**, strong drink itself. Other names include the surname **Knickerbocker**, originally that of one of New York's oldest

Dutch families, and thus applied to all descendants of the New York Dutch, and **Closh** (or **mynheer Closh**: 'Mr Klaus'), properly Klaus and itself an abbreviation of *Nicolaas*, a favourite given name.

Lewis Baboon

Johnny, usually applied to a given national name, here gives **Jean**, France's equivalent of John and thus applied to any Frenchman. **Jacques Bonhomme**, literally John Goodman, is another all-purpose Frenchman, though generally a farmer or farm-worker, while another 'Frenchified' term is **Lewis Baboon**, the direct, and somewhat less flattering response to the concept of John Bull meaning an Englishman (and coined, like Nic Frog, in the same essay – 'Law is a Bottomless Pit' (1712) – by Dr John Arbuthnot; see **John Bull**, below). The Lewis presumably refers to the long line of French kings named Louis. Such 'baboons' were especially popular as caricatured peasants, typically during the French Revolution. The late-19th century saw a brief flowering of the Royal Navy slang **Jimmy Round**, a 'name' which J. Redding Ware, in 1909, suggests comes from the French phrase *Je me rends*: I give up. Whether this idea extends beyond British nautical arrogance cannot be proved. Finally **Alphonse**, the rhyming slang for ponce or pimp, can also mean a Frenchman. The same term, with the same implications, can be found in a variety of European tongues.

Hans-in-Kelder

As far as these terms are concerned there are two primary varieties of German: those called **Fritz** and those called **Hans**. Fritz, a diminutive of Friedrich (Frederick), can be found in the late-19th century, when in a letter of 1883 George Meredith compared 'Fritz' to 'Alphonse', but emerged properly during World War I, when as well as a German soldier, it meant a German shell, aircraft, submarine or anything else pertaining to the German side of the hostilities. It was also found as **Fritzy**, as **Fricy**, in Russian, and as **Freddy**. In Poland **fryc** meant a gullible sort of person, while **frycować**, literally 'to befritz', meant to dupe, to make a fool of someone. The mainly American phrase **on the**

fritz: out of order, working sporadically, emerged in 1929, but may not actually relate to the name. Instead it may be an onomatopoeic version of the sound of sputtering, shorting electricity, or even a euphemism for 'fuck' (as in *fucked up* or *all to fuck*, meaning out of order). That said, another phrase, **put the fritz on**, meaning to spoil, destroy or put a stop to, was coined in 1903 and would seem to have some connection to Germany, perhaps to the clichéd stiff-necked obduracy with which Germans (or at least Prussians) are credited.

Hans, Germany's other name, first appears in England during the 16th century. The equivalent to John or the Dutch Johannes it meant either a German or a Dutchman. During the 17th and 18th centuries it was probably best-known in the phrase **hans-in-kelder (Hänschen im keller** in German), meaning literally 'Jack-in-the-cellar' and translated as a foetus or unborn child. **Hans the grenadier** paid tribute to German soldiering, while **hans-wurst** or simply **wurst** ('Hans-sausage') characterized a 'typical' German. Like Fritz, Hans gained wider use during the 20th century's two World Wars, and was joined in the second by **Heinie**, a diminutive of another popular name, Heinrich (Henry); its Polish version is **Hanysek**.

Other German names include **Greta, Gretchen**, a Polish borrowing that means 'a frivolous girl of easy virtue', **cousin-Michael** (on the pattern of England's **cousin-Jan**, meaning a Cornishman) that translates the German **der deutsche Michel**, to mean the (German) peasantry and **Hohenzollern**. This term, used to indicate Germany's autocratic spirit and belligerent policies refers to the Hohenzollern dynasty, a family originating from Hohenzollern in southern Germany which became successively electors of Brandenburg, kings of Prussia, and emperors of Germany. Finally **Piefke**, used in Austrian slang as a nickname for any German, is based not so much on a single name but on many, pointing up the way so many Prussian surnames seem to end in some harsh, cacophonous syllable.

Mulligan Stew

St Patrick, the patron saint of Ireland, may or may not have converted the entire country single-handed, explained the Trinity through the shamrock (now Ireland's national flower) and rid the country of its snakes – all of which legends accrue to his memory – but one legacy brooks no argument: his name. Patrick, in the forms Pat and Paddy, has generated a large number of metonymic terms, all of which mean Irishman or, in combination, denote some form of 'Irish' activity.

Pat, the simple abbreviation, appears around 1830 on both sides of the Atlantic. Within the next decade come **Patess**, an Irishwoman, **Patland**, Ireland, and **Patlander** an Irishman. Although the *OED* appears to deny such a background, claiming 'origin unknown', **patsy**, meaning a fool or sucker is surely another version of pat, and is based the stereotype of Irish stupidity. Its first use is cited in 1903 and it was soon well enough known for Harpo Marx, complete with prototype red wig and playing alongside his brothers Groucho and Gummo, to appear on the American stage in 1911 as 'Patsy Brannigan', a stock vaudeville character: the dumb Irishman.

Even more popular than Pat is **Paddy**, which reflects the Gaelic form of Patrick: Padraic. A paddy, among other things is a nickname for the ruddy duck (possibly through the ruddy complexion and red hair of many Irishmen), but that use is a by-product of a far larger and more pointed vocabulary. The word appears first in 1780, when it is used by Arthur Young in his *Tour of Ireland* and became well-established, once more in Britain and America, as the 19th century proceeded. The legendary Irish loquacity gave the Irish phrase **come the paddy over**: to hoodwink, to bamboozle, while the employment of many immigrant Irish as manual labourers made **paddy** itself synonymous with a bricklayer or his hod-carrier. **Paddy**, meaning a tantrum, comes from the reputation of the Irish as short of temper and quick to take offence. (The same word has been used in prison slang to mean the padded cell in which prisoners who have in some way 'done their nut' are confined; however one must acknowledge a parallel root: the word *padded* itself.) More recently, at least in Black America since the 1940s, paddy has meant a White man (as have **paddy-boy**, **patty**, **patty-boy** and **White-paddy**) and thus a policeman (given the large numbers of Irishmen who have always been drawn to the big city forces). This link between the Irish and the police can also be seen in **shamus** (*c.*1925) whether a uniformed policeman or detective (and even more commonly a private detective), which comes from *Seamus*, a common Irish name and usually pronounced as such, for all that Humphrey Bogart persists in 'sharmus' in the film of Raymond Chandler's *The Big Sleep*. Variations on **shamus** include **chom, chomus** and **sham**. Similarly 'Irish' are **shamrock** (the national emblem) and **muldoon** (a common surname). Today's gangsta rappers keep the tradition going, characterizing today's officers as **O'Malley**.

There are many combinations based on Paddy. Most take the naïveté or stupidity of the Irish as their touchstone. Thus for sailors **Paddy's hurricane** (or an **Irish hurricane**) is a flat calm, an **Irish battleship** or **Irish man o'war** is no more than a barge, **Irish lace** is a spider's web, **Irish mahogany** the common elder, **Paddy's lantern** the moon, and **Paddy('s) lucerne** (in Australia) a type of shrub – the tropical evergreen, *Sida rhombifolia* – so prolific as to be a pest (whereas lucerne is a form of clover, much used as animal fodder). To **do Paddy Doyle**, in British army slang, is to serve time in the punishment cells and the **paddy wagon**, which of course welcomes in any race or creed of prisoner, is the police van or 'Black Maria'. A **Paddy Wester** is either a second-rate, incompetent seaman; or a fake seaman with a dead man's discharge papers. The latter term comes from one *Paddy West*, a notorious boarding-house keeper in 19th-century Liverpool, who sold fake seamen's papers to thousands of otherwise unqualified men. **Paddyism** is an Irish peculiarity or 'Irishism'. In Australia **paddy's market** was originally the weekly market for cheap or secondhand goods held in the late-19th century near Haymarket Square in Melbourne; it propgressed to mean any kind of cheap market and during World War II also the market in Cairo where Australian troops sold illegally manufactured goods, black market commodities and the like. A **Paddy funeral** referred to any boisterous party (from the drinking traditional at an **Irish wake**, which, when not serving its literal purpose, means any boisterous, noisy event) and like patland, **Paddyland** meant Irish and **Paddylander** an Irishman. A **Paddywhack** is a large and threatening Irishman or the thrashing he is deemed capable of admistering to those who fall foul of his temper; the military phrase **what paddy gave the drum** is, unsurprisingly, a thrashing.

Patrick aside, **Michael** is another typically 'Irish' name and michael,

mick(e)y or particularly **mick** have meant Irish since the mid-19th century. The term originated in America, where it soon extended its range to become a generic for the Roman Catholics (who at that time were still predominantly Irish – Italians and Eastern Europeans began arriving somewhat later in the century). This Catholic link means that **mick** can also mean a Mexican. **Mick** has also come to mean the penis, for instance in James Joyce's *Ulysses* (1922), although this may be less of a tribute to Irish manhood than a parallel naming to that used in *John Thomas* or *dick*. **Mick(e)yland**, inevitably, has been used for Ireland, while the disparaging verb to **mike**, meaning to loiter comes either from *mouch* (which most probably comes from the Old French *muchier*: to hide or skulk) but, as Hotten notes, may be another case of racial stereotyping: Irish labourers were seen as congenitally idle. To *take the mick(ey)*: to tease, however, has no Irish background; it is simply rhyming slang: to take the Micky Bliss, i.e. to *take the piss*. On the other hand a **Mickey Finn** or **Mickey Flynn**, a knockout drug, possibly chloral hydrate, mixed into an unsuspecting victim's drink, certainly is Irish. Or at least the man who created it was. The original Finn was a saloon-keeper who ran the Lone Star and Palm Saloons in Chicago *c*.1896-1906; acccording to his story he had picked up the recipe from voodoo operators in New Orleans.

Mulligan, a well-known Irish surname, has its own stable of terms, at least in America; all seem to have originated around the turn of the 19th century. The best-known is **Mulligan stew**, an old hobo or tramp term that describes a makeshift stew made of whatever meats and vegetables are available and the usual meal in the hobo *jungles* of the 1930s. This generated the **mulligan car**: the railroad car from which meals are served, the **mulligan joint**: a cheap restaurant (from *joint*, meaning small restaurant or café) and **mulligan mixer**, a Western term meaning cook. The US Army's **mulligan battery** was the cook wagon, mocking the standard battery's more bellicose activities. Mulligan, on the same lines as shamus and paddy, can also mean a prison guard, another group who at one time tended to be recruited from the immigrant Irish. The New York stage of the 1870s, or at least its more down-market venues, saw the enormous popularity of a series of 'Mulligan plays', created by the talented song-and-dance duo Ned

Harrigan and Tony Hart. These plays – among them *The Mulligan Guard Ball* and *Mulligan's Silver Wedding* – were the direct descendants of the 'Mose and Lise' Bowery productions mentioned above, mixing themes dear to Irish immigrant hearts, with a solid leavening of contemporary 'dirty realism', using plenty of local colour and sometimes drawing their plots from the well-documented machinations of New York politics. Irishry aside, Harrigan and Hart's work is the bridge between the rough-hewn burlesques of the mid-19th century and the increasingly sophisticated 'musicals' that would dominate the early 20th and beyond.

If Pat, Paddy and Mick stole the honours for the men, then **Bridget**, and her diminutive **Biddy** was the quintessential Irish girl. Grose cites 'Biddy, or Chick-a-biddy, a chicken, and figuratively a young wench' in 1785, but the equation between Biddy (or Bridget) as the typical Irish serving maid or charwoman comes fifty-odd years later. Biddy and Bridget play much the same role, although only Biddy has lasted into the present day, in meaning an interfering, irritating old woman. A less common term is **bridgeting**, extinct by 1918, which in its time meant a confidence trick whereby money was extorted from these often naïve girls, who turned over their wages in the belief that they were helping some Irish Republican cause. Mullingar, a place rather than personal name, gives the derogatory **Mullingar heifer**: a girl with thick ankles an d thus the phrase **beef to the heels, like a Mullingar heifer**. Both come from the supposed physique of Mullingar women.

A few other names also relate Ireland to the names of its people. Among them are the surnames **Donovan** and **Murphy** (also used widely to mean a potato, a 'staple' Irish food) and **dogan**, which is also presumed to be a name. They are all generic for Irishman, as is New Zealand's **doolan**, which can also mean a Catholic. So too is **Mac**, from the Gaelic 'son of' and the prefix of many Irish surnames, while **Teague**, usually found in the context of Roman Catholicism (see *Religion*) can also be used in **Teagueland** and **Teaguelander**. Bark, from a number of northern English dialects, means an Irishman, and Barkshire is Ireland. The reason remains elusive, unless it comes from the idea of an Irishman shouting or 'barking'. Proper names give **Ted** and **Teddy**, from Theodore, and **tip**, an abbreviation for Tipperary (and best known as the nickname of Thomas 'Tip' O'Neil, the American politician). Finally the Anglo-Irish **shoneen**, from the Irish Gaelic *Seonin*, a diminutive of *Seon* or John, refers to a person born and living in Ireland, whose allegiances – cultural, political, even sporting – are predominantly directed against England.

O, O Antonio

Italian names are rather like the general names thrown around London or New York, where respectively 'John' or 'Mac' can serve as all-purpose forms of address, irrespective of the actual given name of the person so addressed. In other words they are mainly generics, such as **Antonio, Carlo, Dino** (presumably the source of **dyno**, a Mexican, and as such a term that deals with a similarly 'Latin' race) and **Tony**, any of which can be used when talking to someone who appears Italian. Dyno is also used of recent Central European immigrants, and while it may merely extend the 'Latin' use to a wider population, it may also come from the Polish imperative **daj-no**: give! Slightly more arcane is **poppie-squalie**, but that seems to be little more than Pasquale and the rarely heard **hike** and **shike** are basically variations on Ireland's Mike.

Abie the Agent

Like the French, who are traditionally enjoined to add a saint's name to those given to every child, Jewish names, or at least traditional Jewish names are a rollcall of theological figures, in this case from the Old Testament, and on that ground could as well be included under *Religion* as here. Abraham, Isaac, Jacob, Rebecca...they and others have all been used as synonyms for Jew for many years.

Abraham, to start with the first of the patriarchs, gives **Abe** or **Abie**, both of which play the predictable role, with an additional use by African Americans in which **abie** means a tailor (a use that reflects the Royal Navy's use of *jew* to mean the ship's tailor). Less well-known these days is **Abie Kabibble**, a name that is based on the American Yiddish *ish kabibble*: who cares, don't worry, and which in turn comes most probably from the synonymous German Yiddish *nish gefidlt*.

Adopted as a catch-phrase by the vaudeville superstar Fanny Brice, the term was picked up by America's 'dean of cartoonists' Harry Hershfield who in 1917 launched a character called *Abie the Agent*, based on one 'Abie Kabibble'. Highly successful, the strip lasted until 1932. The term was further popularized by a swing trumpeter who adopted the name 'Ish Kabibble', and started performing as a comic.

After Abraham, **Isaac** gives **Ikey** in English and **Icek** in Polish. Ikey can also mean a pawnbroker and as an adjective, wide-awake or smart (1900). **Ikey-mo**, which adds Moses to Isaac, just means a Jew. **Jake**, from Jacob, Isaac's son, is a third synonym. Similar names include **Max**, a common Jewish given name, **Sol** (from the wise King Solomon), and **Sammy** or **Šmul** in Russian (both from Samuel, although the *Dictionary of American Slang* suggests that the name comes from the acronym *Sigma Alpha Mu*, a Jewish college fraternity, whose members are called 'sammys'), and the women **Rachel** (Jacob's wife) and **Rebecca** (or the Hebrew **Ryfka**, Abraham's wife). Rebecca was also the name taken by the tall, but otherwise anonymous man who, dressed in women's clothes, led a series of successful attacks on toll-gates in South Wales in 1843-4. These 'Rebecca Riots' as they were known, took as their text *Genesis* 24:60: 'And they blessed Rebecca and said unto her, Thou art our sister, be thou the mother of thousands of millions and let thy seed possess the gate of those which hate them'.

See You, Jimmy!

Sandy, the abbreviation of Alexander, is one of the most common given names in Scotland, and thus it is hardly surprising that it has come to mean any Scot. Cognate is **Sawney**, although the most notorious Sawney, Sawney Beane, leader of a band of incestuous murderous cannibals in the 15th century, is hardly much of a role model. **Saunders**, usually a surname, can also mean Scot, although it would appear to be a mis-spelling or mispronunciation of the original sawney. **Sammy**, while by no means a specifically Scottish term, appears to have been enlisted, although its real background may be in *sammy*, 19th century English slang for a fool. Two quintessentially Scottish terms remain: **mac** or **mack**, used as a prefix in thousands of Scottish surnames, and perhaps most typically of all, **jock**. Jock, a Scottish version of John and equally popular, has meant a Scottish (or northern English) sailor; a Scottish soldier or a member of a Scottish regiment or indeed any Scotsman since the late 18th century. Perhaps not Scottish in national terms, but central to everyday communication in Glasgow, is *jimmy* (from James) which is found through the city as a popular term of address.

John Bull

Writing in 1712, the physician and wit John Arbuthnot (1667-1735), a fellow-member with Swift, Pope and the playwright John Gay of the literary Scriblerus Club, entitled an essay thus: 'Law is a Bottomless Pit. Exemplified in the Case of the Lord Strutt, John Bull, Nicholas Frog and Lewis Baboon: who spent all they had in a Law-suit.' Otherwise known as 'The History of John Bull' it is an ingenious attack upon the war policy of the Whigs. Lord Strutt does not seem to have a nationalist role, but as noted above, **Nicholas Frog** is Dutch, **Lewis Baboon** French and **John Bull**, as generations continue to acknowledge, English. Whether Arbuthnot actually coined the phrase, or merely popularized it, remains unknown, certainly the *OED* has no earlier citation, but it has become one of the best known images of those characteristics that the English cherish as 'theirs'. An extension, **Johnny-Bull**, and a female version, **Joan Bull** both exist, as does **jumble**, used, at least according to the author Colin MacInnes who incorporated it into several novels, by West Africans (either visiting students or immigrants to Britain) during the 1950s; it is an elision of the standard term. That said, claims that **jumble** is also West Indian seem less likely – neither Cassidy & LePage's *Dictionary of Jamican English* (2nd edn 1980) nor Richard Allsopp's *Dictionary of Caribbean English Usage* (1996) include it. The homonymous *jumbe*, itself of African origin, is a demonic creature, half-spider, half-man. Back across the Atlantic the regular term crops up again in Antigua, where it is the name of a traditional Carnival and Christmas parade character who is clad in sacking, the bottom part of which is stuffed with rags and sugar-cane cuttings. As he capers along he is accompanied by a drummer who carries a long whip, frightens the onlookers and extorts money from them. His image, given his name, is presumably that of the English plantation owner, for once suffering beneath rather than wielding the whip. John Bull is often accompanied by a **bulldog**, another term used symbolically to represent the character of the English people, known in their wilder flights to call themselves 'the bulldog breed' (a phrase coined by the usually sceptical Lord Macaulay).

Tommy, usually known as the typical English soldier, has also been used, presumably by those who have mixed with him in wartime, as a synonym for the average Englishman. Like America's *G.I.*, a term that reflects Army paperwork (it comes from Government or General Issue), tommy has its origins in army bureaucracy. To quote the *OED*, the use arises 'out of the casual use of this name in the specimen forms given in the official regulations from 1815 onward... In some of the specimen forms other names are used; but "Thomas Atkins" being that used in all the forms for privates in the Cavalry or Infantry, is by far the most frequent, and thus became the most familiar; thus 1815 (Aug. 31) War Office, Collection of Orders, Regulations, etc. 75 (Form of a Soldiers Book in the Cavalry when filled up). Description, Service, &c. of Thomas Atkins, Private, No. 6 Troop, 6th Regt. of Dragoons. Where Born... Parish of Odiham, Hants... Bounty, 6. Received, Thomas Atkins, his x mark.'

A small group of terms, all based on cousin, are all used of Cornishmen. Dating from the 19th century they include **cousin-jacky** and **cousin-jan**, and if a woman **cousin-jenny**. **Cousin-jack** (and **cousin-anne**) have meant a miner (and his wife) who have come from Wales to work in America. A less affectionate, but undoubtedly cognate term is *cousin betty*, which can mean either a 'loose woman' or a half-wit. (Coincidentally, according to Barrère (1902), *cousine* in French argot means either a male homosexual or as *cousine de vendange*, 'a dissolute girl fond of the wine shop'; a *cousin de Moïse* is her husband, *Moïse* itself being slang for a man deceived by his wife, as befell the Biblical Moses). The last of these terms, **Taffy** – the 'classic' name for a Welshman – is simply an abbreviation of the Welsh proper name *Dafydd* or *David*, which is also that of the country's patron saint.

Yankee-Doodle-Dandies

Of all the names that have come to personify a nation, **yankee**, meaning American in general and New Englander in particular, is among the most used. The word is first cited in 1765, in its New England context and by 1784, as the country expanded beyond its north-eastern roots, came to mean the entire nation (and occasionally one of its ships). Since then uses of yankee have proliferated: it has meant whiskey sweetened with molasses, American stocks or securities as traded on the London stock market, and, far more recently, a composite bet on four or more horses, composed of doubles, trebles, and one or more accumulators.

As far as its origins are concerned, there have been a number of theories, and while these have generally been abandoned, before looking at what is supposed to be the 'true' etymology, some of these suppositions may be considered. The two earliest statements as to its origin were both published in 1789. As noted in the *OED* Thomas Anburey, a British officer who served under Burgoyne in the War of Independence, derives Yankee from the Cherokee *eankke*: slave or coward, and claims that the term was applied to the inhabitants of New England by the Virginians, resentful at their lack of help in their war with the Cherokees. The second mention came from William Gordon, writing in his *History of the American War*, who stated that it was a favourite word with farmer Jonathan Hastings of Cambridge, Mass., *c*.1713, who used it to mean 'excellent'. He makes no suggestion, however, as to where Hastings had obtained it. The theory that, for many years, remained the one most widely accepted appeared in 1822: this suggested that the word evolved from the Native American mispronunciation of the word 'English', moving it through Yengee to Yankee.

All of these have been discarded in the face of what seems to be the real etymology: the Dutch word *Janke*, a diminutive of *Jan* (John) and used as a derisive nickname by either the Dutch or the English in the New England states. Certainly there is substantial documentary evidence, dating to 1683, that bears this out. For the next forty-odd years local records give several examples of sailors and pirates and one Black slave, all of whom seem to have been nicknamed yankey, yanky or yankee. This theory has been extended by Raven I. McDavid, in his abridgement of H.L. Mencken's *American Language* (1963); he claims that the term is most likely an elision of *Jan Kees*, Kees being a diminutive of Cornelius, a common Dutch given name, which was the Dutch equivalent of 'Joe Doakes' or 'John Doe.' In its turn Jan Kees is based on *Jan Kaas*, literally 'John Cheese'. It seems to have been coined as a nickname for the Dutch settlers, then, with the appearance of the English in Connecticut, turned on the newcomers by the Dutch and then extended to the whole of New England. From there it spread to characterize the whole of America, and still does, whether in its English spelling or in such variations as Russia's **Jánki**, the Spanish **yanqui** and so on. Outside America its most common use, of course, is in the phrase that means, whatever the spelling 'Yankee go home!'.

Uses of yankee include **yankee heaven** or **yankee paradise**, otherwise known as Paris, France; **Yankeedom**: the USA, a **yankee hitter**: in baseball a weak hitter (the assumption being that better players come from the southern states; a **Jap liner**, on the other hand is a 'cheap hit', also known as a **Texas leaguer**; the reference is to cheap, badly made Japanese goods), and the adjective **yankee**, which plays upon the New England image to mean shrewd, reserved and mechanically ingenious. In Latin America, where Argentina is stereotyped as a conspicuously aggressive nation, Argentines have been termed by their neighbours the **yankees of the south**. Back in America a **blue-bellied-yankee** (with its reference to the *blue-noses* of Boston) is a Yankee par excellence. Aaside from **septic tank** (see Disease) rhyming slang offers **army tank** and **ham shank**, both meaning Yank.

For many people their first experience of yankee comes in the doggerel nursery rhyme 'Yankee doodle', who came to town 'riding on a pony. | Stuck a feather in his cap and called it macaroni.' Aside from the inclusion of the slang term macaroni, meaning a fop (as well as an Italian, see *Food*) **yankee doodle** itself is slang, noted by Grose as 'A booby or country lout, a name given to the New England men in North America'. Doodle, a silly or foolish fellow, a 'noodle', had been coined in the early 17th century and may have been taken from the Low German *dudeltopf*, literally a nightcap, but was used to mean a fool. At the same time 'Yankee Doodle' had been an American song since 1768, supposedly composed in 1755 by Dr Shuckburgh, a surgeon in Lord Amherst's army, mocking New England's supposedly provincial and thus inadequate soldiery. However the journal *Notes and Queries* cites the song 'Yankee Doodle; or the Negroe's farewell to America' and dates it 1775. One line reads 'Yankee doodle, yankee doodle dandy, I vow, Yankee doodle, yankee doodle, bow wow wow'. The two may be the same, but the 'Farewell' hardly seems to fit Dr Shuckburgh's intention. Two centuries on, the image of a yankee as a would-be sophisticate is seen again in Australia's **Woolloomooloo Yank**: a relatively unsophisticated person who attempts to ape the supposedly hip style of an American. Woolloomooloo, one of Australia's small towns, is a general term for rough, unsophisticated and thuggish; thus the terms *Woolloomooloo bushman*: one who rides a horse badly and *Woolloomooloo upper-cut*: kick to the groin.

In 1839, with yankee long established, the term **Jonathan** began to be used to describe both Americans and New Englanders, especially in the phrase **Brother Jonathan**. It apparently originated in the expression 'Brother Jonathan', as used by Saul, mourning his friend in *II Samuel* 1:26: 'I am distressed for thee, brother Jonathan: very pleasant hast thou been unto me: thy love was wonderful, passing the love of women.' It was supposedly applied to Jonathan Trumbull, Governor of Connecticut, by George Washington, who often sought his advice.

The Yankees, as a group, are perhaps the 'safest' of all Americans, representing the early White, Protestant settlers, and they are the target for relatively few racial slurs. Not so those whom they ousted, the Native Americans. Names for the 'red Indians' are many, typically **Hiawatha** (from Longfellow's much-parodied 1855 poem 'The Song of Hiawatha') or **lo** (plus **mister-lo** and **poor-lo**). In 1936 Mencken suggested that this derived punningly from Alexander Pope's verse: 'Lo, the poor Indian! whose untutor'd mind | Sees God in clouds, or hears him in the wind'. **Chief**, or **Big Chief**, always used sarcastically, gives **chief-rain-in-the-face**, **sitting-bull** (from Sitting Bull [*c.*1831-90] leader of the Sioux and in 1876 victor of the Battle of the Little Big Horn, which wiped out General Custer and his men) and similar attempts at 'humour'; **misterjohn** is an 1870s coinage.

For African-Americans various supposedly polite terms describe the

White man or woman. Among them **Miss-Ann, Miss-Annie, Mister-Charlie, Mr Charles** or **Charles** (and the less than respectful **Chuck**), **Charlene** (the female Charlie), **Mister-Eddie** and **Mister-Jones**. **Boss** stresses the image of an overbearing, racist White man while **captain** is less reminiscent of the navy than the prison yard, where the chief warder is often known as Captain. **Mary**, as it does in many countries, especially the missionary-infested Pacific Islands, means a White woman.

Abdul, Olaf and Tom

Canada, with its Anglo-French population, boasts a pair of names, one from each language. Used to describe the national (English) élite, **Tom** is in fact an acronym, which notes the way that élite concentrates in *T*oronto, *O*ttawa, and *M*ontreal; a secondary meaning may pick up on **tommy**, seen above as meaning an Englishman. It may even hint at the Black use of **Uncle Tom** to mean a Black who is subservient to the White power structure, that power for French Canadians being seen as the Queen and her government in London. The French term, coined in the early 19th century is **jean-baptiste, jean-batiste**, or even an anglicized **john-baptist**; an alternative is **jean-courteau**. In all cases the popular French name becomes a generic for French Canadians.

A male Filipino can, perhaps understandably, be known as a **philip**, the nation takes its name from Philip of Spain. A female Hawaiian, is a **hula-lula**, the latter part a girl's name, the former a Hawaiian dance, associated with grass skirts and tourist posters. (**Hula-land** is thus Hawaii.) The same John that is found in John Chinaman, also prefaces **John Tuck**, a British term for a Chinese mandarin, combining the usual use of 'johnny' with a reference to the tucking of such a mandarin's hands into his sleeves. Other Chinese names include **charlie**, which has been used for other Asians (and was of course the term of choice, culled from the military alphabet, for the Viet Cong during the Vietnam War), and **ming**, which comes from the Chinese meaning bright or clear and presumably refers to the dynasty which ruled China from 1368 to 1644. The derisory **Mary**, an all-purpose proper name that can mean woman in general, is used by Americans to deal with any female Pacific Islander; the word is also used on New Guinea to describe a woman or girl.

Back in Europe Czechs are known, at least in Poland, as **Pepik** or **Pepiczek**, a derogatory term based on a dialect form of *Josef*, a common given name. **Horwat**, a surname, means Hungarians in general, as does **hun**, which in this context is an abbreviation of Hungary and not a reference to the word used to typify warlike Germans. **Hunnry**, an outright pun, plays much the same role, while **Miklos**, a common given name, means Hungarian to Germans. **Gudde** or **Guddas**, a nickname for any eastern and northern Slav – Pole, Lithuanian, or Russian – is found in the German saying, 'When the Prussian speaks, it is for the Gudde to be silent'. **Stashu**, Poland's equivalent of Stanley, is used in America to refer to any Pole. **Ivan**, a Russian name as common as John, means a Russian, and particularly a Russian soldier, to Anglophone countries, while **fonye ganev**, Yiddish for 'Vanya, the thief' or 'foxy Ivan' plays on the low Jewish opinion of Russian honesty,

Tony, which as an abbreviation of Antonio can mean an Italian, also means a Portuguese (both civilian and soldier); **don**, from the title *Don* that sometimes precedes Portuguese names, plays a similar role. The derisive **chico**, meaning a child in Spanish, is used by Americans to describe Puerto Ricans; it was formerly a popular personal nickname among Puerto Ricans and Mexicans, especially during the ascendancy of the baseball heroes Chico Cardenas, Chico Fernandez, Chico Salmon and Chico Ruiz. **Pedro**, a typical Puerto Rican name, is a generic, as is the similar **Jose** for Spain, **Abdul** for Turkey and **Ole** or **Olaf** for Norway and Sweden. Spain can also boast **dago**, from **Diego** (James); a **dago bomb**, like a **guinea football**, is a large firecracker or hand grenade.

Old Crab

ARROGANCE

MUTUAL INTOLERANCE being what it is, the majority of the seven deadly sins are ascribed to one's neighbours at one time or another. Pride and arrogance are no exception and while such terms are relatively rare, compared, say, with those dealing with colour or religion, they do exist. They fit, as one might expect, the various national stereotypes.

A **mof** in Dutch means a muff or greenfinch; it also means a person who consistently sulks and frowns and thus, according to the Dutch picture of Germany, a typical German. England weighs in with the **German gospel**, a synonym for vain boasting, megalomania and self-aggrandizement. The term comes from a speech delivered in November 1897 by Prince Henry of Prussia to his brother Kaiser Wilhelm, which was full of such fulsome phrases as 'The gospel that emanates from your Majesty's sacred person...'. The French phrase **fier comme un écossais** means 'proud as a Scotsman'. The Poles, never over-amicable towards the Germans, talk of an **inina pruska**: a Prussian air, and thus an arrogant expression. **Zabity Niemiec**, also Polish, means a touchy German, while in Provence **auturious coumo un Alemand** and **coulerous coume un Alemand** mean respectively 'haughty as a German' and 'huffy as a German'. Provence also offers

faire l'espagnou: 'To act the Spaniard', a phrase that means colloquially to put on airs; **espagnoulado**: a Spanish stunt and another
term from Provence, is used to mean swagger, bravado and boastful-
ness. Indeed, if any stereotype can be applied to the Spanish, it would
appear to be pride, a virtue in Spanish eyes, less appealing to international onlookers. Thus Italy has **spagnoleggiare**: to 'throw the Spanish', otherwise to swagger, and to show off, and **spagnolismo**: 'Spanish
mannerisms', i.e. haughtiness. Germany talks of **spanischer Ernst**:
'Spanish seriousness' or utter lack of sense of humour, and **spanisches
Gesicht machen**: 'to make a Spanish face' is to affect an over-dignified
air; to show indifference or aloofness. Finally England's **Spanish
athlete** is a braggart, a pompous or conceited talker; the punning
phrase stigmatized anyone who 'throws the bull.' Readers of the tales
of the Three Musketeers, with its Gascon hero D'Artagnan, will have
no problems defining either **Gascon** itself: properly a native of France's
south-western privonce of Gascony and figuratively a braggart and
boaster or **gasconnade**: bravado, braggadocio or bluff.

Czarny jak, 'as black as a Swede', say the Poles when they wish to
categorize someone unprepossessing or ill-natured. **Szwed** by itself is
an unpresentable or filthy person. The Swedes lash out in turn at the
Finns with **arg som en finne**: surly as a Finn. The Dutch talk of the
lompe Deen and the **norsche Deen**, respectively the awkward Dane
and the sullen Dane. The Danes in turn pillory **en vilter Krabat**: a
wild Croat. In Old French **norois**: a Norwegian, described anyone seen
as high-handed or overbearing. The Argentine term **judear**: 'to act the
Jew' is to be tricky or scornful while Portugal's **judia**, literally a Jewess,
means a jeering or sneering person.

What is condemned as excessive Jewish pride has obviously been a
source of worry to fellow-Jews as well as enemies. A number of Yiddish
proverbs warn against such emotions: 'The Lord guard us against
Jewish arrogance, Jewish mouths, and Jewish heads', 'May the Lord
deliver us from Jewish pride and Gentile passion', and 'Every Jew
would like the front seat in his little synagogue' are just three. To the
Jews a **terkish hartz**: a Turkish heart, denotes a callous or truculent
streak. And the **grand Turk**, as a general English phrase, describes not
merely some ludicrously self-important rank in the Ku Klux Klan, but

any proud, arrogant person. The English, to the French, produce the phrase **méchant comme un Anglais**: 'as unpleasant as an Englishman'. **Play the Indian** (1840) plays itself on the image of Native American stoicism and means to restrain one's emotions; **sing Indian** (1829), coming from the same background, means to accept one's death without complaint. **Stoic** itself has a racial background: it refers to the school of Greek philosophers (founded by Zeno, *fl. c* 300 BC), characterized by the austerity of its ethical doctrines; the great hall at Athens (adorned with frescoes of the battle of Marathon), in which Zeno lectured was the Stoa. **Free as an Arab** uses another cliché, that of the desert warrior galloping across the desert's trackless waste, and means unbridled or undisciplined. A **surly-boy** has been used for an Irishman, while **Irish assurance** is shamelessness. Finally **ring-tail**, a generally derisive term which has applied both to Italians and Japanese, is based on the nautical jargon **ringtail**: a small triangular sail, extended on a little mast, and occasionally erected on the top of a ship's stern. Figuratively a ringtail is a worthless object and as such has been used, aside from the racial connotations, to define a tramp with a grudge, an ignorant, loud-mouthed, vulgar person and, in Australia, a coward.

I Cheat all

CHEATS

IT WOULD seem, taken logically, that if one segregates a given
individual, cuts him off from all forms of employment bar one, and
ensures that the one he is allowed to undertake is despised by the rest
of the community, then it is surely to add gross insult to equally gross
injury then to attack and pillory that individual for performing the task
which, willy-nilly, he has been allotted. Taken logically that is, but the
world of racial abuse is not, of course, one of logic. Thus the role of the
Jew: forced by Christian piety to take on the role of money-lender, he
is then cursed by the pious for performing the very task with which he
has been saddled. Jews, as this section makes clear, are not the only race
to be stigmatized as cheats, but they take pride of place, as it were, in
this tawdry lexicon. Of the great racial stereotypes, this one is undeniable.

Look, for instance at the range of sayings that harp on the topic. They
can be German: **a real Jew never sits down to eat until he has been
able to cheat** (the Serbs and Rumanians both run variations on this),
the Jews use double chalk in writing; they can be Russian: **The Jew
will cheat himself, when the idea strikes him, Jews do not learn
cheating; they are born with it**; or Polish: **the Jew is a cheat to**

135

begin with and **only the devil can cheat a Jew**; or Moroccan: **when a Jew smiles at a Moslem, it is a sign that he is preparing to cheat him**. They can express superlatives: **he can cheat a Jew**, i.e. he is a man so cunning that he can even best a Jew, or jokily suggest the near-impossible: **a Saxon cheated a Jew**, the German equivalent of a man biting a dog. They are part of the strange calculus of national abuses: **One Jew is equal in cheating to two Greeks, and one Greek to two Armenians**, or **a Russian can be cheated only by a Gypsy, a Gypsy by a Jew, a Jew by a Greek, and a Greek by the devil** (both Russian).

It is all very respectable. One need only browse the citations offered by the *OED*, which only in its Supplement and subsequent Second Edition agreed to add to its entry on the noun **Jew** 'As a name of opprobrium: spec. applied to a grasping or extortionate person (whether Jewish or not) who drives hard bargains' the note 'offensive'. The verb **to Jew**: to cheat or overreach, in the way attributed to Jewish traders or usurers. Also, to drive a hard bargain,...to haggle. Phr. **to jew down,** to beat down in price' has been treated similarly: its entry now adds that 'These uses are now considered to be offensive.' Nonetheless the uses are there, a positive roll-call of literary stars: Washington Irving, Henry Mayhew, Dante Gabriel Rossetti, Gerard Manley Hopkins, Emily Dickinson, J.M. Synge, T.S. Eliot, Anthony Powell (albeit in the mouth of a fictional character). If the luminaries find no problems with the concept, hallowed by centuries of Christian doctrine, why should the lumpen? And of course they do not.

Apart from these two English terms, there are the nouns **Jewish lightning**: deliberate arson in order to gain the insurance on an otherwise unprofitable business; a **Jewish waltz**: the process of deal-making and haggling; a **Jew trick**: an advantage taken that is not strictly dishonest, although supposedly out of keeping with a notional business or professional code; or the verb to **jew out of**: to use petty, quasi-criminal means to 'do someone out of' something. The use of the bald 'Jew', rather than the notionally softer 'Jewish' merely underlines the aggression in such terms.

And one does not have to speak English to find ways of expressing the same thing. The 'Jew trick' has spawned a variety of synonyms: the

Dutch **Jodenstreek** or **Jodentoer** (the latter also means a night shift in a factory or, perhaps grudgingly, something needing ingenuity or skill); the Greek **tsiphoutia'**, the French **judasserie** (literally a Judas trick); the Argentine Spanish **judearia**, which has an added implication of teachery and betrayal; Portugal's **judiaria** (also meaning coward or indeed a ghetto) and Germany's **judentijcke. Judelei**, also German, translates as 'Jewish ways', colloquially it means 'chiselling'. The Scandinavian **Jodetraek** means both a dirty trick and, in chess, a 'fool's mate.' **Juiverie**, in France, means the Jewish quarter, a 'Jewish stunt' and usury. The phrase **Il m'a fait une juiverie** means 'He has played me a dirty trick'. **Juivoler**, a mix of **juif** and *voler*: to steal, is a slang term meaning 'to rip off'. Other verbs include Holland's **Joden**: to Jew (someone), i.e. to 'do' someone or to engage in petty dealing. **Judzić** (Polish) to trap, to give bad counsel and to importune; **żydowską piosnkę komu śpiewać**: to 'give someone the Jewish spiel' means to sound them out as to the possibility of their accepting a bribe. **Einen Juden anhangen** means 'to fasten a Jew on someone', thus to give one the lie or to show someone up in German, while the Russian **zhidovat'**: to Jew, means variously to haggle, to behave in a Jewish manner, to gesticulate or to speak with a Jewish accent.

That other countries rank 'cheats' among their national stereotypes is undeniable. But the pinning of such labels is not the crusade that centuries of anti-semitism have made of its application to the Jews. Like their American cousins the Yankees, the Dutch have a reputation for driving a hard bargain. But there, as much as anywhere, lies the difference. To drive a hard bargain is, somehow, respectable; it is accepted, it is perhaps not desperately smart (hence the long disdain of 'trade' by the British upper classes) but a hard bargain, however hedged with real-life duplicity and deceit, is in no way equivalent to a 'Jew trick'. If the Dutch have been maligned, it is through their passing role as Britain's one-time national enemy. Some terms have lingered, no doubt, but the genuine animus has abated and the racism, while certainly there in the words, is invisible. It is not, in any sense, a matter of faith.

Dutch cheating is seen in a number of phrases. A **Dutch auction** or **Dutch sale** is a mock auction or sale in which the much-touted 'reductions' have no bearing in commercial fact; the term also describes an 'auction' in which, quite contrary to the usual process, bids start high and are gradually reduced. A **Dutch bargain** can either be the sealing of a deal by drinking to it or, less charmingly, the making of a deal in which the advantages accrue to one side. A **Dutch book**, in horse-racing, is a fraudulent bookmaker's or price-maker's odds line in which the prices quoted come to less than 100%. Similar cheating can be found in the **Dutch reckoning**, a financial account that is generally imposed verbally, without indicating particulars or offering proper paperwork. An alternative meaning is of a bill that if queried will only get higher. In British nautical jargon it implies a bad day's work. A **Flemish account** is an unsatisfactory account, a balance sheet showing a deficit. **Dutch gold**, **Dutch gilding** or **Dutch metal** are all otherwise known as tombac, an alloy of East Indian origin, combining copper and zinc, in various proportions, rolled into very thin sheets and used for decorative purposes; **Dutch foil**, a very malleable alloy of 11 parts of copper and 2 of zinc, beaten into thin leaves, is used as a cheap imitation of gold-leaf. Finally, in poker, a **Dutch straight** is in fact no straight (five cards in sequence, irrespective of suit) at all. It comprises five cards, but the sequence is of alternative, rather than consecutive cards and might only be of use were the game one of 'lowball', i.e. the lowest hand wins. A **Chinese straight** or **Chinese flush** is equally bad: it comprises four cards of any required suit or sequence; the problem is that five is the mimimum needed.

The French, stigmatized for their obsession with all things sexual, come off reasonably lightly in this area of abuse. To **French** is to sham or fake or to 'go through the motions', and a **French seal,** to furriers, is another way of saying 'dyed rabbit'. Like its Dutch equivalent **frantzukaya zoloto**: French gold, as used in Russia, is a variety of gold of the worst grade. (**Moscow gold**, of course, was a staple of Cold War fantasy, fuelling the worldwide revolution that never came.) French itself gives **jouer de la flûte de l'Allemand**: 'to play the German flute' and used (à la Dutch reckoning) meaning to overcharge. The flute in question is the tall, narrow German glass used in a tavern.

Bismarcker or **bismarquer**, literally 'to Bismarck', are two French terms meaning to cheat, especially at cards or billiards. They reflect the activities of the German chancellor Otto von Bismarck (1815–98) whose hard-nosed foreign policy included the deliberate concocting of the spurious 'Ems telegram' which precipitated the Franco-Prussian War of 1870 – an encounter that did nothing for French national pride. **Bismarck** alone, at least in England and its colonies, referred to what is now termed Black Velvet, i.e. champagne and stout. **German goitre** and **German gold** are the equivalents of Dutch gold and both mean tombac. The popular name *Fritz* gives a couple of terms: **befritz** (an English hybrid) and the Yiddish **opfritzeven**, both meaning to dupe or manipulate. The Dutch **moffelaer**, an extension of **moff**, meaning German, means sharper, chiseller or trickster, and this image of German slyness is compounded by the Czech **němec potměšilec**: a 'German sneak', although its colloquial use is to describe the *Parietaria glabr*a, a species of nettle that disguises its sting with a smooth surface. Poland's **oszwabić**: 'to beswab' and as such an attack on the old German province of Swabia, means to cheat.

There is no actual religious proscription of the gypsies, unlike that of the Jews, but like the Jews, alongside whom they were massacred in Germany's death camps, the gypsies have, to put it at its mildest, 'a bad press'. They too are seen, *inter alia*, as innate cheats and the language thrown in their direction has many echoes of that tossed at the Jews. Thus the Serbo-Croat **ciganiti**: 'to gypsy' means to cheat, and the Russian **tsigan**: a gypsy, means also a cheat and a criminal. A **gyp artist** or **gypper** is a swindler, a **gyp moll** the female equivalent; **gyppery** stands for dishonesty, especially in business transactions, and a **gyp racket** is dishonest activity. A **gypsy deal** is a business transaction that never actually happens; a **gypsy's warning** is no warning at all and to **take gypsy's leave** is to depart without settling one's debts. Inevitably the list includes **tsigansky posao**, a Serbo-Croat term that means 'gypsy trick'. Hungary gives **cigánykodni**: 'to act the gypsy', to haggle; to cheat, and **cigányság**: 'gypsydom', that is, trickery and deceit. Back in English **gyp** or **gip**, itself no more than an abbreviation of gypsy, meant swindle or cheat; a **gyp flat** or **gyp joint** was (and remains) any form of dishonest business establishment, typically a 'night club', designed to fleece the unwary visitor. A **gyp artist** is a confidence trickster. South African troops use **gyppo** to mean to dodge or wangle one's way out of a task or duty. In Barbados, the adjective **gypsy** means malicious or interfering, while in the British Virgin Islands, **gypsy-mouth** means a talkative person whose words are essentially nonsense.

Americans of all varieties have been branded as dishonest. The early Dutch settlers branded some of the Native Americans they first encountered as **copperheads**, a reference to the venomous snake (*Agkistrodon contortrix*) which, even more unpleasantly than a rattlesnake, which at least gives some indication of hostility, strikes utterly without warning. The word **snake** by itself was a synonym first for a West Virginian and latterly for an Appalachian. (The Poles have their snakes too: **hadiuiga**, meaning snake, is a synonym for the Ruthenians or Ukrainian peasants living in Eastern Galicia.) The same native Americans were further stigmatized in the phrases **Indian gift** and **Indian giving**, both meaning something presented with the intention of securing its return in the future, a phrase that is echoed in the French **faire l'échange de l'indien**: 'to make an Indian exchange' and translated as to give something practically worthless in lieu of something valuable. The celebrated purchase of Manhattan Island from those same 'Indians' by Europeans, who bartered a handful of trinkets for what is now the heartland of New York City, is presumbly excluded from the definition. (Once more there is a Polish equivalent in **pruski dar**: a 'Prussian gift'.) **Honest Injun**, now an oath of honour for small boys, originally had only a sarcastic usage; given the prejudices of the 19th century, there was no such thing as an 'honest' Indian, unless, of course, he was dead. More recently the **scalper**, one who resells tickets at exorbitant prices, gets at least a portion of its background from the notion that Indians exacted excessive ransoms for those they captured, not to mention the threat implicit in the name.

Last of the American groups are the **yankees** themselves (see *Personal Names* for etymology). In its own way yankee is as synonymous with cheating as Jew, although, once again, there is no religious dimension (other perhaps than that of high Protestant hypocrisy, boasting, with undimmed rectitude of out-doing the very group they cheerfully stigmatized for similar practises). Thus one finds a **yankee trick**: a petty or cheating act of deceit, the verb to **yankee**: to haggle, to cheat, to drive a hard bargain, and **play the yankee** with and **come over yankee**: to cheat.

Other national cheats include the Chinese, in the phrase **Chinese copy**: a perfect copy, capturing the defects as well as the qualities; the Greeks, giving **Greek cry**: cheating at cards, the French **Grec**: a Greek, meaning a card-sharp and a general trickster (and in restaurant use one who does not leave a tip), and a **Trojan Horse**, which recalls the Homeric legend to describe any form of ruse, up to and including downright treachery. The early 19th-century **come the paddy over** means to bamboozle or humbug and adds yet another slur to the many aimed at the Irish – in this case at their verbal skills. England's traditional Euroscepticism surfaces once more in a pair of phrases: **old Spanish customs** are long-standing practices which are unauthorized or otherwise irregular but nonetheless continue. Their *locus classicus* was amongst the print unions of the old Fleet Street, then home to Britain's newspaper industry. A **fine Italian hand**, which on the one hand celebrated the elegance of Italian (Italic) handwriting, over the heavy script of German Gothic, on the other implied a degree of 'foreign' craftiness in the conduct of political, business, or personal affairs. The equation of Italy with Machiavelli dies hard. Germany also distrusts the Italians, and adds **lampartisch Tükki**: Lombardian knavery. **Basquerie**: 'Basquishness', for the French, means a low-down, dirty trick. Finally, belatedly, a couple of Yiddish terms; **calder** or **chalder**, meaning cheat, outsmart or impose upon, possibly reflects on the Biblical story of Laban the Aramean, or Chaldean, who not only tricked Jacob into marrying Leah, but into working for him in addition. And **opton oif terkish**, literally to 'repay in the Turkish manner', means to play a trick or steal a march on.

Tim Vicar

LIARS

THE LINE between cheats and liars is of course thin, but perhaps they can be separated. The former, it might be said, go behind one's back, the latter work directly in your face. Not only that, but lying (other than coincidentally) has no monetary subtext. Anyone, of whatever faith, is equally culpable, and there is no theology involved.

The idea that among one's enemy's national propensities might be something of an economy with the *actualité* is as old as human conflict. Thus the Greeks used the word **kretixein**: 'to Cretanize' to mean 'to tell tall stories', while **Cretan weaponry** was further translated as lies and deception. **Megarian tears** (referring to a city in ancient Greece) were considered as insincere 'crocodile' tears. Sometime later a similar accusation was aimed by Rome against Carthage in the sarcastic phrase **Punica fides**. Coined by the Roman historian Sallust (86-35BC) it meant literally 'Punic' or 'Carthaginian faith' and was translated without any demur as 'treachery'. The term persisted long beyond Rome, thus in 1600 the classicist Philemon Holland wrote in his translation of Livy of 'Crueltie most savage and inhumane, falshood and trecherie more than Punicke.' The Romans were also singularly unimpressed by the Greeks, an emotion borne out most famously in Virgil's line from the *Aeneid*: *Timeo Danaos et dona ferentes*: 'I fear the Greeks, though bearing gifts.' England's **Greek trust**, i.e. no trust at all, and Italy's **fede greca**: 'Greek faith' translated as unfaithfulness or disloyalty, keep up the image.

And from Rome onwards it's been open season when it comes to calling your enemy a liar. America's **Chinese compliment** refers either to the pretended, but actually quite insincere, acceptance of someone's suggestion, or to a display of exaggerated deference that serves only to mask one's unsavoury and probably hostile intentions. **Kína-ezüst**, in Hungary, is China silver, i.e. silver-plate, a phrase that echoes the English **German silver**, in practical terms a White alloy consisting of nickel, zinc and copper, originally obtained from an ore found at Hildburghausen, and figuratively anything fake or sham. In Swedish eyes a **danskt hjärta** or 'Danish heart' is the property of one who is distinctly untrustworthy, while in Germany **Holland und Brabant versprechen**: to speak of Holland and Brabant, meant to make fantastical promises and to deceive in this case, not an enemy, but one's own wishfully-thinking self.

The French, whose manners, as noted elsewhere (see *National Names*), are considered far too smooth for safety, are unsurprisingly seen as less than honest. The Normans seem especially open to such criticisms, with Germany's dismissal of a Norman as 'a crafty fellow', and the rest of France's chiming in with **Normand**: 'a sly fox' and **une réponse de Normand**: a Norman response, or an evasive answer. Not that Normandy is unique. The rest of Europe positively queues up to throw in their tenpenn'orth of abuse. Poland offers **francik**: a smooth fellow or young rogue. Portugal's **francesismo**: a 'Gallicism', is affected or insincere amiability. For the Dutch a **Fransche eed** or 'French oath' is a promise which one does not expect to see fulfilled and **Fransche gedachten**: 'French thoughts' are idle sentiments, emptily pious wishes or superficial ideas. The 16th-century English produced **French faith**, much the same as its Punic variety, i.e. neither faithful nor trustworthy.

Elsewhere, in this catalogue of duplicity, one finds the Bosnian **alarnan**, literally a German, practically a crafty rogue and Germany's own **nordische List**: Nordic cunning, a phrase that targets the Prussians. The Jews, turning on the gypsies, define **tzigeinershe shtik**: 'gypsy stuff' as hollow blandishments. Another group all too popular for their unpopularity, are the Irish. Thus one finds the **Irish compliment**: a backhanded compliment, **Irish evidence**: perjury, and to **weep Irish**: to utter words of apology (or even let fall tears) that are completely unfelt. **Irská samolibost**, Czech for 'Irish assurance', means boasting. Dalmatia joins the game with its condemnation of nearby **lacnianska vira**: 'Italian honour', which is of course no honour whatsoever. And on it goes; Poland hates the Lithuanians, thus **napasci litewska**: 'a Lithuanian attack' or a stab in the back and **skryty jak Litwin**: 'secretive as a Lithuanian', insincere and scheming. Germans have no time for Poles, condemning those hypocrites and liars who are **falsch wie ein Pole**: 'insincere as a Pole' and disdaining the essential emptiness of unctuous, over-elaborate **polnische Hoflichkeit**: 'Polish politeness'. Italy's **spagnolata**: a 'Spanish article' is a bluff or an unashamed lie, Germany's **welsche Treue** is translated not as 'Welsh' but as 'Italian faith' and in either case means treachery; the English sneer at those considered **false as a Scot** (as do the Dutch for whom the term **Schotsch**: Scottish, means variously dishonest, rude, callous, cowardly and stupid). And the world's journalists mock the phrase 'British official' as deliberate, calculated government lying. Finally there is the early 20th-century Afro-American use of **eel**, a creature famed for its slipperiness, to describe the clever, some say unscrupulous, Yankees.

Mefs. VAN SOUR CROUTS.

FOOD

HUNGRY AS ever for an excuse to abuse, the language of difference seizes on yet another obvious example of 'otherness' – food – and renders what might otherwise be appealing quite unpalatable. Gastro-nationalism, as it were, gets the benefit of several antagonistic worlds: not simply racial difference, but those ever-absorbing bones of contention, manners and taste. What you are, as the old 1960s slogan used to proclaim, is what you eat, and never more so than in this arena of squabbling particularism. In some ways, of course, it is also a reverse on the traditional snobberies of consumption, in other words it's not so much a matter of whether or not you know how to eat, say, an artichoke, but whether or not you'd want to be seen eating the wretched foreign thing in the first place.

As ever one can discern certain stereotypes – the chilli-chomping Mexicans, British *rosbifs*, French frogs and German potato-eaters – each locked into the demands of their stomachs, but no-one, whatever their personal culinary preferences, has any monopoly here. When it comes to food, with so many contending 'dishes' on offer, the best resort is to read the menu.

French Canadian Bean Soup

Soup is a relatively rarified category and concentrates on the French, or precisely the French Canadians who are known variously as **Johnny-peasoup**, **Jean Potage**, **Johnny Soup**, **French-peasoup**, **peasoup**, and **peasouper**. Quite where it fits in is a mystery, but such immigrants may (or may not) have fascinated the American gangster Dutch Schultz, whose last words – a long, rambling and ultimately disjointed tirade – requested, 'Helen please take me out. I will settle the incident. Come on, open the soak duckets; the chimney sweeps. Talk to the sword. Shut up, you got a big mouth! Please help me to get up! Henry! Max! Come over here. French Canadian bean soup. I want to pay. Let them leave me alone.' South of the border America offers **metzel**, a German immigrant, from *Metzelsuppe*, a soup made with sausage; in Germany itself **Suppenschwabe**, literally a 'soup-Swabian' describes anyone truly dedicated to soup. Last of these 'dishes' takes one back to America where the **Borsht Belt** describes that part of the Catskill Mountains where the great Jewish resort hotels are to be found. Less massively popular than once they were, they still, no doubt, serve *Borscht* – chilled beetroot soup with sour cream – to their clientele.

Macaroni

Pasta, literally paste, i.e. flour moistened with water or milk and kneaded, comes from the Greek *paste*: barley porridge, via a Latin use that meant 'a small square piece of a medical preparation'. Brought from China, where it appeared in the form of noodles, by the Venetian explorer Marco Polo at the end of the 13th-century pasta, in its many and varied forms, has remained a staple of Italian cooking. Thus pasta, or at least its two best-known varieties – spaghetti and macaroni – has become synonymous with Italians too. **Spaghetti** itself, plus **spaghetti-bender**, **spaghetti-eater**, **spaghetti-head** and the abbreviation **spag** all mean Italian. **Spaghettiland** can mean Italy while an **Italian special**, or less affectionately a **wop special**, means a dish of spaghetti in the world of short-order cooking. With garlic-flavoured sauce it becomes an **Italian hurricane** (the garlic itself is **Italian**

146

perfume). The **spaghetti western**, of course, is any of those movies, pioneered by Sergio Leone at Cinecittà in Rome, and initially showcasing the young, monosyllabic Clint Eastwood, which depend on maximum violence, minimum chat and the moodiest of scores.

Macaroni, the fatter version of spaghetti, with a hole running its length, is equally popular, and in language terms has a far longer pedigree. A symbol of things Italianate since the 18th century, it crossed from the Italian kitchen into the English dictionary with the institution of the *Macaroni Club*, 'which is composed of all the travelled young men who wear long curls and spying-glasses' (*Letters of Earl Hertford*, ed. Horace Walpole, 1764); the travelling, suggests the *OED*, probably gave the members a taste for foreign foods, hence the name. They dressed extravagantly – monstrous, blue-powdered wigs, red high-heeled shoes – and gambled for high stakes. Their club, Almacks, became today's Brooks. The essayist Joseph Addison attempted to make a link with another Italian word, *maccherone* in its senses of 'blockhead, fool, mountebank' but it does not exist; Addison was perhaps writing facetiously. The macaroni, however he may have delighted in his own image, was never popular. By 1770 the *Oxford Magazine* noted that 'There is indeed a kind of animal, neither male nor female, a thing of the neuter gender, lately started up amongst us. It is called a Macaroni. It talks without meaning, it smiles without pleasantry, it eats without appetite, it rides without exercise, it wenches without passion'; Horace Walpole, writing in 1774, when the craze had passed, noted that 'They have lost all their money...and ruin nobody but their tailors.' By the end of the 19th century it meant no more than 'an over-dressed, or gaudily-dressed person', an effeminate fop. More recently the term has dropped all references to fashion and like spaghetti means simply 'an Italian'. In Australian slang, since the 1920s, it has also meant nonsense or meaningless talk.

Pasta is eaten across the world, and thus the term is not exclusively English. Synonyms are found in Russia – **makarnscik** and **makarnnik**, literally 'macaroni-man' – and in Greece, **makaronas**. Cognate are the Yiddish terms **loksh** and **lukichen**, both of which mean noodles and thus, once more, an Italian. The German **spanische Nudeln** or Spanish noodles, however, means not a food but a severe and painful flogging. (**Spanischer Ritt**: a Spanish ride, means the same, presumably from the fact that floggings took place across a 'horse'.) A **meatball**, which traditionally adorns the dish in its American incarnation, is also an Italian.

Guppy-Gobblers

As with the Jews and pork, so the Catholics and meat, an item which is, for the truly pious, off-limits on Friday. Instead fish is mandatory. Such fish-days, or fasting days once included Wednesdays too, and were – religion aside – a way of dealing with the realities of Medieval and Tudor economics. Thus **fish-eater**, **guppy-gobbler**, **mackerel-snapper** and **mackerel-snatcher** all mean Roman Catholic.

That said, aside from the **conch** (from the Greek *koncha*: a cockle or mussel) which has served variously as a nickname for the natives of the Bahamas, for West Indians in America and for a 'poor White' native, often a fishman, living in the Florida Keys or North Carolina, the remaining fish terms, culled mainly from central Europe and Russia, concentrate on the herring. In Canada a **herring-choker** is Newfoundlander or a native of any of the Maritime Provinces; the same term is used in America for a Swede. Still in the US, a **herring-snapper** is both a Swede and occasionally a Catholic, while a **herring-punisher** is a Jew and a **herring-destroyer** or **herring-choker** a Norwegian. In the West Indies a **herring-Jew** is a Jewish or Syrian immigrant, referring to those made their fortunes peddling salt-fish. Jews themselves call a herring a **Litvack**, a Lithuanian, a reference to the Lithuanian and Ukrainian Jews who were so fond of the fish. Other major herring eaters include the Poles, whose unsatisfied appetites give the derogatory German phrase **polsche Hering**: 'a Polish herring', i.e. diluted vinegar and onions plus an imaginary herring, and the Dutch. A **Dutch red** is a smoked Dutch herring and a **pickle-herring** a Dutchman; Russia's terms **Hollandskiya** and **selyedki Hollandskiya**: 'Dutch herrings', refer to any food bought from street-pedlars but which is scarcely edible. The **herring pond**, of course, is the Atlantic (although *to cross the pond at the King's expense* referred to transportation to Australia). Nicknames for the herring, masking its

common-ness with a variety of terms that reflect a rather more luxurious table, are **Alaska turkey, Billingsgate pheasant, Californian
pheasant, Crail capon, Digby chicken, Dunbar wether, Glasgow
magistrate, Gourock ham, Halifax mutton, Taunton turkey** and
Yarmouth capon, all referring to centres of the herring industry.

German Ducks and Indian Hens

Like fish, which in mainstream slang can refer both to a woman or her
vagina (and indeed carries a wide variety of alternative definitions),
meat also comes with sexual overtones. **Dark-meat, black-meat**, a
piece of dark meat, a **hot piece (of dark meat)** and a **rare piece
of dark meat** can all signify a Black woman, viewed invariably as a sex
object. **White** or **light meat** can mean just the same of a White woman.
But in terms of meat as food rather than, as the US slang has it *PEEP*
('perfectly elegant eating pussy'), the language throws up a whole
platter of possibilities.

To continue in the world of Black America, **nigger steak** is liver
(substituting cheap offal for the more expensive 'White' cut), while
nigger and halitosis is steak and onions. **Alligator-bait** or **'gator-
bait** refers to any black human being, especially a child; an **Aussie
steak** (at least to the Australian army) is a piece of mutton, predictable,
given the vast number of sheep 'Down Under'. A **Dutch steak**, taking
Dutch for Deutsch, is a hamburger, as is a **German dog** (referring to
the great American dish, the hot dog), and a **French pie**, presumably
as a result of some heavy-handed culinary humour, is stew. The West
Indian **nyam-dog**, however, is a Chinese persdon, from *nyam*: food
and a reference to their appetite for canines. **Goulash** means a Hungarian in America as does the same dish, translated as **madarik**, in
Czech. A **frog-eater** (or **Froschesser** in German), unsurprisingly, is
a Frenchman. In the world of poultry, a **German duck** (in late
18th/early 19th century England) was half a sheep's head boiled with
onions; the term (which in less appetizing contexts referred to a
bed-bug) acknowledged the popularity of the dish amongst the German sugar-refiners and confectioners of London's East End.

Russia's **kolbassnik**: 'sausage-glutton' is a German, while **Fritz**, in

Austria, is a German sausage, bland but large. A **choucroutemane**, literally a 'saurkraut maniac', meant a German in France; saurkraut, a form of pickled cabbage, is popularly eaten as *choucroute garnie*: 'garnished' with boiled sausages. Saurkraut, *garnie* or not, gives **kraut**, still popular as a nickname for a German, and **krauthead**. **Sausage** also meant a German in late-19th century England and **baloney** or **boloney**, meaning nonsense or rubbish and which is generally accepted as referring to a Bologna sausage (although the *OED* claims the connection is 'conjectural'), appeared in the 1920s. Against the Oxford verdict, lexicographer Ramon Adams refers in his dictionary of the American West, *Western Words* (1968) to 'bologna bulls: animals of inferior quality whose meat is used to make Bologna sausage'. A **Polak**, in German, can mean variously a sausage, a carved fowl, a kind of potato and the dregs at the bottom of a glass.

Chilli, chile or chili con carne (a stew of Mexican origin containing minced beef flavoured with chillies) gives several terms for Mexicans, who are thus disdained as **chilis, chili chokers, chili eaters, chilipickers, chili-beans, chilli-bellies** and **chilli-chompers**. A **chili chaser** is a US border patrolman, employed to prevent Mexicans entering the country illegally. Chilli itself does not, popular belief to the contrary, refer to the nation, Chile, but is a Mexican word, in place long before the Europeans arrived. Other classic Mexican dishes give other terms. The *taco* (a Mexican snack comprising a fried, unleavened cornmeal pancake or tortilla filled with seasoned mincemeat, chicken, cheese, beans) gives **taco-eater, taco-head** and **taco-bender**. (A **taco wagon** is an automobile with the rear end lowered.) The *enchilada* (literally 'seasoned with chilli', and in practice a tortilla served with a chilli-flavoured sauce) gives **enchilada-eater**; peppers in general lead to **pepper, pepper-gut** and **(hot) pepper-belly**; a **hot-tamale** (in culinary terms made of crushed Indian corn, flavoured with pieces of meat or chicken, red pepper, etc., wrapped in corn-husks and baked) is an attractive girl. Chilli is also used figuratively to mean second-rate (since Mexican) and thus gives a **chili chump**, a pimp who has only one girl working for him or an inexperienced pimp. Such a pimp may well be Black, but the reference is to the supposed incompetence of small-time Mexican pimps.

For a bird of such weighty stolidity, sitting stuffed and uncomplaining on so many Christmas and Thanksgiving tables, the **turkey** has a surprisingly confusing background. In the first place it suffers from a fundamental misnomer: it doesn't come from Turkey. Its first appearance seems to have been as the *Guinea-cock* or *Guinea-fowl*, known to Greeks and Romans alike as *meleagris*. The reference to Guinea reflects the fact that the Portuguese began importing the bird from Guinea, in West Africa. The synonym *turkey-cock* appeared in the 16th century, and in turn underpinned the fact that Guinea, at that time, was under Turkish rule. The 16th century also saw, in 1518, the conquest of Mexico by Spain; among the booty the Spaniards enjoyed was the bird that would become known as the American turkey, and which had already been domesticated for some time. When C. F. Linn (1707-78), better known by his Latinized name Linnaeus, set about classifiying flora and fauna, he took the African name, *Meleagris*, and gave it to the Mexican bird. Its African cousin, a somewhat smaller, slenderer creature, remained the Guinea-fowl.

None of which has much bearing on the naming of the turkey around the world, but might cast a little light on what otherwise appears a rather confused system. The English turkey itself sets the pattern, leading generations into the erroneous belief that the bird began life in the eastern Mediterranean. France's cant term **Jesuite** refers to the original importers of the bird: Jesuit missionaries. The majority of other names attach it to 'India', or perhaps (with a little more accuracy) 'the (West) Indies', which might just about stretch to Mexico. Thus the French **coq-d'Inde** or **dindon**, the German **Indischer Hahn**, the Italian **gallo d'India** and the Greek **indianos**, which can also mean 'Red' Indian (plus the abbreviations **dianos** and **diana**). The same 'Indian' image persists in Arabic and in Turkish itself, where the bird is **dajaj Hindi**. Both Dutch and Germans underline the theory with **Kalkoen** and **Calecutischer Hahn** (the Calcutta hen). Indeed, the 18th-century Italian traveller Padre Paolino believed that Calcutta, or Calicut as it then was, meant 'Castle of the Fowls'. Though, as *Hobson-Jobson* observes, 'being herein, as he often is, positive and wrong.' In the majority of Indian languages the bird is **peru**, a term that comes directly from the Portuguese name: **galo de Peru** (with the assumption, based on its existence in Mexico, that the turkey comes not from Africa but South America). *Hobson-Jobson* further suggests that the term may have arrived, as did chilli, from South America. However Hindi also offers **sutra murgh**, 'ostrich' or 'camel-cock' (reflecting the Latin name *struthio camelus*), **fil-murgh** ('elephant-cock', from Persian) and the Tamil **van-kori** ('great fowl'). Native Americans, in the 18th century, referred to turkey (and venison) as a **White man's dish**.

The slang use of turkey, meaning a disaster or flop, emerged in American showbiz jargon in the 1920s, when it was cited in *Variety* magazine as 'a third rate production'. It would seem to be linked to the slightly later turkey: a stupid, slow, inept, or otherwise worthless person, and in both cases the image is of a large, waddling creature, of no real worth. **Turk**, meaning an Irish immigrant (**Greek** was synonymous) was sometimes expanded to **turkey**. The synonymous **saltwater-turkey** underpinned the journey from Ireland, across the 'saltwater'. The Irish connection reappears in **Irish turkey**, meaning corned beef and cabbage, a classic 'Irish' dish and one in which (in a similar 'role-reversal' to French pie) the image of poverty is deliberately contrasted with the presumed 'luxury' of eating turkey. It seems to have been coined in the US comic strip, 'Jiggs and Maggie'. The dish is also known, facetiously as **la bullie Hibernian**, fake restaurant French for a distinctly plebeian dish that is also known as an **Irishman** or simply a **boiled dinner**. The Irish do no better out of **Irish horse**, which refers to tough, undercooked salt beef (especially as served to sailors) although it can also, in the gay lexicon, mean an impotent penis. Only the **Irish wager**, a rump of beef and a dozen bottles of claret, improves their image. Normal service is resumed with **chaw** or **chawbacon** both of which mean variously a yokel, a peasant and an Irish immigrant. Finally **banjo**, an Australian coinage, refers both to the shovel wielded by so many of these immigrants (otherwise known as the **Irish banjo** and the **idiot stick**), and to a shoulder of mutton

'Let the goyim sink their teeth into whatever lowly creature crawls and grunts across the face of the dirty earth, we will not contaminate our humanity thus...Let them eat eels and frogs and pigs and crabs and lobsters; let them eat vulture, let them eat ape-meat and skunk if they like – a diet of abominable creatures well befits a breed of mankind so hopelessly shallow and empty-headed as to drink, to divorce and to fight with their fists... Thus saith the kosher laws, and whom am I to argue that they're wrong.' Thus also saith the fictional Alexander Portnoy (Philip Roth, *Portnoy's Complaint*, 1969), and along with circumcision and a big nose, nothing defines the Jew like his abstention from pork. It has also engendered a number of put-downs. Like the 'jokes' that term Blacks 'snowballs', the charm is apparently in the opposition. The pig is **the Hebrew's enemy** and pork and its other by-products **Jew food**, while the Jew himself is a **porker**, **porky** or **pork-chopper**. In the language of America's short-order cooks, a **sheeny's funeral** is roast pork. It also gives wide-ranging opportunities to offer such sayings as 'If the Jew knew that the sow had swallowed half a kopek he would have made a meal of it', and 'Give the Jew a ruble, and he will devour the whole young sow', a pair of Russian examples that conveniently conflate two stereotypes for the price of one. The pig and its processing also give **smokey** and **smoked ham**, for a Native American; **pork-chop**, for an African American and **Pork and Beans**, a term that means Portuguese, both from the approximate assonance and from the fact that during World War I this appeared to be their troops' staple ration.

Other than Scotland, otherwise known as **haggisland**, from the haggis (sheep or calf offal minced with suet and oatmeal, seasoned, and boiled like a large sausage in the maw of the animal) which is seen as a typically Scottish dish (although prior to 1800 it was equally popular south of the border), Britain, or rather England, BSE notwithstanding, is the country of beef. France's **rosbif** (1850s onwards) sums up the type, and the Dutch add **Engelsch gaar**: the 'English way' when they mean undercooked or half-raw. The English have also been termed **beefeaters** (from as early as 1620), mixing the animal with the uniformed custodians of the Tower of London: the Yeomen of the Guard. These developed from the Beefeaters of the Guard, a name that referred, not especially kindly, to an earlier use of *beefeater* (or *loafeater*): a well-fed menial who earned his board and keep. Beefeater was even extended to describe a briefly fashionable woman's hat, modelled on those worn by the Yeomen.

Finally the East, which gives **chow**, meaning both food and a Chinese person and which comes from the Cantonese *cha'ao*: to fry. Thus **Chowmeinland** is China, referring to *chow mein*, the artificial dish concocted by America's mid-19th-century Chinese immigrants as a sop to those unsophisticated Western palates who nonetheless wanted some ersatz Chinese food. **Jap hash** is also Chinese food, and refers to chow mein or chop suey. An **egg roll**, still in the Eastern context, while ostensibly another form of Chinese food, refers to one of America's most recent groups of Far Eastern immigrants, the Koreans.

'The Home of the Bean and the Cod'

Although the nation most usually linked with beans is Mexico, as will be seen below, both Jews and African-Americans have been credited with what might be called 'fabophilia'. Thus a **black bean** can be a Black person, while a **nigger bean**, like so many other terms thus categorized, is a dark bean. Meanwhile Spain has **judia**, both a string bean and a Jewess; **judia de careta**, a small spotted French bean, **judion**, a large variety of kidney bean; and **judihuelo**, a small French bean or a Jewish child. The Czechs, where **žid** means variously a Jew, a spotted bean and a bitter-tasting mushroom, make the same equation.

But beans primarily means Mexican and **bean-eater** and **beaner** have branded Mexican immigrants for a century. The same terms have been grafted onto the Cubans who have been appearing, in Florida rather than California or Texas, since the 1960s. Combinations with beaner give **beaner shoes**: *huaraches*, the typical Mexican sandals and **beaner wagon**: an old, dilapidated car seen as the basic form of immigrant transport. **Frijole-guzzler**, based on another Mexican dish, also means Mexican. The jargon of short-order cooking gives **Mexican strawberries**, reddish-coloured beans and the **Mexican navy**, as in the order 'a bowl of fire and Mexican navy': a plate of chilli and beans. Mexico notwithstanding, North America has its own bean-orientated enclave: Boston, Massachusetts. 'Good old Boston,' as John Bossidy's 19th-century doggerel put it, 'the home of the bean and the cod.' Bostonians were termed **bean-eaters** in 1800 while Boston itself is still known as **Bean Town** to American truckers. **Beantown** returns to a Mexican inference in a parallel meaning: the poorest, immigrant section of a town or city.

Cabbage-head, otherwise denoting a fool, referred to both the Dutch and the Germans in late-19th-century America and like Bean Town, **Cabbage Town** meant the poor area; it could also mean that section inhabited mainly by German immigrants. A **cabbage-eater** refers both to a German and a Russian.

Germans like cabbage, at least in racial clichés, but not as much, apparently, as they adore potatoes. The equation of the German with a 'potato-eater' can be found in Polish, **kartoflarz** and **kartoflannik**: a potato-glutton; Italy, **tedeschi patatucchi**: German potato-swallowers; Russia, where **kartoshkl** means the same thing; Czechoslovakia, **nemceata**: literally 'German stuff' and actually potatoes, and Portugal where the term is **al(1) emao batata**: potato-swallower. In Holland a popular variety of potato is the **Pruisen** or 'Prussian'.

Bulba, a potato, means a White Russian to Muscovites, while **niggertoe** means a potato in America, and **french fries** refer to the Québecois in Canada. But the only real rivals to Germany in the potato stakes are the Irish. And while the German delight in the vegetable seems to be linked simply to their gargantuan appetite for the tubers, Ireland's link, as in so many other areas, is with peasant stupidity and poverty as much as with the actual food. Thus the sneering usages **Irish lemons, grapes** and **apples** all refer to the potato. So too does the **Irish apricot**, occasioning Francis Grose's remark in 1785 that 'It is a common joke against the Irish vessels to say that they are loaded with fruit and timber, that is potatoes and broomsticks.' The **Irish cherry**, another fraudulent 'fruit' is in fact a carrot. Similar terms include **bog-oranges** and **Munster plums** (Munster being an Irish county). **Navigators** (and the rhyming slang *navigator scot*: potatoes all hot) refer to the job undertaken by many mid-19th-century Irish immigrants to Britain, that of a 'navigator' (and thus the slang *navvy*): a labourer on Victorian Britain's railways and canals. Contemporary life was further indicated in **home-rulers**, baked potatoes cooked and sold in the street, which emerged during the late-19th century, a period marked by Sinn Fein's agitation for Irish Home Rule. **Spud**, a popular nickname for a potato, was also one for an Irishman (the **spuddy**, a seller of bad potatoes in 19th century London, possibly combined both) as was **Murphy,** which started with the person and moved on to the vegetable. Finally, predictably, the Irish have been known as **potato-eaters** and **potato-heads**. A **potato-fingered Irishman** is clumsy and maladroit.

Spinach, at least in America, refers to a Spaniard while in Czechoslovakia **Spanelka,** at least when capitalized means a Spanish woman; without the capital it means a red onion. The leek is the Welsh national emblem, thus to **wear the leek** means to be Welsh while in slang a **leek** has meant a Welshman since 1695. An **Indian turnip,** also known as a *Jack-in-the-pulpit,* is a tuber which, when eaten raw is burningly pungent; just as Indians supposedly hide their true nature from the White man so the tuber hides its sharpness from its eater. A Jerusalem or 'Jewish' artichoke (also known as a Jerusalem potato) is a **jewboy,** although the slur is totally misdirected on both counts. The 'Jerusalem' is a perversion of *Girasole Articiocco* or Sunflower Artichoke. First cultivated in the Farnese garden in Rome, it began its spread around Europe in the early 17th century.

Czechs in general have been termed **mushroom-pickers** (and the occupation is well-known throughout Central Europe). The **Jew's ear** is a form of edible fungus, growing on wood and the **Scotchbonnet** is better known as the 'fairy-ring' mushroom. In Sweden a **Karl-Johanes-svamp,** or Charles XIV mushroom, is a cèpe. Charles XIV, who had been Napoleon's General Bernadotte, was a great lover of cèpes, and introduced them into Sweden. A **nigger killer** is a yam (at least *c.*1895), whether from the resemblance of some varieties of yam to a club or to its sheer stodginess choking an eater to death; while an **eggplant** (or aubergine) is another name for African-American, a reference to the vegetable's black-purple, shiny skin. A synonym **molonjohn,** used by Italians of Blacks, presumably comes from the Italian *melanzana*: an eggplant. An eggplant can also be a **Jew's apple**. Last of these vegetable terms are the Australian **vegetable John,** a Chinese greengrocer, of whom there were many in the 1920s, and the French **macédoine,** a term that means a mixture of chopped-up fruits or vegetables, but which has its roots in Macedonia, the empire of Alexander the Great, and as such home to a huge variety of peoples. A **Dutch grocery** is an ill-kept, run-down, third-rate grocery although given the usual Dutch reputation for financial acumen and a devotion to cleanliness, this seems paardoxical (it is, perhaps, another example of Dutch actually meaning *Deutsch*: German).

Prisoner of Mother England

Three fruits dominate as far as racial references are concerned: the pomegranate, the lime and the banana. **Pommy**, or in its most popular combination **pommy bastard**, is widely known to mean a British immigrant (or indeed visitor) to Australia. It is equally widely accepted that pommy is an abbreviation of pomegranate (itself from the Old French *pomme grenate*: the seed-filled apple). From there on the problems begin. In short, no-one seems properly to know why the term was adopted. The most popular assumption is that pomegranate 'rhymes' with immigrant, as does another once-popular nickname, *jimmygrant*, and certainly there are many citations of young people, now old, recalling shouting 'Pommygrant' after still pallid Britons, newly arrived from what, of course, was known as **Pommyland**. Certainly W.S. Ramson, editor of the *Australian National Dictionary* (1988), backs up this interpretation. One alternative suggestion is that it began life as *pome*, an acronym for Prisoner Of Mother England, but given that no citations for pommy predate 1912 (pommy bastard comes in 1915 and **whingeing pommy** or **whingeing pom**, an allusion to what other Australians see as the tedious characteristic of the newly-arrived British, in 1962, and thus the old hippie joke; 'Grow your own dope – plant a pom'), and that these prisoners stopped arriving some sixty years earlier, this seems unlikely.

Lime juice, long recognized as a prophylactic against scurvy or vitamin C deficiency, was doled out to sailors who might otherwise have been struck down on the long voyages of the age of sail. Among them were those whose ships went from Britain to such colonies as South Africa, Australia and New Zealand, and this intake of limes gave rise to the nickname **limey**, first for the sailors and gradually for all Britons. It began in the 1880s as **lime-juicer** and the abbreviation followed around 1910. It was at this time that the term was adopted by America, a much older colony. Synonyms included **lime-juice, lemon-eater** and **lemon-sucker** and for a while **Limeyland**, in Australia, referred to the 'mother country'.

As for bananas, this fruit touches equally on the inhabitants of Queensland, Australia and Natal, South Africa. Thus **bananamen, banana-benders** and **bananaskins** are all Queenslanders. **Bananaland** is Queensland (and a **Bananalander** a native of the state), and **Banana City** is Brisbane, the state capital. At the same time it can mean Durban, capital of Natal, while **banana-boy** refers to a resident or native of Natal.

Still in Africa, if figuratively, an **African grape** is that most clichéd of foods, the watermelon, supposedly *the* African American favourite, as is **nigger special**. **Canteloupe**, another kind of melon, is used similarly by the Italian community to mean a Black person. A **raisin** can also be a Black person, perhaps a reference to the 1959 play *A Raisin in the Sun* by Loraine Hansberry (1930-65), while in German a nag or pedant is a **Korinthenkacker**, literally a 'currant-crapper', a term that embodies the traditional home of the currant, Korinth in Greece. A **židovka**, which in Czechoslovakia means a Jewess, can also mean a kind of plum (as well as a brand of whiskey, a lady-bird and a tam o'shanter), while a **Jew plum** is properly known as an otaheite apple, which, while its flesh is edible, has rind that tastes like turpentine. **Pineapple**, with little originality, refers in America to to a Pacific Islander, while in New Zealand these same islanders are **coconuts**.

Italian Heros

Bread means an Afro-American while one of the many definitions for **negro-** or **nigger-head** (both sailors' terms) is a loaf of brown bread. The Dutch **Franschje**: 'a little Frenchman' means variously a type of flat bread without a crust, and a kind of cheese; a **pretzel**, a crisp biscuit shaped like a knot (the word comes from the medieval Latin *bracellus*: a bracelet), is a German. The French pun **japon**, meaning bread, plays on the French *du pain*: some bread. A **bagel** or **bagel-bender** refers to the doughnut-shaped bread popular among Jews and logically means a Jew, as does **motza**, the unleavened Passover biscuits, which can also mean money. Lox, or smoked salmon, the 'automatic' accompaniment

to bagels (and cream cheese) gives **lox jock**, another synonym for Jew.
Bagel has another meaning in South Africa where it denotes a spoilt,
wealthy, upper-class young man; his female equivalent is a **kugel**, the
Yiddish for cake. Although such young people were originally (and
mainly still are) Jewish, there are equivalents – at least among the girls
– in the Black community (**ebony-kugels**) and among the Afrikaaners
(**boere-kugels**). The jargon they speak is **kugelese**. (Slightly dis-
tanced from food, but definitely related to the kugel is the **JAP** or Jewish
American Princess, sisters, as it were, under the sun.) An **Italian hero**
is a large sandwich (whether the distinctly phallic look of such snacks,
usually in a long roll, reflects on Italian masculinity is debatable), while
in Papua New Guinea **bretskin** or 'bread skin' is used by country
people to describe someone from the capital, Port Moresby, who eats
more bread than is felt to be necessary and is thus seen as self-indulgent,
fat and lazy by his country cousins.

Chocolate Drops from the South

Despite the wide variety of sweets there is, at least in the racial lexicon,
only one major brand: the dark one. Thus America's **licorice** and
licorice-stick and France's **jus de rélisse**: licorice juice, all of which
refer to a Black person. Thus too America's **brown sugar**, as memorialized in the Rolling Stones' song title, and **toffee** or **taffy**. Like
brown sugar, most 'sweet' terms tend to the sexual, thus **chocolate,
chokker, choco, chocolate drop, hot chocolate, sweet-chocolate,
chocolate-bar, chocolate-chip**, all of which refer to Black girls, who
are doubtless seen as 'good enough to eat'. Between the World Wars the
French used **petite chocolatière**: 'little chocolate bon-bon' to describe a Black woman. Specific brand-names – **Hershey-Bar** and
Tootsie-Roll (both best-selling American chocolate-based sweets) –
underpin the image.

The fact that chocolate, like rum, sugar, tobacco, coffee and cocoa,
was at one time the product of Black slave labour, only points up the
ironies. Advertizing furthered the image: a brand named 'Assorted
Chocolates' was adorned by a picture of a couple of 'cute' Black girls,
while in Germany a variety of chocolate cake termed itself 'the edible

negro'. In an American book of comic stories entitled *Chocolate Drops from the South* (1932) its author, Edward V. White, asserted that America's 'greatest source of laughter and good humor' was her Blacks. For 'he looks funny, he acts funny, he is funny. Moreover, he is serious about it all'. White, presumably, would have lauded the term **nigger spit**, another way of describing lumps in cane sugar. Other sweets, such as Canada's **eskimo** or South Africa's **eskimo pie** – both meaning what in Britain is termed a 'choc-ice' – refer to the Inuit, for whom the name Eskimo, it should be recalled, means those who eat their meat raw – hardly an especially 'sweet' concept. One anomaly in this toothsome list is the **Mexican jelly bean**. No sweet this, but a vintage Chevrolet lowered in the rear and fitted with a **Mexican window shade** (a Venetian blind) in the rear window. Not strictly a sweet, the peanut is best noted here. **Peanut** itself meant a Black person; the obvious link is to the growing of peanuts in the south, and to the Black agronomist George Washington Carver, whose introduction of peanuts and sweet potatoes essentially saved the southern economy. However, peanut can also mean a person of small value, and relates to such cognate terms for Black as **dink** and **jit**. Dink itself, which was also used by US troops to describe the Vietnamese, is an abbreviation of the slang *rinky-dink*: worthless, second-rate. Another 'peanut' image is that of **goober-grabber**, used as a catch-all term for the south. The word *goober*, widely used for peanut, probably comes from the Congolese *nguba*: a type of peanut. As for jit, it is an abbrevation of the slang term *jitney*, meaning five cents; the Black person is equated with the low-value coin.

A French Pancake is not a Crêpe

Like sweets, what one might term 'national' desserts also seem to have a bias towards the Black. Thus the American **niggers in a snowstorm**: stewed prunes and rice, and the cowboys' favourite **nigger-in-a-blanket**: a dish made of raisins in dough. **Prunes** by themselves refer to a Black person or to a Black head, and **nigger-toes** are brazil-nuts. The French phrase **Anglais á prunes** refers less to a dish than to a characteristic: meanness. (*Prunes* translates strictly as 'plums'.) To the amusement of the French, the English – careful, penny-pinching travellers – note the highly priced fruit in restaurants and ask instead for a handful of (cheap) plums as their dessert. This image of parsimony persists elsewhere: **faire une anglaise**: to do it English style, refers to the practice of tossing coins to decide on who is to pay for a round of drinks, or to divide the bill (like impecunious students) in exactly equal portions. **Anglaise** refers to that share (and can also describe the various investments each partner makes in a business). French cabbies talk of **Anglais de carton**: a mean (English) tipper.

But there is more to dessert than prunes or plums. The Scots call their English neighbours **pock-pudding** or **poke-pudding**, which is a synonym for bag-pudding (from the Scots *poke*: a small bag or sack and thus any pudding boiled, like a Christmas pudding, in a bag), while in Canada French Canadians are mocked as **johnny-cakes**, a term that can be found in a doggerel verse, popular amongst Montreal children around 1900: 'French peasoup and johnnycake | Make your father a bellyache.' The cake, which exists in Canada, America, the West Indies and Australia and which is made of maize or wheat-meal and either toasted at a fire or baked in a pan, may be of Black origin; the 'Johnny' may also be a red herring: some authorities claim that its original form was 'journey-cake' and, given its basic ingredients and the simplicity of its cooking, this may well be true. A **French pancake** is not, alas, a crêpe, but is in fact a rectangular academic hat or a beret.

Buttermilk Bottom

Dairy products in language as well as the marketplace typify the Dutch. Thus Britain's **butter-mouth** (1547), **butter-box** (1600) and butter-bag (1645) all meant a Dutchman, on account of the vast quantities of dairy products consumed and produced in Holland. A **Dutch cheese** is a bald person, as is the South African **cheesehead** or, in Afrikaans, **kaaskop**. A **limburger**, the very smelly yet paradoxically bland cheese is a German (although the cheese is a Belgian speciality). Like the Polish herring, which is in fact no herring at all, Germany's **polsche Botter** or 'Polish butter' lacks butter; it is, instead, salt on bread. Still with butter, there are a number of African American terms, notably **butter baby** or **melted butter**, both of which mean a mulatto 'yellow' girl;

butterhead: a Black who, for whatever reason, is considered an embarrassment to his race, and **Buttermilk Bottom**, a name coined for the Black section of Atlanta, Georgia, but which spread to many towns and cities in the Southern states and in all cases means the Black part of town. Last in the butter stakes comes **Jew butter**, which is not actual butter, but goose grease, the equivalent of dripping and a popular spread on bread. The Jews' own term for such a spread is *schmaltz*, literally 'fat', and which, while devoid of racial overtones, can be found as a pejorative itself, implying excessive and mawkish sentimentality, especially in the world of show business.

Gris Pik

With a few exceptions, words based on grease refer exclusively to the unfortunate Mexicans. A **polnische Nudel**: 'a Polish ball of fat' is a slovenly woman, while in Papua New Guinea the Highlanders, who grease their bodies with pig fat, are known in Tok Pisin as **gris pik**: pig grease. However, given the Highlanders' association with entrepreneurship, *gris* can also mean a bribe (as in the English slang verb *to grease*). Paradoxically, the term pig is not an insult as such, there are no assumptions of 'uncleanness', yet actually calling someone 'a pig' remains an insult.

British service slang adds **gippo**, **gippy** and **gypoo** which can mean variously stew, gravy, bacon fat, butter or any form of greasy sauce. Quite why the gypsies should be, as it were, smeared with the term is unexplained, but it may come from the simultaneous World War I use of *Gyppo* to mean an Egyptian, a race who being Middle Eastern, might, in the way of such slurs, be presumed to be greasy. From there on the focus is strictly on Mexico. Aside from **frito**, meaning fried and itself emphasizing the Mexican love of fried food, and **oiler**, which refers to the cooking rather than the commercial liquid, Mexicans have been **greasers** – supposedly from their 'greasy' appearance – since the 1840s. Similar terms include **greaseball**, which has also been used for a Greek, just as **greaser** can occasionally denote an Italian, **grease-gut** and **grease-boy**.

Wheatfolks and Maize Puddings

Rice, being the staple it is, means Chinese or Oriental, especially as **ricer**, **rice-belly**, **rice-eater** and **riceman**. A **rice queen**, in gay use, favours Easterners as lovers, while the recent **rice rocket** refers in America to a Japanese-made off-road or four-wheel drive vehicle. Less common is **rice Christian**, which from the 1890s to the 1930s described those inhabitants of rice-growing countries who volunteered for conversion less through religious fervour and more through a desire to obtain food from gullible missionaries

Buckwheat, a species of *Polygonum* (*P. Fagopyrum*), a native of Central Asia, whence it was introduced into Europe by the Turks in about the 13th century, is used in Europe as food for horses, cattle, and poultry; in North America, however, its meal is made into buckwheat cakes, regarded as a dainty for the breakfast-table. In slang it also means a Black person, either another play on the Black/White jokes that produce 'lilyWhite' and 'snowball', but possibly an acknowledgement of 'Buckwheat' Thomas, the Black actor in the 'Our Gang' Saturday morning movie series of the 1930s. Nor is buckwheat restricted to the US; **greckosj**, a Ukrainian term based on *grecka*: 'buckwheat' is used by Russians to mock their Ukrainian neighbours who eat *kasha*, a gruel or thick porridge made from boiled buckwheat. **Wheatfolks**, an occasional name for White Americans, appears to link in to buckwheat, as well as punning on the common description 'White folks'.

Sago, a form of starch prepared from the pith of various palm trees, and much used as a food in the Pacific, is found in Australia as a slur on the natives of the Pacfic Islands, while back in Europe **Mamalznik**, from *mamaliga:* 'corn meal mush' – and which is the Rumanian national dish – means a Rumanian to Russians. Similarly other Jews call their Rumanian cousins **mameligge**: 'maize pudding'. Maize, which comes originally from the Cuban Spanish *maiz*, has gained a number of names including the Dutch and German **Turkish corn**; Italy's **gran Turco** : the Grand Turk and the Russian **koukouru**, which last term is fact a direct theft of the Turkish word for corn. Maize always seems, as it were, to come from 'next door': In the Congo it is **mas ma Mputa**

(literally 'the ear from Portugal') while in America it can be **Indian corn**, in Tuscany **Sicilian corn** and in the Pyrenees **Spanish corn**.

The Black Teapot

Unlike the majority of these terms, which identify the properties of a given food or drink with the perceived deficiencies of a given nation, the bulk of terms that deal with tea and coffee seem more preoccupied with the drinks themselves. Thus, other than **pepsi**, which in Canada pokes fun at the French Canadians' alleged propensity for the fizzy drink (possibly even greater now that its cans resemble the blue of France's rugby and football teams), **cocoa**, meaning a Black person and **black teapot**, which referred to the Black servants who were once *the* fashion accessory in any smart European household, the rest seem to deal with intrinsic quality – or lack of it.

English winter and **cold English** are both iced tea, although the American phrases, albeit subsconsciously, underpin the British reputation for sang-froid; an **English martini** is tea spiked with gin. What sounds like the very repellent **Scotch coffee** is no more than hot water flavoured with burnt biscuit, while **Negro coffee** is coffee senna. **Indian coffee**, a 'Wild West' coinage, is coffee made from old grounds; the derisive assumption was that such coffee was all an Indian deserved. **Cowboy coffee**, on the other hand, was properly brewed. Likewise **svensk kaffe**: 'Swedish coffee' is, to Danes and Norwegians, watery or poorly made coffee. **Brazil-water**, another term for coffee, sounds little better (especially given Brazil's much touted reputation for the stuff), but the contruction probably does no more than reflect such phrases as *scandal-water,* which to the 18th century meant tea. In mainstream use *Brazil water* was in fact the reddish dye extracted from the local species of the Sappan tree, native to eastern India. Indeed it is this dye, which was known as *brasil* (Spanish) or *brésil* (French) that gave its name to the entire country, which was originally named *terra de brasil*: red-dye land. Why the dye itself was termed 'brasil' remains conjectural. It may come from the French *briser*: to break (since the wood tended to crumble on its voyage to Europe), from the Spanish *brasa*: a glowing coal (indicating its colour) or even from the Arabic *wars*: saffron. Poland's **kawa niemiecka**: 'German coffee', is coffee flavoured with chicory, while in South Africa **Boeretroos**: 'Boer's solace' is strong, flavoursome black coffee.

As Bilong Sospen

Utensils do not figure highly in these lists, but there are a few noteworthy terms. A **stove-lid** is an African American, as is a **skillet** (otherwise a large stew-pan, often made of cast-iron); a **skillet blonde** is a Black woman in a blonde wig. The **Japanese knife trick** is the use of one's knife to convey food to the mouth, presumably reflecting on the obtuse 'trickiness' of any Oriental, as well as on the fact that the Japanese do not customarily use Western knives and forks. A **Spanish spoon** is either a long-handled dipper or narrow shovel, while a **Spanish toothpick** is a nickname for Bishop's-Weed or *Ammi viznaga*, a form of 'hot' herb. In Papua New Guinea the North Solomon Islanders, who generally play the role of the Irish in Britain and the Poles in America, are known in Tok Pisin as **blak sospen**, a black saucepan (from the darker tone of their skin) and are further insulted by the phrase **as bilong sospen**, literally 'your arse belongs in a saucepan', which carries a dual meaning; on the one hand 'your skin is so black it looks burnt' or 'you are such an appalling person that you deserve to be tossed into a cannibal cooking pot'. It is in Indonesian New Guinea that a related phrase is found. The Asmat tribe of the Casuarina Coast of Irian have two categories of people, the Asmat ('the human beings') and the rest of the world, **Manowe**: 'the edible ones'. Last of these terms is **Samoyed**; this is the name of a tribe of Tartaric origin, who inhabit the province of Tomsk in Siberia. It not an insult as such, but a term that translates as 'self-eater', in other words, consuming food without utensils or even fire.

Hash-House Greek

The American term *joint*, which began life in the mid-19th century as a cant term, meaning a place where criminals could get together or 'joint up' and later as an opium den, before becoming more generally a room or place, gives **Chink joint** (a Chinese restaurant). In England both **Chinese** and **Indian** mean the restaurant and the meals it serves, thus the common 'Let's get an Indian'. However **chinois**, in France, means no more than a cafeteria, irrespective of the menu. The Afro-American equivalent is a **nigger joint** (a cheap, low-class café, and thus one frequented by poor Blacks). Synonymous are **nigger juke** or **nigger jook**, both of which incorporate the term *juke* (also found in jukebox) which means variously the cheap, raucous music played at similarly inclined roadhouses, cafés and brothels (and which give the term *juke it*: to play piano in a cheap bar or brothel), to dance, to have a good time and to have sex. From there it came to mean any building used for drinking, dancing and generally enjoying oneself. The origins of juke are debatable but may lie in Africa – in the Bantu *juka* or Wolof *dzug* – or possibly Scotland, where a *jouk* is a place into which one may dart for shelter. It is in such a café that the patrons eat **blackplate**, a synonym for soul food and, as such, traditionally Black dishes. Black-plate puns on the mainstream **blueplate**, usually as 'blueplate special', coined during World War II, which refers either to a restaurant dinner plate divided into compartments for serving several kinds of food as a single order, or a main course (as of meat and vegetables) served as a single menu item.

Other restaurants include America's **wophouse**, which uses *wop*: Italian to make a pun on *flophouse*: the lowest level of transient hotel used by vagrants and tramps, and Australia's **steakdahoyst** or **steaka-da-oyst**, mocking Italian speech patterns to describe an Italian restaurant specializing in steak and oysters. Among its various meanings France's **chinois**: a Chinese, meant *c*.1900 the proprietor of a coffee-house. Greek restaurants, like Indian and Chinese ones, pop up all over the world. In Russia the **grecheskaya kukhinisterskaya**: 'Greek restaurant' is a euphemism for badly cooked food. In Australia, a Greek is known as a **grill**, from the number of immigrant Greeks who run cheap cafés specializing in mixed grills, while in America a **Greek hash-house** is a lunch-stand. This last gives what is called *hash-house Greek*, a reference not so much to the café's owner, but to Greek in the same sense as it has been used since the 16th century: an unintelligible jargon, in this case that of short-order cookery. Such jargon includes *slaughter in the pan*: beefsteak, *red mike with a bunch o' violets*: corned beef and cabbage, *two of a kind*: fishballs and *Adam and Eve on a raft and wreck 'em*: scrambled eggs on toast.

Doing a Tightener

As far as gluttony, greed and over-eating are concerned, the onus seems to have devolved upon the Germans. Thus Poland's **grubość niemiecka**: 'German bulkiness' refers to any glutton, while the French talk of **une saignée d'Allemand**: 'a German bleeding' when describing the way one loosens the clothes after a hearty meal, and **un saut de l'Allemand**: 'a German leap', i.e. a jump out of bed straight to a well-covered table, and thence, laden with food, back to bed. The Provençal **desboutounat coumo un beure à ventre alemand** also refers to post-prandial relaxation or 'loosening up like a German beer-belly'. Similarly inclined is France's **ventre suisse**: 'a Swiss belly'. It means a large paunch and refers not simply to the Swiss, whose appetites are not otherwise that celebrated, but to the word **Suisse** which in France, as elsewhere, means a hotel porter. Such men, at least in theory, are seen as browsers and sluicers of gargantuan appetite. For a people so heavily identified with food, the French themselves get off rather lightly. Perhaps the rest of the world has swallowed their propaganda; however there is **Frankish fare**, meaning excessive or over-*generous amounts of food (though Frank too can, and did originally refer to the Germans), and **gabaï**, a term used by Gascons to attack their northern neighbours and which means glutton. The Dutch, seen as undiscriminating if enthusiastic trenchermen are credited with a **Dutch palate**: a coarse palate, with no appreciation of the finer comestibles, while their South African cousins, the Boers, talk of a **Kaffir's tightener** to mean a heavy meal, which, despite the reference implicit in kaffir, could hardly have been an exclusively Black phenomenon. (The slang term *tightener* itself had been coined, with no racial overtones *c*.1850, and *do a tightener* meant to gorge oneself.) The Czechs, who use **polákavati**, thus attacking the Poles, to mean gorge or stuff oneself, also equate **židek**, usually the disparaging 'Jew-boy', with a greedy-guts or glutton.

A Piss and a Look Around

From excess to deprivation, and starvation gives as many 'national' words as does gluttony. Typical are a variety of notional 'meals', the point of which is that there is no meal whatsoever. Thus America's **Mexican breakfast** or Australia's **Pommy's breakfast**, both of which entail no more than a cigarette and a glass of water. In different contexts Australia also offers the **dingo's breakfast**: 'a piss and a look around', and a **drover's breakfast** in which a cough is substituted for the passing of water. The 'Pommies' have their alternatives too, a **vegetable breakfast** and a **Spitalfields breakfast**, both of which refer to judicial hanging. The Spitalfields meal is a 'tight necktie and a short (wind)pipe' while the 'vegetable' in question is an 'artichoke (hearty choke) with caper sauce.' An **Irish** or **Irishman's dinner** is no dinner at all, a phrase that emerged in America and was reinforced by immigrant memories of the deadly famine of 1845-6, although a modern joke describes such a dinner as 'a boiled potato and a six-pack of beer'. The slightly longer **have an Irishman's dinner** is to be forced to forgo an expected meal.

The Spanish, perhaps on the grounds of their much-celebrated pride, seem to volunteer starvation – echoing those who claim that one can never be too rich nor too thin. Thus to **take a Spanish supper** is to tighten one's belt rather than actually offset one's hunger with food, while in French **un ventre à l'espagnol**, 'a Spanish belly', is one that is swollen, but only from starvation. Provence, in the south of France, is responsible for two apparently contradictory phrases. **Aver lou ventre de l'espagnola**, 'to have a Spanish stomach' is to stint oneself in food and drink (*see* Spanish belly above) while **buffa** (or **boufa**) **coume un espagnou**, means puffed up like a Spaniard (although this perhaps refers to pride rather than pudding). To pursue the motif of emaciation, African Americans have termed Whites **the thin people** while they in turn have been called **bones**, although this presumably refers to the 'Mr Bones' character, once a staple of 'black' cross-talk vaudeville acts between 'Mr Bones' and 'Mr Jones'. (The original 'Mr' or 'Brudder Bones' played on the castanet-like 'bones' that were a feature of such shows).

Some diets make you fat, others merely place something in one's stomach. Geophagy, literally earth-eating, has been found in various parts of the globe, typically Tierra del Fuego, but as these terms indicate, it has also cropped up in the so-called 'civilized' West, specifically the poorer states of America. Thus **clayeater** means a poor White, especially a native of North or South Carolina or Georgia; a synonym is **grit-sucker,** while **clover-eater**, substituting grass for earth, is a nickname for a Virginian. Similar are **rosin-chewer** and **hay-eater**. Equally strange is an appetite for wax, found in the American **candle-eater**, meaning a Russian, and Italy's **tedeschi magnasego** or 'German tallow-eaters'. Both of these, however, may not be quite as bizarre as they seem. The candles that the Russians 'eat' may well be a reference to the burning of candles in Russian Orthodox churches, while the German consumption of tallow, or animal fat, may refer to the innate greasiness of pork.

I Smoak all

DRUGS & DRINK

THE ROLE of drugs in this lexicon is slightly ambiguous. On the whole, with the exception of heroin (and its precursor opium), which carries such negative baggage that any link to a country involved in its processing or distribution makes that country inevitably suspect, these labels are not usually tossed at an individual with malice aforethought. Yet they are included on the grounds that drugs, especially to Western eyes, are of themselves in some way threatening – and in the discussion of drugs, as of race, dull facts are rarely considered, let alone debated coolly – and as such carry some brand of evil. They fall, if anything, into the category of 'foreign': exotic, different, other and therefore bad. Indeed, the perceived link between drugs, be it the opium and cocaine scares of the inter-war years, or the hysterical response to the growing use of cannabis in the 1950s and beyond, cannot be divorced from race. Irrespective of the actual effects of the drugs in question, the idea that their consumption might lead to the mixing of White women with yellow or Black men, terrified the authorities. It was for those reasons, to a far greater extent than any medical research, that Britain, and like it America, has always propagandized so enthusiastically against 'illicit substances'. Not surprisingly did Sax Rohmer, creator of Fu Manchu, pen a lurid best-seller entitled *Dope*, playing cheerfully on the perceived links between the 'yellow peril' and the varieties of White powder. The exploits (and media exploitation) of such allegedly corrupt exotics as the Chinese restaurateur 'Brilliant' Chang or the Jamaican jazz drummer Edgar Manning, the era's drug-dealing bogeymen, thrilled Britain in the 1920s. Nor has the link entirely vanished; at a time when overt racism is largely absent from public discourse certain 'drugs' have become a useful code-word for 'race': for the much touted 'war' on 'crack' cocaine, one can invariably read: 'a fear of young Black men'.

Double standards, invariably under-pinning any supposedly 'moral' discussion, are never so evident as in the debate between those drugs that have been declared illegal, and those, typically tobacco and alcohol, which, if for no better reason than the revenues they generate for the world's governments, are considered acceptable. Such niceties, however, do not impinge on the world of race, and accusations of drunkenness are as much a part of the nationalistic lexicon as any other. Indeed, as will be seen, drink-related slurs far outweigh those that deal in drugs.

Sticks, Bush and Temple Balls

Hashish and marijuana, respectively the resinous and herbal forms of cannabis, produce two varieties of terminology, both referring to what might be termed brand-names. There is the country of origin, the great majority of terms, and a few references to religion, noting the spiritual side of the drug, whether valid or not.

For the first group one finds **Af**, an abbreviation for **Afghani** (Afghanistan being a great source of top-quality hashish prior to the Russian invasion of 1979 and the civil war that has followed), **Lebanese Red** (and **Gold**), **black Russian** and **black Pak** (from Pakistan): all of these refer to hashish. Marijuana seems to attract more 'national names', including **Panama red**, **African** or **Congo bush**, **Thai sticks** (grown in Thailand and sold tied around a thin stick resembling a satay skewer), **Nepalese temple balls** (widely reputed to be cut with opium), **Indian hay** (which refers to Native Americans, although

Indian weed, coined in 1730, refers to 'straight' tobacco), **Injun**, and **Indian hemp**, once the cover-all term for any form of cannabis, based on the use of the drug, in resin form, in the sub-continent. More recent coinages include **indo**, an abbreviation for Indonesian, **Nam black**, **Nam shit** and **Nam weed**, all grown in Vietnam, very dark green and notably potent. **Acapulco Gold**, the hippies' favourite back in the 1960s, refers to Mexican marijuana (the name marijuana itself being of course Mexican), a form that gives the slightly racist **Mexican cigarette** – a poorly rolled marijuana cigarette or joint – and **fly Mexican airlines**: to smoke marijuana. **Mexican green** is yet another variety, as are **Chicago green** (presumably a homegrown variety from America's major mid-West city), and **Durban poison** (from South Africa).

Religious references – a regular sidebar to hallucinogens – come in **buddha**, which can either describe a potent form of marijuana, currently popular with American youth and much hymned in rap music, or a mix of marijuana and crack cocaine. A **booda** (presumably an alternative spelling) is a large cannabis-impregnated cookie. The older **maharishee**, which essentially puns on marijuana, recalls the Maharishi Mahesh Yogi, an Indian guru who became hugely popular in the 1960s with the Beatles and others in search of raized consciousness. Finally a **dutchmasta** (from the brand-name cigar) is a cigar from which the tobacco has been removed and replaced by marijuana.

Kicking the Gong around

The role of national names as regards cannabis is one of default: cannabis is, while in no way actually dangerous, nonetheless deemed illegal, thus if nations are linked to it there is an implicit slur. When one turns to the harder, 'class A' drugs like heroin and the opium from which it is obtained, then one is back with an old acquaintance: the yellow peril, i.e. China and the mystic East. That opium was in fact introduced to China by European traders may be an historical irony, but is of little relevance. **China White**, **chi**, **china brown**, **chinese H**, **chinese rocks** and **Chinese No. 3** all refer to forms of heroin, processed in the Far East (although rarely if ever in China itself) and sent West. **Chinese tobacco** meant opium, while **Chinese needlework** refers to the injection of narcotics, and to have a **Chinaman on one's back** is to crave narcotics (the more common term replaces the Chinaman with a monkey, a substitution that may reflect an underlying racism in itself). **Dragon**, a symbol of China, can also be heroin, although it may be a back-formation from the phrase **chasing the dragon**, the most common way of smoking (rather than injecting) heroin: the user sucks up the smoke of the drug – in powder form – which is burned on a piece of kitchen foil; the heated heroin liquifies and flows across the foil, gradually giving off smoke which is sucked into the smoker's lungs by a tube, also usually made of kitchen foil. (If a matchbook cover is substituted for the usual tube, the term becomes *playing the mouth organ*.)

Heroin, although it was first synthesized in 1898 (its name comes ultimately from the Greek *heros*: a hero, a reference to the sense of omnipotence and emotional painlessness that the drug confers), was not the first major painkiller to take on a secondary role as a 'recreational' drug. Opium, from the Greek *opion*: poppy-juice, culled from the opium poppy or *Papaver somniferum*, could be found in the British pharmacoepia as early as the 14th century, and had doubtless been known for centuries prior to that. How early it moved from the physicians to the fun-seekers is unknown. It would seem to have arrived during the mid-18th century; certainly Horace Walpole, in 1751, can quote an aristocratic lady declaring that prior to having her daily dose, she still felt herself to be 'without my wit'. Thomas de Quincey's well-documented experiences as an 'opium-eater' were published in the *London Magazine* in 1821. Thirty years later, with Victorian earnestness swamping the greater sophistication of an earlier era, the opium 'dens' of East London gave Dickens a convenient and custom-built backdrop for the villainies of *Edwin Drood*. But it was not England, but America, that witnessed the serious use of opium, outlawed and fascinating, and tied directly into the Chinese population.

America's opium users found their supplies in the Chinatowns of the big cities, typically New York and San Francisco, and as well as the drug found an elaborate vocabulary linked to the pipe. Opium itself was known as **yen**, a word that came from the Mandarin **yan** or Cantonese **yin**, both of which meant opium. Thus, by extension it meant one's

craving for the drug, and, in a wider world and wider use, craving or
desire, pure and simple. Amongst users the term was also found as
yen-yen, mixing the original word and its English derivation.

Kick the gong around means to use drugs, especially narcotics.
Film buffs will recall its appearance, slightly adulterated, in the film *To
Have and Have Not*, when the pianist Hoagy Carmichael sings of a
'coloured man' who liked 'to kick old Buddha's gong'. Other heroin
terms include the **Spanish cure**: the treatment of addiction, as practized in Spain, by forced, total abstinence, and the 1960s slang **'Frisco
speedball**: a drug cocktail containing not just the usual 'speedball', i.e.
a mix of heroin and cocaine, but a little psychedelia (hence ''Frisco':
San Francisco, the home of contemporary hippiedom) in the form of
some LSD. Mexican heroin, which is dark brown, is known as **tootsie
roll**, from the brand-name of the US *Tootsie Roll*: a chocolate cake.

Mexican Jumping Beans

Amphetamines, which first appeared under the name Benzedrine in
1933, the properties of which are most succinctly explained in their
slang name *speed*, have attracted a few 'national' names. Their popular
use as a stimulant for otherwise less than enthusistic soldiers, has
created **German marching pills**, referring especially to methedrine,
a very potent form first created in Germany. **French blues**, otherwise
known as *purple hearts*, were the drug of choice for many young people
in the early 1960s. More recently **borders** has been coined to describe
the non-proprietory capsules of barbiturate powder (a depressant, and
as such the opposite of amphetamine) sold on the black market and
which have been made up in Mexico before being shipped across the
border into the US. **Mexican jumping beans**, punning on the small
beans in which lurk an insect, causing them to 'jump' as it moves
around, are also amphetamines.

Driving French Horses

Alcohol, other than within such liquor-free cultures as Islam, is a
universal. (And even the hapless Arabs have to suffer the British phrase

a mouth like the inside of an Arab's underpants, referring to such ghastly physical feelings as are concomitant with a hangover.) A drug with infinitely more deleterious effects than the much vilified cannabis (which gleans the bulk of its 'national' terminology from its various 'trade-names'), it is tolerated, from long habit, not to mention the revenue it offers the world's governments. Language too benefits: there are for instance around 2,500 slang terms meaning drunk, and while the bulk are inapplicable here, the language of drinking and drunkenness has impinged, as it does everywhere else, on the language of race.

To start in America, where drunkenness, like rape, is one of the supposedly 'natural' characteristics of the African American, one finds **nigger gin** and **nigger rum**, both inferior versions of the spirit in question (but considered good enough for poor, Black consumers), **jig water**, which means liquor in general, and **nigger-pot**, which is moonshine. (In Barbados, Jamaica and other West Indian islands, however, a *nigger-pot* is a rich one-pot meal of meat, vegetables and spices, cooked for a festival.) **Nigger day** is Saturday, when it is presumed that every African American, temporarily liberated from work, sets out to get **nigger drunk**. (**Nigger night** is also Saturday, a time for what were once termed 'courting couples', of whatever colour, to enjoy a little fun; the term was coined *c*.1850.) White America offers the **Coney Island head**, a beer which has more frothy head than actual beer and refers to the way vistors were defrauded by the bartenders of Coney Island, New York's leisure centre. A **yankee** was a glass of whiskey sweetened with molasses. College students **go Borneo**: get crazily drunk, a reference to the presumed antics of the 'Wild Man of Borneo' and **go to Mexico**, another synonym for getting drunk, this time noting the way US teenagers from Texas, California and other border states make brief trips into Mexico for 'lost weekends' of non-stop excess. **Smoke**, which has been a derogatory term for Black people since the late-19th century, can also mean any cheap, rotgut alcohol, especially denatured alcohol shaken up with water and drunk by down-and-out alcoholic tramps. In Britain, **African lager** or **Nigerian lager** mean Guinness stout: apart from its creamy head, the drink is virtually black. In France, a **négresse** is a bottle of red wine and **une négresse morte** is not a dead Black woman, but an empty bottle. The military slang **il est senegalais**: 'he is a Senegalese' means that he is dead drunk.

Unsurprisingly, there's nothing like national enmity to sharpen up the racial slurs, and how they linger. It is, after all, more than two centuries since English ships fought Dutch ones across the breadth of the North Sea, and the two countries engaged in the militant rivalry of empire-building in oceans somewhat farther afield; but if the Dutch have any image in late-20th-century Britain it comes from such phrases as **Dutch treat**, **Dutch uncle** and above all **Dutch courage**. This last, defined as cowardice that, fortified by generous quantities of alcohol, becomes (temporary) bravery was indeed coined during the Anglo-Dutch wars. It has yet to fade from the national vocabulary. **Dry Dutch courage** offers the same comfort, this time based on the use of drugs. Other terms appeared too, although they, on the whole, have faded. Among them are **Dutch milk**, **Dutch sods** (from the 17th-century English *sod*: steeped in liquor) and plain **Dutch**, all of which mean beer; **Dutch gleek** (possibly taken from the word *gleek* meaning trick or joke) means any liquor. A **Dutchman's headache** is a hangover, following so much drinking, while a **Dutchman's drink** is an emptied pot. Of the many similes that denote drunkenness, **drunk as a Dutchman** was always popular (the Czechs echo the sentiment with **pije jako holundr**: he drinks like a Dutchman) and a **Dutch feast** combines drunkenness with another sterotype, meanness, to describe any meal where the host gets drunk before his friends; the assumption is that he has hogged the supply of alcohol.

The Dutch phrase *op zijn*: 'on his' (other theories give the etymology *op zee*: over seas or imported), and transliterated as *upsy* or *upsee* gives rise to a small group of terms, once common in 17th-century England, and all of which refer to drinking habits. Thus **upsy-Dutch**: in the Dutch manner, **upsy-English**: in the English manner; and **upsy-Freeze** in the Friesian manner; to drink **upsee-freeze cross** is to drink with arms inter-twined. The exact meanings of upsy-Dutch and upsy-English (i.e. what *were* the Dutch and English manners of drinking?) are lost in some long-gone boozy tavern but all three terms can simply mean strong liquor itself or just heavy drinking; **upsy-friesy**, for instance, is defined as 'addicted to drinking deeply', to **upsy-friese** is to empty a pot and **upsee English** is 'strong, lusty London beer'. Across the Atlantic, in America, Dutch, as has been noted, can often mean Deutsch or German but whatever the national reference a **Dutch doggery** is a low grog shop, while **Dutch garden** (this one certainly meaning *Deutsch*) is a beer garden. A **Dutchman**, in England, is or was a bottle of Deutz and Gelderman champagne. The Dutch themselves use the phrase **de Rus gezien hebben**: 'to have seen the Russian' to mean to be dead drunk.

Fransche, in Dutch, means brandy, and if the French duly succeeded the Dutch as Britain's national bugbear, then their principal export, via customs office or smuggler's cove, was brandy. And the English appetite for what was known variously as the **Frenchman**, the **French article**, **French elixir** and **French lace** remained undiminished, whatever other sacrifices their patriotism demanded. **French cream** was also brandy, especially when added to afternoon tea (then still something of an aristocratic preserve) and as Francis Grose noted in 1785, 'so called by the old tabbies and dowagers when they drink their tea'. Aristocratic taste or not, an excess of brandy caused one to **drive French horses**: to vomit, and in America, where no such pretensions supposedly obtained, the **French walk** referred to the posture adopted by those in the process of being tossed bodily from a saloon. 'French' here is a pun on **frog**, since the unfortunate drunkard, his limbs splayed out as he flew through the air, might be seen, for just that moment, as resembling a frog, its limbs akimbo. (The **Spanish walk** describes a similar form of progress, but can also mean a cautious, tippy-toeing pace, apparently reminiscent of a victim of the pirates of the Spanish Main, making his or her fearful walk along 'the plank'.) Around 1900 the Italians used **Francoso**: a Frenchman, to mean a drunkard. More recently, and germane not to brandy but to wine, has appeared the term **châteaued**: punning both on the wines of Bordeaux, which are always labelled as to the Château in which they are produced, and on yet another slang synonym for drunk: *shattered*. Turning the tables, the French phrase **faire brûler Moscou**: to 'make Moscow burn', reminiscent of Napoleon's unhappy arrival at the city in 1812, means to mix a large bowl of flaming punch.

If the Germans are perceived as gluttons when it comes to food, then in alcoholic terms they're simply drunks. Thus Denmark talks of a **Tysker**: 'a German', and means a drunk, Provence uses the phrases **sadou coumo un alemand** and **pinta coumo un aleman**, both of which translate as 'drunk as a German', as well as the synonymous **flabuta coumo un alemand**: 'fluted' or soused like a German; old French has **iouer de la fluste de l'Allemand**: 'play the German flute' as well as the more recent **faire une Prusse**: 'to do a Prussia', meaning to be dead drunk. America's **hophead**, more usually found with reference to *hop* meaning opium and thus meaning a heroin user, began life meaning a drunkard and focussed on the hops in what was once termed, especially when strong, **German conversation water** (a term that sets the pattern for the 20th-century **German marching pills**, i.e. amphetamine and the even more recent **Columbian marching powder**: cocaine). A **German garden**, like a Dutch garden, is a beer garden. Lastly **on the fritz**, punning on the popular German name and usually found in the context of machinery that sporadically ceases to function, has also meant drunk.

Like the reviling of Jews for money-lending, a role which they had no option but to assume, the attacking of Native Americans for drinking, to which they were introduced by their European conquerors, seem somewhat otiose, but that does not, of course, diminish the practice. Thus **Indian liquor**, **Indian rum** and **Indian whisky** describe, in the way of Indian coffee (see above) the vilest, most adulterated and most gut-rotting versions of the liquors in question; to **see Indians** is to be drunk, while to **play the sober Indian** is to resist any form of communal drinking – with a subtext that hints at the impossibility of such strength of character. A further 'Indian' term is found in the late-19th-century **hootch**, meaning a form of rough liquor, manufactured from sugar and graham flour (a form of unsifted wheat flour) by the Hoochinoo (itself an alteration of Hutsnuwu), an Alaskan Indian tribe. It has come to mean any rough alcoholic drink, especially whiskey.

If when they drink, the Germans drink a great deal, then the Irish, so we should believe, do nothing other than drink. Alcohol, after all, is 'the curse of the Irish' and as the sneering American saying has it, renders one 'resolute as a drunken Irishman.' A **whisky-mick** is an Irishman while **St Patrick**, the patron saint of Ireland, is a nickname for any particularly good whisky. (*Paddy* itself is a long established whiskey brand-name, patented in 1925 by the Cork Distilleries Company Limited.) **On a brannigan**, taking a popular Irish surname, means out on a drunken spree, while **rileyed**, meaning drunk, is a formation based on the phrase *the life of Riley* (or Reilly or O'Reilly). The source of the phrase seems to be the staging in February 1881 of the Ned Harrigan and Tony Hart play *The Mulligan's Silver Wedding*, described as a 'low-life comedy', which featured among other high points the song 'John Riley's Always Dry', which listed the eponymous Riley's prodigious drinking. The Irish and drink, though in a somewhat different context, gave late-19th-century London the opportunity for the grimmest of humour. The term **Fenian**, which flourished briefly in 1883, meant three penny-worth of cold whisky and water and punned on the order 'three cold Irish', itself referring to the Fenian activists Allen, Larkin and O'Brien who were hanged for the Phoenix Park murders of Lord Frederick Cavendish, the Chief Secretary and Thomas Burke, the Under-Secretary for Ireland, in May 1882.

Soul comme un anglois: 'drunk as an Englishman' is an old saying, dating in fact from the Hundred Years' War (1337-1453), as the archaic form *Anglois* indicates; it related originally to the excessive drinking of the invading British troops, who gorged themselves on the rare and unknown wines they found in the cellars of France. The image has yet to die, nor will it so long as England sends her football supporters abroad in their anti-ambassadorial role, and the modern **John Bull**, Australian rhyming slang for 'full', i.e. drunk, makes it equally clear. Similarly, **corkney** means an Englishman, a double pun on the London Cockney and on his supposed drinking habits. **English manufacture** is shorthand for cider, ale or beer, while **British champagne** is porter (a kind of beer, of a dark brown colour and bitterish taste, so-called from its popularity amongst porters and other 18th-century manual labourers), and **British brandy** is artificial or 'cooking' brandy. **Scotch chocolate** is brimstone (better known today as sulphur, and featured in Dickens' *Oliver Twist*) and milk, while a **Scotch pint** was a bottle containing not one but four pints. This played, as usual, on Scots parsimony, and in this case gives the image of the Scot asking for 'just a pint', but proferring this quadruple-sized container.

Being Mediterraneans and less terrified of liquor than the Puritans of the North, Italian drinking terms fail to carry any burden of sin; it is their quality that is impugned. Thus **Dago red** or **guinea red** both refer to cheap red wine, usually Chianti, which is often manufactured at home by Italian immigrants or by their descendants. **Wino**, at least in Chicago, means an Italian (rather than a drunkard as it would in the wider world) and refers to this same homegrown wine; an identical term was used in the Far West for grape pickers and winery workers. Not that Italians get off entirely without moral censure: in France **avoir pincé son italique**: 'to have one's Italian (leg) caught' means that one is unable, thanks to an excess of alcohol, to walk straight. In the Breton dialect **Italien** means rum.

The Scandinavians have a fair reputation for drinking, but it has generated relatively few phrases. The Dutch mock the **dronkelap** or **dronken Lap**: 'the drunken Laplander', while Sweden's **torstig som en dansk**: 'thirsty as a Dane' applies to anyone desperate for a drink. The Danes retaliate with **full som Svensker**: 'drunk as a Swede'. Other phrases have no special favourites. A **maroquin**, in France, is a 'Moroccan' or a complete drunkard; **soul comme un polonais**: 'full as a Polack' means disgustingly drunk (supposedly mocking the Polish-French Maréchal de Saxe, a great tippler) as does the Dutch **drinken gelijk een Polak**. Late-19th-century Britain offers **drunk as a Polony**, which supposedly picks up on the French phrase, but may also refer to the slang term for a sausage, a *polony* (from Italy's *Bologna* sausage), which, given its shape, patently cannot 'stand up'.

Still in France **faire suisse**: to do it the Swiss way, means to drink in solitude (once more there is, possibly, the image of the porter drinking in his cubbyhole). **Suissesse**: a 19th-century French slang term meaning Swiss girl (the standard term is *la Suisse*), means a glass of absinthe and orgeat or almond syrup. The German **Schweizerblut**: 'Swiss blood' is a sort of wine. The **Swiss itch**, or **Swiss hitch**, which one might have related to insects rather than liquor, refers to the popular method of drinking any liquor that one fears might be contaminated. Created for the 'bathtub gin' of the Prohibition era but these days generally found in the world of tequila-drinking, it describes the process by which one places a pinch of salt on the back of the hand, then licks it off, and takes immediately a jigger of tequila, and follows that by immediately biting into a segment or a slice of lime. The salt and lime are presumably a prophylactic against disease.

Cape smoke, in South Africa, was a form of banana liquor drunk around the end of the 19th century. It was distilled from bananas and its roots lie not in the English *smoke*, but in Swahili *moshi*: banana liquor. **Turkenwein**, literally 'Turkish wine' and generically 'sour wine' was coined in 1529, during the Turkish siege of Vienna. The winter was almost unbearably cold, the suffering was great, and not only the wine but even the vegetation seemed to turn sour, and the word was thus applied to everything that was disappointing. To **play the Greek** is to drink excessively and **Greek fire** (properly a weapon, used to ignite the enemy's ships) once meant rotgut or cheap whiskey; **uherčina**, in Czech means variously Hungarian wine and fever, otherwise known as the 'Hungarian disease'. Finally in Australia **Northern Territory champagne** is methylated spirits mixed with health salts (which gave them a fizzy head), and which is popularly drunk by many Northen Territory Aborigines.

Swedish Condition Powder

Last of all come a quartet of legal intoxicants. The **Indian drug** is tobacco, so called because the Native Indians introduced Europeans to the plant in the 16th century; **Swedish condition powder** is snuff, a loggers' term, as are the synonymous **Scandihoovian dynamite** and the 18th-century **Irish blackguard**. The story behind this last is that it was coined indirectly by one Lundy Foot, the Dublin snuff-merchant. When still a shop-boy, Foot made a mistake in the preparation of some snuff, for which his master called him an 'Irish Blackguard'. Despite this the new type of snuff proved a great success and, established as his own boss, Foot sold great quanitities under that name that had hitherto been only an insult.

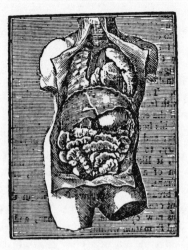

THE BODY

TRUTH BE told, we all have much the same body. The pigment may differ – and that topic is sufficiently large to have its own area of discussion (see *Colour*) – but otherwise you're talking the usual four limbs, nose, ears, other orifices and extensions and so on. Some may be more attractive than others – and that depends on the culture in question – but such judgements are marginal. Genitals divide 50:50, of course, but in terms of pure objectivity they simply complement each other. But then objectivity, let alone disinterested truth plays the least of parts in this sort of prejudice, and physical characteristics, perceived or even actual, have taken on a disproportionate importance. Like those pictures of naked men, showing how the importance of the penis to its owner is generally in direct disproportion to its actual dimensions, the minor physical differences are blown up grotesquely so as to provide yet another weapon in the squalid armoury of racial abuse.

While certain nations, predictably, have been saddled with certain physical stereotypes, a chapter on the body should concentrate on the body itself, and accordingly one can begin with the head, indeed with hair that surmounts it.

Fuzzy-Wuzzy

For reasons that in an ideal universe would be obscure but in the contemporary one are all too obvious, the world, or at least that section of world from which most of these terms are plucked, has long since chosen to accept the primacy of straight, in other words 'White' hair. Literally White hair, i.e. blonde hair, of course, is better yet, but straight is what matters. Straight, in other words not kinky, nappy, curly, in other words not Black. Or indeed Jewish. And if blondes have, as we are told, more fun, their opposite numbers have infinitely less.

Black people have tight curly black hair. Not all, but predominantly, and for that they will not be forgiven. **Brillo-head**, taken from the popular steel-wool scouring pad, is one of a number of cognate terms, including **wire-head**, **velcro-head** and **burr-head** (from *burr*: any rough or prickly seed-vessel or flower-head of a plant) that equate Black people with the texture of their hair. (Not everyone need, of course, be Black, as Andrew Neil, the former editor of the *Sunday Times*, and known to *Private Eye* and its readers as 'Brillo', can doubtless attest.) **Linthead** (1940s) refers to those who moved north from the small Southern mill-towns, seeking to take advantage of the wartime boom. Similar terms include **nappy**, which comes from the nap or pile of a cloth, and as a word, if not a pejorative, dates back to the 16th century when it simply meant shaggy. Nappy has other uses too: **nappy music** is synonymous with Black music, while nappy as an adjective means dirty and messy, especially of the hair – whether black or not. With the predictable absence of subtlety **nigger wool** means Black hair, while **woollyhead**, another synonym and one coined by James Fennimore Cooper in his book *The Prairie* (1827), simply means an African American. **Niggerknots**, used by West Indians as a mutual insult, refers to a Black person's natural hair, thick, tough and demanding much combing. Through metonymy (the use of the name of a thing to describe an abstract concept), woollyhead was also used to mean an abolitionist, i.e. a pro-Black, anti-slavery activist. Less obvious is **buffalo**, which may be linked to the *buffalo soldier*, a nickname for America's segregated mid-19th-century Black soldiery. The ostensible background is that Black hair was supposedly reminiscent of a buffalo's coat; few contemporaries would have failed to notice another, general slang use of *buffalo*: a large, slow, stupid person.

To stay with what mainstream slang has termed the *weathercock*, the *crumpet* and the *bean*, a **negro head**, or even less flatteringly **nigger-head**, has a number of meanings, although none refers directly to the head or indeed the hair. Like woollyhead, **niggerhead** meant a pro-Black activist, but there was much besides. In nautical jargon, a *Negro's head* is a loaf of brown bread and a *niggerhead* a bollard or winch head; elsewhere a nigger-head is variously a heavy, black cobbling stone, a large boulder, a brand of dark Virginia tobacco, a tussock of moss that is formed in swampy ground, a spherical prickly cactus belonging to the genera *Ferocactus* or *Echinocactus*, a synonym for the black-eyed Susan (*Rudbeckia hirta*), a yellow flower with a dark centre, and a variety of rocks, shells, lumps of coral and similar formations.

Not all Blacks are American, nor are all racists. **Fuzzy-wuzzy,** runs the nursery rhyme, was a bear, but he was also a Sudanese warrior, and thus christened by the British troops who fought in Sudan at the end of the 19th century. Rudyard Kipling apostrophized them in the *Barrack Room Ballads* (1892), toasting 'Fuzzy-Wuzzy, at your 'ome in the Soudan'. But Kipling, carefully discarded aspirate and all, has at least the excuse of his era. He seems positively benign in the face of the casual dismissal of Nancy Mitford, writing in *Pigeon Pie* (1940) of 'Chinks and Japs and Fuzzy Wuzzies and Ice Creamers and Dagos', while the BBC's *Listener* magazine wrote, with no apparent irony in 1965 of 'Tibetans, Zulus, and other relatively speaking unarmed fuzzy-wuzzies.' This was in a sports review. Not for nothing did George Orwell define sport as war minus the shooting. Whether Tibetans quite fit the bill is debatable, but at one time or another Fijians, Papua / New Guineans and other South Pacific Islanders have all been labelled with the dubious epithet. Finally, there is **frisé**, a term that began life as a description of a raized design in silk, and is best known as a recent up-market lettuce of choice. For these purposes and in France (fittingly no doubt for that culinarily-obsessed nation) rather than the pride of the local Waitrose, it describes a Jew, or at least Jewish curly hair. **Judenhaar** or 'Jew-hair' is an Austrian term for the down some babies show at birth.

The Black take on White hair is somewhat more forgiving, even envious. If Blacks' own hair can be condemned as **bad hair**, then 'White' hair is logically *good hair*. **Silk** describes White hair, especially that of a blonde woman, who herself has been known as a **silk-broad** (*broad* being a 20th-century slang term for a woman, albeit not the most moral of her gender). Less luxurious, but synonymous, is **cotton-top**. **Righteous moss** means White people's hair in general, a blend of *righteous*, meaning first-rate or excellent, and *moss*, meaning in this context hair, but more usually its pubic variety (a usage that extends to *moss rose*: the vagina, *mossy bank*, *mossy cell* and the *mossy face*). That said, it can also mean Black hair. Other hair-related terms include **pigtail**, meaning a Chinese person (from a hairstyle enforced by the 19th-century Manchu dynasty), and thus **Pigtailiana**, meaning China. In the West Indies a **chinee bump** (or a *corkscrew* or *nigger-plait*, an example in itself of the way nigger, when used between Blacks, can be a neutral term) is a temporary hairstyle for Black women whereby the hair is tied into neat rows of regular clumps to facilitate drying after it has been washed. It can then be styled as required. Poles call Germans **kasztan** or chestnut, because of what they see as a typical German hair colour, while Russians depict Ukrainians as **xoxól**, a reference to the characteristic topknot sported by the Cossacks.

Short hair too has its national styles. A **Dutch cut**, in America, can either be a crewcut or a style in which the front of the hair is brushed forward and 'banged' or cut in a dead-straight line (from the standard English *bangs*: a fringe), while the back is cropped almost to the bone. A **German pomp** is short for a pompadour, so popular in the 1950s, or, once again, a very short cut. In the former Yugoslavia, everyone called Swedes **siso**: cropped, in tribute to their demonstrable affection for the scissors. In Germany **Schwedenkopf**, 'the head of a Swede', means closely cropped hair. Finally comes the **croppie** or **croppy**, ostensibly one who has his hair cut short, but in fact a direct reference to the Irish rebels of 1798, who chose to cut their hair defiantly short, as a tribute to their sympathy with the still unfinished French Revolution. A few years later, as the transportation of convicts to Australia gained impetus, a croppy became synonymous with a convict, his hair slashed viciously short in preparation for the lengthy, squalid voyage. Sometime earlier the word had also meant Roundhead, a term that it appropriated from criminal cant. Once a description of those who while in prison had not merely lost their hair, but their noses and ears as well, it came to mean a Puritan (some of whom had suffered in this way), and thus a Roundhead, an opponent of Charles I and his cavaliers.

From short hair to no hair. The smooth, round, red-coated Edam cheese gives **Dutch cheese** as one definition of a bald person, while the West Indies in general, and Rastafarians in particular use **ball-face** and **ball-head** to characterize Whites. Not all may actually be bald, but compared to Rastamen, with their flowing, knotted locks, the meagre crop of White man's hair is indeed tantamount to baldness.

To extend the hair a little further, to its grooming, one should note a variety of combs. The **German comb** or **peigne d'allemand** in France, the **Welsh comb**, and the synonymous **Irish rifle** all represent the same thing, a quick smoothing of the hair with the thumb and four fingers. The inference is that the people in question lack the sophistication to buy the real thing; whether the 'target' of the 'rifle' is fleas or nits, is not specified. The Polish **pejsak**: earlocks, refers to the long sidecurls or *peies* (pronounced 'pious') that denote a Hasidic Jew, of whom Poland, prior to World War II, had a substantial community.

And last of all another term from Blacks for Whites. Wig. Although in terms of wigs perhaps the most bizarre is the late-18th century's **Nazarene foretop**: an ornamental wig made in imitation of Christ's head of hair (thus Nazarene meaning Jesus of Nazareth), as represented by painters.

An Irish Shave is no Shave at All

You don't have to be Jewish to like Levi's Rye Bread, as the old ads used to say (in New York City anyway) and you don't have to be Jewish to get cursed out on the grounds of your unattractiveness either. But like a taste for rye bread it would appear that a touch of semitism does predispose you, or at least your accusers, to such attacks. **He must have passed through the wilderness with the Children of Israel**, say the Germans of a deformed or unprepossessing person; **he looks like a Jew who lost his forfeit**, runs the Italian comment on a scornful expression; **what a pity**, say Muslims with a nod to the Jew's supposed financial acumen, **that the Jew has his eyes**. The twin terms **Jew-face** and **Judengesicht**: Jewish looks, used respectively by Arabs and Germans, imply an unprepossessing, crafty appearance. And the Czech term **židačisko** or **židisko** (**Żydzisko** in Polish), literally an 'ugly or hideous-looking Jew', can be thrown at anyone seen as generally unlovely. In Poland **żydogłowy** or 'Jew-headed' should not be interpreted as a compliment, while in Portugal **cara de judeu**, literally 'Jew-face', refers to anyone looking somewhat under the weather.

In fairness, such epithets are available to all. The well-known assumption that nothing in China runs at 90 degrees to the horizontal is seen in **slope, slope-head, slopie** and **slopie-gal**. **Flange-head**, like these a coinage of World War II, compounds the fantasy, although bizarrely; a *flange* is usually a form of projecting neck or collar, used to anchor one (usually metal) object to another. The Japanese, who might be seen as 'suffering' the same problem, offer **chanchanbozou**, literally a poppy capsule but in practice a comment on the shape of Chinese heads. **Cabeza** or **cuadrada**, both meaning squarehead, are used in Spanish to berate the Germans (and occasionally the Scandinavians), and **squarehead** itself was popular among the Allies in two world wars. Ironically it had started life as thieves' cant, meaning one who is not a criminal, a forerunner of the *square* (used by teenagers) of later years. In Sweden lower-middle class, petty-bourgeois Germans are known as **ippeltysk** or 'apple Germans'. The reference is to their round and rosy cheeks – all that fresh air and *lederhosen* no doubt. And if Germans have rosy complexions Blacks it seems have ashen ones. Thus **zombie** and **spook,** in other contexts phantoms and ghosts (although zombie can also imply a dull, lifeless person) both mean a Black person, as too does **boogie**, a term that is usually taken to refer to dancing, but may equally well stem from *booger-* or *bogeyman*: originally another take on demon or ghost. An **ash-cat**, otherwise known as a dirty, dishevelled child, also describes a thin, wasted, ragged Black person. This image of Blacks as invisible is epitomized in Sam Greenlee's novel *The Spook That Sat By The Door* (1969), in which the FBI's 'token nigger' turns out to be a fifth columnist for militant Black revolution. Other ghost-related terms include **shade** (otherwise a ghost or disembodied spirit), **shadow** and the female **shady-lady**, a term that usually implies a dubious character, rather than a dark skin. **Seedy**, meaning shabby or looking pallid and unwell, has also been used to mean Black. The compliment is returned by the use of **wrinkle-face** to describe White complexions. A face, any face, in France can be **Maroquin**: Morocco leather, giving rise to the combative phrase *On lui donnera sur le maroquin*: he'll get his face knocked in. In late-18th-century America a **roundhead**, with its deliberate overtones of Puritan, Republican rebelliousness, was a New Englander.

And all these faces, if male, need shaving. The (American) **Indian razor** was a pair of clam shells or, as technology advanced, a pair of crude metal tweezers used to remove facial hair. A **Jew shave** describes the covering of unsightly bristles with talcum powder, while an **Irish shave** is no shave at all, simply a visit to the lavatory, an experience that is also described, in America as, **going to Egypt**. While still lavatory-bound, **une installation à la turque** is a toilet without a seat, while **la face du grand turc** (the face of the Grand Turk) is the posterior and Hungary's **törökülés**: 'Turkish seat' means sitting crosslegged on the floor. A latrine can also be a **Scotch ordinary**, although in standard English *ordinary* usually means a tavern dining room, or the meals one gets there. The implication, presumably, is that while other people offer food in an ordinary, the mean Scots offer only its waste product. The 19th-century **Dutchman's razor** had nothing to do with shaving, other than in the Irish sense; it was animal excrement, as found in fields or farmyards; thus the phrase **cut one's foot with a Dutchman's razor**: to step in excrement.

If the Asian head is sloped, then the Asian eye slants, and the all-embracing terms **slant** or **slant-eye** (more World War II coinages) mean variously Chinese, Korean, Vietnamese, Japanese and indeed anyone living in the Far East, especially when pitted militarily against Uncle Sam. Such terms, varying as to the conflict, have existed since the 1930s. Not that you have to be American to proselytize the canard. Russians use **kosoglzye**: 'squint-eyed', or 'cross-eyed' and **uzkoglzye**: 'slant-eyes' in just the same way. Marginally less opprobrious are America's **almond-eye** and **li'l-eyes** (not to be confused with the cant *short-eyes:* a child molestor). **Squint-eyes** echoes the Russian while **moon-eyed leper** mingles physique with disease. The opposite term,

roundeye, is used by Orientals, and American Blacks, to mean a Caucasian or Westerner (in America it can also mean the anus, irrespective of colour).

The skewed image persists in the wider world, thus for film crews the term *Chinese* is used when the *barn doors* (adjustable flaps fitted to a light) are adjusted to diffuse light through horizontal slits, reminiscent once more of those sinister, slitted eyes. The concept also underpins the aviator's **Chinese landing**, a landing in which one wing is lower than the other and which both puns on the Oriental sound of the words 'one wing low' and makes the usual racial equation of Chinese as meaning off-angle or unstable. The flyer who makes suhc a landing is a **Chinese ace**. A similar contruction, at least as to the pun, comes in Australia's **chinese consumption** denoting a sufferer with smoker's cough or 'wun bung lung'. It also provides a couple of pieces of cricketing jargon. A **Chinese cut**, blending Chinese wiliness with another supposed Chinese attribute, undeserved luck, is a glancing stroke, quite probably intended to go in another direction, which edges the ball between the stumps and the fielders and earns lucky runs.

One final 'eye' reference leaves China for the US, to the Appalachian mountains, America's poorest area. An Appalachian is known cruelly as **one-eye**, a reference that, at least according to the *Dictionary of American Slang*, points up the inbreeding of these isolated mountain communities: generations of incestuous lust has supposedly bred a tribe whose eyes are unnaturally close together.

From the eyes to the nose, and before moving to the masters of nasal excess, the Jews, one should note **nickel-nose** and **Pinochio**, both of whom are Italians, the second of which recalls the anthropomorphic puppet (whose nose expands the harder he lies) in the story by Carlo Lorenzini. The **Roman nose**, a relatively desirable appendage, is one that has a prominent bridge. In the anglophone West Indies **straight nose** is a European. A **blue-nose**, a Black term for White people, is on the one hand the result of icy weather on pink flesh, on the other a synonym for a Puritan; the image underpinning both is of chilliness. A blue-nose can also be a native of Nova Scotia (or one of their fishing vessels) and a purplish potato grown in the same area. The puritanical reference is to the notorious 'blue laws', passed by New England's religious fanatics in the late 18th century. Still in America, the flat 'African' nose of some Blacks gives **broad-nose**. The slang term *beezer* or *bezer* has meant nose since the early 20th century, thus **black beezer** is occasionally used for Black face.

'The Jew is written all over his face', declares the German saying, backed up by a Silesian rhyme which translates, in every sense roughly: 'Jew Ikey, nose spiky, nose pointy, nose shitty'. Terms that equate the Jew and his nose are legion. On a physical level, only circumcision is an equally infallible guide to the semite in our midst. In no special order one can choose from Russia's **zhidovskaya morda**: Jewish snout, America's **hook, hooknose, banana-nose** and **eagle-beak** (not, of course, to be confused in any way with the proud aquilinity of the Roman nose) and **schnozzole** or **schnozzola**, best known for its application to the comedian Jimmy 'Schnozzle' Durante, (1893-1980), whose Italian surname, if nothing else, proves that physiognomy and ethnicity are not always so easily linked. Schnozzle comes from the Yiddish *shnoitsl* and, in turn, from German *Schnauze*, both meaning snout. The big nose imagery extends into nature, where Australia's **Jew lizard** has an especially prominent snout, while in America the **jew-bird** is a nickname for the ani, a type of cuckoo, with an arched and laterally compressed bill, and the **jewcrow** is the chough, another bird with a big bill. A **Jew wattle** is a coloured skin projection on the carrier pigeon's bill (*wattle* itself meant ear in 18th-century slang) and a **Jew monkey** a type of macaque, once again sporting an outsize nose. Finally **jew nail**, in Poland, is a small headless nail of corrugated sheet metal almost as wide as it is long.

A phrase more usually associated with another organ – it's not how big it is but how you use it – underpins a last pair of nose-related terms. The German **einen Polnischen machen**: 'to do a Polish' and the Provençal **moucade dous alemans**: 'German nose-blowing' both mean exactly the same: blowing one's nose not into a handkerchief, but into one's hand.

Nose for Jews, thick lips for Blacks. Thus **bootlips, bongo-lips, saucer-lips** (with an added reference to the lip-plates sported by certain African tribes) and **thick-lips** all mean Black. America's **shad mouth** (resembling the shad, a fish) is a person with a large upper lip and thus a Black person. **Nigger tone** and **nigger vibrato** both mean a low buzz produced by the throat muscles on a wind instrument. The verb **nigger-lip** means to moisten the tip of one's cigarette while smoking, an act especially frowned upon among marijuana users, where the communal joint passes from mouth to mouth. Still smoking, the **French inhale** refers to the act of exhaling smoke and then inhaling it back through the nose; this seemingly grotesque manoeuvre is apparently attributed to the alleged sophistication of the French. For Italians, to smoke heavily is **fumare come un turco**: to smoke like a Turk. Next to the lips comes the mouth and while buck teeth, at least in France, are **dents à l'anglaise**: English teeth, a **Dutch oven**, most commonly a large pot heated by surrounding it with fuel, and placing hot coals on the lid, can also be a mouth. Not only that – it can also be the smell of a bed in which someone has just farted. A fart itself is a **Scotch warming pan** (although the object in question can also be an accommodating young woman). An **Irish** or **Irishman's fart**, in America, is an Irish immigrant, because, like the bodily function they're 'always making a lot of noise, raising a stink and never want to go back where they came from.' In France **rêver la suisse**: 'to dream in Swiss fashion', is to gaze into mid-air with gaping mouth and bulging eyes.

Continuing the downwards journey, a **Spanish beard** can be a lengthy beard, as well as a species of moss, while any piece of notable face-fungus in Germany is a **Schweizerbart**: a Swiss beard. A **beardie** is a Jewish convert to Christianity, so-called because, while he was happy to accept a Christian God, he was less so to shear his facial hair, once a sign of piety. Beneath the beard the neck, and in Germany again a **Judenapfel** is what English calls the Adam's apple. **Redneck** or just plain **neck** has been in use in the US since the early 19th century. Although today's kneejerk definition turns on porcine Southern sheriffs beating hapless civil rights protestors, or no-brain religious maniacs shooting pro-abortion medicos, the term, in its earliest incarnation *c*.1830, held no such pejoratives. By the late-19th century, however, the low-rent, bigoted image was in place and it has stayed. The term comes, apparently, from the sunburnt necks of such figures, who were primarily agricultural labourers. South Africa's cognate **rooïnek** (Cape Dutch for redneck and coined nearly a century later) refers to the country's

English immigrants. Its original reference was to a brand of merino sheep imported into the Orange Free State by an English farmer; this was transferred to the red-coated British soldiers of the Boer War, and latterly to any English settler.

Have you Heard the German Band?

Moving through **American shoulders** (a tailoring term that refers to the square cut of a coat emphasizing the breadth of the shoulders à la movie gangster) one reaches the arm. Here the humerus or funny bone, whether German or French, takes on a Jewish aspect. In Germany it is the **Judenbeinchen**: the Jewbone, while in France it is **le petit juif**: the little Jew. The **Jew bone**, however, is the sacrum, also known as the *resurrection bone* and more properly as one of the bones forming the dorsal wall of the pelvis. Hands are **German bands**, at least in rhyming slang (where ethnicity also presumes some burly peasant's *maulers*), while the **Australian grip** is a handshake that feels a bit too cordial for the shakee's comfort. In Russian **Polish fingers**, symbolizing the typical Polish peasant, are unmanicured, work-coarsened fingers.

To look, as it were, at the big picture, body-related terminology can refer to large and small, fat and thin, pretty or plain. A **Dutch build** implies a squat, stocky figure; the Germans translate **Hollanderei** as both dairy-farming and a large female bosom; thus the phrase **Sie hat ei tüchtige Hollanderei**. The image persists in Danish and Norwegian where one meets the phrase **tjukk aom en hollaender**: fat as a Dutchman. Around 1700 nearby Belgium offered **flanderkin**, properly an inhabitant of Flanders, to describe a fat man. Black America's **Bahama Mama** stigmatizes a fat, unattractive 'Black Mammy', supposedly typical of the West Indies, and the US also offers **German aunt** for a fat, frumpish woman. A **French aunt**, on the other hand, and albeit predictably, is flighty and attractive. The Yiddish **zaftig**, meaning plump or well-rounded and originating in the German *saftig*: juicy, is applied to an overweight girl, although such girls appeal greatly to what slang terms *chubby-chasers*. A **German goitre** is a beer-belly as is a **Milwaukee goitre** (a reference to the American brewing city and indirectly to Schlitz 'the beer that made Milwaukee famous'). From large to small, and in France **rabourgris**, literally 're-Bulgarized', means one of arrested, stunted growth, as does **azteque**: Aztec, while a **Lapon** or Lapp is a dwarf. In Rumania **jidov**, a Jew, means a giant, while **narrowback**, in America, is yet another synonym for Irishman.

Nor are good looks immune. While America's **Greek**, elsewhere the source of number of sexual references, is an adjective that implies fine physical form and facial beauty (taking its imagery from classical Greek sculpture), and the phrase **like a trojan** (the individual in question being the hero Hector, in Homer's *Iliad*) implies great strength, endurance and energy, things are not invariably positive. **Turner** (a reference to the *Turnverein*, the popular athletic or gymnastic societies attended by many German Americans), also meant fit and healthy, but for all the touted attraction of its sculptured bodies linked in mass calisthenics, there was a sinister side to this so-called 'sport'. The *Turnen* (literally 'body contortions') movement was itself deeply nationalist. Founded by Frederick Ludwig Jahn (1778-1852), known as the *Turnvater* or 'contortion father', it was a direct response to Napoleon's occupation of Germany and asserted hard, Germanic sport in the face of supposedly decadent team games. To perform these exercises, often to a background of torchlight parades and similar near-pagan festivals, was to demonstrate one's loyalty to the state. A parallel movement, heavily influenced by the turners was the *Nordische Freikörperkultur*, a cult of physical beauty which, as the author Ian Buruma has pointed out (in *The Missionary & the Libertine*, 1996), reached its apotheosis under the Nazis, with their obsession with perfect Aryan flesh (and its downside, the dismissal of all and any alternatives).

Not strictly physical perhaps, but certainly falling the realms of attractiveness, is **Wop**, which, along with **Eyetie**, is perhaps the most commonly used term for an Italian. It most probably comes from *guappo*, a Neapolitan and Sicilian word that is best translated as dude, fop, dandy or swell; this in turn is synonymous with 'good-looking' and goes back to Latin *vappa*, literally translated as sour wine and thus, figuratively, a worthless fellow. Wop, without an article, can also mean the Italian language, and it is of course frequent as an adjective. The term originated in New York around 1910 and one of its earliest uses was to describe Italian gangsters, especially those who worked as pimps. In 1914 Jackson and Hellyer's important *Vocabulary of Criminal Slang* defined wop as 'an ignorant person; a foreigner; an impossible character...' although there is an argument – on the basis of their citation – that they actually missed the ethnic side of the word. **Wopstick**, a showbiz term, means a clarinet, underpinning the popularity of the instrument among American-Italian jazz musicians; **Wopland**, as one would assume, is Italy.

Dutch Pegs and German Flutes

Dutch pegs and **Scotch pegs** are both legs, although the reference is more to satisfy the demands of rhyming slang than from any direct racial assumption. Rhyming slang also equates **German flutes** with boots, although the relevant meaning here has no rhyme, but simply means thin legs. Both **Irish legs** and **Irish arms** mean thick, heavy legs. The 18th-century slang lexicographer Francis Grose, whose own substantial physique was best summed up in his surname, suggested that 'It is said of Irish women that they have a special dispensation from the Pope to wear the thick end of their leg downwards.' (Grose, unashamedly a man of his politically incorrect age, also gave the judiciously bowdlerized definition 'C—t: a nasty name for a nasty thing'.) Still in Ireland, **redshanks** means a Celt, an allusion to the colour of bare legs reddened by exposure to wind and weather (although **red-shanks** and **red leg**, both mean a poor White in Barbados). For the French, Italian legs are obviously particularly risible. **Avoir les jambes en italique** is to be bandy-legged, and **pincer les jambes** is to stagger around, another slur on Italy. In an ironic reversal on the usual 'slanted' imagery to **walk in Chinese fashion** is to walk single file (otherwise known as **Indian file**), and in Australia the **Chinkie-jog** or **Chinaman's trot** once referred to a horse's slow but steady trot, a nod, presumably, to the steady pacing of Australia's Chinese immigrants. Neither leg nor body, but somewhere in between, the **Australian flag** is a shirt-tail rucked up between trousers and waistcoat.

Feet offer few examples, although **long-heel** refers to an African American and America's fundamentalist Baptists were once known as footwashers, from the religious rite whereby Primitive Baptists wash each other's feet, as commanded in *John* 13:14 'If I then, your Lord and Master, have washed your feet, ye also ought to wash one another's feet.' **Flatfoot**, also known at various times as a slang term for a soldier, a sailor and a policeman, has also stood muster as an immigrant – whether Irish or German. The large representation of Irishmen in the 19th-century New York police force underpins the former while the latter were known as the **flat-footed Dutch** (i.e. *Deutsch*).

Siamese Twins

Given the primacy of the genitals, whether male or female, in main-stream slang, *down there* as one of many euphemisms has it, is remark-ably under-represented in racial terminology. At least, that is, in their non-sexual aspect. This is dealt with properly elsewhere (see *Sex*).

For Poles, both Tatars and Jews are **obrzezaniec** or **obrzynek**: 'a circumcised one', while in France the testicles are **les Siamois**: 'the Siamese twins'. Jews, in any case, are not seen as overtly sexual crea-tures, or at least not threatening ones. Other than the **Jewish compli-ment**: a large penis but no money (although gay use defines it simply as a circumcized penis), the position is best summed up in the middle European saying: 'If the Jew is of gold, his testicles are of copper'. The one mysterious and possibly specious link is the use of the term **goolie** to mean Icelander. Goolies, most likely from the Hindi *gol*: a bullet, ball or pill or possibly from the UK dialect *gullies*: marbles, seems to have no simple link to this chilly northern island. In the warmer climes of South Africa **soutpiel**: literally 'salt-dick' is an English immigrant who is described as having one foot in South Africa, one in England and his penis dangling in the ocean in between. Finally, a single reference to women: in France **avoir ses anglais** is to have one's period. The phrase supposedly reflects the role of the pre-War (and indeed post-War) English as regular visitors to France.

Uriahs beauteous Wife
Made David seek his Life

SEX

SEX, ESPECIALLY for those nations reared beneath the shadow of the Judaeo-Christian myths, and all the dark threats they pose when faced with the thought of untrammelled pleasure, is a wonderful source of inter-racial hatreds. If making love is seen, for whatever reason, as a sin, then those who not only enjoy it, but actually permit themselves to be seen enjoying it, and perhaps worst of all, are not ashamed to admit the fact, are surely open to chastisement. In the context of this book, that chastisement is of course strictly verbal; in the wider world it can reveal itself in more painful incarnations.

Given the general popularity of love-making – among the people if not the priesthood – it might be felt that of all the racial, stereotypes those involving sex would be, at least within this context, relatively enviable. Yet it is not so; the opposite impetus is if anything the rule. Once the world of nationalisms grasps a topic, it is unlikely to embellish it in a positive manner. Thus sex, ostensibly a pleasure, is rendered, if not a pain, then at least a threat. Dirty, diseased, dangerous – like any other of the stereotypes that delineate racial types, it is not one with which one would wish to be associated.

Hotter than French Love

While the race/sex equation is best seen in the context of centuries-old fantasies as regards the supposed insatiability of Black sexuality, and its concomitant threat (and allure) to Whites, especially White women, in linguistic terms, it is the French who seem to attract the most opprobrium when it comes to sex. Perhaps it is the very fact that the French, in Puritan eyes, have no excuses. Unlike the bestial 'darkies', whose men, wielding outsize members, yearn for constant release, and whose brutalized women fall naturally into the role of slut, breeding a mongrel race that will undermine the very foundations of social order, the French are White, they are western, they are European, and they should not be so willingly ensnared in the sins of the flesh.

Indeed, although for anglophones there were undoubtedly 'French' words contingent upon that nation's role as England's national enemy – an image that was intensified by the supposed (and genuine) horrors of the French Revolution and reached its peak during the Napoleonic wars that succeeded it – the great weight of such terms has evolved during a period when the French, while perhaps not truly loved, have been at least nominally allies. And these terms, almost invariably, hinge upon one of the great nationalistic stereotypes: the French and sex. At best they are obsessed with it, at worst their entire culture is presented as downright pornographic and 'dirty'. 'As sluttish and slatternly as an Irishwoman bred in France' runs the Irish saying, and the target does not lie on the Dublin side of the Irish sea.

Quite why this should be is debatable. In the first place the French are mercifully influenced by the Mediterrnanean culture of the South (a culture that focusses not on the chilly, puritanical Protestantism of the north but on the somewhat more flexible world that seems to exist in Roman Catholic countries). This finds sex so much less terrifying than do, say, the British or Americans. One need only glance at the output of two of the greatest novelists of the 19th century: England's Dickens and France's Balzac. The former can deal with idealized mothers and comical charwomen; he is rendered as gauche as a teenage boy at his first dance when facing the complexities of flesh-and-blood female sexuality. Indeed, such figures are virtually absent from his pages. Balzac exhibits quite the reverse: his women, be they actress-courtesans, provincial social climbers, *grandes horizontales*, housewives or mothers are genuinely three-dimensional. Dickens' less than saintly private life must have pointed out the realities quite clearly, but Victorian Britain could not countenance such honesty. In England the word liberty, especially sexual liberty, is easily conflated with libertine.

But the stereotype was in place some time before Dickens. Henry Fielding, narrating his novel *Tom Jones* (1749), notes that 'I am so far from desiring to exhibit such Pictures to the Public' and compares the forbidden plates to those that appear 'in certain French novels.' But if Fielding, and after him such writers as Thackeray (who railed against the immorality of **French prints**) or Robert Browning ('My scrofulous French novel | On grey paper with blunt type!' *Bells and Pomegranates*, 1842) kept the flame alive, it took World War I, and the arrival of British, Imperial, and perhaps most importantly American troops in real-life France, to make the label properly stick. There they met **Ou-la-la girls** and **Madamoizooks**: French women of a flirtatious bent and doubtless related not too distantly to that other charmer and subject of the war's most widely sung lyrics, **Mademoiselle from Armenteers** ('she hasn't been fucked for forty years'). 'How do you keep 'em down on the farm, after they've seen Paree?' ran another popular song, but you (or rather economics) did and back on some Mid-Western prairie they sweated beneath the sun and told their knowing buddies that the day was **hotter than French love**. Unsurprisingly the French, disdainful of the dough-boys' nods and winks, used the adjective **americain** to describe ogling, leering, 'goo-goo eyes'.

And 'French love' itelf, was something a euphemism. Of all the clichés that bind France to sex, the nation's supposed predilection for oral sex is perhaps the strongest. The verb **to French** arrives in the slang dictionaries – the mainstream works were still far too prudish – in the early 1960s. Its currency must have been much earlier – American troops talked about **the French way** in 1917 – although such terms as *eat* (1927), and *blow* (1933) preceded it, at least for lexicographers. The synonymous *go down* emerged during World War I (in 1916). Its more rarified version, the mutually satisfying *soixante-neuf* or 'sixty-nine' appeared in 1888, when one P. Perret explained that 'In familiar language this divine variant of pleasure is called: *faire soixante-neuf* (literally, 'to do 69').' (Thus the facetious *68*: 'you suck me and I'll owe you one'.) It is in that same year that *fellatio*, still the 'respectable' word for **Frenching** also appears, defined by the notorious publisher Leonard Smithers (1861-1907, a friend *inter alia* of Wilde and Beardsley and characterized as 'the most learned erotomaniac in Europe') in his translation of Forberg's *Manual of Classical Erotology* thus: 'The verge [penis, from Latin *virga*: a rod], introduced into the mouth, wants to be tickled either by the lips or the tongue, and sucked; the party who does this service... is a fellator or sucker.'

It had had two notable predecessors. Irrumation, still to be seen in the older medical textbooks, came from the Latin *irrumare*, a word found in the works of the poet Catullus. Thus in his sixteenth poem he writes 'Pedicabo ego vos et irrumabo | Aureli pathice et cinaede Furi... As translated by J. P. Goold (Loeb Classical Library, 1987) this runs 'I'll bugger you and stuff you, you catamite Aurelius and you pervert Furius...'. 'Stuffing' in this context may not specifically describe fellatio, but for the next few centuries it served, at least as medical jargon. By the mid-19th century a new word, *gamahuche* or *gamaruche* (which gives the modern slang *gam*: to fellate) had emerged. A direct steal from the synonymous French it became the word of choice in such classics of Victorian pornography as *My Secret Life* or Edward Sellon's wonderfully titled *The New Epicurean; or, The Delights of Sex, Facetiously and Philosophically Considered, in Graphic Letters Addressed to Young Ladies of Quality* (1865): ' "Quick, quick, Blanche!" cried Cerise [Sellon's nubile heroine], "come and gamahuche the gentleman".' (Sellon [1818-66], a soldier turned hack writer, and whose other works included *The New Lady's Tickler; or, the Adventure of Lady Lovesport and the Audacious Harry* and who in 1866 entitled his autobiography *The Ups and Downs of Life*, also offers the dictionary early citations for *cunny* and *frig*). Its corollary was **minetting** (i.e. cunnilingus, and once more taken from a French word, meaning literally 'little kitty' and thus linked to such English slang synonyms as *kitty*, *pussy* and *puss*).

Such coyness aside, in the sphere of oral sex 'French' and variations upon it dominate the sexual vocabulary, especially in America. Fellatio itself gives **the French art, French culture, French tricks** and a

French head job. A **French language expert** or one who was **French by injection**, terms from an older, pre-gay liberation gay vocabulary, described anyone considered particularly well-versed in fellatio; to **speak French** was to enjoy any variation on 'straight' sex, while the **French active** was the passive or sucked partner of a fellatory pair. Still in the gay world of the 1940s and 1950s, **French language training** was to teach one's partner fellatio, a **French abortion** described the ejaculated semen, spat out by those who preferred not to swallow it. To **tell a French joke**, however, is to indulge in anilingus, the licking not of the phallus but of the anus.

Not that oral sex is the only subject of 'French love'. The **French letter**, the **French safe**, the **frog** and the **French tickler** all mean a condom, the last featuring extra protrusions for added stimulation. The French hit back with **capote anglaise**, 'an English hood'. **La vice anglaise**, of course, is flagellation (usually enjoyed as a recipient), supposedly imbibed by every upper class **rosbif** across his public school prefect's knee. **Dancer à l'anglaise**: 'to dance in the English style', refers to up-market whores who pretend that they are off to the opera or to a ball, but actually leave their carriage at a restaurant where they solicit clients. **Mariage à l'anglais**: an English marriage arrangement is one in which, soon after the wedding, the partners take up lives in separate domiciles. It is employed also to describe a period of living together after no more than a casual meeting, as at a dance. **Frenchy**, another term for condom can also mean a White slave (espeically in the East) and White slave – a girl forced into prostitution, a story that gave tabloid fodder to the early 20th century – itself is worthy of comment, not so much as a term of abuse, but as regards the defining addition of the term 'White'. A Black slave is simply a slave; such, one might feel, was the natural order of things – no colour qualification was apparently deemed necessary.

Other terms include the **French article**: a prostitute (like **French goods**, meaning syphilis, it can also mean brandy), and **French curves** (usually a drawing instrument which permits the drawing of non-circular curves), a shapely figure. A **French kiss** is a deep kiss, using the tongue as well as the lips (also known as a **soul kiss**) and a **French kiss filter** is any filter-tipped cigarette. **French dip** is vaginal precoital fluid, and **French dressing** semen. Those last two are once more archaic American homosexual jargon, as is the **French embassy**, a YMCA where homosexual activity is extensive and unchecked, a **French photographer** (a gay photographer) and, more recently, the **French revolution**: the movement for homosexual rights. Finally, a **French postcard** is a pornographic picture, regardless of its real origin, and **French stuff** is either pornography or any sexual activity judged 'unusual'.

'They Cohabit with their Sisters'

The obsession with Black sexuality, and the threat it presents, is as old as European contacts with Africa. Travellers as early as the 12th century were reporting on 'the sons of Ham' who 'like animals...go about naked and have not the intelligence of ordinary men. They cohabit with their sisters and anyone they can find...'. By the 16th century the fantasy was widespread. Shakespeare's *Othello*, with its 'black ram tupping your White ewe' may, given the lack of actual Blacks in contemporary England, be interpreted as a comment on class rather than racial tension, but the image is unmistakable. The concupiscent, rutting Black stud, with his outsize penis (that myth seems to have come on stream around 1620, when another explorer talked of Mandingo men whose 'members are...burthensome to them') was a staple of fearful fascination. It would take the 19th century, however, to bring such fears into real prominence, with its ever-expanding European colonization of the 'Dark Continent' and, across the Atlantic, the American obsession with the twin myths of the rapist Black slave (or ex-slave) and his helpless prey, the virgin White 'belle'.

In both arenas, the already tricky relations between the races were exacerbated by the role of sexuality. The White missionaries, descending like spiritual locusts on African culture, loathed what they saw as open, unrestrained and thus immoral African sexuality. That tribes had age-old, complex systems of boundary and taboo meant nothing to these earnest votaries of the Cross. Religion was less bothersome in America; there the impetus was simple fear. The Black 'buck' had to be castrated, both metaphorically, and often in bloody fact. Between

1889-99 there was one lynching every day in the American South, ninety per cent of the victims being alleged 'black rapists'. And in both cases sexual repression, whatever its proclaimed justification, served as a convenient addendum to the greater need: social repression.

Linguistically, the emphasis is definitely on female sexuality rather than male. Logically enough in a system where Black men were to be marginalized as far as possible, while Black women were seen as freely available to White men. Thus one finds a wide range of references to the female genitals: **black jack** (although this can also refer, in gay parlance, to the penis), **black joke, black maria** (also a black prostitute), **black meat** and **black mouth**. **Black bagging** refers to the pursuit of Black women. As noted in *Food* (above) **Dark meat** and **brown sugar** both deal with black women unified into one amorphous sex object. Still in a food idiom, **love chocolate** is a White person who specializes in Black partners. (**Love vanilla**, logically, reverses the partnership.) Other terms include the uncompromising **nigger wench** (18th century) and **black bitch**, plus **dinge-broad** (from dinge and the slang *broad*: a woman) and **poontang**, a word that means both a Black girl and a vagina and which comes from the French *putain*:a whore. **Jungle fever**, a term originally coined for the White man's desire to have sex with Black women, has been reversed (as seen in the title of Spike Lee's 1991 movie) to describe the same emotion, but with the Black man and the White woman as the protagonists. Dealing with men, a **black pencil** is a Black penis as is a **black pudding**. Amongst Hells Angels getting one's **black wings**, according to Hunter Thompson's celebrated study of the outlaw bikers (*Hell's Angels* 1969), refers to the initiatory rite (a positive compendium of White male fears) of performing cunnilingus on a menstruating Black woman. Native Americans, while more usually vilified as drunks, give the students' punning **Pawnee Indian**: a sexual inadequate who 'paws' his unfortunate partner. (The actual Pawnees occupied lands near the Loup, Platte and Republican River valleys in Nebraska).

Such language is by no means restricted to America. In Australia, where **nigger** is (or at least was) used to refer to the Aborigines or Native Australians, **black velvet** (otherwise known as a mixture of Guinness and champagne) refers to Black women, specifically in a sexual context. A **creamy piece** or a **Darwin blonde** is a half-Aboriginal girl, once again viewed as sexually available. The word **gin**, meaning Black woman and taken from the Native Australian language Dharuk *diyin*: woman and also (quite coincidentally) an abbreviation for *Aborigine*, gives a number of terms. **Gin-banger, gin-burglar, gin-cuddler, gin-dozzler, gin-hunter, gin-jockey, gin-masher** and **gin-stealer** all refer to White men whose preferred sexual partner is a Black woman. Only the **gin-shepherd**, usually some form of missionary, who attempted on moral grounds to keep the races apart, stands out from the group. A cognate phrase, the dismissive **weak as gin's piss**, refers to thin beer, among other drinks, and is Australia's take on the English equivovalent: *cat's, gnat's* or *horse piss*. Occasionally, in the early 19th century, the term **White gin**: a White woman, is found.

Africa itself offers relatively few terms. An **African queen** is either a Black homosexual or, on the model of *size queen* or *felch queen* (where the adjective refers to the sexual taste rather than to the person) a White homosexual who prefers Black partners. An **Egyptian queen** means much the same, but the image is of a proud and stately person. (Keeping up the pattern, a **rainbow queen** is someone who likes mixed-race sex.) In 19th-century Britain a **City Road African** was a prostitute working on the City Road, one of a sisterhood whose numbers had included over the years the *Bankside lady, Covent Garden nun, Drury Lane vestal, Fleet Street dove, Fulham virgin, Haymarket ware, St John's Wood vestal* and a *Whetstone Park Deer*, a succession of slang terms in which the names changed as did the focus of London street whoring, moving gradually north from the stews of Southwark. Quite why she should be termed an 'African' remains a matter of mystery, other than that perhaps the City Road, for many customers, would be a relatively 'undiscovered continent' compared to the more traditional red light zones of London's West End. In Guyana in the West Indies, to **go back to Africa** is for a light-skinned man to marry a woman whose complexion is much darker than his own, while a **chachundar** (from Hindi *chhachuudar*: a mole or shrew) is used by those of Indian descent to describe an Indian woman who has close friendship or even a child with a Black man.

The Cleopatra Clip

Still far beyond European shores, the East (always good for a little exotica) provides a few terms. America's **China doll** makes the obvious pun in its description of a Chinese girl (more likely an immigrant than anyone encountered *in situ*), while India gives the Australian **Indian dick**: a long, thin sausage. **India** itself means the female genitals, presumably from the inverted triangular shape of the sub-continent, reminiscent of pubic hair.

Like those of any black or brown-skinned races, Japanese women have been casually categorized as being, if not actual whores, then freely available. Thus the American navy blithely termed such women as **skibby** or occasionally **skippy**. Both terms are rooted in the Japanese *sukibei*: randy or lecherous. It had also meant a courtesan and the sense was extended, after its dilution, to mean 'loose' or 'unchaste'. In American mouths it tended to refer to a female domestic servant, but the seeming synonymity of the term skivvy, also a maid-of-all-work, may in fact be coincident. A similar term, **moose**, was used to describe a young Japanese or Korean woman, especially the wife or mistress of a serviceman stationed in Japan or Korea. Based in the Japanese *musume*: daughter or girl, it had also begun life meaning prostitute but had, at least in Japanese, lost this pejorative overtone and meant any girl or woman. **Geechee, geechie** or **gheechee**, used by Americans to describe Pacific Islanders, may have its roots in the Japanese *geisha*: a female entertainer or, loosely, a prostitute. (**Geechee** or **geech** is also used in the US to refer to Southern African Americans, the root lying in the Ogeechee River, Georgia, where the local dialect, similar to Gullah, the dialect spoken by Blacks living on the sea-islands and tide-water coastline of South Carolina and Georgia, is also known as *geechee*).

Moving gradually west from Japan one reaches **Babylon**, defined in the *OED* as 'a magnificent city, once the capital of the Chaldee Empire; also, the mystical Babylon of the Apocalypse; whence, in modern times, applied polemically to Rome or the papal power, and rhetorically to any great and luxurious city'. Babylon, hanging gardens notwithstanding, has suffered a bad press for many years and for all its former magnificence has been a synonym for 'glamorous vice and magnificent de-bauchery', at least in English, since the early 16th century. Then Protestants, seeking to pillory the Church of Rome, compared its rule with the **Babylonian captivity**, properly that of the Jews some two millennia earlier. A century later, the Church is assailed again when a preacher declares that 'the Scarlet-whore of Babylon spawnd it with her menstruous profluviums'. Babylon could also refer, erroneously, to the tower of Babel (its root, as far as has been ascertained is the Assyrian *bab-ilu*: the gate of God) and in 1816 the etymologist James Gilchrist attacked the work of his predecessor Samuel Johnson as a 'kind of Babylonish lexicography'. More recently **Babylon** has been featured in Rastafarian iconography as the world of (White, Western) oppression, to be set against the promized Ethiopian land of Zion. Specifically Babylon means the police, both in Jamaica and Britain. Less threatening, and most immediate is the punning American teenage **babylon**, pronounced babe-y-lon, and as such a place where attractive young girls (*babes* in slang) are to be found.

The Middle East also offers **bint**, a young girl; the Arabic word for daughter *bint* was picked up by travellers and latterly soldiers. When used in English, and outside the Arabic context, it tends to be dismissive, if not actually derogatory. **Keifer**, as in 'have a bit of keifer' or have sexual intercourse, is another term that probably comes from Arabic, in this case *keyif*: 'the amiable beauty of a fair woman'. Not exactly Arabic, but certainly Middle Eastern, is the **Cleopatra clip**, named for the infamous Queen of Egypt and on offer in louche bars across the world: it is an example of muscular control whereby a woman can pick up objects – coins, cigarettes – with her vagina. (It was this trick, supposedly, that endeared Mrs Simpson to King Edward VIII). Finally the mid-16th to early 18th century term **bardache**: a male homosexual, comes first from the standard English *bardash*: a catamite, itself probably linked to the Arabic *bardaj*: a slave. Araby, to use a suitably romantic description, is also responsible for **sheik**, properly an Arab term meaning tribal chieftain, but adopted in America, at least during the 1920s, to mean 'lady-killer', womaniser or romantic lover. The whole fantasy of hawk-faced desert warriors, sweeping away innocent Western women only to arouse their heaving breasts (and much more – albeit unwritten and certainly unfilmed – besides) stems from E.M. Hull's wildly romantic novel *The Sheik*. Published in 1919 it was filmed two years later, starring Rudolph Valentino, *the* Latin lover of the period. When he died in 1926, aged barely 31, grieving fans would toss themselves into his grave; in the interim they simply added the title of his hit movie to the national vocabulary.

Cut-Cocks and Clip-Dicks

Predictably, the role of the Jew in this area of language is linked to the penis, the circumcision of which is seen as defining the male Jew's image as regards sexuality. Thus, starting with the Latin **curtius Judaeus**: 'the curtailed Jew', such terms include **clip(ped)-dick**, **snipcock** (coined by Britain's *Private Eye* magazine), **cut-cock** and **skinless**. The US gay lexicon offers a **Jewish compliment**, a **Jew's lance**, **Jewish corned beef** and **Jewish National**, which last refers to America's Hebrew National brand of kosher salami. One who is circumcized but not Jewish is **Jewish by hospitalization**. A **Jewish nightcap** is the missing foreskin. Finally there is **Abraham**, an acknowledgement of the oldest of the Jewish patriarchs.

Abraham's bosom, however, refers not to the penis but to the female genitals, and refers to the New rather than the Old Testament, specifically *Luke* xvi. 22, where the phrase is used to describe 'the abode of the blessed dead'. It is the 'lying on' inference, with its image of sexual intercourse, that counts. As far as the Jewish woman is concerned her image underpins the way in which racist stereotyping demands (and creates) extremes, even contradictory ones. She can be a wanton slut, from whose lascivious eyes no simple *goy* is safe, and almost simultaneously a frigid, sexless, castrating *kvetch* or 'nag'. Thus while the Poles talk leeringly of **Żydoweczka**: a darling Jewess (the coarser **Żydówicka**, however, means simply 'Jew woman'), and their American cousins once hymned the **kosher cutie** (using dietary laws to identify an entire race), the Hungarian saying declares that **He, whose sweetheart is a Jewish girl, | should tie a rope around his neck and whirl**; and the popular joke defines **Jewish foreplay** as 'the man pleads for sex, his partner refuses all physical contact'. And if the most alluring

of all Balzac's courtesans is the Jewish Esther (errant, beautiful, ultimately tragic daughter of the miser Gobseck), the **JAP**, or **Jewish
American Princess** (all shopping, no fucking), is the fount of myriad
jokes. 'What does a JAP do with her arsehole? Send him off to work
every morning'. 'Why does the JAP like sex doggy-style? She hates to
see anyone else having a good time.'

The Russian Blessing

As far as sexuality is concerned, Russia is relatively restrained, offering
only **elds**: 'prick', 'cock' as a derogatory synonym for a native of
Kazakhstan or a member of any of the other Central Asian peoples (a
group also termed **black-arses**. However, Central Europe exhibits a
number of versions of what is loosely known as the **Russian blessing**:
a verb form accompanied by the words for 'your mother'.' e.g. **idi u
picku materinu**: 'go (in)to your mother's cunt'. A synonym for the
American English *motherfucker*, it echoes the Afro-American *dozens* or
mamma's game, a form of ritualized insulting in which the participants
take it in turn to attack each other's mother. A Rumanian version of the
'blessing' is translated 'go climb up your mother's cunt with your cock
in pieces'; Yiddish returns to euphemism with **russisher mi-she-
beyrakh**: a 'Russian blessing'. Less abrupt is the catch-all term **Balkan
prince**, characterizing a romantically adventurous prince from one of
the small Balkan states as depicted in operettas and musical comedy.
Whether many such charming **lotharios** (itself somewhat racist, given
the Italianate style of the name) are in fact princes, other than in their
own minds, is of course open to speculation.

If the Poles are seen as peasants in other form of stereotyping, than
as far as sex goes they appear as easy-going, sluttish even, tending to
short-lived relationships, notably devoid of 'benefit of clergy'. And the
image offers one area where for once Poles and their generally loathed
neighbours the Jews, who lived amongst and alongside them, were
forced into the same position. Their Lithuanian or Russian sisters
showed little solidarity when they described a Polish peer (whether
Jewish or Christian) as **poilishe dripke**: a Polish slattern. The same
image appears in Germany's **pulke** or **Polsche** (both dialect terms)

meaning literally a Polish woman, but in practice a slut. The image crossed the Atlantic to Argentina where **polacca**, once more 'a Polish woman', meant a prostitute, a term that gained some justification from the numbers of Polish girls recruited (whether voluntarily or as 'White slaves') into the brothels of Buenos Aires. The apparent predominance in Polish society of what modern census takers would term POSSLQs (persons of the opposite sex sharing living quarters) gives the Scandinavian **polsk ekteskap**: literally 'Polish marriage', but meaning concubinage, and **polsk forbandt**: a 'Polish bond' and thus a fleeting attachment. **Leve paa polsk**: 'to live (together) in Polish style' meant to live as common law husband and wife. The German term **flandrische Liebe**: 'Flanders love' credits Belgium with equally short-lived affections. Thus also Britain's **Scotch marriage**. While on matters Scandinavian, a **Swedish headache** refers to abdominal pains resulting from sexual excitement, a problem that is more usually apostrophized in slang as *blue balls*.

Neither the Germans nor the Italians, for all the latter's identification with womanizing, feature substantially here. A **German helmet** is the glans penis (thus **polish the old German helmet** means to perform oral sex), while the Latin **libido Suevorum** is translated as Swabian lust, a reference to the supposed appetites of the natives of that German duchy, now absorbed into Baden-Württemberg and part of Bavaria. Italy gives **Italien**, French for a jealous person, while sex **in the Italian manner** refers to anal intercourse (a practice usually linked to the Greeks and presumably referring to one of the few 'natural' methods of contraception available in a Catholic country). The phrase was probably popularized by the French; certainly the Italian Benvenuto Cellini, in his autobiography, speaks of being accused of such a 'perversion' by his French neighbours. However it seems to have been coined by an Italian, Luisa Sigea (*c.*1530-60), known by her contemporaries as the Minerva of her era and the author of *Satyra Sotadica*, (?1659). This, when translated into French by Nicolas Chorier (who according to some experts was *himself* 'Sigea') became *L'Académie des Dames*, originally printed in Latin as *Aloisiae Sigeae Toletanae Satyra Sotadica de arcanis Amoris et Veneris*, and allegedly first unearthed by the Dutch philologist and historian Jan de Meurs (1579-1639). On either count, in its 1707 translation as *The School of Love* it would become the earliest surviving piece of prose pornography in England.

Spanish Fly

Appearing in the late-18th century the **Spanish padlock** is cited by Francis Grose as 'a kind of girdle contrived by jealous husbands of that nation, to secure the chastity of their wives', and Germany's **spanisches Kreuz**: 'Spanish cross' describes a form of kissing whereby the man kisses the woman on the forehead, on the two cheeks, and on the mouth. However Spain's best-known gift to the world of erotica is **Spanish fly**, otherwise known as the supposed aphrodisiac *cantharides*. This term, known as **spaansche vlieg** in Dutch, **spanische fliege** in German and **mouche d'Espagne** in France was coined in the 1630s and has remained a staple of erotic folklore ever since. Cantharides itself, from the Greek *kantharis*: a blister-fly, and known properly as *Cantharis vesicatoria* was known to medicine in the late-14th century and by the early 1500s had taken on its aphrodisiac image. Dried and ground into powder, the insects were used externally to produce a redness or slight inflammation of the skin and internally as a diuretic and most importantly as a stimulant to the urino-genitary organs. Whether it ever actually worked as required remains arguable, but its image is undimmed.

Over the border in France the phrase **ne pas quitter les basques de quelqu'un**, kin to England's 'tied to one's apron-strings', means never to leave someone alone. The *basque* in questions duly refers to that disputed territory lying in the north-west of Spain, but its specific reference is to a basque: a form of long waistcoat; these days the basque has been incorporated into the wardrobe of erotic adornments, along with **French knickers** and kindred aids to arousal. The word can also refer to a (generally) unerotic beret, as well as, in quite another context, a dish of minced mutton, mixed with bread-crumbs, eggs, anchovies, wine, lemon-peel and baked in the caul of a leg of veal. A final Iberian term comes from Portugal: **Portuguese pumping**, which one must assume to be masturbation, whether performed by oneself or by another's hand; the phrase managed to bring a blush to the cheek of both

Redding Ware and Eric Partridge, neither of whom seems to have found himself able to describe it properly.

Low Countries

The Dutch, whose image (the spying dancer Mata Hari – properly Margarete Zelle – apart) is hardly one of libidinous excess, have nevertheless contributed a number of sex-related terms.

America's **Dutch kiss** is one in which both participants grab the other's ears (as opposed to New Zealand's **Maori kiss** which involves the rubbing of noses), while a **Dutch nickel** is a stolen kiss. The theft comes from one of America's stereotypes for the Dutch – that of robber – and thus makes the phrases synonymous with **Yankee dime**, used to mean the same thing in the Southern states, where *yankee*, symbolic of all things northern, denotes the same negative image. That yankee may possibly have a Dutch origin is, however, pure coincidence. Britain's **Dutch widow** means a tart, reflecting the role of the 17th-century Dutch as the national enemy, but the **Dutch wife** is a bolster, otherwise defined as a 'masturbation machine'. More properly it was a long roundish bolster filled with strips of paper and used in beds in the tropics as a rest for the limbs. A **Dutch girl** is a lesbian, with a heavy-handed pun on *dyke,* a term commonly used to mean lesbian and which, although no proper etymology has been established (it may possibly be a corruption of *hermaphrodite*) has no relevance whatsoever to Holland's defences against the sea.

Dutch dumplings describe the buttocks, while in America **Dutch by injection** means any woman living with a foreigner. Similar terms include **French by injection** (anyone considered particularly well-versed in fellatio) and **Irish by birth but Greek by injection** (a homosexual). The **Netherlands** and the synonymous **Low Countries** refer to the sexual organs (whether of male or female, although the pun on *cunt* does underpin a generally female use), as do France's equally punning **pays-bas**: low countries. Back in England **upper Holloway** (the vagina) and **lower Holloway** (the anus) are informed by the same geographical games, in this case referring to the less salubrious suburbs of North London, as is **lapland**: the vagina. One other 'Dutch' term is **xuj gollndskij**: meaning 'Dutch prick' and used in Russia as an all-purpose curse.

*'A **** and a Clap'*

Other than **anglais**: a man who keeps a mistress, and the self-congratulatory **britannia metal** and **English sentry**, both of which refer to the erect penis (although the former also means something fake), terms that mix England and sex are, perhaps predictably, somewhat deprecatory. Most, indeed, seem to rest on the necessary prostitution that is seen as the logical result of female poverty. Thus the late-18th-century **Cambridge fortune**: a woman who has no fortune of her own and must rely for attraction on her personal charms alone. It puns on two staples of the Cambridgeshire countryside and the term is defined by Grose as 'a wind-mill and a water-mill', i.e. the unhappy woman can talk and urinate but that is all. **Whitechapel**, from the yet-to-be-solved Jack the Ripper killings of the late 1880s, meant for a while a sex murder, but the **Whitechapel portion** ('two torn smocks and what Nature gives', i.e. the vagina, in the late-17th and early 18th centuries; 'a clean gown and a pair of pattens' in the mid-19th) referred more directly to sex itself. Similar formations included the late 17th-century **Rochester portion** and the **Tetbury portion**, defined crudely by Grose as 'a **** [cunt] and a clap'. (Whether 'Rochester' also refers to the notably libidinous aristocrat, John Wilmot, Earl of Rochester, is unknown; more generally, from the geography of the town, it was a popular Kentish proverb). Across the Irish sea the **Tipperary fortune**, bowdlerized as 'an Irish woman with no fortune other than her body' was further explained by Francis Grose as 'Two *town lands* [the breasts], *stream's town* [the pudenda] and *ballinocack* [the anus].' This last comes itself from the name of a fictitious town, combining the Irish *baile*: a town with *cack*: excrement. The **Irish fortune**, still referring to the vagina, was defined, rather like its Whitechapel equivalent as 'pudendum muliebre and pattens'. The patten, another artefact of poverty, was a very basic overshoe, composed of a wooden sole secured to the foot by a leather loop passing over the instep, and mounted on an iron oval ring; its use was to raise the wearer an inch or two from the ground.

A Map of Ireland

For all the unpopularity of the Irish in 19th-century England, when their role as labourers condemned them to class-based as well as racial opprobrium, the majority of 'Irish' terms, in the sexual or any other context, stem from their mid-19th-century arrival *en masse* in America. That said, a good many, being used by English-speakers, have naturally made their way back across the Atlantic. Some, however, are English English: to **play Irish whist** means to have sexual intercourse – where the 'jack' (the penis) takes the 'ace' (the vagina) – and in hotel jargon a **map of Ireland** is a semen stain on the sheets. (In France the same problem is **une carte de France**: a map of France.) **Irish confetti**, an American term, is a heavy ejaculation, especially as resulting from fellatio. As for the rest, they should be seen as forged primarily in the great cities of America where the Irish, however powerful they may have become, were far from welcome initially.

In no special order, they include the **Irish clubhouse** (1960s): a refined house of prostitution (elswhere it can mean a police station); an **Irish dip**: sexual intercourse; **Irish draperies**: pendulous breasts and the **Irish root**: the penis. An **Irish tootchache, Irish rise** or **Irish promotion** are all terms for an erection, although the 'toothache' can also refer to pregnancy, and the 'promotion' can equally well refer to detumescence. The **Irish toothpick** is the erect penis. An **Irish marathon** is an extended session of lovemaking, while an **Irish kiss** is a slap in the face. An **Irish wedding** is masturbation, an **Irish virgin** a spinster (perhaps from the image of the pious nuns, whose only 'husband' is Christ). Last of all the **Irish way** (like the **Italian manner**) is heterosexual anal intercourse. This variation on the more common **Greek way** (homosexual anal intercourse) refers to the belief that pious Catholics, when not risking their future with a throw at **Vatican Roulette** (the notoriously unpredictable 'rhythm method' of contraception; the only form permitted even now by the Catholic Church), used anal intercourse as their sole means of contraception. In every case, as ever, the image is of the 'dumb mick', too stupid to tell the difference, even when it came to sex.

Hot Tamale!

In all of those terms, no matter what their provenance, the hapless Irish are daubed with the usual smears: poverty, ignorance and boorishness. Sex is almost an afterthought. Similarly the Mexicans, America's 'other Irish' (although the Poles run them a close race) are tarred with their usual epithets: poor, cheap and obsessed with spicy food. Once more, the sexual aspect of the terminology is secondary. Thus the Jewish **kosher cutie** is echoed in the **Mexican dish** or **tamale** (which as a dish is made of crushed Indian corn, flavoured with pieces of meat or chicken, red pepper, wrapped in corn-husks and baked). Both of them are, of course 'hot' – a term that has carried sexual implications since 1500. The **sexy-mex** needs no translation. To **Mexican it** reflects more on Americans than on their southerly neighbours: it means to get a quick divorce, more easily granted in Mexico than in the US. **Chili,** a term commonly meaning Mexican (see *Food*) and properly referring to the hot pepper that is part of Mexican cuisine, occurs in this context as a **chili pimp**: a low-rent, thus Mexican, pimp. And the **Tijuana Bible**, also known as an 'eight-pager', is a small pornographic comic book popular during the 1940s; they usually featured the ill-drawn but nonetheless identifiable exploits of well-known movie stars, or in the case of Popeye, for whom spinach played its usual role, cartoon characters more regularly found in other milieux. One last Latin-American term is **coño**, used by Peruvians of the Spanish. Literally meaning 'cunt', it exhibits an unequivocal loathing.

'The Quintessence of Debauchery'

Of all the many, and almost invariably insulting synonyms for homosexual, one of the oldest and most widely used is **bugger**. It has been the accepted standard English term for a sodomite since the 16th century and, whether its many users appreciate the fact or not, began life as a racial insult. First cited in English in 1555 it comes from the French *bougre* (dating to 1340), which in turn originates in the Latin *Bulgarus*, a Bulgarian, a name given to a sect of heretics who emerged in Bulgaria in the 11th century. The term was transferred to the

Albigensian heretics, who it was believed were largely homosexual. The term has also been applied to usurers, while in 19th-century Britain it meant a stealer of breast-pins (*bugs*) from drunks. **Bulgare** in French and **bulgaros** in Rumanian both mean huge, chunky or enormous. Terms allied to bugger, and meaning homosexual, include **bunker**, **burglar**, and **budli-budli** (which in 20th-century India means sodomy). It also remains common as a general term for a man, especially in such combinations as **silly bugger**, **daft bugger** and the like. **Bug** (18th-century and incontrovertibly slangy) is defined as one who incites others to sodomy. Bugger is not itself a slang term, but its use in a wide number of combinations is. The lexicologist Geoffrey Hughes, writing in *Swearing* (1991), describes **bugger** as 'the most flexible of all obscenities', serving equally well in each of the eight categories he specifies as the areas in which such terms work, ranging from the personal ('You ——!'), to cursing ('—— you!') to usage as a verb ('To —— about'). Even *fuck*, which seems to work in so many different ways, and in so many combinations, is not so prolific.

If bugger is rooted in religion, then so too is another word for the same practice: **sodomy**. The Biblical tale of the twin cities of Sodom and Gomorrah – in *Genesis* xviii-xix – talks of the sins of the 'cities of the plain' and it has long been accepted that the sin of Sodom, at least, was that of anal intercourse – and thence equated, rightly or wrongly, with homosexuality. That said, Lord Rochester's infamous play *Sodom, or, The Quintessence of Debauchery* (1684), featuring a *dramatis personae* that includes Bolloxinion, King of Sodom, Cuntigratia, his Queen, General Buggeranthos, Princess Swivia, the maids of honour Cunticula and Clitoris, seems to be pan-sexual in its appetites. Likewise the characters who populate the Marquis de Sade's gruesome (and indeed tedious) *One Hundred and Twenty Days of Sodom* (1785-9) certainly have no intention of restricting their polymorphously perverse activities to a bit of 'bum-banditry'.

All that is true, but Sodom still remains primarily identified with homosexuality. When a writer spoke of 'Sodomes and Spintries' in 1649 his meaning was clear: a *spintry* was a male prostitute and thus a site of 'unnatural' practices. The term **sodomite**, dating to the early 14th century is clearly defined in its first appearance: 'that is not twixt woman and man', and when in 1474 the pioneeer printer William Caxton refers to the Sodomites he delineates their 'vnnaturell synne'. Less well-known are **sodomiter** and its female equivalent **sodomitess**. The Catholic Church, elsewhere equated with Babylon, could also, in Protestant eyes, be 'sodomitical Rome'. **Sod** appears around 1850; it is simply an abbreviation of sodom and carries the same import. Its sexual side has gradually fallen away, and current use, especially in combinations such as *sod-all, not give a sod* and *Sod's Law* (what can go wrong, will go wrong), lacks any such overtones.

Greek Culture

In the world of national/sexual stereotyping, the Greeks, thanks to their ancestors' refusal – unshackled by Judaeo-Christian terrors – to stigmatize same-sex affections, have long since drawn the gay card. Not that their image was ever that good. The 16th century used **Greek** as a synonym for a cunning, wily person; a cheat or card-sharp and a man of loose habits. Quite when these 'loose habits' were specified as homosexuality cannot be pinned down, but mid-20th-century slang, especially as encountered in the world of contact advertising and the 'menus' of prostitutes' services, not to mention the carefully guarded euphemisms of what was now an illegal subculture, all made the link. **Greek love** is first cited in 1931, in the context of the lack of 'normal' sex within a prison, and it was followed by such cognate terms as **Greek fashion** and **Greek way**, both meaning anal intercourse. **Greek**, whether as verb or noun, also referred to anal intercourse, while **Greek culture** added to the lexicon. Culture itelf is a widely used euphemism in the world of sex, underpinning the various sterotypes. Thus **English culture** is bondage and 'discipline' (i.e. whipping), **Swedish culture** the use of rubber garments in sex (one sweats as if in a sauna, although **Swedish**, *tout court*, means mutual masturbation), **French culture** is fellatio, **Roman culture** an orgy (from fantasies of some lubricious 'decline and fall') and **American culture** the most Whitebread variety of sex, love-making in the 'missionary' (face-to-face) position.

The **Greek side** is the buttocks, although **Greek bottom** refers to a method of cheating at cards whereby one deals the second card from the bottom of the pack. **Low Greek** is heterosexual intercourse, whereas **high Greek** is anal: the anus is 'higher' on the body than the vagina. **High Russian**, a somewhat rarified term, refers to the simultaneous indulgence in anal and oral sex. The Russians themselves seem to bypass the Greeks in this area, stigmatizing instead the Armenians. Thus **zpocnik**, literally 'ass-man' or 'ass-fucker' means Armenian, as does **mialsk**, which translates literally as 'homosexual'. Back in English the usually non-specific anti-gay insult **asshole-bandit** can also be used as a derogative for a Greek, whatever their sexual predilection. In French **debauche grecque**: Greek debauchery, means pederasty. Perhaps the only country where 'Greek' does not automatically mean gay is Germany where the phrase **Wie steht's um Griechenland?**: 'How about Greece?' means 'How's your girl-friend?' And although neither country would relish the fact, for some people **Turk** has become synonymous with Greek, at least as far as pederasty is concerned. A further 'Turkish' connection is found in **hummum**, originally a Turkish bath, but generally recognized in the 19th century to be synonymous with a brothel. The first such establishment, named the Hummum, was set up in Covent Garden in 1631; it later became a hotel.

Greek provinces also came in for their share of opprobrium. **Locrian lewdness** referred, apparently, to the excesses practiced by the inhabitants of Locris, but one wonders whether such pleasures proved worthwhile. According to a *Homily against Adultery*, printed in 1547, 'Among the Locrensians the adulterers had both their eyes thrust out'. Better known is the traditionally preferred sexuality of the island of Lesbos: **lesbianism** or woman-to-woman sex. Coyly described as 'tribadism' as far back as the 17th century (from the Greek *tribeo*: to rub), female homosexuality has long been attributed to the island's best-known inhabitant, the poet Sappho (*c.*600BC) whose name is thus the source of another synonym: **sapphic love**, dating from the late-19th century.

Other than the term lesbian, the most frequent references, however, are to the city-state of Corinth, which was viewed as the very embodiment of decadence, albeit hetero- rather than homosexual. Ancient Greek offers such terms as **korinthia chorei**: 'Corinthian wench', to mean prostitute and **korinthiasteis**, a whoremonger, and the image persisted well into the 19th century. In 1755 Samuel Johnson defined the term **Corinthian** as 'Relating to the licentious manners of Corinth' and subsequent dictionary definitions have added 'a debauchee, a gay fellow', a 'sport' or 'swell' and a profligate, 'given to elegant dissipation'. Perhaps the most influential use of the term came in 1821 when the sporting writer and slang collector Pierce Egan published his best-selling chronicle of 'fast' society: *Life in London* 'or, the Day and Night Scenes of Jerry Hawthorn, esq., and his elegant friend, Corinthian Tom, accompanied by Bob Logic, the Oxonian, in their rambles and Sprees through the Metropolis' appeared on 15 July, 1821.

Egan's creation was an enormous, instant success, with its circulation mounting every month. Pirate versions appeared, featuring such figures as 'Bob Tallyho', 'Dick Wildfire' and the like. Print-makers speedily knocked off cuts featuring the various 'stars' and the real-life public flocked to the 'sporting' addresses that Egan had his heroes frequent. There was a translation into French. At least six plays were based on Egan's characters, contributing to yet more sales. One of these was exported to America, launching the 'Tom and Jerry' craze there; the New York first night featured as its star one Tom Hyer, a well-known saloon-keeper, gang-leader and boxer and a century later a Tom and Jerry was a form of hot toddy. The version created by William Moncrieff – whose knowledge of London and of its slang equalled Egan's – was cited, not without justification, as 'The Beggar's Opera of its day'. It ran non-stop for two years. And while Egan died in 1849, his creations are still with us. The celebrated duo have been perpetuated in Warner Brothers' cartoon cat and mouse and as the male protagonists of BBC television's sitcom *The Good Life*. By the end of the 19th century the term was mainly synonymous with an amateur sportsman, playing for the love of the game rather than for any coarse, pecuniary reward, but the old meaning still lingered; in 1890 the *Daily Telegraph* could still refer to the 'wild Corinthian element' that was to be found in such watering holes as Monte Carlo.

Macaroni

CLOTHES

NATIONAL COSTUME is not all one might suspect. Despite their ostensible innocence and neutrality, clothes can cause as much trouble as anything else if the dedicated racist decides to enter them into the arena. One person's tourist trap is another's red rag to a nationalist bull. In the grim fertility of racist vocabulary-making, anything can be adopted to serve as a goad to hostility. Even the humble sock or trouser. The cut, as it were, of their jibe.

Rags, Towels and Diapers

If one ignores **blue-bonnet** or **blue-cap**, twin terms that both mean a Scot, and which are based on an early national costume (a broad, flat bonnet of blue wool) the other terms that equate head-coverings and race, deal with the citizens of the East. **Raghead, towel-head** or **diaper-head** (nappyhead, were the term used in English English) were first used to describe citizens of the Indian sub-continent in the 1920s; rooted in the underworld, the terms were extended to take in the Arabs of the Middle East in the 1980s, a usage much promoted by the Gulf War of 1991, when **handkerchief-head** or **hankie-head** (previously used to describe the stereotypical Black 'mammy') joined the lexicon. (The war also encouraged the use of the highly derogatory **sand nigger** and **dune coon**, terms that describe an Arab or any other native of the Middle East (bar the Israelis, who naturally take on the wide vocabulary for which Jews are automatically eligible). The 'mammy' use has also influenced **raghead**, which in Afro-American vocabulary initially referred to anyone seen as not being absolutely up to date with current information, and, up to the 1960s, anyone, male or female, who sported a bandana or scarf tied round their forehead. A somewhat laboured use has India termed **Land of the Rag-head**; the only surprise is that unlike other national names, no-one seems to have coined *ragland* as a nickname for India.

'My Jewish Gaberdine'

Moving to the upper body, both **highpockets** and **short-coat** have been used by Americans to describe their Black neighbours. Blacks in turn have called Whites **long-coats**. The Polish **kusielec** and **kusal** both mean short-coated, and thus a German, from the German fashion for wearing a 'sack' coat (with a swallow tail).

Mocking the Jewish propensity to set themselves up as experts in whatever occupation they pursued, however inexperienced they might actually be, the Yiddish proverb notes that 'When the Jew buys a gaberdine, he becomes an expert on cloth'. What is interesting here is not the self-deprecation, but the term **gaberdine**. First encountered, in a racial context, in Shakespeare's *Merchant of Venice* (1596), when Shylock accuses his enemies 'You...spit upon my Jewish gaberdine', the word seems very far from the homely gaberdine which, well known to generations of English schoolchildren, is usually called a macintosh. However the religious link is far more valid than the modern one. The term appears to come from the Old French *gauvardine*, *galvardine* or *gallevardine*, perhaps a derivative of Middle High German *wallevart*: a pilgrimage (in the same way France's *pelerin*: a pilgrim, gives *pelerine*, a long narrow cape or tippet, with ends coming down to a point in front, usually of lace or silk). Other Romance languages then picked it up, giving the Italian *gavardina* and Spanish *gabardina*, probably the immediate root of the English word. As used in English gaberdine has meant a form of loose smock, the garment worn traditionally by almsmen or beggars, a child's loose frock or pinafore, a type of twill-woven cloth, usually of fine worsted, as well as the 'Jewish' reference. The Polish term **chalaciarz**: 'begaberdined' meant a Jew, identifying the person with their topcoat. One last term, a **coat-and-suiter** (with its cognates **suit-and-cloaker** and **ready-to-wear-set**) refers generally to the Jews, traditionally prominent in the clothing trade.

The Croatian Cravat

Reaching the shirt, or at least the throat, one finds **cravat**, a word best associated with golf clubs, the Home Counties and a type of man, long retired from the forces, yet still loathe to abandon his rank and blazer. But cravats, far from being as English as those who sport them, in fact come from Central Europe. The *Hravati*, Napoleon's Croatian mercenaries, wore cravats as part of their uniform. The garment had in fact come into vogue in 16th-century France, as an imitation of the linen scarfs that were part of the Hravati uniform. In civilian use it was of lace or linen, or of muslin edged with lace, and tied in a bow with long flowing ends. The name wasadopted for a linen or silk handkerchief passed once (or twice) round the neck outside the shirt collar, then tied with a bow in front; it can also describe a long woollen comforter.

The shirt itself gives a **Puerto Rico Pendleton**, i.e. an old work shirt; the name contrasts Pendleton, an up-market American shirt-maker, with the implied poverty that accompanies anything termed Puerto Rican. A form of shirt also gives the name **camorra**, the Neapolitan equivalent of Sicily's Mafia. The word *camora* appeared first in John Florio's *New Worlde of Wordes* (1599) where it was defined as an 'Irish rugge or mantle, a Mariners frocke'.

A Grecian Bender

From trousers one gets Poland's **pludrak**: a 'pantalooner', and thus a German, because of his wide breeches; Iceland's **finnabraekur**: 'Finnish pants', a phrase that is used to mean a dead man's breeches, 'and the euphemistic **Turkish medal**: an undone button on the trouser fly. A **Welshman's hose** refers to anything that is not quite straight. **Grass-skirt** supposedly identifies the Pacific Islanders while a **Scotchbum** was a 17th-century colloquialism for a type of bustle. References to a bustle can be found in the late-19th century's **Grecian bend**, a particular, stooping style of walking adopted by fashionable women *c*.1872-80; one who adopted this exaggerated stance was a **Grecian bender**. The Danes used the equivalent phrase **graesk Bjoning**: 'Greek inflection' to describe an exaggerated bustle in a dress. Slightly earlier in the century came the **Roman fall**, defined as a way of walking in which the shoulders were thrust back, thus creating a droop backwards; it stemmed from the French Empire when officers were forced to adopt the un-natural posture due to the tightness of their uniforms.

Porter des Chausettes Russes

The primary use of shoes or socks (or lack of socks) in these contexts comes from Russia where the French term **Russes**: Russians or **chausettes russes**: Russian socks, refers to the foot-wrappings that were for many years (even into the 20th century) worn by Russian soldiers. Socks were a relatively late invention, occasioned by the Revolution of 1917 and the organization by Trotsky of the Red Army. Thus the phrase **porter des chausettes russes** is another way of saying 'wearing no socks.' The Russians themselves used **lápotnik**: 'one who wears bast sandals' (sandals made of plaited lime bark, also known as **Russian matting**) to decry the impoverished peasantry. **Russian boots**, however, were leg chains, as affixed to prisoners. Still on the theme of socklessssness, America's **California overshoes** or **California socks** refer to a form of makeshift 'sock' made by wrapping the foot in a sack, often a flour sack, over which the boot can then be put on. **Black-silk-socks**, on the other hand, is a way of describing an older Afro-American man, who tended to favour such footwear. **Boot** refers to a fellow Black person, possibly from the fact that boots are regularly thought of as black. A **wooden-shoe** is a Dutchman, the image being of the traditional Dutch wooden clogs.

A Jew Spat On This

Non-specific clothes-related terms include the French cant **indiennes**: 'Indians', meaning clothes, **kilty** or **kiltie**, an 1840s term that means a Scotsman, especially a Scots soldier, based on the kilt, a word that comes from the Danish *kuilte*: to tuck up (one's skirts). The world of second-hand clothing is generally associated with the Jews and Germany's **Judenglanz**: 'Jew-shine' refers to the sheen that well-worn old clothes tend to acquire. A couple of German sayings also link Jews to clothes: **a Jew spat on this** is said when a hole is found in their clothing, while it was generally believed that **a Jew is of as much use as the moths in clothing**. However, old clothes are not simply 'Jewish'; the Ghanian phrase for second-hand clothes, reflecting the imperial legacy, is **the White man died**.

An Italian on Sunday

Fashionable people also attract their own names. Thus the Sicilian term **francisinu**: a Frenchman, i.e. a 'swell' or fop; and Ireland's **patent Frenchman**, which also means a well-dressed, even showy person, and refers both to the gleaming patent leather of his shoes and, perhaps, to the word 'pat', an automatic reference to an Irishman. **Un anglais**, however, represents a carefully made-up showroom or shop-window dummy. In South Africa **jewish** means smart, expensive clothing while in 19th century England a **jewbarker** was a foppishly dressed person, the term based on the slick appearance of the clothing-stores' 'pullers-in', who stood in the street and extolled their stock to passers-by; many of these young men were Jews. A **jewlarker** was a dandy, although the etymology is inconclusive. Yiddish, in turn, offers **oisgeputzt vi an italiener urn zuntik**: 'dressed up like an Italian on Sunday', a term that refers to any garments that feature loud, gaudy colours, a slur that one commentator notes carefully 'takes into consideration the labourer; for Italian taste is not to be ridiculed by any people'. Germany's **polnisch aussehen**: 'to look Polish' has a similar implication, although the Poles fail to attract a defender of their wider aesthetic. For **macaroni**, perhaps the best-known of all, see *Food*.

a Swine

ANIMALS

THE CO-OPTING of members of the animal and allied kingdoms as agents of insult is a tried and tested variation on the larger theme. Anthropomorphism is not restricted to fairy-tales, sanitized or otherwise. It is only 500 years ago that dogs, cats and pigs, among other creatures, were tortured and executed for supposed blasphemy. The negative aspects of animal behaviour, for all that they are creations of human beliefs, lend themselves admirably to the language of abuse. In a non-specific sense, terms like cat, dog, bitch, pig and louse have a long, if undistinguished pedigree in the field. Cat, for instance, has been variously synonymous with whores and gossips since the 16th century; dog was a general term of abuse by 1325 and bitch by 1400. Pig may be a 19th-century usage, but swine is another 14th-century coinage. Louse, initially in the phrase *not worth a louse*, emerges around 1580. And these are a fraction of the whole.

It is hardly surprising, then, that the form has been adapted to the world of racial insult. As in many other categories, the application works on a variety of levels. On the one hand there is the supposed physical resemblance, usually as regards colour. Thus America's (and occasionally Britain's) use of coon for Black. There is the deliberate taunt, thus the linkage of Jews and the pig, and the extension of the national animal, the kangaroo for Australia, the bear for Russia. Finally there are the supposed links between the characteristics of a given animal and that of a particular race. All these are illustrated below.

Gone Coon

Coon (*c*.1860) is an abbreviation for raccoon, an American nocturnal carnivore of the genus Procyon. The common North American species is *P. lotor*, 'a greyish-brown furry animal with bushy tail and sharp snout' (*OED*). Today its extra-natural associations are invariably racial, but it had an earlier, non-racial life. Around 1832 it described any man, especially a sly and shrewd one; a further meaning, *c*.1840, was of a member of the old US Whig party, which for a while had the raccoon as its emblem. By the late-19th century the meaning was unequivocally racist, and used as such in Australia too, where it described another Black group, the Aborigines. It also generated three 20th-century rhyming slang phrases: **egg and spoon**, **harvest moon** and **silvery spoon**. By then the 'chocolate coloured coon' (usually a White person in blackface) had been for years a staple of mass entertainment, typically as in British television's *Black and White Minstrel Show* (a programme that for all its dedication to 'olde time entertainment' at least resisted the original name for such performances: a **nigger show**). The first ever 'minstrel show' was staged in 1843 in New York and starred Dan Emmett and his 'Virginia Minstrels'; it would also be Emmett who in 1859 popularized the totemic song 'Dixie', that in the Civil War to come (and ever after) would become the anthem of the South. (Thus **Dixieland**, which can be both a form of jazz, and a name for the whole South.) Another term for such performers, **moke**, referred to *mocha*: coffee-coloured and described both a White 'minstrel' and a light-skinned Black person. And for all that coon is undeniably rooted in America, it was, of course, the term of choice in the long-running Sixties sitcom *Till Death Us Do Part* when its devotedly racist anti-hero Alf Garnett wished to abuse Britain's Black populace.

It is show business that offers a pair of coon-related terms, to wit **coon song** and **coon shouter**, the first, which is also known as a 'shout song', is typically in ragtime and is usually a sentimental popular song based on the repertoire of America's Southern Blacks. The second refers to any performer (Black or White) who sings in the manner of a black-face minstrel. (A later term, **jazz-bo**, which would also come to mean a White jazz fan, the male equivalent of a *flapper*, could also mean a minstrel.) Indeed, the first use of coon in a racist sense is also entertainment-related, coming in the sheet music, printed in 1834 (and possibly in 1829) for the minstrel song 'Ole Zip Coon' ('he is a larned skoler'). Its singer was one George Washington Dixon and the song proved so iconic to America that some time later, at the height of the theatre riots which, for political or nationalistic reasons regularly erupted in mid-19th-century New York, one manager only managed to quell the hoodlums by sending out a performer waving large US flags and singing the popular ditty. By the time of the great anti-slavery novel *Uncle Tom's Cabin* (1852), the phrase 'tree a coon' (to capture an escaped slave) had entered common parlance and coon was still one of the basic terms of kneejerk racism, not merely in the US but now in the UK too, as the new century dawned. With the unconscious brutality of that age, the word is defined in the *Westminster Gazette* (May 1903) as the 'modern slang for a nigger.' Unsurprisingly South Africa espoused the term, but, despite the state of the nation's race relations, used it mainly in its show-business sense.

Back in the States one finds more specific terms in **coon-ass** and **coonie**, both of which single out Louisiana's French speaking Acadians, a group whose forbears can be found in the 18th-century French colony of Acadia which at its height dominated Canada's Maritime Provinces (Nova Scotia, New Brunswick and Prince Edward Island). It was descendants of this colony who moved south after the British conquest of Canada and resettled in another French colony, Louisiana. And it was these settlers whose ancestry and whose name lies behind the state's modern *Cajans* or *Cajuns*. Indeed, by the time these coon references evolved, it was Cajuns, rather than Acadians proper who were thus vilified. It should be noted, however, that coon-ass, at least has an alternative etymology: the French word *conasse*: the vagina or vulva. Unassailably American are **gone coon** (one who is considered doomed or otherwise beyond help), **go the whole coon**, a synonym for going the whole hog and **hunt the same old coon**: to carry on doing the same thing. A **coon's age** (1840s) meant a very long time, synonymous, no doubt, with 'coloured people's time'. While **coon squall** (loud, senseless talk) reflected an image of loud-talking Blacks, and **coon out** (to leave surreptitiously) that of their slithering away from a difficult situation. Last of all the coon terms is the modern **dune coon**, meaning Arab and another take on parochial America's contempt for all things Middle Eastern.

Show business, or at least entertainment, whether commercial or otherwise, appears to be responsible for another widely used term, **jigaboo**, often abbreviated to **jig** and sometimes found as **zigaboo**. It most likely comes from the standard English *jig*: a dance, itself coming from the French *giguer*: to leap, gambol and frolic (the classic 19th century Black stereotypes). Alternatively it is modelled on *bugaboo*, which in 13th century Europe was the name of a demon, and since the 18th century, the fear of demons in general. One last possible etymon is the Bantu *tshikabo*: a meek and servile person, used derogatively by the once-African slaves

Aside from coon, America's woods provide another small group of terms, linking animal life to anti-Black racism. Other than the Warner Bros' cartoon anti-hero Pepe DePew, the **skunk**, with its loathsome smell, has never been ranked with the list of 'cute' animals and as well as being synonymous with a notably mean or contemptible person has also been used to define an Afro-American. Last of all is **possum** (properly an *opossum*: a small marsupial mammal, living mainly in the trees) which, already used in the US to mean a coward, meant an Black person by 1890. Australia has always used possum too, although there the word's uses, while certainly negative are not racist. Among its meanings are a thief, and a confidence trickster's victim. Perhaps best-known of all its use by 'Dame Edna Everage' who opts for a use that has continued since the 1890s: a generally affectionate term for an unspecified person. The phrase *stir up* or *rouse the possum* means to liven things up (the corollary, presumably, of the static art of *playing possum*). Finally **Brer Terrapin**, from the *Uncle Remus* tales created in the late 19th century by Joel Chandler Harris, has sometimes passed muster as a generic Black.

'Hop Off, You Frogs!'

Frog, meaning simply a contemptible or offensive person, dates to around 1330, and it was well established in English when in 1626 it was used more specifically, to decry the fact that 'these infernall frogs are crept into the West and East Indyes'. The 'frogs' in question were the Jesuits, but barely thirty years later the term had moved from religious to national vilification, qualifying England's then national enemy, the Dutch. A century later and Britannia faced a new threat: France. And it was to the French that frog would henceforth be attached. France itself became **frogland**, taking over the name from Holland, while its inhabitants became **froglanders** (formerly the Dutch), **frog-eaters**, **frog-legs**, **froggies** or just plain **frogs**. Like one who spoke it, the French language became **frog**. Just to confuse things a real-life frog, back-referenced to the earlier put-down, became a **Dutch nightingale** (1769). (An **Irish nightingale** is also a frog; here, inevitably, the inference is that the Irish peasant wouldn't know the difference.) As a glance at today's tabloids makes clear, the link is as strong as ever, for all that Napoleon is long since dead. The *Sun*'s response to what it saw as excessive EC interference was the unequivocal: 'Hop Off You Frogs!' Back in the 1700s, America soon picked up the mood and frog was synonymous with all things French even before the War of Independence. On both sides of the Atlantic he was often, at least during the 19th century, prefixed with an honorific 'Mister' or even, in a mocking mish-mash of the French *Monsieur*, 'Mounseer'. There were the occasional jokes about 'fricassées' and other froggy dishes.

Logically, a **tadpole** was a French child while frog itself might, via the consonantal reverses of 'pig-Latin', become **ogfray**. Extending from one amphibian to another, the French *crapaud*, a toad, gave **crappo**, **crow-poo**, **Jean-Crapaud** and, with the addition of the generic 'Johnny', with which Britons apostrophized so many other nations (Johnny Turk, Johnny A-rab), **Johnny-Crapaud** (which can also mean a French Canadian) and **John Crapose**. Crappo and **cropoh** leave the original spelling even further behind, although the definition remains the same. During World War I both the British and French armies used crapaud/crappo as the nickname for a French trench-mortar, the squat dimensions of which looked vaguely like a squatting toad. There is not the slightest etymological link, but the punning hint at the old term *crap*: excrement cannot be ignored, especially in the context of the Anglo–Saxon's blanket resentment of the 'dirty foreigner'. And the French, as noted elsewhere, are considered 'dirty' in every sense.

Nor is the French/frog link restricted to English. The Russians, who also suffered a French attack in 1812, have **ljagstnik**: frog and **zabod**: frogeater, both fulfilling their predictable role. However a pair of toads who are not French are the Turkish variety, known as **ne met rak** or a German crab, and the American one where, for a change, it means a Black person.

Man of the Woods

The concept of evolution may have been part of the international consciousness long since, but the intermingling of monkeys, apes and men is never so pronounced as in the vocabulary of racism. Nor, however much the religious right pushes for the acceptance of its narrow, anti-evolutionary agenda, has it ever restrained itself from accepting what it sees as the endemic stupidity of African Americans, and thus the use by such conservative diehards of the terms **ape** and **monkey** to describe them. That said, major dictionaries, for whatever reason, are remarkably restrained in this area. While the slang phrase **go ape** has been defined as 'to go crazy; to become excited, violent, sexually aggressive, etc.; to display strong enthusiasm or appreciation; also, to malfunction', that is as far as such anthropomorphism goes. The world in which Black people are dismissed as 'just down from' or even 'still up in' the trees, is absent.

The real world, however, is less fastidious than the lexicographers, and racist terminology is more than happy to embrace the supposed equivalence between the anthropoids and homo sapiens, at least those species who do not come equipped with a White skin.

The missing link, as it were, appears in mid-19th-century America, when it was expanded from the basic ape, to **African ape** and **black ape**. More recently, *c.*1970, Australians have opted for **rock ape**. With the grim logic of such terminology, synonyms soon extended to include

baboon and **orang utan**, a word that, ironically, comes from the Malay *orang utan*: man of the woods. (For all that, *baboon*, without racial overtones, is used in the West Indies to mean an ugly, ill-behaved person, as is *rangatang*, meaning one who is belligerent, aggressive or coarse.) The 1920s saw the inclusion of **monkey-jane**, used of a Black woman and a tip of the hat, presumably, to Jane, the heroine of Edgar Rice Burroughs' *Tarzan* stories. **Pongo**, a Black person, especially an African, comes from the Angolan or Loango *mpongo*: a large anthropoid ape, the chimpanzee or gorilla; coined in the 17th century the name was transferred to the orang-utan of Borneo and Sumatra a century later. The racist use came much later still, in the 1960s, although it has been used in slang throughout the 20th century, first by World War I sailors to mean a soldier or marine (the use was general throughout the forces by World War II), then by Australians to mean an Englishman.

And what works for ape works even more efficiently for **monkey**, a term which emerged as an all-purpose insult in mid-17th-century England. It has remained a negative term, although it only gained its White vs. Black connotations this century. Both racial groups use it of each other, and both imply that same lack of essential humanity that underpins the most elemental racism.

One should not, indeed, restrict monkey's racist use. If it works for Whites it can work equally well for Blacks. **Porch-monkey** can mean a Black person (presumably from the image of his or her lounging around the house, preferring not to work) but it has its equivalents. The term **monkey-man** is a Black one; it emerged in 1924 and meant a fool, lacking savoir faire and sophistication. More recently the Rolling Stones have used it as a song-title. By extension it meant a weak man, especially one who accepted his wife's or some other woman's domination. It was such a man who was 'made a monkey out of' by his partner. Paradoxically, a monkey-man, or **monkey-woman** can also be the adulterous third party in a 'love triangle'. The perceived imbalance in civilization between America's Blacks, especially those living in the major cities, and those who emigrated from the islands of the West Indies gave monkey-man a new twist: a West Indian. Such individuals were also branded **monkey-chasers** (a term that was applied by White America to the inhabitants of Papua New Guinea; it can also mean a cocktail made of gin, ice, plus a little sugar and a trace of water) although contradictorily, **monkey-catcher**, a US Black term, means a shrewd and intelligent individual.

One last US use of monkey, often abbreviated to **monk**, is to mean a Chinese person and it is this that leads one east, primarily to Japan. Here one finds the Russian **makaki** ('little monkeys') meaning a Japanese, and thus the once-popular boast *makaki shapkami zakidayem*: 'we'll catch the little monkeys by throwing our hats over them'. Coined at the onset of the disastrous (for Russia) Russo-Japanese War of 1904 it was a piece of arrogance its users would soon regret. In addition are America's **monkey-nip** (a far from subtle blend of monkey and nipponese) and the less obvious **jocko**. Jocko, which sounds Scottish but is in fact an English name for a chimpanzee, comes from a mistake by the French naturalist Georges Buffon (1707-88) who misheard the Gaboon word *ncheko*: a chimpanzee as *engeco*, and then transliterated it as 'jocko'. From there it entered the textbooks, and equally importantly took on a role as a popular name for circus and other chimps.

Although monkeys and apes have tended to categorize people of colour, there are two contrary instances, one simple, the other a little obtuse. The obvious one is **brush-ape** (1920), used by other Whites of the poor Whites of Appalachia, arguably America's most backward and deprived area; 'brush' here is the undergrowth and scrub amongst which they can be found. The other is the Dutch **steertman**, meaning literally a 'tail-man' and translated as an Englishman. According to Otto von Reinsberg-Duringsfeld's collection of nationalist proverbs, the Dutch once believed that ever since the murder of Saint Thomas à Becket in 1170, the English were punished by being born with tails.

The Hapless Porker

Although the tale of Circe turning Odysseus' men into figurative and physical swine dates back to Homer, the use of **pig** as a derogative, racial or otherwise, takes what might be seen as a surprisingly long time to develop. That said, the ancient Greeks condemned their neighbours as *Boeothios sus* or Boeotian pigs, but the name Boeotia, a district of Greece proverbial for the stupidity of its inhabitants, was already synonymous for dullness or lack of intelligence.

Given the hapless porker's role as the taboo object in both Islam and Judaism, one might have assumed that its reputation would have earned it a wide variety of uses. But no. In fact pig enters English, at least, as an affectionate rather than a derogatory term. The soldier-poet Sir Philip Sidney, in 1586, talked of a 'pretie pigge' and he was not alone. And although the Bow Street Runners, those early 19th-century predecessors of the Metropolitan Police, were known as *pigs*, it was from their supposed 'rooting around' for criminals that they earned the name (*grunter* was a popular synonym) and not from any personality defect. (The use of pig when it re-emerged in the hippie Sixties was another matter.) Indeed, it would be three hundred years before pig became a term of abuse, and even then the emphasis was in one direction: a pig was a slut, a girl who was both promiscuous and drunken. It is a synonym for the French *cochonne*, literally sow, defined in 1902 in Barrère's *Dictionary of Argot* (French slang) as a 'popular, lewd girl' (that 'popular' providing evidence, no doubt, that the French are indeed as dirty as any xenophobe could desire).

All this is logical enough. Pig, as primarily defined, is the young of the swine, and *swine* was an undoubted term of abuse from the 14th century on. Wyclif, Shakespeare and Browning, among many others, used it. But it was a personal, rather than political use: individuals, not nations were the target. One needs to abandon English and turn to Europe for a more general use of pig. On one level the term depends on no more than the physique of the animal. To the Pole a Prussian is a **prosiak** or sucking pig, a pun on **Prusak**: a Prussian; to the Czech the Pole is **polach**: a Polish hog (a pun on *Polak*, meaning simply Pole). To West Indians a **Berkshire hog** is either an ugly person or a notably dark-complexioned Black man. (That said, it is hard to ignore completely a link, however subconscious, to *Berkshire hunt*: the vagina, the 'darkness' of which has given such slang synonyms as *bottomless pit, cave of harmony* and *stench trench*). The modern Greeks term Turks **gourouni**: pigs. **Porco tedesco**, say the Italians: German pig. The American breed of large, meaty pig is known as the **Poland China**, scorning two nations for the price of one. In culinary-national stereotyping, if the Irish are not eating potatoes, they are gorging on bacon.

Thus in England around 1810 **Murphy's countenance** or **Murphy's face** combines physiognomy and a typical Irish surname to mean a pig's head, while seventy or so years later the **gentleman who pays the rent** was, in Ireland, a pig. At the same time the phrase **poor as paddy Murphy's pig** means very poor indeed. The pig/Ireland relationship is perhaps best seen in the phrase **as Irish as Paddy's pig**, and the popular early 20th-century American verse, 'Oh they kept the pig in the parlor | they kept the pig in the parlor | they kept the pig in the parlor | And the pig was Irish too.'

But it is the pig as dirt, as religiously unclean that dominates these usages. **Among the Jews it is better to be a swine than a human** runs the German proverb, a line that has been attributed to the Roman Emperor Augustus, on hearing of King Herod's massacre of the innocents. The fact that Herod, although King of Judea, was not a Jew but in fact an Idumean (belonging to a kingdom between Egypt and Palestine) did not temper the remark. Another saying, also a German coinage, characterizes a dish of pig's knuckles as **unsalted, it tastes like a dead Jew**. The link between Jews and pork has remained popular. Those medieval Spanish Jews (and indeed Muslims) who ostensibly converted from their own pig-hating religions to Christianity, but still maintained their own traditions in secret, were known as **marranos** or 'pigs'. The term was used as an adjective to mean simply filthy. In the Balearic island of Majorca, the descendants of such converts, sincere or otherwise, are still known as **chuetas,** once again pigs. The term comes from *chuya*, literally pork, and thus a pork-eater, although there may be extra input from *jueto* (the Catalan for 'little Jew') and even *chuco* (a word used to call a dog). The term **Judeschwein**: 'Jewish pig', has yet to vanish from Germany's vocabulary.

Headquarters of the Scots Greys

Talking of his political rival Lord John Russell, Britain's 19th-century Prime Minister Benjamin Disraeli remarked that 'If a traveller were informed that such a man was the Leader of the House of Commons, he might begin to comprehend how the Egyptians worshipped an insect', and a century later a biography of the American muckraking journalist Drew Pearson was entitled *All American Louse*. The use of insects as terms of vilification has always been widespread.

The cockroach, that less than appealing denizen of steamy kitchens and damp basements, provides an all-purpose term of abuse. The Romans talked of the **latta germanica,** or German insect. The German word **Russe,** literally Russian, means both cockroach and black beetle. The apparent indestructibility of the species gives the phrase **er ist ein Russe**: he'll stand for anything, he's a glutton for punishment. A **German cockroach** is a cockroach or Croton bug (the species *Blatta orientalis),* named for the Croton river, Westchester county, New York state. The theory is that such insects began plaguing New York about the time (1842) that the Croton aqueduct brought water to the city. The Russians return the favour with **Prussak,** which means both cockroach and Prussian, while the Hungarian **russzni,** once more literally 'Russian', is a cockroach or any other form of bug. (It also means a small, spiced fish.) The Yiddish **preissn,** Prussians, is another synonym for the creepy-crawly. The French, always open to abuse on grounds of physical or moral pollution, get their share of entomological slurs. In Poland the roach is a **francuz** or 'Frenchman' while the German **Franzose:** 'Frenchman' performs the same role. Somewhat farther afield lives the **Persak,** an oriental variety of cockroach, here equated with Persia, today's Iran. Finally natives of the often-vilified German state of Swabia (now overtaken by Bavaria) have been designated as cockroaches by the Austrians (**Schwaben**) and the Hungarians (**sváb** or **sváb-bogár**: a Swabian beetle).

The roach is far from the only insect to offer a term of abuse. The louse, a parasitic insect of the genus *Pediculus,* which infests the human hair and skin, has been tied to a number of nations, most notably Scotland, where the early 18th-century *Dictionary of the Canting Crew* (by the otherwise anonymous B.E., Gent.) defines **louseland** as Scotland and a **Scotch louse trap** as a comb. Sixty years later, another slang collector, Francis Grose, underlines the slur by citing both **itchland** and **scratchland** as Scotland (thus Scots are **itchlanders**), and adds the punning **Scotch greys,** meaning lice. This play on the name of a respected regiment also gives the **headquarters of the Scots Greys**: a lousy head, and the phrase **the Scots Greys are in full march by**

the Crown Office: lice are crawling on one's head. This pun, without any national reference can be further found in **light infantry** and **light troops**. In the 20th century the regiment reappears in Australia, where **Scotch greys** are a virulent species of outsize mosquito, carrying yellow fever. Surprising though it may seem, Samuel Johnson, usually so keen to savage dwellers north of the border, restrains himself from slurring the Scots on this front but a successor, the slang lexicographer John Camden Hotten offers the Doctor a slight tip of the hat when he remarks that 'our northern neighbours are calumniously reported, from their living on oatmeal, to be particularly liable to cutaneous eruptions and parasites.'

If not the Scots the Spanish, at least in French. **Espagnol**, properly a Spaniard, means a louse when left uncapitalized; its feminine version, **espagnole**, which should mean a Spanish woman or girl, is used in slang to mean a flea. Another French usage is **négresse**, which can mean, as well as a bottle of red wine (thus *une négresse morte*: an empty bottle) a flea or insect. In Japan the **Nanking insect** is a bedbug (presumably with reference to Japan's 1930s invasion of China), while in America a **nigger killer** is a whip scorpion, and a **chigro**, a punning blend of chigger (an insect) and negro, is an Afro-American as well as a flea. A **nigger bug** is a black bug of the genus *Corimelaena* which feeds on plants and gives a foul taste to the fruit. Paradoxically, a **nigger-flea** is a broomstraw covered with a tallow coating. Back in Europe, specifically Czechoslovakia, **zidovka**, properly a Jewess, is a ladybird, as well as a tam o'shanter, a kind of plum and a name for whiskey. Native Americans called the honey-bee, imported from Europe, the **White man's fly**. Finally the Russians, ever-keen to damn the Jews, manage to smear them yet again with the saying **Our lice are on our heads, but the Jew's are in his heart**.

'Jump Jim Crow!'

The bird, with its generally positive connotations, has not attracted a particularly wide range of slurs, but, inevitably, there are some. While Shakespeare's *arabian bird* (used in both *Cymbeline* and *Antony and Cleopatra*) refers literally to the phoenix and is used to mean a marvellous or unique person, and the *kiwi*, the popular nickname for a New Zealander since World War I, are hardly opprobrious, there is a little more edge in some related terms. **Crow**, meaning African American and coined in the 1790s, is undoubtedly negative as is the US **blackbird**, meaning a Black slave. More recently blackbird, in Afro-American use, has come to mean an especially dark-skinned person. Crow must also be linked to the phrase **Jim Crow**, which meant a Black person, initially a slave, and was popularized via an early 19th-century Kentucky plantation song with chorus 'Jump Jim Crow'. The term is occasionally found as **John Crow** in Jamaica. With the ironies of such things, it was a blackface (i.e. White) entertainer Thomas Dartmouth Rice who first made it a hit. Crow was a general putdown, and the Elizabethan playwright Robert Greene, knocking his fellow dramatist William Shakespeare, termed him 'this upstart crowe' in 1590.

In Papua New Guinea **buka**, literally a crow, is used to brand the local butts, the North Solomon Islanders, whose complexion is notably dark and who are generally seen as backward peasants. The term originated, however, in White use, and meant anyone in the area, North Solomonese or whoever. The female version is **meri buka**, a 'dark woman' (*meri*, from the English name Mary means woman). Once again it refers to the North Solomons, but can also mean rum, from a popular brand which features a Black girl on its label. Not crow as such, but presumably related to Jim Crow, is South Africa's **Jim Fish**, used of any Black male. **Blackbird**, which also gave Australia a sneering synonym for Aborigine or Native Australian, gives the verb to **blackbird**, to kidnap Blacks for slavery, and **blackbirder**, the man who did it. Perhaps the nastiest extension is Australia's **blackbird shooting**: the killing of Aborigines by White settlers, who in the early years of the 'lucky country' hunted them like any other disposable animal, for sport.

Not all birds are black, and their colouring has influenced a number of terms. In pre-revolutionary days, when China had not yet turned its tailoring over to Mao suits, Russians called their Oriental neighbours **fazán**: pheasant, a reference to the perceived 'plumage' of their colourful formal dress. Similarly 1930s Germans called Americans **Papageien**: parrots, as a tribute to their colourful dress sense. Modern Americans, in turn, see the brightly dressed immigrants from Puerto

Rico as **parakeets**. **Flamingo**, at least in Holland, can mean both the bird, with its bright pink plumage, and a Fleming. Other bird-related terms include the heavily punning **cree-owls** (Creoles or Acadians), **ringtails**, used for both Italians and Japanese, the Czech **židatko**, literally a crested lark, but for slang purposes a Jewish youngster, and the German **Litauer** or Lithuanian, a term meaning jackdaw and generated by the harsh 'kr' noises in Lithuanian speech, supposedly reminiscent of the bird. A **French pigeon**, stressing a general disapproval of what is seen is innate French duplicity, is a pheasant that, supposedly by accident, is shot out of season. The German phrase **den russischen Adler machen**: 'to do the Russian eagle' is to turn one's back (upon someone). The phrase comes from the imperial eagle, a two-headed creature that can be seen, as it were, looking both ways simultaneously. Finally, blending bird-life and the traditional slur on the 'yellow' Chinese is **canary**, an Australian term used of early 20th century immigrants from China. (The original Australian use had been to describe a transported convict, forced to wear a yellow uniform, and the punishment of one hundred lashes.)

Boo to a Goose

The goose, aside from any culinary charms, is in great linguistic demand. Racial uses aside, one has a variety of phrases featuring the bird, among them 'all (his) geese are swans' (he invariably exaggerates or over-estimates), America's 'all right (or sound) on the goose' (to be politically orthodox), 'say bo' or 'boo to a goose' (to speak, usually found in the negative, implying timidity or cowardice), and to 'kill the goose that laid or lays the golden eggs' (to destroy a source of one's wealth by one's own heedless action).

In the world of nationalisms France, whose national bird is of course the cockerel, dismisses someone as **comme une oie Belge**: '(as silly as) a Belgian goose'. **Geese**, as a simple abbreviation, means Portuguese, as do such allied puns as **portugoose** and **porchgeese**, while **goose** means a Jew. Whether, as H.L. Mencken suggests in 1936, this is a reference to *goose*: a tailor's smoothing iron and as such the basic tool of many immigrant Jews, or whether it is no more than a deliberately coarsened mispronunciation of Jews, i.e. *Joose*, cannot be ascertained. Reversing the usual pattern, the French cant **angluce** and **angauche** both mean goose, a formation based on the claim by the Emperor Charles V that when conversing with birds he spoke English. The English themselves were popularly viewed as being obsessed with birds, especially game. A **nigger goose**, like so many such terms, uses 'nigger' to mean dark and describes the cormorant, while the **nigger duck** (1876) is a duck with a reputation for stupidity. A **black duck**, however, is a Native American, a figure, who like Australia's Aborigines a century later, were seen as legitimate prey by the 18th century's 'sporting' colonists. A **ruddy-duck** was an Irishman, a usage that was boosted by the animal's nickname, a **paddywhack** or **paddy**.

The Land of Cockaigne

One last barnyard species, the cock, lies behind a term that is at the very heart of slang (and the originator of its 'rhyming' variety): **cockney**, a slang word coined in the early 16th century and meaning first a town-dweller, and then a Londoner, specifically one 'born within the sound of Bow Bells', and thus an East Ender. Alternatively it means an overly squeamish or wanton woman

Cockney comes from the 14th-century standard English *cockney*: originally a mother's darling or a spoilt child, and thus a weak, effeminate adult. This was adopted in rural dialect to describe the supposedly 'soft' inhabitants of cities and large towns, who compounded their unpopularity by their ignorance of country ways and words. The famous, indeed clichéd link to 'Bow bells' is first cited in 1600 and appears for the first time as a dictionary definition in John Minsheu's dictionary *Ductor in Linguas* (1617). As he put it 'A Cockney or Cockny, applied only to one borne within the sound of Bow-bell, that is, within the City of London, which tearme came first out of this tale: That a Cittizens sonne riding with his father out of London into the Country, and being a novice and merely ignorant how corne or cattell increased, asked, when he heard a horse neigh, what the horse did his father answered, the horse doth neigh; riding farther he heard a cocke crow, and said doth the cocke neigh too? and therefore Cockney or Cocknie, by inuersion thus: incock, q. incoctus i. raw or vnripe in Country-mens affaires.'

Minsheu's tale notwithstanding, the standard English itself seems to be rooted in *cocken ay*: a cock's egg, or a small or malformed egg. Eric Partridge also suggests, on the basis of a rhyme attributed to Hugh Bigot, Earl of Norfolk (died *c.*1177) that a parallel root of *cockney* lies in the fabulous land of *Cockaigne*, and is as such a synonym for London; the *OED*, however, notes that the reference is probably to the traditional 'King of Cockneys', a kind of Master of the Revels chosen by the students at Lincoln's Inn on Childermas Day (28 December). Another cliché, that of the 'chirpy Cockney sparrer' gives **chirper**.

Engländer Schweinhund!

As every schoolboy knows, or at least every schoolboy brought up on the diet of reheated World War II propagandist leftovers that pervaded the popular culture of the 1950s (and indeed has yet fully to vanish), the most popular German shout, whether in victory or defeat, was *schweinhund!*: 'pigdog!', usually prefaced by *Engländer*. The porcine segment of this mutant creature has been dealt with above, the canine is almost equally popular. **Dog** and **bitch** are both popular terms of abuse, racist or otherwise. Dog and its synonym cur have been applied to those of whom we disapprove since the 14th century (although the more congratulatory *sly dog*, *jolly dog* and the like suggest more than a modicum of grudging envy). Bitch, which began as a less than flattering synonym for whore, became a term of more general abuse at the start of the 19th century.

Husky, the name of the basic Eskimo dog seen tugging sleds across the frozen wastes, has been used as a nickname for the Inuit population since the mid-19th century. *Eskimo* itself is a nickname; the individuals in question call themselves the Inuit – which like many tribal names around the word means simply 'the people' – and Eskimo is an Inuit word meaning eaters of raw meat.

Turek, literally Turk, is a popular Polish name for a dog, while **terrier**, a dog breed, has also been used to denigrate an Irishman, although terrier usually has more positive connotations. Terrier or tarrier was also late-19th-century slang for a tough man, or a loafer. **Tyke** is of course a Yorkshireman. It began life as a term of contempt, meaning a low-bred dog, a cur or mongrel. Applied to humans from 1400 onwards it was similarly unpleasant – 'a low-bred, lazy, mean, surly, or ill-mannered fellow; a boor' (*OED*) – but Yorkshire people, who took it on around 1700, see it, some might say with stereotypical Yorkshire cussedness, as a wholly admirable description.

Less charming are a couple of synonymous Polish phrases: **psiak-rew holynder** and **psiakrew Niemiec**: literally 'dog-blood of a Dutchman' and 'dog-blood of a German' and meaning a respectively a 'goddamed Dutchman' and a 'goddamed German'. Still in Poland, **suka,** literally a bitch, was the everyday term for a Jewess. In Germany the equivalent of the phrase 'man bites dog' is **a Saxon cheated a Jew,** an event similarly representative of a world turned upside down. For Spaniards **gabachos**, curs, is another way of referring to the French. In America a pun on the German dog the *dachshund* (properly badger-dog), gives **Dutch-hound**, working on the common Dutch = Deutsch to give a new term for a German person. A **Negro hound**, however, was simply one used in hunting slaves. Perhaps the strangest dog is China's **running dog**, one of the great clichés of the Cultural Revolution of the late 1960s and early 1970s. A translation of the Chinese *zou*: to run and *gou*: a dog, it meant, in communist terminology, one who is subservient to counter-revolutionary interests, and thus also the capitalist West.

Finally the dog's cousin, the wolf gives **Indian devil,** a 19th-century American name for the wolverine, an animal seen as just as crafty as the 'Red Indians' themselves, and **Wolfland**, which was sometimes found as a synonym for Ireland.

Riding The Spanish Mare

Terms based on the horse, once so central a creature in human daily life, now relegated to the mainly sporting or recreational sidelines, fall into two categories. One group deals with national attitudes to the animal, the other with a variety of general terms in which horses, and sometimes mules and donkeys, provide the primary image.

Thus the French **monter comme un cosaque**, 'to mount like a Cossack' refers to Russia's much-feared mounted soldiery. Taken literally the term means to make a skilful rider; used ironically, as was more common, it means quite the opposite: to mount a horse awkwardly. These same Cossacks presumably influenced the **Russian drag**, a rodeo term that describes a method of riding with one foot in a strap and the rider's head hanging off the side the horse. The English habit of 'nicking' the tail of a horse, making a cut at its root in order to make the animal carry it higher, has given the Hungarian **anglisovati** and the French **anglaiser**, both of which mean 'to English'. **Avoir d'anglais**, however, refers to a horse that has been whipped so hard that it is bleeding. Nor do the French themselves get off completely free: the German name for an equine skin disease is **Franzosenwurm**: French worm.

French horse-racing fans call any snags that occur during the race **banquettes irlandaises** (literally 'Irish seats', in slang), while in America an **Irish horse** is not strictly equine at all, but is actually a piece of salt beef, especially when tough and undercooked. A **Mullingar heifer**, however, is a girl with thick ankles; thus giving the phrase **beef to the heels, like a Mullingar heifer**. The slur is on the supposed characteristics of women living in Mullingar. Still Celtic, both **Welsh** and **Scotch bait** refer to the allowing of a tired horse to stop for a rest and a feed after trudging its way up a steep hill. The Scotch variation, according to Grose (1785), offers a similar rest to an exhausted human. (*Bait* has meant a snack, for humans or horses, since 1570.) A **Scotch hobby** is a scrubby, diminutive Scottish horse.

Horses are gelded the world over, but Hungary seems to have taken on the main linguistic responsibility. The Romans talked of **equus Hunnicus**: 'a Hungarian horse', to mean a gelding, and the term has persisted in French where **hongrer**: 'to Hungarian', means to geld. The Polish word **Wegier**, literally 'a Hungarian', means an abscess found on a horse. Germany's **wallachen** takes one back to gelding, although here the target nation is Wallachia, modern-day Rumania.

America, keen as ever to use its Black community as the source of myriad slurs, describes a saddle sore on a horse as a **nigger brand**, and a horse that has its front toes pointing outwards is **nigger-heeled**.

Equally unsubtle is **mare-nigger,** a Black woman, a **mule,** any Black person and a **nigger horse,** any black horse.

To move from the specific to the figurative, horses pop up in a variety of environments. The English phrase to **ride the Spanish mare,** is defined by slang collectors Farmer & Henley as 'To sit astride a beam, guys loosed, sea rough as a punishment'. Germany's **spanischer Reiter** or 'Spanish rider' refers to the *cheval-de-frise.* Used in fortification, this is a heavy bar criss-crossed by stakes, often surrounded by barbed wire, which serves as a barricade or is used to close a breach. The shape of the whole contrivance suggests a horse and rider. The *cheval-de-frise* is itself a race-based term, and means 'horse of Friesland' in French. The device was initially employed by the Friesians in their struggles for freedom during the latter half of the 17th century. They lacked cavalry for offensive manoeuvres and were forced to rely on defence. The term is also found in the Dutch *Vriesse ruyters* ('Friesian horsemen') and in 17th-century England's *Horse de Freeze.*

In Russia, where France once played an important role in defining the standards (both good and bad) of upper-class life, **shval,** a simple transliteration of the French *cheval:* a horse, meant a confidence trickster. Such figures were seen as smooth, sleek operators, reminiscent of a well-curried horse, and, as the language of choice indicates, of a glossily polished, over-mannered Frenchman. A similar term is found in **sharamýzhnik,** a transliteration of the French *cher ami:* dear friend; the allusion is to the charming French confidence man, calling the slightest aquaintance his 'dear friend' with the same enthusiasm as he brings to depriving them of their money. That the 'sh' sound in both terms requires the speaker to bare his teeth in a (false) smile may be just an amusing coincidence.

Jews, as ever, gained their share of opprobrium. For Americans a **Jerusalem pony** is an ass or donkey, a reference to the Biblical episode in which Christ rode into Jerusalem on a donkey. In Yorkshire dialect a *Jerusalemer* is, or perhaps was, a donkey. The donkey theme persists in Ancient Greece where **gadarogámai,** literally ass-kissers, was a synonym for the Jews. The popular myth, echoed even by celebrated Greek and later Roman historians, was that the Jews worshipped the ass. Leaving Jews, but staying with the donkey, Mexicans, at least in

American eyes, are inevitably equated with the unfortunate burro. Thus the **Mexican car, Mexican carriage** and **Mexican jeep**, all mean, with heavy-handed jokiness, a donkey. It should also be noted that **burrito**, a little donkey, not only represents anyone of Latin American or Spanish descent, but also means the penis (which in a *macho* world is presumed to work equally hard). A **Mexican hairless**, seemingly punning on the eponymous dog breed, is in fact an ancient, worn-out tennis ball. Still in the same linguistic area, England created the punning **Spanish trumpeter** (alternatively the **King of Spain's trumpeter**), a phrase that means ass or donkey and as such puns on the fictitious Spanish grandee 'Don Key' (a relation no doubt of the modern **Spanish archer** or **El Bow**). The **Spanish trot**, on the other hand, is simply a pleasant, undemanding trot.

Stout as a Stockfish

The Romans called a variety of the common crab, characterized by a short abdomen, the **brachyurus Israelita**. Quite why they chose this image – it is hardly a common stereotype of Jewish physiognomy – remains obscure, but the idea persisted and the Croatian word **čifutče** means both a crab with a small abdomen and a Jewish child. The Croats have also characterized one species of marine gastropod as **židovo uško**: a Jew's ear. (*Jew's ear* in English means either a fungus growing on trees, a variety of tomato or a type of lichen). The **jewfish** itself, a blanket name for a number of varieties of the species *Serranidae*, appears to be so called less from any similarity to Jewish features, but because, as the explorer William Dampier explained in 1697, 'it is a very good Fish, and... so called by the English, because it hath Scales and Fins, therefore a clean Fish, according to the Levitical Law'. In other words, it was a properly kosher fish and could be eaten by Jews, unlike such 'unclean' creatures as the lobster or squid.

The etymology of the **pollack**, a sea-fish of the genus *Pollachius*, allied to the cod, but having the lower jaw protruding (typically the European whiting pollack or America's green pollack or coalfish), remains a mystery. The *OED* assesses, and then discards, possible links to the Gaelic *polag*, which is a freshwater species; popular usage, apparently comparing the pollack's unappealing features to those of a human, goes straight from the Latin *Pollachius* to the modern Pole, with one authority suggesting that it is quite possible that the appearance of the fish is associated with the physiognomy of the underworld Pole. Across the border in Czechoslovakia, a **ruska**, which properly (when capitalized) means a Ruthenian, and occasionally Russian woman, is also used, in lower case, to mean both a pale yellow cow and a sardine.

Back in the West, the **Spanish flag** is either a California rockfish (from its red and yellow colouring) or a West Indian fish of the *Serranidae* family; a **Spanish lady** is the ladyfish, or Spanish hogfish. A **Portuguese man-of-war** is properly known as a siphonophore of the genus *Physalia*; it has long tentacles and can sting unfortunate swimmers very severely. A **yellow-fish** was an illegal immigrant to America, although the fish, in this case, may be linked to the slang *new fish*: a newcomer, rather than to the real yellow-fish, a common name for the rock-trout, *Pleurogrammus (Hexagrammus) monopterygius*. To Americans a **nigger chub** (1884) is neither black nor a chub, it is simply a blanket term that covers any fish of no economic importance – only a poor, hungry Black would see it as worth catching. A **niggerdick** (1896), however, is a black fish, while in France a **nègre** or **négresse** is a fish of the mackerel variety. It can also mean a drudge, factotum, ghost-writer, hack, and general literary 'do-all' (thus the phrase 'il me faut un nègre': I need someone to do the donkey-work), a satyr butterfly and a monkey. The American **niggerfish** is a nickname for a number of fish, primarily the grouper, while **niggerhead**, among a plethora of other meanings, can be a large, blackish, smooth-shelled, freshwater mussel. A **nigger knocker** is a hog-fish, otherwise known as the hog-molly or log-perch, and properly as *Percina caprodes*.

Siamoise, literally Siamese and a word that also means the testicles in French slang, and which otherwise translates as a stockfish, has also been used as 'an Englishman'. The stockfish, a name for cod and other cod-like fish which are cured by splitting open and drying hard in the air without salt, has some non-standard use in English too. Phrases like 'stout as a stockfish' referred to the need to beat the dried, salted fish as a way of rendering it edible, and Shakespeare, in *Henry IV, part I* (1596) uses it as a term of abuse.

'The Rats are underneath the Piles'

Notwithstanding the oft-repeated statistic that rats far outnumber the world's human population and that, alongside the insects, they alone would come to rule a post-nuclear world, other than for dedicated rat-fanciers the rat's finest hour is probably as a term of abuse, the *locus classicus* being James Cagney's much pastiched cry of 'You dirty rat!'. (That said, Cagney never actually pronounced the phrase in one of his 70 movies; the nearest he came was in *Blonde Crazy* (1931), when he condemned a fellow gangster as 'You dirty, double-crossing rat!'.) **Rat** here means informer, a usage that had been coined in the early 19th century. As to nationalistic use, a **swamp-rat** is a Louisiana Acadian or Cajun, while a **muskrat** or **musk** is an African American. (So too is a **bat**.) Across the Atlantic, a Czech rat is known as **německa myš**: a 'German mouse', while in Britain the saying **No rats** used to mean 'he or she is a Scot'. The background to this, claims Ware (1909), is the fact that when the bagpipes start playing, all adjacent rats make themselves scarce, although this jibes with the Pied Piper legend, when the rats *followed* rather than fled the pipes. The use of rats as visual shorthand for the loathed Jew in a number of German Nazi propaganda films, where they pour from sewers before meeting their well-deserved fate at implacable Aryan hands, and as 'cartoon'-fodder in such hate-filled journals as *Der Stürmer*, should not of course be overlooked. The Nazis were hardly the initiators of such imagery. Rats and Jews had been a convenient linkage for the Middle Ages. But even in the 20th century there were those who pre-empted Nazi efforts, among the most celebrated being the Anglo-American poet T.S. Eliot, a devoted High Anglican, whose deliberate juxtaposition of the two kinds of 'vermin' ('The rats are underneath the piles | The jew is underneath the lot') leave one in no doubt as to his position.

Jungle Bunnies

Rabbit, like so many of these terms, is a general term of abuse, usually meaning a weakling or victim. It has but a single nationalistic link, but it is, unfortunately, one of the best-known. **Jungle-bunny** (or **chungo-**

bunny) and its less popular synonyms **african-bunny** and **Nairobi-jack-rabbit**, have meant a Black person since the 1920s. A grimly ubiquitous term, it can be found in Britain, America and Australia.

The Portagee Lawnmower

Goats give rise to a strangely assorted trio of terms. In America the **Portagee lawnmower** is a goat used to keep the grass down, a method presumably employed by impoverished Portuguese immigrants, while in Germany the **polnischer Bock** or 'Polish billy-goat' is a bagpipe. In the Ukraine **katsap**, a goat, is a term used to mock the Great Russians and has its origins in the Ukrainian ridicule of Russian beards; Ukrainians went clean-shaven, whereas the arian Russians preferred a distinctive, hirsute chin.

'The Bear shall not have Constantinople'

Domestic and local animals tend to provide the majority of insults, but the wilds offer a number of other epithets. A **bull-nigger** and a **buffalo** both mean African American, while an **Indian signboard** is in fact the bleached shoulder bone of a buffalo, used in the 18th century as a form of signpost. A giraffe can be, in America, an **African skyscraper**. The lion that appears (alongside the unicorn) on the British national coat of arms, is known as a **British roarer**. A **paper tiger**, on the other hand, is the translation of a Chinese expression first used by Chairman Mao, and refers to a person or country that appears outwardly powerful or important but is in fact weak or ineffective. Mao coined the term in the early 1950s; his target was reactionaries in general and the United States in particular.

Buck, in standard English the male of the goat, deer, chamois, hare and a number of other animals, was transferred to slang usage by the early 18th century, when it meant a dashing fellow, a dandy, fop, or 'fast' man. In Ireland **buckeen**, otherwise describing a younger son of the impoverished Anglo-Irish aristocracy (and as such aping the better-known *squireen*: a petty landowner; the suffix *-een* is an Irish diminutive, thus such words as *colleen*: a young girl and *spalpeen*: a young boy, a rascal) meant a bully, whose activities might be seen as a less appealing form of dash. The term persisted into the 19th century, and at the same time took on a new, less glamorous meaning, that of a man, specifically a non-White man. It was applied initially to the Native Americans, the 'Red' Indians, but soon spread to encompass any male Indian, whether of South or Central America, as well as African Americans and Native Australians. The term was often used in combinations, thus **buck Aborigine, buck Indian, buck Maori, buck Negro** and even more common, **buck nigger** (1842). **Buck nation**, in the West Indies, refers to the Amerinxians of Guyana. Somewhat illogically, given the image of rutting maleness that underpins the term, there was also **buck-woman**, a Black woman. Buck usually refers to non-Whites; one exception is the Hungarian **bakszász**, or buck Saxon and as such is an attack on male Germans. Despite the apparent English origin, Richard Allsopp (1996) has noted that in the West Indian context the immediate source may have been the Dutch *bok*: he-goat, a term applied to the natives of Guyana *c*.1790.

Like buck, **greenhorn**, used in a racial sense to denote a newly arrived immigrant, refers to the deer. The standard English sense describes the young animal (it can also be an ox), with 'green' or fresh horns. The first non-standard use referred in the 17th century to a new recruit to the army; it was then adopted by the 18th-century 'sporting' world to describe (as Grose (1785), who also has the synonym *green-head*, put it 'a novice on the town; an undebauched young fellow, just initiated into the society of bucks and bloods'.) Greenhorn was the least distinguished of an ascending list of sophisticates, laid out in the *Scots Magazine* of October 1753 as 'Greenhorn, Jemmy, Jessamy, Smart, Honest Fellow, Joyous Spirit, Buck, and Blood.' Its use in the immigrant context emerged in the West Indies, where it dealt with newly arrived Europeans, but the term gained far wider currency in America, where it described any member of the wave upon wave of the country's 19th-century immigrants. Another animal, the kangaroo provides at least fifty per cent of the Australian **jackaroo** or **jackeroo**, defined in the *AND* as 'a young man, (usually English and of independent means) seeking to gain experience by working in a supernumerary capacity on a sheep or cattle station'. Such young gentlemen came out to Australia in search of 'colonial experience' (in effect an apprenticeship which would end in their elevation to station owner in their own right) and were thus nicknamed – the other half of the blend was the basic name 'Jack') – by the hands with whom they worked. The *jack* plus *'roo* etymology is not the only one. Other sources suggest that the term is simply an elision of another term for a 'new chum': *Johnny* and later *Jacky Raw*.

Germans are also singled out in the French **ours du nord**, the 'the Northern bear', while the Russian **bear** is as stereotypical a figure as the American eagle or the British lion. The term is a late-18th-century one – although there had in earlier times been Persian bears – initiated perhaps by W. B. Stevens who wrote in his *Journal* for 15 December 1794 that 'Those Russian Bears after having devoured the Unhappy Poles are...to direct their fell tusks against France.' The term really caught on during the Crimean War of 1854, when British patriots confirmed in song that 'The Bear shall not have Constantinople', a promise that was underpinned by the fact that 'We have got | the Gatling Gun | and they have not'. In the 1890s Kipling, never one to let cliché stand in his way, urged his government, pondering the Czar's calls for a general disarmament treaty to 'Make ye no truce with Adam-zad – the Bear that walks like a Man!' Bear remains a synonym for Russia, notably in the NATO nickname for the Tupolev TU-95 long range bomber, Soviet Russia's equivalent of America's B-52.

Last of all come the **copperhead** (properly the venomous snake *Agkistrodon contortrix*, common in the US) which has been used variously to name the Dutch citizens of early New York, Native Americans and Northern sympathizers with the secessionist South during the Civil War; **kangaroo**, any European-born Australian; a **Russian,** which in Australia refers to any animal that is especially difficult to handle, and the Russian **zver**, literally a wild beast and a term that is applied to any of Russia's Asiatic nationalities.

DISEASE

THE ARRIVAL of immigrants in a country, or the presence of groups that are considered alien to the greater national majority, has been characterized in medical terms – the invasion of a bacillus, a plague, a sickness – on many occasions. The same Nazi propaganda films that made so much play with rats, also equated the Jews with disease. Indeed, as they gained an increasing stranglehold on first Germany and then Europe, they were able to transmute the fantasy into self-fulfilling prophecy. Starved, beaten, tossed into far from healthy quarters, their genuine illness made them so much easier to exterminate with a clean conscience. One must, after all, extirpate the plague-carrier.

Thus that a number of racial terms are linked to illness and disease is thus hardly surprising. It is true, undoubtedly, that the bulk of these refer to venereal diseases, and especially to syphilis (most venomous of all), but there are others too. Sexually transmitted diseases, therefore, will be considered later. More general problems come first and since they appear, on the whole, to fall into national groupings – a disease for every country, as it were – it is perhaps simplest to look at them as a succession of nation-based problems.

Under the Influence

'The stone,' declares the German saying, 'is a German disease; the gout a British one.' That said, the Germans seem to come off reasonably lightly in this particular area of abuse and the stone or gallstones, does not manifest itself amongst the terms of German-orientated abuse. The **German duck**, elsewhere a popular meal, is a bedbug, while *Roseola epidemica* or *Rubella*, one of the most frequent childhood diseases (although it can also attack adults), has been known as **German measles** for the last century. It has, albeit very rarely, been also known as **French measles** and even *false measles*, a reference to its dissimilarity to 'real' measles. It should be noted, however, that measles, in whatever form, takes it root from an Old High German root *mas*, meaning a spot or blemish on the skin. During World War II, when all things German became impermissible, the illness was temporarily renamed 'Victory measles', a term that, in retrospect, smacks all too much of Orwell's *1984* and its grim 'Victory Gin', Victory Mansions' and the propagandist rest. In Hungary, **német-has**: 'German bowel', means diahorrea.

Despite the German saying, gout itself involves a 'stone', although in this case the painful chalk-stone that forms through the continual deposits of sodium urate (typically in a big toe) that constitute the disease. But saying or not, the supposedly typical 'English diseases' are the sweating sickness, and to an even greater extent, rickets. The sweating sickness, known in medical Latin as **anglicus sudor**: English sweat, was a feverish disease characterized, logically enough, by profuse sweating. A number of epidemics hit England in the 15th and 16th centuries; they spread fast and killed with equal alacrity. As well as the Latin it was known, in Sweden, as **engelska svetten**: 'English sweats' and in Holland as **Engelsch zweet**: English sweat.

Sweating sickness had all but vanished by the 17th century but it soon found another 'national' replacement: rickets, a disease that resulted from a deficiency in vitamin D (found typically in egg-yolk, liver, and fish-liver oils) and which especially targeted children. It is characterized by softening of the bones, especially of the spine, and consequent distortion, bow-legs, and emaciation. A similar disease is found in sheep, where it is known as corn blights or the staggers. Every European country seems to have taken note of this English propensity, and commented accordingly. All these can be translated as the English disease: **angliyskaya boliezn** (Russian), **angolkór** (Hungary), **Engelsche ziekte** (Netherlands and Belgium), **engelska sjukan** (Sweden), and **englische Krankheit** (Germany). In England itself the phrase **English melancholy** was synonymous. Still in the British Isles, neither Wales nor Scotland has been accorded any diseases as such, but Anglocentric speakers branded both countries as the homes of unpleasant infestations. As seen under *Animals*, **Scots greys** and **scotsmen** meant lice, and on these grounds both the **Scotch** and **Welsh fiddle** meant 'the itch'. A **Welshman's hug** meant the same thing. Americans have also nicknamed Serbs and Croats **itch** or **itchy**. It comes most likely from the -itch or -ic suffixes that terminate so many of their surnames, but the implication of dirt is never far away.

The **Grecian bender,** which in other contexts referred to a bustle (a small pad or wire framework that expands the rear of a woman's dress), also refers to Caisson disease or 'the bends' (properly described by the *OED* as 'the acute attacks of pain in muscles and joints suffered on over-rapid reduction of the surrounding air pressure, chiefly by workers in compressed air who are decompressed too quickly, with consequent liberation of dissolved nitrogen from the body tissues'). And Greeks, as well as Italians and Yugoslavs, are the target of Australia's sneering **Mediterranean back** or **Greek back**, a simulated illness, which serves as an excuse for malingering. Other Australians, stereotyping Mediterraneans as naturally lazy, exclude themselves from such specious malingering, and add a synonymous phrase **Mediterranean gut ache,** generally known as **MGA**. This stereotype of Mediterranean laziness also crops up in the late-18th century **Lombard fever**, jokingly translated as 'the disease of laziness or a spree of idleness'. It comes not from Lombardy but from the British dialect *lomber*: to idle, and the *OED* links the term to the dialect *fever-lurden, fever-lurgan, fever-lurgy, fever-largie*, all of which mean the same: idleness. In the end, however, bias wins and the popular association with a supposed Italian trait remained the deciding factor. Lombard in a geographical sense refers properly to presumably hard-working bankers, who had come from Lombardy in northern Italy and made new homes in England, where they were at the heart of the financial world from the Middle Ages onwards. It is these Lombards that underpin the phrase **Lombard Street to a China orange** (and variously **to an egg-shell** or **to ninepence**) meaning the longest possible odds and thus an absolute certainty. The **China orange**: the sweet orange (*Citrus aurantium*) first turned up in London in the mid-17th century; by the 19th it was used figuratively to mean anything of minimal value. **LOMBARD** is also one of the more amusing acronyms of that Eighties crop that was headed by *yuppie*. It means 'loads of money but a right dickhead' and summed up many of the newly (if temporarily) rich young men (and women) who populated the City of London in the artificial boom years of the 1980s.

Hungarians, it seems, are the target only of their neighbours the Czechs. Thus **uherčina**, which properly means the Hungarian language, or the Hungarian manner, and also means Hungarian wine, in this context means 'the Hungarian disease' or a fever. **Maďar**, literally Magyar or Hungarian, means a boil or pimple, as does **uher**, 'a Hungarian' when the U is capitalized, which can also mean ringworm. (Poland's **Żyd**, ostensibly a Jew, can also mean a boil and indeed an ink-blot.) To the Hungarians themselves **kínabor**, 'China wine', is quinine wine, a drink that helps to counter fever and, since the days of the Raj, malaria. The link to China is somewhat odd, since quinine comes from the *Cinchona*, a Peruvian tree, and *quina* is the Peruvian term for bark.

The Irish, so popular in other stereotypes, barely impinge here: one need mention only the **Irish posture**, a faked fainting fit, which, like the Mediterreanean back, is presumably called upon for the purpose of avoiding work. The Jews, for whom no stereotype seems too extreme, have another story. **Mockie**, a slur nickname for a young Jew, may come from the proper name Moses or it may, especially in its alternative form **mouchy** relate to the *smous* or *smouse*, a German Jew and thus a Jewish pedlar. However a third etymology is also feasible: the Yiddish word *makeh*: meaning sore, pest or plague. In Poland **Żydowska niemoc** or the Jewish disease means hemorrhoids or piles, but in Austria and elsewhere it can mean both diabetes, an undoubtedly 'Jewish' ailment, or, in psychiatric use, idiocy. One should note the suggestion of the acerbic Viennese journalist Karl Kraus, whose own Judaism never restrained his scattershot savagery: 'Psycho-analysis is the disease of emancipated Jews; the religious ones are satisfied with diabetes.' The American term **Jerusalem parrot**, meaning a flea, with its implication of the 'dirty Jew', may well be linked to the earlier **parchaty Żyd**: a Polish phrase meaning mangy or scurvy Jew. The adjective *parszywy* has the same meaning, as do a variety of terms such as *parchacz, parchol, parchula*, and *parszywiec*. All have a common root, *parch*: a scab. Dirtiness (and thus disease) is equally central to another Polish epithet **smierdzi Żyd**: the stinking Jew, a figure who atttracts the same form of opprobrious fantasy as does the African American or any other Black person: that in some way they carry their own repellent odour. The Czechs keep up the smear with **židovina**, a term that means variously a Jew, a Jewish stink and, oddly, whisky. However, as one commentator remarked, with regard to the Jews, 'after a sprinkling of baptismal water, the Jew ceases to stink'. **Yiddish cologne**, on the other hand, would not help, in American slang it means gasoline. The **foetor judaicus**: the Jewish stench, a medico-theological term coined in the Middle Ages, could still be found in supposedly authoritative, if undisguizedly anti-semitic, tomes of the 20th century. **Stinkjude** remains a common (if these days private) German epithet. The equally malodorous Black, however religious, cannot 'change his spots' so easily.

In Germany **Judenzopf**: 'Jew-braid' translates as the Polish plait or *Plica Polonica*, a disease of the scalp (*plica*), endemic in Eastern Europe, which results in the matting of the hair. The same problem is also known as the **Polish disease**. The earlier **coccus Polonicus**: 'Polish microbe', was an insect of the louse family, a usage that underpinned Rome's disdain for the barbarians beyond its fiefdom.

One last link between Jews and illness is less unpleasant. **Jewish penicillin**, a joking description of chicken soup, that staple of the Jewish kitchen, and prescribed by Jewish mothers for a widc rangc of illnesses, really does seem to work. At least as far as colds and 'flu are concerned. The hot soup encourages the flow of mucus through the nose, which is of proven benefit to such diseases.

For all its popularity, mass tourism comes with a number of draw backs, not least the effects on one's stomach of hitherto unconsumed foreign food. The language has responded accordingly, coining a number of synonymous terms that register the horrors than can follow hard upon a less than palatable meal in a variety of stopping-off points. And none of these surpasses Mexico, from which we have gained the **Aztec hop, Aztec two-step, Mexican fox-trot, Mexican toothache, Mexican two-step** and most celebrated of all, **Montezuma's revenge**, this last referring to the hapless Emperor Montezuma, ruler of Mexico around 1500, whose own glories came to an abrupt end at the hands of the Spanish *conquistadores*. Not that Mexico has a sole lien on the concept of diarrhoea or in worse cases, dysentery as suffered by tourists with tender stomachs. **Delhi belly, Gippy tummy** and **Cairo crud** (both from Egypt), **Rangoon runs, Spanish tummy** and **Hong Kong dog** all mean the same thing. The **Bronx cheer**, an oral sound of contempt that is intended to resemble what is euphemistically called 'flatulence' allegedly originated in the Bronx, New York City.

References to Spain's identification with venereal diseases will be considered shortly, but the other sickness to which Iberia has given its name is **Spanish influenza**, the great post-World War I pandemic, which in the four years of its rampage across the globe killed four times the number of human beings than had the notably bloody conflict it succeeded. In linguistic terms *influenza* – which can run the course from a worldwide scourge to a worse than usual cold in the head plus runny nose – is not itself Spanish, but Italian and means literally 'influence'. Such an 'influenza' is on the one hand synonymous with the English word, but also implies, from the idea of astral or occult influence, a visitation or outbreak of any epidemic disease which attacks many people at the same time and place. This sense, as in *influenza di catarro*: 'influence of catarrh', *influenza di febbre scarlattina*: 'influence of scarlet fever', was known as early as 1504 and by the 18th century was synonymous with 'epidemic'. In 1743, when 'la grippe' (the French for 'flu) raged through Europe, the Italian 'influenza', given an English pronunciation, became the term of choice in Britain. (An outbreak in Hong Kong in 1957 of what was properly termed *virus A+/Singapore/1/57*, was popularly known as **Asian flu**.)

The combination of Spanish and influenza followed the early 20th-century outbreak, and the spread of the sickness is reflected in the spread of the terms. In Russia it is **ispanka**, in Italy **spagnola**,: both meaning the Spanish girl or woman. In Sweden it was **spanska sjukan**, and in Iceland **spánska veikin**, both meaning the Spanish disease. In Anglophone countries it was, naturally, Spanish influenza or **Spanish 'flu**. Two further 'Spanish' terms should be noted. **Spanish measles**, defined as black measles, is a form, like German measles, of the disease *rubella*, and Germany's **spanischer Kragen**: 'a Spanish collar' has twin meanings. On the one hand it refers to the complete wrapping of a patient in wet blankets, otherwise known as hydrotherapy; on the other it refers to the strangulation of the glans penis, a treatment presumably prescribed on the highest of medical principles.

Before turning to venereal disease, and thus returning substantially to France, there are a few miscellaneous terms that also mix ill-health and national sterotyping. In France the **feu persan** or 'Persian fire' means erysipelas. This local feverish disease is accompanied by diffused inflammation of the skin, and turns it a deep red colour; it is often called *St Anthony's fire*, or the *rose*. The synonymous **Persian fire**, as used in English, meant anthrax (listed as **Persicus ignis** in an English translation of *Blancard's Physical Dictionary* of 1693). Anthrax itself, best known today as a 'splenic' disease that afflicts cattle, and by cross-species infection, man too, was once a carbuncle, or malignant boil – literal translations from the Latin and before that Greek. Scythia, a large country that once covered areas of what today is both central Europe and Russia, gives the **Scythian disease** (coined by the Roman historian Herodotus), and describes the atrophy of the male genitals, and the subsequent 'loss of masculine attributes' (*OED*). The knock-on effect of this was the **Scythian insanity**, in which the newly emasculated man attempted to make the best of his new, ambivalent status by adopting female dress and habits. All of which, despite the discretion of a dictionary citation, would appear to imply that Scythian disease, with or without its supposed physical manifestation, may have been no more than a euphemism for transvestism.

Swiss cheese brain, in the grim jargon of joking doctors, refers to a condition of the brain in which gas bubbles have formed, while in German **Schweizerkrankheit**: 'the Swiss malady', is home-sickness or nostalgia. A **scabby-neck**, to 19th-century US sailors, was a Dane while the rhyming slang **septic** (as in **septic tank**) has meant Yank, i.e. American, in Australia since the 1970s. Finally comes the term **juliana**. Normally a cloth that is manufactured in Uganda and exported throughout Africa, the word has been appropriated by Tanzanians to mean AIDS, another item, rather less appealing than textiles, which is popularly associated with Uganda (although most theories see its naissance, at least in African terms, as the Congo) and spread thence all over the continent.

The French Disease

Maliciously or otherwise, the medical Latin in which the names of most diseases were once enshrined (and which indeed survives in medical jargon to this day) included in its listings a number of racial slurs. Perhaps the best known, and widest spread of these is **Morbvs Gallicvs**, the **French disease**, or more properly syphilis.

The word *syphilis*, and its association with France, go back to the publication in 1530 of a poem *Syphilis, sive Morbvs Gallicvs*, by Girolamo Fracastoro (otherwise known as Hieronymus Fracastorius (1483–1553), a physician, astronomer, and poet of Verona. The poem tells the story of the shepherd Syphilus, supposedly the first sufferer from the disease (the name Syphilis, which was taken by metonymy from that of the unfortunate sufferer, was formed on the analogy of the -is suffix used in such names as Æneis and Thebais). Fracastoro then used the term again – now as a definite piece of medical jargon – in his treatise *De Contagione* ('on Contagion', 1546). The poem arrived in English in 1686 when it was translated by Nahum Tate with the title *Syphilis: or, a Poetical History of the French Disease*. The name Syphilus itself may have come from a corrupt, medieval version of the name Sipylus, who appears in the Latin poet Ovid's *Metamorphoses* as a son of Niobe, the daughter of Tantalus who foolishly challenged Apollo and Artemis, who promptly killed her entire family – some fourteen children. She then wept copiously before being turned into stone, as part of Mount Sipylon. The death of Niobe's children, and their mother's lamentations, have been a popular subject for many artists. Thus names that link France to syphilis abound. In England there is **the French-man**, the **French gout, French crown, French disease, malady of France, French goods** (which can also be brandy, given the source of the liquor) and the **French pox**; to **take French lessons** is to contract the disease, and **frenchified** means infected. The **French pig** refers to the disease in general, but specifically to the syphilitic pustule or bubo that indicates its existence. A **blow with a French faggot-stick** refers to the loss of one's nose through the advancing ravages of the illness, and one whose nose has already rotted away has been **knocked with a French faggot** (despite the modern slang use of *faggot* as homosexual, this means nothing more than stick). Danes and Norwegians refer to **Franzoser**: the Frenchman, and **den franske syge**: the French disease. In Poland it is **franca**, once more 'the Frenchman', while in Russia **frantzukaya boliezn** means the French disease, as does **vranclijiv** or **francuzljiv** in Croatia, **o gallico** in Portuguese, **französische Krankheit** in Germany and **fransos** in Iceland. And on the list goes. Synonyms for the Frenchman include **galico** in Spain and **francouze** in Czechoslovakia. The French disease becomes **mal francez** in Spain and **mal francese** in Italy. Yiddish, which talks of **frantzn** or Frenchmen, describes a sufferer as **farfrantzevet**: 'frenchified', a synonym for Spain's **galicoso**. With so relentless an identification, it is hardly surpising that St Denis (in his more respectable guise the patron saint of France and of its capital city Paris) is also patron saint of syphilitics.

Nonetheless, not all sufferers, linguistic or otherwise, are French, and France even hits back at her persecutors with a couple of phrases. Faced by the German Franzosen she retaliated with **prussiens**: 'Prussians', to characterize the disease, while **aller en Bavière**: 'to go to Bavaria' is to be treated for syphilis; an extra punch was given to the phrase by the pun on **baver**: to drivel, a fate that tended to overtake advanced sufferers as the brain gradually collapsed. Similarly **aller en Suede**: 'to go to Sweden' meant to take the once popular sweating cure for syphilis. Once again there is an inbuilt pun, in this case between the proper name *Suede* and the French *suer*: to sweat. The French have also termed the illness the **Italian disease** and Italy, or at least its great cities, provides the backdrop for Portugal's **mal de Napoles**, and

France's **mal florentin**, respectively the maladies of Naples and of Florence. The **onguent napolitain**: 'Neapolitan ointment' was a salve, the active ingredient of which is mercury, which was used in the treatment of syphilis. Probably quite unconnected is the US term for Scandinavian immigrants: **salve eaters**. The **German pepper**, the fruit of the mezereon, and as such used in the adulteration of pepper, was also occasionally used to form the basis of a decoction which in pre-penicillin days, was used to cure sexually transmitted problems.

Syphilis offers an excellent means of conveying national rivalries and, while Japan uses **mankabassam**: literally 'the Portuguese sickness', and Portugal hits out with **mal de Castilla**: 'the Castillian sickness', ancient Greece referred to the **korinthion chanon**: 'Corinthian ill', another knock at a people who were generally pilloried for their alleged decadence. England, as ever, targets Ireland, with **Irish mutton** and the **Irish button** (presumably a reference to the syphilitic bubo that develops in the groin; a **Welshman's button**, however, is an artificial fly, used by anglers), and throws in a swipe at Spain in the **Spanish disease** and the **Spanish gout**. In the county of Somerset any form of venereal disease is known as the **Welshman's hug**. The Dutch, who fought many bitter battles against Spanish rule, used **gezien hebben Spanje**: 'to have seen Spain', to mean that one was suffering, although the phrase could also mean to have suffered punishments other than venereal ones. The Netherlands also uses **Spaansche pokken**, Spanish pox. Germany backs up its excoriation of France with that of Spain, offering **spanische Krankheit**: the Spanish disease, and the polysyllabic **Spanischfliegenpflaster**: Spanish-fly plaster refers to a syphilitic blister.

'Crows and Ravens...'

Some terms of abuse could not be more simple. **Dirty Arab, dirty Jew** leave no-one in any doubt. Nor indeed do Germany's **Scheissfranzose**: a 'little shit of a Frenchman' (**Fransoos** or **Franzoos** by itself means Frenchman in a pejorative sense in Dutch), the Chilean equivalent **aleman de mierda**: a 'shit of a German', **bromoblachos**, a Greek term for a 'stinking Wallachian', especially a Rumanian from the provinces, who uses a dialect and cannot understand the 'literary' language and the Polish phrase **kiepski po wegiersku**: foul as a Hungarian. Other references to dirt imply national habits rather than literal dirtiness. A **Dutch bath** is a very cursory wash, and to **French bathe** is to use perfumes as a deodorant in lieu of bathing. The French appear, from these phrases, to eschew the laundry: the Dutch phrase **Fransche verschooning**: 'French laundering' refers to the turning of soiled clothing inside out, thus making it reasonably presentable. Another Dutch phrase, **zijn hemd in de Fransche wasch doen**, 'to put his shirt into the French wash' means to wear a soiled shirt on the wrong side; and the French turn on their own, notably the Gascons, with **faire la lessive du gascon**: to 'soap the Gascon way', i.e. to turn one's soiled shirt inside out, before wearing it again.

Like crows and ravens, states the German saying, **the Jews will gain nothing from a bath**. Thus the Polish adjective **parxtyj**: scabby, is used to mean a Jew and in Germany the phrase **einen Juden begraben**: 'to bury a Jew' also means to make inkblots. Mid-18th-century Ireland termed Englishmen **bugs**, the premise being that English settlers imported bugs to the country.

RELIGION

GIVEN THE role of the world's organized religions in the creation, encouragement, proliferation and on-going maintenance of racism it is suprising that there are not more terms that actually focus on religion *qua* religion. There are, perhaps naturally, more that use colour as the background (although no institution has been so assiduous in making the equation between Black or brown and 'inferiority' or 'paganism' than has White Christianity), but one would hardly have imagined that 'food' terms, for instance, would outpace those of religion by more than two to one. After all, it was the arrival of missionaries, rather than their empire-building predecessors, the traders, that really saw an upsurge in the demonology of 'Black' as 'bad'. Yet so the vocabulary shows. Not only that, but looking through the words that do equate religious difference with some endemic evil, it seems to be the Christian sects – Protestantism and Roman Catholicism – who are most enthusiastic in their denunciations. And even these are further restricted by colour.

On the whole this is a White-on-White phenomenon. Perhaps the role of 'idol-worshipping' by Blacks was too easily lumped together

259

with their other 'backward' characteristics for anyone to single it out for special targeting. Perhaps to credit those same idols with any credibility, even that afforded by the negative pronouncements of racial abuse, was to allow them too much importance. It was safer to abuse one's own; and of course when one tired of that, or even sooner, there was always another target, sanctified in every Christian creed: the Christ-killing Jews.

The Bible Belt

The main fault that has been laid at Protestant feet is that, as it were, they 'protest too much'. In other words some of the creed's more extreme followers, usually those tied to one or other fundamental sect, are just too religious. Such followers tend, at least in the past couple of centuries, to be found in what has been termed the **bible belt** of America, states such as Mississippi, Alabama, Kansas and others encompassing the Mid-West and South. The phrase was coined by the critic and philologist H.L. Mencken, a sceptic with little time for the fantasies of the credulous, whose own take on theology dismissed it as 'an effort to explain the unknowable by putting it into the terms of the not worth knowing', and who defined these earnest Puritans as those with 'the haunting fear that someone, somewhere, may be happy'. Writing in 1926 in the pages of his magazine the *American Mercury*, he referred to 'Jackson, Miss.,...the heart of the Bible and Lynching Belt'. Such an area, with its vast constituencies of conservative, religious White Christians, has always been prey to the extremes of their religion. These are the people to whom the Catholic Church (as it is for such preachers as Northern Ireland's Ian Paisley) is still the 'Scarlet Whore of Rome' (an image first coined in 1530 and taken from *Revelations* xvii) and for whom the concept of the apocalypse and the 'end-time' is no mere fantasy, and certainly no joke. Such extremism has always attracted taunts, among them **bible-belter, bible-back** and **black Protestant**, this last used by Catholics to define these sanctimonious, oppressively pious and dedicatedly anti-Catholic folk; the term can also be used to describe a lapsed Protestant. Their natural espousal of any form of censorship, typically those laid down in Boston's late-18th century *blue laws* (which came to influence large tracts of American culture) gave another 'colour' name: **blue-skin**.

Many such Protestants were and are Primitive Baptists, a sect that expanded hugely in mid-19th-century America, and their fanaticism, and their rite of baptizing converts and neophytes through total immersion earned them such terms as **forty-gallon baptists** and **footwashers** (from the commandment in *John* 13:14 'If I then, your Lord and Master, have washed your feet, ye also ought to wash one another's feet'). This immersion was not invented in America: a century earlier one finds the German term **dunker** or **tunker**, both meaning 'dipper' and referring to the same practice. **Dipper** has the same meaning in England, where other terms for Baptists include **crying Willie** and **hardhead** (for their fundamentalism, although the term also covers, irrespective of religion, the Germans, Dutch and English). Extreme Baptists were (and remain) **hard-shell** (the image is of a turtle or crab) while their milder peers were **soft-shells**. (The image is reminiscent of that enshrined in *mossyback*: an extreme political conservative, whose views change with the slowness of a turtle's progress.) Immersion gives the 20th-century **wetwash Baptists**, the opposite of **dry-clean Methodists**. A member of the west Indian Spiritual Baptist Church, who tie their heads in White scarves, is a **tie-head**. Water-sports aside, the sheer enthusiasm of the fundamentalists, typically the Pentacostalist sects who were known for their ecstatic religiosity, gave other names: **holy roller**, **shouter** and **jesus-screamer**.

One does not have to rant or censor, however, to earn opprobrium. The Quakers, or Religious Society of Friends, founded by George Fox in 1648-50, are quite the opposite of the bible-belters, opting for pacifism, for simplicity of life and of dress. If hard-shell Baptists live by aggression and an unswerving belief in incontrovertible truths, then Quakers seem to personify compromise and debate. This has not saved them from dislike. Their dress sense earned them the names **broadbrim** (from their hats) and **shad-belly** (from the name of an old-style coat, a popular article of dress among Quaker men). Rhyming slang termed them **muffin-bakers**, while the popular name **Obadiah** became a generic for the entire group and **yea-and-nay man** reflected their professed predilection for simple, black and White answers.

Speech also lay behind **cohee**, a term that apparently came from the common Quaker usage of the phrase 'quoth he'. The word Quaker itself, for all that it is neutral term today, began as a slur. Methodists, another Low Church sect, were also known as **swaddlers** in the 18th century. Charles Wesley, brother of John, the Methodists' founder, explained in his *Journal* for September 10, 1747: 'We dined with a gentleman, who explained our name to us. It seems we are beholden to Mr. Cennick for it, who abounds in such like expressions as, "I curse and blaspheme all the gods in heaven, but the babe that lay in the manger, the babe that lay in Mary's lap, the babe that lay in swaddling clouts", &c. Hence they nicknamed him, "Swaddler, or Swaddling John"; and the word sticks to us all, not excepting the Clergy.' According to Barrère (1902) swaddler, as cited in Harman's *Caveat for Common Cursetours* (1566, one of the earliest of all slang glossaries), also meant an Irish Catholic who pretended, for the purposes of begging, to have been converted. Methodist could also mean fanatic, and allied pejoratives, similar to those based on *pope* or *Jesuit*, include **methodistical**, **methodisty** and the prefix **Methodistico-**.

Back in the world of fundamentalism, this time in Northern Ireland, Protestants are known (as they are in the Catholic enclaves of Scotland) as **soap-dodgers** (from their supposed abhorrence of washing), **yellowbacks** (where the term reflects their 'Orange' sympathies, Catholics of course are 'green') and **right-footers**. This last, the opposite of the better known **left-footer** for Catholic, apparently stems from the positioning of the lug – that part of the implement upon which one presses one's foot when digging – on their peat-cutting spades. Poland, a fiercely Catholic country, has a number of religiously based epithets. **Niemczyk**: 'the German fellow' means the devil, while **niedowiarek**: an infidel, is a German. Both terms reflect German Protestantism. **Wencliczki**: 'Wenceslaus' is generic for Czech, being that nation's patron saint. Other terms include **Mas John** or **Messjohn** (Master John), used in 17th- to 19th-century Scotland and meaning a Scots Presbyterian minister, as opposed to an Anglican or Roman Catholic, the verb **Japan**, to ordain as a minister (from his wearing of a black coat, as does furniture than has been 'japanned'), **Paris bun** and finally the Papua New Guinea term for 'an impotent man' (which can doubtless be extended to Catholics too): **misinari** or in English, missionary.

Box the Jesuit

Like Protestantism, Catholicism can be stigmatized by its rituals and, given the nature of the rival faiths, these are rather more extensive in the world of 'smells and bells'. Thus one finds **beadpuller** and **beadhunter**, both allusions to the rosary; **crossback**, an American reference to the cross that is found on the priestly vestment or chasuble; **statue-lover** and **statue-worshipper**, both of which refer to the many images to be found in a Catholic church (and never in a Protestant one). The beating of one's breast as part of the ritual confession of sins gives a number of terms starting with **craw-thumper**, listed in 1785 by Francis Grose as a generic term for Catholics, and moving on to **claw-thumper**, **breast-beater**, **breast fleet** and **brisket-beater**. **Chest-pounder** is an American equivalent although **craw-thumper** was initially used as a specific description of the 17th-century settlers in Maryland, who, as opposed to the Puritans of New England, were Catholics. The traditional avoidance of meat on Fridays gives **fisheater**, **mackerel-snapper** and **mackerel-snatcher**, all Americanisms. A **candle shop** is a Roman Catholic church, reflecting the many candles that burn in one.

R.C., **roman**, **cat-lick** or **cat-licker**, all mean Catholic, as does Australia's **rock-chopper**, which combines the 'r' and 'c' with a reference to the Irish Catholic convicts, transported to Australia in the early 19th century and condemned to perform hard labour, i.e. breaking rocks. The role of the Pope as the head of the Church gives **papist** (a slur since Martin Luther coined its German equivalent in 1521, after which it was promptly translated into English) and **poper**. The 16th century saw a number of allied, and equally pejorative terms: **popish**, **popery**, **papistical**, **papistic**, **papish**, **paism**, **popestant** and **popeling**. The much earlier Pope-holy, meaning hypocritical, dates back to Chaucer. The Reformation was a great generator of inter-denominational slurs: both sides, for instance termed each other **Antichrist** and **whore**, while religious differences were savaged as 'fornication', 'harlotry', 'carnality' and other terms redolent of sexual, rather than spiritual deviation.

The **Pope's nose** – the rump of a fowl – appears in Grose's slang dictionary in 1796; its 'Protestant' sucessor, the *parson's nose*, arrives a century later. In Papua New Guinea, where *papa santi* (holy father) is the more respectful term (and a Catholic is simply a *katolik*), **popi** is the negative form, an equivalent to papist. Even less respectful is 18th-century England's **holy father**, defined by Grose as 'A butcher's boy of St Patrick's Market, Dublin or any other Irish blackguard'; and a **touch of the holy bone,** a phrase that originated in Ireland and then migrated to America. It means sexual intercourse, and teases those who believe in the supposed power of saintly 'relics'. Rome itself gives the English adjective **Romish** (1531) and the French **romaine**: a 'Roman thing', i.e. a lecture or telling-off. The practice of noting Saints' days or other Church festivals on the calendar by printing the date in red gives **red-letter man**, and red is found again in **redneck**, a somewhat paradoxical term in this context which in its time has meant both a Presbyterian (from which its use extended to encompass the mainly Presbyterian/Protestant poor Whites of southern America) and at the same time Roman Catholics and thus Irish immigrants. The Catholic use, as opposed to the American, Protestant one, comes from Lancashire, where it was a 19th-century dialect term. Another dialect term, Suffolk's **jesooiter** (a Jesuit) described a tiresome, empty talker.

The simple word **Jesuit** was itself highly prejudicial for a time. The sect, founded by St Ignatius Loyola in 1533, was one of the Catholic church's most efficient arms in the fight against the Protestant Reformation. Thus, in Protestant England, they were loathed, typically in Stubbs' denunciation, in his *Anatomy of Abuses* (1583) as 'the devil's agents'. Characterized as casuists, preaching that any means, however devious, justify an end, Jesuit became a term of opprobrium, especially in the adjectival form **Jesuitical**: 'deceitful, dissembling; practising equivocation, prevarication, or mental reservation of truth.' (*OED*) Jesuits were also seen as perverse: Rochester portrays them as sodomites in his peom 'A Ramble in St James's Park', while the slang phrase 'box the Jesuit', meaning to masturbate, is defined by Grose as, ' a crime that is said much practized by the reverend fathers of that society'.

'Take away an Irishman's religion, and you make a devil of him' claims one saying, and the link between the Irish (whether in Ireland or America) and their predominantly Catholic faith is undeniable. The majority of these terms developed in 19th-century America, although the quasi-blasphemous 'oath' **by the holy poker and the tumbling Tom!** is reported in Hotten's *Slang Dictionary*, first published in Piccadilly, London in 1859. **Teague**, from the Irish name *Tadhg*, and usually rendered as Thaddeus in English has lasted since the 17th century, and by the way spawned **taig**, the usual modern use, and **tad**, an abbreviation of Thaddeus, as well as **tyke**, Australia's version of teague. **Mick**, which means an Irishman, religious or not, also means a Catholic in the US, as does **Turk**, which itself may be one more perversion of teague. **Far-Down** is an Irish-American Catholic whose forebears came from Northern Ireland (from County Down, one of the six counties of N. Ireland), where a **left-footer** still means a Catholic. Last of all **Irish triplets**: translated as the birth of one child a year for three years in succession mocks both the Irish themselves, seen as ignorant of the proper meaning of standard use of 'triplets', and the church's refusal to permit contraception.

A word that mixes Catholicism, politics and even good old fashioned banditry, is **Tory**, a contemporary synonym for the British Conservative party, and prior to the Conservatives, the name of those Irish who became outlaws, subsisting by plundering and killing the English settlers and soldiers who, under Cromwell's troops, had dispossessed them. It comes from the anglicized spelling of the Irish *tóraidhe*: pursuer, although some sources define a tory as the one pursued, and therefore an outlaw. Around 1680 it was adopted as the nickname for those who opposed the exclusion of James, Duke of York (a Roman Catholic) from the succession to the British Crown. According to Roger North writing in *Examen* (1740), The Bill of Exclusion 'led to a common Use of slighting and opprobrious Words; such as Yorkist. That did not scandalise or reflect enough. Then they came to Tantivy, which implied Riding Post to Rome...Then, observing that the Duke favoured Irish Men, all his Friends, or those accounted such by appearing against the Exclusion, were straight become Irish, and so wild Irish, thence bogtrotters, and in the Copia of the factious Language, the Word

Tory was entertained, which signified the most despicable Savages among the Wild Irish'. The Tories' rivals, the **Whigs** (the ultimate fathers of the modern Liberals), were originally Presbyterian Covenanters, i.e. those Scots who did not wish to see James or Catholicism in power. The word itself, which elsewhere means sourmilk or cream, buttermilk or a dish of whey fermented with herbs (all of which presumably come from whey itself), is thought to have been based on the Covenanters' motto *We Hope In God*. In the larger world a whig came to mean an irresolute person, someone who constantly changed their mind (based on the Parliamentary party's perceived propensity for dithering). As might be expected, **Whigland** was Scotland and **Whiglanders** Scots.

Lastly, a small subset of Catholic-related terms can be found in the Greek use of **frankia** ('the land of the Franks'), to mean Western Europe. **Frankos** refers to a Roman Catholic, rather than the Greek Orthodox church that dominate Christian worship in the Eastern Mediterranean. **Frankopappas** is a Catholic priest and **frankepho** is a convert to the Roman Church from that of Greek Orthodoxy.

'One Who Killed Our Lord'

'Now a Jew, in the dictionary, is "one who is descended from the ancient tribes of Judea...", but you and I know what a Jew is: One Who Killed Our Lord... a lot of people say to me "Why did you kill Christ?' 'I dunno, it was one of those parties, got out of hand, you know". We killed him because he didn't want to become a doctor, that's why we killed him.' Thus the position of the Jewish-American satirist Lenny Bruce, but the black humour masks centuries of grim propaganda. The fissiparousness of Christianity may have led within its own ranks to some of the terms listed above, but as far as the Jews are concerned, the main product of nearly two millennia of Christian theology found its logical conclusion in the ovens of Auschwitz, Treblinka and the rest.

The term **Christ-killer** is absent from the *OED*, a tribute perhaps to Sir James Murray's admirable liberalism but not to his usually all-encompassing lexicography. The term is used by one of Henry Mayhew's interviewees in his 1857 study *London Labour and the London*

Poor, and the concept, even then, was moving towards two thousand years of use. Its first dictionary citation is in Ware's *Passing English of the Victorian Era* (1909), a supplement to Farmer & Henley's multi-volumed *Slang and Its Analogues*. He notes that it is 'passing away – chiefly used by old army men' and indeed it does seem shortly after the Mayhew citation to have taken up a more prominent residence in America, its use fuelled, no doubt, by the predominantly Catholic Irish, Polish and other Central European immigrants who continued to flood the country. Nor has it vanished. One can find citations as recently as the late 1980s, and these are not historical references. (A secondary meaning of Christ-killing, of noisy, radical oratory – the reference presumably to the crowds of Jews supposedly beseeching Pilate for Christ's death – was briefly fashionable among tramps *c*.1930.)

As Bruce says, 'you and I know what a Jew is', and those who spread the concept and coined the term would have had little time for his painful irony. It is, perhaps, to be harping on a point to say yet again that the Jews have been singled out as a racial scapegoat rivalled only by the Blacks, but such is the reality. For every positive there must be a negative, and if Christianity has long-since seized the metaphorical White hat, then Judaism, home of the Christ-killers, has been forced to adopt the black.

'How odd | Of God | To choose | The Jews': thus the clichéd jingle, but odd or not, the idea of the Jews as being chosen for a special role in the divine scheme can be found throughout the Bible. *Exodus* xix has God promising the Israelites a role as 'my treasured posession among all the peoples' and *Deuteronomy* x claims that 'He chose you...from among all peoples'. If, even to believers, these are not 'God's words' but a rationalization by the Jews of their apparently unique role in the world, then so be it. The image of a **chosen people**, a term that starts appearing in English in the mid-16th century, has persisted, as much mocked as celebrated. **Chosen Pipples**, delivered with a fake 'European' accent, tends to the former category. Another collective term is **ghetto-folk**, a much newer phrase, but one which stems from the placing of Jews in carefully segregated areas of towns and cities, sometimes surrounded by an actual wall. The first ghetto appeared in Venice in 1516 and possibly took its name from the site of its foundation, a disused foundry or, in Italian, *getto*. The extension of ghetto into its modern use, an urban area (often one of its poorest) in which a given minority group is concentrated, emerges in the late 19th-century, and while it has come to encompass any such group, was initially used to describe the East End of London – then the home of England's Jews. Allied is the American **go-ghetto**, meaning a Jew and punning on the standard word go-getter.

Like chosen people, the **Hebrews**, and thus the modern abbreviations **hebe, heeb, heebie** and occasionally **heebess**, start life in the Bible. The word began life in the Aramaic *hebrai* (and Hebrew *hibri*) which literally meant 'one from the other side of the river'. Thus *Abraham ha-hibri*, in Hebrew, meaning literally 'Abraham the passer over' or 'immigrant' (to Palestine), becomes 'Abraham the Hebrew'. The word lost its 'h' in Middle English, and became *ebreu* but regained it by the 14th century. Quite when Hebrew gained its pejorative usage (paving the way for the modern abbreviations) is hard to pin down, but by the time Shylock, in *The Merchant of Venice* (1600), talks of his 'Hebrew gaberdine' the negative meaning was fully in place. Italy's **ebreaccior** and **ebreuzzo** (both 'Hebrew') have exactly the same connotation. As a language Hebrew, like Greek and Dutch, is a synonym for gibberish.

Several other names have been used as part of the abusive lexicon. Initially neutral, descriptive terms, they work almost as euphemisms, as if the simple word 'Jew' is too much for a fastidious person to utter. Royal decrees, pontificating on the status of the Jews during the Middle Ages used the Latin term **Secta nefaria**: the nefarious sect. **Israelite**, like Hebrew is another word that began as a simple description, but gradually, as anti-semitism gathered strength, came to be an implicit term of criticism. **Levi** refers literally to a descendant of the tribe of Levi, the third son of the patriarch Jacob; like the Cohens, the Levites are hereditary priests, in their case responsible for such temple rituals as animal sacrifice. In the 18th century the *levi* was briefly a fashion accessory: a form of dress popular among women but described by Horace Walpole as 'a man's nightgown bound round with a belt', resembling, supposedly, some *haute couture* version of Levitical garb. Late 19th-century Britain read the **Daily Levy** or the *Daily Telegraph*,

a London newspaper so named for its former owner, Joseph Moses
Levy while the navy's HMS *Leviathan* was known by nautical wits as
the **Levy Nathan**. **Moses**, another Biblical figure (*inter alia* the man
who brought the Ten Commandments from Mount Sinai) has also been
a source of abuse. Moses simply means Jew but in 1785 Francis Grose
notes the term **stand Moses**, used of a man who 'has another man's
bastard child fathered upon him, and he is obliged by the parish to
maintain it'. As defined in New York police chief George Washington
Matsell's *Vocabulum* (1859, America's first homegrown slang dictionary) Moses is 'a man that fathers another man's child for a consideration'. The phrase appeared, according to Randal Cotgrave's *Dictionarie
of the French and English Tongues* (1611), because traditional images of
Moses show him 'hauing [sic] on either side of the head an eminence,
or luster arising somewhat in the forme of a horne', an image reminiscent of the cuckold's horns, and as such causing 'a prophane Author to
stile Cuckolds, Parents de Moyse'. From there Moses himself became
the cuckold, and thence the common phrase. **Mose**, or **old man mose**
can also mean an African American as well as stand as a personification
of time. Moses is also found in the Polish **Mosiek**: a Jew, and possibly
in Germany's **mauscheln**: gesticulating, intoning words, or talking
Yiddish. **Abram**, which is found (see *Crime*) in a variety of cant
combinations, has been used to mean Jew in Russia.

Ishmael, Abraham's son by Hagar, means literally 'God will hear'
and has been used to mean both a Jew and an outcast, thus the
celebrated first line of Melville's *Moby Dick* ('Call me Ishmael') and
Ishmael's description in *Genesis* xvi. 12 as 'one whose hand is against
every man, and every man's hand against him'. In the theological
partitioning of the Hebrew patriarchy, the Arabs claim to be his
descendants. Ishmael's outcast role links to another staple figure of
Judaeo-Christian mythology: what France calls **le juif errant** and the
Germans term **ewiger Jude**, the eternal Jew or the **wandering Jew**
and give the phrase 'Er ist schon ein ewiger Jude': he can't stay put.
The legend of the wandering Jew, who supposedly insulted Christ as
he toiled up the via Dolorosa towards Calvary and was thus condemned
to wander the earth eternally, appears during the 13th century. According to Roger of Wendover's *Flores Historiarum* (*c*.1235) an Armenian

archbishop, visiting England, claimed that in 1228 he had entertained at his own table a Jew named Cartaphilus, once Pontius Pilate's porter, who had foolishly uttered the insult, asking 'Go faster, Jesus, why dost thou linger?' Christ's response, 'I indeed am going, but thou shalt tarry till I come', set Cartaphilus, off on his travels, never to cease until the Day of Judgement. The story took on its modern form in 1602 when a pamphlet claimed that in 1542 Paulus von Eizen, bishop of Schleswig, had met a man, this time calling himself Ahasuerus, who claimed to be the wanderer. This name has stuck and prompted a variety of literary works. A species of vine, that 'wanders' at random, is also known as the wandering Jew. Combining both Moses and Ahasuerus is **moisher**: to wander around, used in Derek Raymond's seminal novel of upper class low-lifes, *The Crust On Its Uppers* (1962).

Another Jew, even more vilified in the Christian pantheon, is Judas Iscariot (literally *ish-qriyoth*: 'man of Kerioth'), the betrayer of Christ. Thus **Judas** itself means an informer, Germany's **Judaskuss**: Judas-kiss, is a kiss of betrayal (as indeed is the **Judas kiss** in English), and France's **judaizer**: 'to Judas', means to betray. The **Judas-colour**, used of the hair or beard, is red (from the medieval belief that Judas had red hair and a red beard); it is a myth that has been sustained for centuries, typically in Dickens' allotting the evil Fagin with matted red locks. A **Jew's thorn** (or Christ's thorn), is the *Paliurus Spinacristi*, from which Christ's crown of the thorns was allegedly constructed while the German phrase **auf den Juden Christtag**: 'until Jewish Christmas', means never.

The Crucifixion also gives **pharisee**, when not a synonym for Jew, then defined as a bigot or overliteral devotee. The Pharisees were the dominant Jewish sect when Christ was preaching and it was they, allegedly terrified by his message, who persuaded Pilate to have him executed. **Rabbi**, the Hebrew term meaning 'my master', is generally used as a Jewish synonym for 'vicar' or 'father', but it can be a negative generic for a Jew. It is also used, in a variety of professions, typically the police, as a senior figure whose advice and aid can be sought by those he favours. Other 'Biblical' references include America's **house-of-David boy**, which refers to the second King of Israel, David, whose story is found in the book of *Samuel* (but, it should be noted, in no

ancient non-Biblical work whatsoever). It was David who defeated
Goliath, had a best friend called Jonathan, duplicitously seduced Bath-
sheba by sending her husband off to die in battle, wrote the Psalms and
fathered the wise Solomon. It was also King David to whom God
promized that his kingdom would endure for ever and it is thus that
the New Testament sees Christ as one of his lineal descendants. The
'House of David', nonetheless, is seen as a Jewish phenomenon, and it
is that image that is mocked in the phrase. **Dave**, by itself, has also been
used to mean a Jew. Another phrase, the **stiff-necked people**, quotes
Moses' outburst when his patience with his flock, forever backsliding
to set up Golden Calfs and the like, became over-stretched.

One of the most interesting, coined *c*.1820, and until the last World
War most common of anti-Jewish terms has been **sheeny**, and it has
been one of the most elusive to pin down. A variety of etymologies have
been proposed: the American lexicographers Wentworth and Flexner
suggest, in the *Dictionary of American Slang*, the German word *shin*, a
petty thief, cheat or a miser. Leo Rosten, the great popularizer of
Yiddish, prefers the German-Jewish pronunciation of the German
schön, beautiful, fine, nice, and a word Jewish peddlers supposedly used
to describe the merchandise they offered. More complex, but perhaps
most feasible, is that proposed by Nathan Süsskind in 1989. His
etymology is based on the Yiddish phrase a *shayner Yid*: a pious
(literally 'beautiful-faced') Jew and thus an old-fashioned and traditional Jew and one who, according to the Talmud sports the religiously
proper full beard. The term was then taken up, mockingly, by assimilated German Jews who had immigrated to England, as meaning 'an
old-fashioned Jew', i.e. in habits, clothing and religion. These 'modern'
Jews mocked their less sophisticated successors, who followed them
from Germany and clung on (at least initially) to their old-fashioned
ways. The first half of the phrase, which the 'uncultured' Jews pronounced *sheena* rather than the more Germanic *schön* was taken up by
gentile Jew-baiters to create *sheeny*. Sheeny itself gives the late-19th-
century **snide and shine** (or **S and S**), East London Gentiles' slang
meaning a Jew, especially an East Londoner. The term seems to pun on
'rise and shine', mixing sheeny with the older slang term *snide*: meaning, fake, counterfeit and generally dubious – a reference no doubt to

the supposedly poor quality of the goods they hymned as *schoen*.

A small group of religiously inclined places complete this section. The Croatian **avra** and Rumanian **havra** both refer to a synagogue or Jewish school, and play upon the hebrew *chevra*: a society. An extension, America's **cinemagogue**, a cinema with a Jewish owner, puns on synagogue. In 1930s England the **Holy Land** was any predominantly Jewish neighbourhood; the **Holy of Holies** was the Grand Hotel at Brighton, which around 1890 became a favourite with Jewish customers, while Brighton itself was known facetiously as **Jerusalem the Golden**. Before the Nazi era in Germany, Grünewald, a suburb of Berlin, was similarly termed the **golden ghetto** from the wealth of its succesful Jewish residents.

Unchristened Turks

Unlike Judaism and the various branches of Christianity, Islam and the Muslims whose religion it is, have been given a comparatively gentle ride until relatively recently. It is only in the increasingly embittered commentaries for and against the Islamic position in the Middle East, the 'fundamentalist' revolution in Iran, the *fatwa* pronounced against Salman Rushdie, the attritional horrors of the civil war in Algeria and the upsurge of religious ideology in Egypt that **Islam** has become a demonized term in itself. So too has **fundamentalist**, an adjective which in this context rarely requires a noun. In a religious world the Jews were pilloried for 'killing Christ', in a more secular one the Muslims in turn are attacked for seeking, so it appears, to 'kill' the comparatively 'liberal', and undoubtedly irreligious ethics of the modern Western state.

Not that the past is an unbroken succession of benevolence as regards Islam. Mahound, a name synonymous with that of the Prophet Mohammed, was commonly used in the Middle Ages to mean a devil, a false god (or prophet) or a monster. The term continued as one of opprobrium into the 19th century, and Mahound was regularly partnered with Termagent, characterized as another Muslim deity. The earlier terms **mawmet** and **mawmetrie**, both based on Mohammad, also provided names for false gods and idolatrous religiosity. In the 16th century, when the threat of Islam was in retreat, the term was given a new lease of life, used by Protestants to attack their Catholic rivals. The word **Moor** (*see* Colour) is a synonym for Muslim, and in 19th century India southern Indians and Sri Lankans referred to the people and languages of the north as Moorish. The Arabs themselves branded Black people **kafirs**: atheists or infidels, giving modern South Africa's kaffir and the Yoruba **kèfèri**, an unbeliever. The lands around the Hindu-Kush were known as **Kafiristan**, literally 'infidel-land' to the Persians. The term **fakir**, used in America to mean a confidence trickster or hoaxer, mixed the English *faker* with a new exoticism by combining the Hindu *fakir* (from Arabic *faquir*: a poor man) meaning 'an indigent person, but specially applied to a Mahommedan religious mendicant, and then loosely, and inaccurately, to Hindu devotees and naked ascetics' (Hobson-Jobson). **Turki nekrescenye**: 'unchristened Turks' meant Moslems in Russia, while in Scandinavia fanaticism is **Tyrkertro**, literally Turkish fatalism; **to go turkey** plays on the clichéd fatalism of Islam by meaning take potluck, and thus divide up the spoils. And if America used **infidel** to mean a Turk, then the Turks themselves called a non-Muslim **giaur**: a blasphemer or an infidel, and lending itself to *The Giaour*, the title of Byron's 1813 poem.

This stereotyping of the Muslim as a fatalist, unmoved by worldy events (Islam itself means submission), is seen in the German term **muselmänner**: 'mussulmen', used by the prisoners of the Third Reich's concentration or extermination camps to describe those of their fellows who had reached a state of physical and emotional exhaustion in which they displayed fatalism and loss of initiative, as Gerard Reitlinger put it in *The Final Solution* (1953), such men were no more than 'a walking skeleton wrapped up in a bit of blanket'. They may as well have been dead; invariably they soon were.

Woe to the Uncircumcized!

One man's gentile is another's true believer, and as H.L. Mencken noted in 1922, after listing in the *Smart Set* a page-and-a-half of defunct 'pagan' deities, 'They were gods of the highest dignity – gods of civilized peoples – worshipped and believed in by millions. All were omnipotent, omniscient and immortal. And all are dead'. Yet religion remains the great divider and language continues to worship at its altars. For Jews the best-known term to define a gentile is the Yiddish **goy**, which means simply 'nation' in Hebrew (as initially does gentile itself, via the Latin *gens*: a people). Goy gives a variety of combinations, including **fressn vi a goy**: 'to gobble like a gentile', to eat piggishly; a **goyishe kop**: a 'gentile head', i.e. a fool or a bonehead; the phrase was coined for peasants, but the inference is that no gentile, however cultured, can really be seen as on a par with Jewish intelligence and wit; thus the phrase **a goy bleibt a goy**: 'a gentile remains a gentile': however optimistic one may become, the goyim remain, at heart, the same; and **goyisher mazzl**: 'gentile luck', said of someone whose fortune is undeserved. The female goy is a **shikse**, a term that, in many Jewish households, became synonymous with charwoman. Like **shaygets**: a gentile youth, of which it is the feminine form, it comes from the Hebrew *sheques*: a blemish.

Lesser terms for non-Jews include **arel** and **orel**, both of which mean uncircumcized, and **okum** a Hebrew acronym meaning *o*ved *k*okh'vim *um*azolot, 'a worshipper of the stars and zodiacal signs', thus any gentile. More specific are terms for various middle European races, not all them actually *goyim*. Thus **tzeylem-kop**: 'cross-head' was a Lithuanian or White Russian Jew as named by other East-European Jews. The origin is obscure but it may come from the alleged keenness of Lithuanian Jews (knows to their peers as **Litvaks,** as opposed to the Polish **Polaks**) to embrace Christianity in order to make a literary or professional career, or at any rate, to delve into secular learning, forbidden though it was to the pious. Amalek, in the Bible, was a celebrated and much-vilified persecutor of Jews; thus the analogous **amolek** refers to the Rumanians, who ever since gaining their own independence seemed to have been desperate to deny the Jews theirs, and **zaks-amolek**: literally 'Saxon Amalek', refers to the Saxons, a group of Germans who were considered even more anti-semitic than their fellows. One last Biblical Hebrew word, **tirnkhe**: 'thou shalt obliterate' also refers to Amalek, the hereditary foe of the Israelites. It was used by Polish Jews as a nickname for the Armenians, whom they saw as direct descendants of Amalek and his Jew-hating tribe.

While the modern **buddha-head** is a simplistic American putdown of all Asians (**marble head**, evoking images of statuary, is a Greek term), irrespective of their actual religious faith, and **hermit kingdom**, meaning Korea, referred in the early 1900s to that (still undivided) country's relative isolation from the rest of the world, the term **celestial**, in a variety of Chinese contexts, is more problematical. Such terms include the **Celestial empire**, the **Celestial emperor** and the **Celestial kingdom** and evolved in the early 19th century. Celestial, from the Latin *caelum*: the sky, means in figurative terms 'of or pertaining to heaven, as the abode of God (or of the heathen gods), of angels, and of glorified spirits' (*OED*) and thus of a heavenly nature. Prior to the Revolution of 1949 China called itself *djing-kuo*: the centre of the world or the *Middle Kingdom*. A synonym was *t'in chow*, which has been translated as 'Heavenly Dynasty' and thus 'Celestial Kingdom': the sense being that the Kingdom in question is the one that is ruled by a dynasty appointed by heaven. China's attitude to foreigners is simple: **yang kuei tse** or **gwei lo** both mean 'foreign devil'.

A few other terms can be included. **Aunt Jane** refers to an Afro-American woman whose world is defined by spiritual rather than secular values; thus a regular church-goer and religious believer; the reference in *Genesis* to man being 'God's own image' is extended, when dealing with Black people to **God's image cut in ebony** and those who are happy with the images presented of quiescent 'darkies' may also term themselves **all-god's-chillun**. Russia, at least during the atheist Communist hegemony, was the **Godless country**, while in Rastafarian use **Babylon** (see *Sex*) is the non-Rasta world. The French term **Thebaïde**, meaning deep solitude or even a state of mental barrenness, refers to the Egyptian city of Thebes where early Christian monks once retreated. The Norwegian phrase **dra til Blokksberg**, go to Blokken, a peak in Germany's Harz Mountains, refers to the belief that covens of witches once gathered beneath its icy crags.

The last Biblical term is a positive minefield of ambiguities. **Philistine** is defined in the *OED* as a member of 'an alien warlike people, of uncertain origin, who occupied the southern sea-coast of Palestine, and in early times constantly harassed the Israelites'. Although the precise etymology remains debatable, the link to the territory of Palestine is undeniable. Translating the prophet Amos for his English-language version of the Bible in 1382 Wyclif conflated Philistines and 'Palestines' and the connection has remained. The use of Philistine as a pejorative began developing around 1700, when the *Dictionary of the Canting Crew* defined Philistines as 'Serjeants Bailiffs and their Crew; also Drunkards'. From there, with its implication of 'enemy', the term seems to have been picked up by early 19th-century German students, who used *Philister* to mean what Oxbridge calls 'town' as opposed to 'gown', i.e the local, non-academic citizenry of a university town. (The French slang *épicier*, literally a grocer, means much the same, and has been extended, like philistine, to mean uncultured and boorish; similar too was the original usage of *snob*.) From there the word took on its current meaning, defined (once more in the *OED*) as one who is 'deficient in liberal culture and enlightenment, whose interests are chiefly bounded by material and commonplace things... sometimes a mere term of dislike for those whom the speaker considers "bourgeois"'.

Clodhopper

PEASANTS

THE IDEA of unsophistication, of provincialism, of boorishness strays into many abusive terms. A number can be found elsewhere in this text: words designed to describe, for instance, America's poor Whites or the mixed-race citizens of the West Indies are often laden with metropolitan disdain and such terms can be found under *Colour*. Others are listed as *Fools*. This chapter attempts to isolate peasants as peasants, those who are criticized simply because, rather than join the urban world, they remain tied to the soil.

Of such terms the most odious, generally seen as transcending mere description and moving into dedicated abuse, is **kanaka**, used throughout the Pacific basin and a word described by the writer Nigel Lewis as 'an ugly, pejorative word meaning something between native and nigger' (*The Book of Babel*, 1994). Its origin, the Fiji term for 'man' is obviously neutral, but once it moved into the wider world it took on more negative connotations. From the mid-19th century onwards the term described the Pacific Islanders who were brought to Australia to work as indentured labourers on the Queensland cotton and sugar plantations. As a number of historians have noted, the indentures were merely cosmetic; the kanaka system was to all intents slavery. The number of labourers increased throughout the late 19th century, to such an extent that Queensland, known already as Bananaland, for its primary crop, gained a secondary nickname: **Niggerland**. Nor was the term restricted to Australia or even the Pacific. The American West Coast used it to describe Hawaiians in the late-19th century; in Ecuador and Peru it took on a new twist, and **canaca**, the local spelling meant either a Chinese person or a brothel-keeper. It could also, by its Chinese association, mean yellow. In Germany **kanake** means both foreigner and immigrant.

Its base, however, remains the Pacific, notably Papua New Guinea where the derisory exclamation **kanaka, bikpela samting**!: 'yokel, it's a big thing!' can be freely translated as 'it's obvious, dickhead!' So common is the exclamation that it is often abbreviated to **KBS**! Other uses include **buskanaka**: 'bush yokel', meaning a peasant, a savage or a teetotaller, and **kanaka bilong kunai**: 'yokel from the grass country' and thus a Highlander. Kunai is a tough grass that grows in the Highlands as a result of years of slash and burn cultivation. Highlanders are also **Chimbus** or **Simbus**, technically the name of both a cultural group and a Highland province, but in effect a putdown of the people so named. Grass underpins another local word, **asgras**: 'arse grass', or a loincloth made from grass, actually coconut palm or sago. Those who wear such loincloths are seen as backward, savage or unsophisticated. Like **buskanaka**, **busman** or **bushman** means a yokel as well as an outcast. One final PNG term is the uncompromisingly negative **smellbek**: 'a smelly bag'. This too means yokel and refers to those who work filling bags of copra, a malodorous occupation. The Papuans themselves were originally known as **netif**, or native in Tok Pisin, the local pidgin. This has gradually been seen as offensive and has been replaced by *wontok*: one talk.

Whether or not **canuck** (also spelt **canack**, **cannuk**, **cunnuck**, **kanuck** and **kunuck**, and sometimes found as **johnny-canuck**), which has meant a Canadian or French-Canadian in patois since the 1830s has any link to its Pacific cognate is unknown. While it may well come from the first syllable of Canada, some sources suggest a link both to kanaka and to the French *canaque*. Certainly at one time both

Frenchmen and Pacific Islanders worked side-by-side in the Pacific North-West fur trade. However, given the essential geographical distance, there are other theories: the word Connaught, a reference to the early Irish immigrants (although this is generally felt to be wide of the mark); the first syllable of Canada itself, as mispronounced by Native Canadians; a mix of Canada (again) and the Algonquin suffix *-uc* or *-uq*; a mix of Canada and Chinook and finally, and possibly most feasibly, and English version of the Iroquois *kanuscha*, a word meaning the resident of a *kanata* or community. As for Johnny Canuck, he made his first appearance in a cartoon of 1869, symbolic of young Canadians, whether British or French.

Moving south of the border into America one finds a number of terms calling on a 'peasant' identification. Aside from a variety of 'typical' names, which can be used by Blacks and Whites in common – **Clem**, **Rube** (from Reuben), **Hiram** and **Jeeter** (from *Jeeter Lester*, the poor White protagonist of Erskine Caldwell's novel *Tobacco Road* [1932]) – the simple term **farmer**, usually standard English, is found in slang meaning a backward, unsophisticated individual. More specific are **briar** and **briar-hopper**, both of which refer to dwellers in the Appalachian mountains. These mountain people, and indeed a wide range of poor Southern Whites are more generally known as **hillbillies** (or in the rarer female version: **hillnellies**). As described in the *New York Journal* (23 April, 1900), 'a Hill-Billie is a free and untrammelled White citizen of Alabama, who lives in the hills, has no means to speak of, dresses as he can, talks as he pleases, drinks whiskey when he gets it, and fires off his revolver as the fancy takes him'. He is also, by urban standards, a backward rustic. The word itelf comes from *hill* plus *billy*, using the proper name to mean a person, a fellow. Among other terms, usually used of poor Whites by their Black neighbours, are **gulley-digger**, **hoe-sager** (possibly from hoe plus the dialect *sager*: a sawyer, thus one who 'saws' a hoe backwards and forwards) , **leatherneck** (which also refers to any dirty, uncouth person, as well as meaning a US Marine), **snuff-dipper** (taking snuff, by both men and women, is or was a common hillybilly recreation), **squatter** or **White-arab**. **Buttermilk-swallower** refers to diet, while **butternut**, used by northerners of the South, is based on the colour of the dye used for home-spun clothing. Both *butter* and *cheese* have also been used to define a rustic – the reference is to dairy-farming – but without any racial overtones. Southerners have also been known as **pikes** and **pikers**. This may be a specific reference to Pike County, Missouri: as Mencken (1936) has noted 'The...first example is dated 1869, when *piker* meant a yokel from Pike County, Mo., then the common symbol of everything poverty-stricken and uncouth'. Nonetheless, there may be a link to the UK slang *pikey*: a gypsy, as well as to the turnpike, along which many poor people wandered, looking desperately for work. **Sharecropper**, usually a specific term describing those who work a small farm for a landlord, sharing such profits as there are with the owner, has been used as a generic term for all poor Southerners. Last of the US terms are **blanket-indian** and **stick-indian**, both of which describe a supposedly backward Indian who has in no way assimilated to modern life.

Still farther South the despised Mexicans are good for a number of words that emphasize their poverty and rural subsistence – **native**, which is also used in New Mexico, **paisano,** from Spanish *paisano*: a peasant, **pelado**: from Spanish *pelada*, a poor ill-bred person and perhaps most insulting of all, **peon**, from Spanish *péon*: an unskilled farmworker. Properly pronounced 'pay-on', the term is even more offensive when pronounced, as is general in American 'pee-on'. One more term, this time from the West Indies, is **bungo**. Meaning a crude, boorish, ignorant Black person it comes, more than likely, from the African language Hausa, in which the word *bungu* means a nimcom-poop, a country bumpkin. Africans, specifically the Bono people of Ghana, ask someone who stares **wo yę akuraseni?**: are you a villager?, mocking the gawing peasant 'come up to town'.

Judging by the terms that follow, Russia, the Ukraine and their neighbours in eastern or central Europe seemed locked into a compe-tition to see who is the most backward and the least sophisticated. Russia and Poland both use **chachol**: 'a clown' or 'a lout' to mean a Ukrainian; the Ukrainians retaliate with **burlak**: 'a churl, a boor and a lummox'; back come the Russians with **khokhol**, literally 'the crest of a cock', hence a bushy forelock and thus, apparently a Ukrainian and a boor; finally the Ukrainians, not to be outdone in the realm of facial hair, offer **katsap**, a burly, crude and bearded rustic. Nor is either limited to the other's failings. For Ukrainians a German is **shvabanok**: a hulking great Swab, while **cuxnj** or **cuxonec** (from *Cud*, a Baltic tribe) condemns, in Russia, the various nationalities of Finnish or Baltic origin such as Estonians, Karelians and Mordvinians. And so it continues across the area. Serbians typifty Hungarians as **sirov**, literally raw or crude; the Yiddish word **Moldevan**, literally Moldavian, is synonymous with a boor or lout; the Czechs denounce the **moravec nemravec**: the uncouth Moravian; elsewhere a **ruman**, a Rumanian, is the equivalent of a serf. Once these groups have made their way to America, there are new names. A **Polack**, literally a Pole, implies a slow, crude peasant; **bulak** means a Czech as does **honyok**, a word that can also mean a German; the essence of the term is not the racial origin, but the boorishness. Somewhat out of place is the extension **Filipinyock**, a Filipino, which appears to be another use of honyok. A link has been essayed with the Yiddish *yock*, another name for a gentile, but the effort seems contrived. Last of all is **slob**, which presumably has some link to Slav but is more immediately linked to the cartoon nation of 'Lower Slobovia', a snow-bound land of fur-clad people who spoke with a burlesque Slavic accent, created by Al Capp for his strip 'L'il Abner'.

Other 'peasants', less nationally specific, include **bushwhacker**, which can mean variously an outback Australian or a Pennsylvania 'Dutchman' (i.e. a German immigrant); in both cases the word denotes a backwoodsman. **Dutchy**, in America, refers to that same group of newly-arrived Germans, yet to adapt to America and still retaining their old-country crudities; by extension it means low-class, dowdy and slovenly. France's **râpé comme la Hollande**: 'shabby like Holland', emphasizes the negative image. Last of all is the French term **Boeotian**, meaning a stupid peasant. The Athenians of classical Greece traditionally regarded the natives of neighbouring Boeotia as churlish, rustic and ungainly.

Beggar

THE POOR

THE COMFORTABLE are the great coiners of abuse, and who are more comfortable than the comfortably off? To pontificate from a beachfront villa, a Left Bank apartment or Central Park triplex is easy. But who said unpleasantness had to be hard? The poor, as the cliché has it, are always with us. And it is not enough, simply, that they should lack money and thus 'our' advantages; it must be someone's fault. Theirs, naturally. And if they have no other raison d'être, let alone adequate resources, then at least let them pay, if only in terms of verbal slings and arrows, for our inconvenience and embarrassment.

Mexican Schlock

Stupid, avaricious, animalistic, dirty, over-sexed, there's always a stereotype going begging, which in the case of Mexico is the *mot juste*, since the people of Mexico, especially when they move over the border and set up home alongside their wealthy, northern neighbours, have long since been branded as poor, and made to suffer accordingly.

The simplest form comes in the adjective **Mexican**, which without further qualification implies the second-rate and the cheap, irrespective of which noun it qualifies; similarly generic is **adobe**, which is equally significant of poverty, and which comes from the Spanish *adobe*: sun-dried mud or clay, widely used as a building material in Mexico. From thereon in, it's all combinations. A **Mexican nightmare** is a piece of gaudy ceramic crockery, typical of that sold to tourists, while **Mexican schlock** (from *schlock*: cheap, inferior merchandise; anything defective or in poor taste, itself from the German *schlag*: a blow, thus meaning merchandise that has been 'knocked about') refers to the sort of art, all donkeys, sombreros and señoritas, that gets peddled to the country's visitors. In the realm of sports a **Mexican athlete** is an unsuccessful candidate for a college or school sports team, a **Mexican nose guard** an athletic supporter or jock-strap, a **Mexican hairless** (punning on the standard use, as the name of a breed of dog) is a worn-out old tennis ball and **Mexican liniment** is petrol. **Mexican Bogner's** are jeans worn as ski pants (Bogner's proper being the brand-name of choice in luxury ski-wear) and **Mexican cashmere**, referring to another up-market fabric, is a sweatshirt.

It is, however, in the world of automobiles that the Mexicans are comprehensively put in their place. A **Mexican Maserati** is a Mercury while a **Mexican Buick** is a Chevrolet, both phrases emphasizing the relative values and status of the pairs of cars in question. A **Mexican valve job** requires the flushing of the carburetor of a running engine with kerosene; a **Mexican window shade** or an **aztec** is a Venetian blind mounted in the rear window of a car. To give one's car a **Mexican carwash** means to leave it out in the rain, a **Mexican motor mount** is inner tubing used as a shock absorber, rather than the purpose-built material, and a **Mexican muffler** is a home-made silencer made from a tin can stuffed with steel wool which is then attached to the car's exhaust pipe

Generics and Off-Brands

After so exhaustive a listing, it may be hard to imagine poverty any-where other than in Mexico. Certainly no other nation can lay claim to the stereotype. But poverty is widespread and in terms of abuse is as useful a stick as any with which to belabour one's enemy. Thus one finds the **starving Armenians,** a phrase that refers not simply to Armenians, who suffered an appalling famine early in the 20th century, but to any starving people, Iceland's **eiga ekki danskan túskilding**: 'not to have even a Danish two-shilling piece', i.e. to be absolutely impoverished, and New Zealand's **British treasury note**: a blanket which soldiers found too thin to keep them warm.

A large tranche of insults are aimed at America's Black population. **Generic** and **off-brand**, usually used in merchandizing, both mean a Black person; the implication being that in their poverty they display no 'fancy packaging' or figurative form of producer's brand-name. Generic, off-brand goods are cheap and plain. **Nigger-rich** means having barely enough to live on, and thus to **nigger it** means to live at the very limit of subsistence. Afroican Americans in turn have their say. A White can be a **no-count** (of no account, worthless) person, a **pineywood rooster** (a counter-attack to all those images of Blacks being equated with crows), a **drifter** and a **punk** (in the sense of inferior, cheap and second-rate – one that long predated the rock 'n' roll version). **Cheap-john,** used by rather than of Blacks, can also mean a pawnbroker or even his shop, while its synonym **cheap Charlie** can be a corner candy store. Both are based on the 19th century's 'Cheap Jack', an itinerant hawker who would set up his stall, price his wares at grotesquely inflated prices, then gradually reduce them until the customers – still massively over-charged – were willing to buy.

The 18th century's **beg-lander** underlines the role of the poor Irish as tenants, rather than landlords, and America's **hoper** refers to an Irish immigrant who regrets the fact; they go to bed 'hoping they'll be Yankees when they wake up.' These were dreams unlikely to be fulfilled; in the meantime these same Irish divided on class lines; the **lace-curtain Irish**: genteel and petit-bourgeois, and the **shanty Irish** or **shanty-micks**: the lower-class, impoverished Irish whose windows, if theyir shacks sported such things, were covered in sacking, not lace. In France **être en ecossais**: 'to be in a Scottish plight' means effectively to be down at heel, to be reduced to the point of starvation, suggesting that not all Scottish parsimony is seen as voluntary.

an Ideot

FOOLS & MADMEN

LIKE THE wider world of slang, where terms for fool draw widely on the suffix –head – _dickhead_, _lunkhead_, _jickhead_, _fuckhead_, _prawnhead_, _poophead_, _rubblehead_ and _chucklehead_ are but a random selection – race follows the same path.

Thus **hardhead**, which variously denotes the generality of American Whites (from their insensitivity), Appalachians (from the equation of 'poor' and 'foolish') and African Americans (who can also be **thickheads** and **boneheads**). Only one use, dealing with the sort of tough, aggressive and independent Black American otherwise known as a **bad-ass nigger**, counters the norm. And even this usage reinforces one White cliché: he may not be a fool, far from it, but still it underpins the belief that one can never knock out or hurt a Black man by hitting him on his head, since it is too solid to damage. That image is sustained in **rock**, used for Blacks, and presumably an abbreviation of the slang _rockhead_. **Coconut head**, with its 'jungle imagery' further qualifies America's Blacks, while **pumpkinhead**, a coinage of the late-18th century and based on the local diet, deals with the Whites of New England. Leaving America, more head imagery can be found in Holland's **koppige Fries**: the 'pig-headed Friesian', the Flemish or Belgian Hollandsche **kaaskop**: 'Dutch cheese-head' or the **pig-headed Dutchman**. Sweden's **finnhuvud** extends the picture to the 'Finnhead' or stubborn person while the Yiddish **yapmoldevaner getsh**: 'a Moldavian icon', is a dummy; a lumbering blockhead'. Even **Jap**, which is generally accepted as an abbreviation for the standard English Japanese, may also be a version of the slang *yap*, short for *yaphead*: any stupid, worthless person. (The mock-language **jerkanese**, appears to be a mix of *jerk*: a fool and Japanese.) **Zip**, used for Japanese and later the Vietnamese, may have come from the army slang acronym ZIP for *Zero Intelligence Potential*. But zip is also an old slang term for zero, hence perhaps for anything of small value, a term that links to another word used for Blacks and Orientals: **dink**. **Loogan**, used for Central Europeans, has no ascertainable etymology – it means fool in general slang – but it may be a term, like Brannigan, that has adopted an Irish surname, in this case Logan, for metonymic purposes.

As are the Irish in Britain and the Highlanders in Papua New Guinea, so are the Swabians in Germany. Thus **Schwabenalter**: the Swabian age, in fact the age of forty, prior to which it is assumed that Swabians have no sense; **Schwabensprung**: 'a Swabian jump' or very short distance; **Schwabenstreich**: 'a Swabian trick' or stupid prank. The Poles weigh in with **glupi swabi**: 'the stupid Swabians', a generic for all Germans, who were thus compared with the Swabians, generally seen as the 'worst' of any Germans in Polish eyes, and **oszwabka**: 'a Swabian article' and thus something second-rate or ersatz.

Gullibility, a sub-set of stupidity, gives Russia's **armyanskiy anekdot**: 'an Armenian story', a tale told at the fool's expense – the fool usually being an Armenian – or a plain lie (in which case, however, the liar is the Armenian); the Afro-American **homeboy** and **homegirl**, while usually meaning a good friend, usually from one's urban neighbourhood, and lacking any pejorative implication, can also mean a simple, naive 'country cousin', a term allied to **home folks** and the adjective **down-home**. The Yiddish **kirre deitsh** means both German or Austrian and 'sap', while a **German Michel** defines the German as a gullible individual, particularly in a political sense; **Trick Willy** is a gullible Black man, as used by his peers; trick carries the implication of its alternative meaning: a prostitute's client. In Spain the question **somos indios?**: are we Indians? means, with a sneering reference to the simplicity of South American tribesmen, do you take us for suckers? The Spanish use of **primo**, to describe a Mexican, is a direct transfer of the word's usual use, meaning a dupe.

Strong and silent may still win out in romantic fiction, but elsewhere it tends to get identified with the world's shorter, thicker planks. Both inarticulacy and muscle-tone can also equate with foolishness. Thus the classical Greek phrase, **inarticulate as the Cappadocians**, the Polish **gluchorniemcy**, meaning 'deaf Germans', and used as a nickname for German colonists in Galicia, and the Dutch **zwijgen als een mof**: silent as a German and therefore both glum and dumb. America's **big Dutchman** and **big Swede** are both less than complimentary, while **stolid as a Dutchman** means especially impassive and stupid-looking. The same image can be found in **botte Hollander**, Flemish for the blunt Dutchman, and **finritamp**, Swedish for a lumbering Finn and thus a Finnish chump. The Swedes also mock the **finna-student**: the Finnish student, i.e. the dunce (the proper term would be *Finsk student*), who presumably gains much the same qualifications as the **Dublin University graduate**, yet another example of the clichéd condemnation of the Irish as fools. Still in dumbo mode are France's **l'Allemand lourd**: the clumsy German, the Czech **německopitomý**: the stupid German and the German dialect term **poalsch**, properly Polish, but realistically clumsy or clownish. And Germany's own **deutscher Baccalaureus**: a German graduate, can mean an ignoramus and a boor. The Americans, pointed as ever, prefer **dumb Polack**. **Dumb sock**, also American, means a fool, especially when a Scandinavian immigrant as well, and in Spain **hacer ci sueco**: 'to play the Swede' means to act as if one were too stupid to understand.

From here on in it's all much of a muchness. Different is dumb and can be categorized as such. Stupidity pure and simple can be found in the Russian **Efióp**: an Ethiopian, but used colloquially (and bizarrely) to describe a stupid German, a concept that was used centuries earlier by the Romans who mocked **stultitia Saxonum**: Saxon stupidity. (The **Sciavus saltans** or 'prancing Slav' is another Romanism; on what grounds one cannot at this distance say.) The Jewish use of **yekke**,

Yiddish for a German, has overtones of Teutonic rigidity and intellectual inflexibility. The theory that the word is actually a combination of three Hebrew letters meaning 'a Jew of scant intelligence' is thrown aside as 'folklore not philology' by Leo Rosten. Denmark's **dum som en skotte**: 'stupid as a Scotsman' and Hungary's **buta topt**: 'the stupid Slovak', may be equally folkloric, but such slurs are enshrined in the national beliefs.

Apart from the supposed standards of 'Dublin University', the Irish suffer a variety of other insults based on ignorance. The **Irish comics** are the obituary columns in a newspaper; an **Irish hint**, in America, is a hint so broad that it is virtually a declaratory statement, while the phrase **you're Irish** 'translates' as 'you're talking nonsense'. The oldest, and most ostensibly respectable is the **Irish bull**, a blunder, or self-contradictory proposition, especially that which is made by an Irishman. Typical examples would be 'The British landlords have taken all from their tenants' empty pockets' or 'taking a post graduate course in the freshman class'. Bull comes from a variety of similar words; the Old French *boul* or *boule*: fraud, deceit, trickery; modern Icelandic *bull*: nonsense and Middle English *bull*: a falsehood. It does not, despite theories to the contrary, come from a papal bull or religious edict (despite the obvious Catholic connection) nor, despite the backing given by Francis Grose (basing his belief on an earlier piece in the *British Apollo* (No. 22. 1708), is there an eponym, one Obadiah *Bull* 'a blundering lawyer of London, who lived in the reign of Henry VII'.

Mongol or **Mongolian**, a medical term that has been replaced by the less contemptuous Down's Syndrome baby, was coined in 1866 by the English physician J. Langson Down (182896), who noted that there was 'the possibility of making a classification of the feeble-minded, by arranging them around various ethnic standards...The great Mongolian family has numerous representatives, and it is to this division, I wish...to call special attention. A very large number of congenital idiots are typical Mongols'. The term, with its initial implication of imbecility has survived, in such uses as the Australian nickname for Chinese immigrants, in the playground mockery of *mong*, a term cognate with *spaz* (spastic) and *malco* (malco-ordinated) and in *monged*, an adjective that means enjoying the effects of MDMA or Ecstasy.

Gooney (and its female equivalent **gooney-gal**) have both been used by Americans to describe the Pacific Islanders. The term, which may possibly be linked to a much older word meaning albatross (and thus parallels the use of *booby*, meaning both bird and simpleton), echoes the British dialect word *goney* or *gawney*, meaning a simpleton and which, most likely, comes from the Anglo-Saxon *ganian*: to gape. The phrase **in a Portuguese pig-knot** means confused, and especially not knowing where to begin telling a story, while **n'entendre plus raison qu'un suisse**: 'he'll no more listen to reason than a Swiss', is a French term based on what is seen as Swiss stubbornness. Italy's **svizzero**: a Swiss, means a conceited simpleton. **Czerkieski**, a Polish word meaning literally Circassian (a people of the northern Caucasus) is used of one who is frivolous and superficial. **Monaco**, in Spain, means a Dalmatian, or colloquially, one who is merely pretending to be more stupid than he actually is.

'Are you Russian, Boy?'

With that fine disregard for national sensibilities that marks pretty much every entry in this book, the term **asiatic**, usually a neutral standard English adjective, has been purloined by America, and especially by its armed forces, to mean insane, crazy or wild. Like the British term *doolali*, which came from the experiences of troops serving in the Indian army, this term comes from the effects suffered by troops serving lengthy tours abroad. Similar disdain underpins a whole raft of comparisons, typically Holland's **Croaet**: a Croat, and thus, apparently an eccentric; a **flying Dutchman**, used in America to describe a fantasist, a wild-eyed individual, and an eccentric; the French **Iroquois**, which translates not as a member of a Native American tribe, but instead as a perverse individual, whose actions make no sense. **Rysk** or Russian means crazy in Sweden, where anyone acting oddly is asked **Ar du rysk, poike?** Are you crazy, boy? The French phrase **être en Flandre**: 'to be in Flanders' is to go crazy, especially in someone else's reluctant, terrified company, and **Sint som en finne** is a Danish/Norwegian saying meaning without any comment, 'mad as a Finn'. The Danes and Norwegians also offer **sint som en tyrk** and **vred som en**

tyrk, both of which mean crazy as a Turk but are better translated as 'mad as a hatter'. Afro-Americans have been called **buggy** or even **buggywhip** (which despite its overtones of slave-driving is in fact a euphemism), the term comes from the general slang *bugs*: crazy, with perhaps an added influence from boogie: a Black person.

The East provides two further terms. One is America's **asiatic**, a term coined by American troops serving in a variety of Oriental postings. Rather than describe the locals, for whom there are a wide variety of unpleasant synonyms, it refers to Americans who, unable to deal with the various aspects of life 'out East' have succumbed to greater or lesser forms of insanity. The word then came, as did America's forces, back home and can now be found as a general term, for which military service is not required. The second, Britain's **doolally**, is also military and refers to the Indian Army's base at Deolali, where discharged soldiers waited, bored and increasingly tetchy, for the next ship home.

The final term here is **dingbat**, which has occasionally been used to mean a Chinese person, although its more general use is to refer to a madman. Dingbat is a remarkably prolific word. Bartlett's *Dictionary of Americanisms* (1877) specifies such meanings as a bat of wood that may be thrown (or 'dinged'), a piece of money, a cannon-ball, and a bullet, while in volume 1 of *Dialect Notes* (1895) Mr. Philip Hale, of the *Boston Journal*, cites 'the following definitions...:(1) Balls of dung on buttocks of sheep or cattle. (2) Blow or slap on the buttocks. (3) Flying missile. (4) Squabble of words or pushing. (5) Money. (6) In some of the N.E. schools, the word is student slang for various kinds of muffins or biscuit. (7) Affectionate embrace of mothers hugging and kissing their children. (8) Term of admiration.' It is, despite this plethora of alternatives, the later use of dingbat to mean a foolish person, and thus an eccentric, coined in America and transferred to Australia, that probably influences its racial use. An additional definition in Australia cites dingbats as DTs or *delirium tremens* and, last but not least, as an army batman.

Tom Fearfull

COWARDS

W E LEAVE when the time is ripe; you wander off a little early, *they* run away. One person's timely prudencce is another's rank cowardice. Race, always keen to spot a loser, is in there with a raft of phrases to grind them down a little further. The idea of slipping away unnoticed, even on the most innocent of grounds, has long provided a wide range of phrases.

The best-known of these, in English at least, is to **take French leave**, an 18th-century coinage which refers to a social habit, initially fashion-able in French society, and thus imported across the Channel, of quitting a reception or party without taking official leave of the host or hostess. In fairness, this early form of departure was apparently taken with the best intentions: to avoid breaking up an otherwise pleasant social occasion, but a more negative image soon developed, and would totally displace the original usage. By the 19th century, to take French leave was to make a hasty departure, and generally said of one who absconds or is unwilling to face an embarrassing situation – as likely financial as social. Thence a **French leave-taker** was a military de-serter. The image was obviously appealing, and other languages vied to offer their own version. Spain has **despedirse à la francesa**: 'to disappear like a Frenchman', Dutch **een Fransch kompliment maken**: 'to pay a French compliment', Danish **tage fransk Afsked** and German **französischen Abschied nehmen**.

All those mean 'to take French leave', but France is by no means the only country so accused. The English, for instance, are the subject of Poland's **wyrne si po angielsku**, of Hungary's **angolosan tavozni**, Germany's **sich englisch empfehlen**, the Italian **andarsene all'inglese** and, naturally, of France's **s'en aller à l'anglaise**. Dutch leave means much the same, as does **do a Dutch**, the German equivalent **wie ein Hollander auskratzen** (or **laufen** or **durchgehen**): 'to scurry away like a Dutchman' and **polnischer Abschied**, translated literally as 'Polish leave' as well as the phrases **den polnischen Abschied nehmen** or **mit polnischem Abschied weggehen**: 'to slip away on the quiet'.

If one is to take note of German folk wisdom, **the Jew is afraid of his own shadow** and indeed **his own fur coat frightens the Jew**; despite the on-off condemnation of Israel, a Jewish state, as war-mongering and bloodthirsty, the Jews are simultaneously not considered brave, and there are several terms to bear this out. German student slang has **Juden**: the Jews, better known as 'the jitters'. (**Mohren**: Moors, is used in exactly the same way; here the image is of rolling-eyed 'darkies', jumping at every unknown creak,) **Judenangst**: 'Jew anxiety', is a racial characteristic, while the Russian **mytar** or worry-wart is a nickname for a Jew. **Judische Hast**: 'Jewish hurry' is seen as unnecessary haste and generates the mocking phrase **Nur keine judische Hast**?: 'Where's the fire?' or 'What's the rush?'

Other phrases include the Polish **abszyd niemiecki**: a 'German farewell', which is in fact a synonym for being tossed out into the street or 'shown the door'. Denmark and Norway use **en polsk Forstraekkelse** to describe a 'mortal funk' or abject terror while the links between the colour yellow and cowardice give America's **yellow-belly**: a Mexican. In France the phrase **ressembler le Picard**: to be like a Picard, means to act extra-cautiously, to keep out of danger at all costs.

Robber

CRIME

Lanthorn and Candlelight

THE IMAGE of gypsies as Bohemians, as a group who flaunt the conventions of 'respectable' society, has been addressed under *Aliens*, but they have a parallel and less romantic role, that of 'natural-born criminals', a people for whom larceny is in their blood. It is an image that persists throughout Europe, whether the tribe is termed gypsies, Egyptians or the words cognate with the Polish *cygan*.

However, the first term for gypsy that emerges in England is none of these; rather it was **moonman**, cited by the playwright Thomas Dekker in his study of the London underworld, *Lanthorn and Candlelight* (1608). Gypsies had obviously been found in England for many years – the 19th-century slang lexicographer John Camden Hotten suggested that it is to them we owe the origins of British cant, or criminal jargon, and they certainly made a major contribution to cant and to mainstream slang – but Dekker's discussion is the first ever to be printed. Moonman, in its Latin form *lunatic* or *loony*, usually referred to the insane, but as he explains, 'these moon-men...are neither absolutely mad, nor yet perfectly in their wits. Their name they borrow from the moon, because, as the moon is never in one shape two nights together, but wanders up and down Heaven like an antic, so these changeable-stuff-companions never tarry one day in a place...'. Moon-man, however, was not Dekker's coinage: it already meant 'a robber by night', and can be found as such in Shakespeare's *Henry IV, Part I* (1598). It may be safely assumed that the gypsies and the robbers were conflated in Dekker's term.

Other terms for gypsies included **Egyptians**, which Dekker claimed ' they call themselues', a term echoed in France's **Egyptien** and the derivative **affaires d'Egypte**: 'Egyptian affairs', i.e. smuggling and theft; (it is from Egyptians, of course, that what is effectively an abbreviation, gypsies, is itself taken); **broom-squires**, a name also used for those dwellers of the New Forest who eked out a living making brooms from heath; the **fair-gang**, from the gypsies' attendance at fairs, and the 19th-century **pikey** or **piker**, which refers to their moving along the turnpike or toll roads. Piker had also meant, from the 14th to the 16th centuries, a robber or petty thief, and it is hard to believe that the terms were not related, if only in the popular image of the gypsy. Across the Atlantic, the term described a poor Southerner who moved to California in hope of a better life, and, more widely, a cautious person, whether in gambling, where this usage originated, or in the wider world.

Outside English, the terms, other than the French **foi de Bo-hemién**: 'gypsy faith', or honour among thieves, tend to reflect variations on **cygan**, which in Polish means a gypsy and thus a crook or swindler. In Russian, while once more literally a gypsy, it stands as a derogatory synonym for Hungarian and Rumanian, both of which states hosted large numbers of gypsies and both of whom were seen as equally criminal. **Hungarian** itself can mean a thief or vagabond (as well as the punning 'hungry person'). **Tsiganit**, also Russian, meaning 'to gypsy' translates colloquially as to scoff at, to 'make a monkey of', to beg or to engage in shady deals. **Tsiganstvo**: 'gypsying', means swindling. The Greek **Torkogýftos**, literally a 'Turk-Gypsy', is an Armenian, a race who rank with the gypsies, Greeks and Jews as the personifications of dishonest tradesmen. Iceland's **hundtyrki**: 'dog

Turk' or scoundrel, while making no reference to the gypsies, is equally uncomplimentary to the Turks.

Usual Suspects

As for alternative examples of the meeting between race and villainy, it's very much a tale of rounding up the usual suspects. African Americans, who in any case suffer from a wholesale branding as criminals, offer the **Harlem credit card**: a short hose used for siphoning petrol from the tanks of unguarded automobiles (**Mexican credit card** and **Mexican filling station** mean just the same); and the idea of a dark-skinned man, up to no good and prowling through the dark has given **night-fighter** (sometimes **Alabama-night-fighter**), **night-creeper, night-owl** and **midnighter**. Perhaps the best-known crime-related 'black' term, however, is **nigger in the woodpile** (or **nigger in the fence**), a phrase that was coined *c*.1850 and means a catch, flaw or anything otherwise suspicious in a situation. The image it promotes is of a Black robber, hiding in one's woodpile, preparing to steal either the wood, or worse still, the contents of the house it serves. For poker-players, a **Mexican straight** is any hand, plus a knife. The Provençal **braiman**: a Brabanter or Fleming, means a freebooter while the Czech **flamendr**: a Fleming is a tramp. Such Czech phrases as **flamamovati** and **Vesti flámovský život**, both meaning 'live Flemish style' and thus live a vagabond life, turn the tables on the usual identification of Czech 'Bohemia' with vagrancy. The identification stems from the flood of Flemish soldiers, deserters from their own army during the wars of the 16th and 17th centuries, who lived as tramps on Czech territory.

In France **picart**: a Picard is a rogue, or a man who lives by his wits; **un bouchon du Lombard**: 'a Lombard's mouthful' is poison, referring to the image of Italy as a land of Borgias, endlessly pouring noxious powders into their rivals' food. An **Italian quarrel** stands for treachery, poison and remorselessness. Germany's **welsches Süpplein**: literally 'Welsh' but effectively 'foreign' (and thus 'Italian') 'broth', means exactly the same. **Grèce**: properly Greece, can also mean the underworld while **vol à la grecque**: 'Greek theft', is a confidence trick. The nearby Bulgarians, already saddled with their identification with buggery, can also be known, in a predictable pun, as **burglars**. Poland's traditional loathing of Germany gives **Swabić**: 'to Swab', i.e. steal, while **Indian up**: meaning to sneak up stealthily, refers to the Native Americans' reputation for guile and craftiness. **American tweezers**, a cant term, refers to a specific tool used by burglars to open locked doors. **Go to the Bahamas** means to be sent to the punishment cells.

The Irish, traditionally associated with their recruitment into the police, have also formed their links with crime. An **Irish theatre**, in British army slang, is a military guard-room, presumably alluding to the likelihood of finding Irish soldiers incarcerated there; America's **Irish clubhouse** (elsewhere a brothel) is a police station (punning on *club* and *baton* or *truncheon*); in the 1920s an **Irish dividend** meant a shakedown by the police and the French cant **envoyer à l'Irlande**: to send to Ireland, means to send or smuggle items – goods, letters – out of prison to the free world. Somewhat earlier the 16th-century **Irish toyle** or **swigman** (a far distant predecessor of modern Australia's wandering *swagman*) was a mendicant villain who posed as a tinker or peddler to fool his victims (*toyle* comes from the standard English *toil*: a net or trap); such villains toured the country, pretending to peddle pins, lace and similar haberdashery in order to obtain access to houses which they then pilfered.

Nor are the Jews spared. **So many Jews, so many thieves**, declares the sanctimonious German proverb, and libellous or not, there are certainly a number of pertinent terms. The **Abram-** or **Abraham-man** emerged during the 16th century, meaning a wandering beggar, adopting tattered clothing and posing as a madman. Two centuries later Francis Grose defined his successor the **Abram-cove** as 'a naked or poor man; also a lusty strong rogue' and in the 19th century he could also be a thief specializing in pocket-books. On whatever count, the term **Abram** came from the Biblical *Abraham* and the reference is possibly to the parable of the beggar Lazarus in *Luke* xvii. It may also have have been related to the *Abraham Ward* of London's Bethlehem Hospital, in which the insane patients were housed; the hospital, known popularly as Bedlam (and as such engendering a well-known English word), allowed certain inmates to go begging on a number of fixed days each year; the *abram-man* posed as one of these licensed beggars. Allied terms include the verb to **sham Abraham**: to feign insanity, a phrase that, as noted by John Camden Hotten, created a punning anecdote: 'When Abraham Newland was Cashier of the Bank of England, and signed their notes, it was sung: "I have heard people say that sham Abraham you may, but you mustn't sham Abraham Newland".' **Abram work** was any form of swindle, and thus to be **on the Abraham suit** was to be working as a begging-letter writer, the pursuit of many small-time 19th-century confidence tricksters; an **Abrahamer** was a tramp; to **maund Abraham** to beg while posing as a madman (from *Abraham* plus *maund*: to beg, itself probably derived from the French *mendier*: to beg, which is linked in turn to the Latin *mendicus*: a beggar and the Romany *mang*: to beg). **Jack the Jew** or **Jack Jew** was a Jewish thief or fence while in France **la petite Judée** was the nickname for the late-18th-century prefecture of police in Paris, then sited on the Rue de Jérusalem.

One last criminal term, **Alsatia**, is English, although its target is France. (That said, the word is used by the French in just the same way.) Taking its name from *Alsace-Lorraine*, the marginal, disputed border area between France and Germany, it meant the underworld in general, and the criminal 'no-man's-land' of 16th-century London in particular. This was divided into two: *Higher Alsatia* (Whitefriars in the City) and *Lower Alsatia* (around the Mint in Southwark). *Higher Alsatia*, its earlier manifestation, was once the lands of the Whitefriars Monastery, extending from The Temple to Whitefriars Street and from Fleet Street to the Thames. After the Dissolution of the Monasteries in 1538 the area went downhill, and, as allowed by Elizabeth I and her successor James I, its inhabitants claimed exemption from the jurisdiction of the City of London. As such the area became a centre of corruption, a refuge for villains and a no-go area for the law. Any attempt to arrest a criminal, wrote Lord Macaulay, was met with a united counter-attack by 'bullies with swords and cudgels, termagent hags with spits and broomsticks' and many others beside. The privileges were abolished in 1697, but it was decades before the old habits died out. A related term is the **Squire of Alsatia**, a slang phrase that gave itself to the title of Thomas Shadwell's play, first staged in 1688. This title had various meanings, notably that of a gentleman who has been drawn to the criminal world and there found himself fleeced, robbed and generally rendered destitute by its larcenous denizens; as well as an overly generous man and a rich, gullible fool.

Dancing at Beilby's Ball

Once captured, tried and incarcerated, the criminal would encounter a number of race-related terms among the cant that thrived behind prison walls. Many are or were related to the Dutch: to **take the Dutch route** or **do the Dutch** is to commit suicide; as the **Dutch act** or **Dutch cure** is the suicide itself. Quite why the Dutch have been thus branded is odd; it is, after all, the 'drunken' Swedes rather than the phlegmatic Dutch who are more usually associated with self-destruction; one must assume that it is no more than one additional example of their role as a national enemy. **Dutch distemper** is jail fever (this time from alleged Dutch lawlessness). In today's South African jails, where most prisoners are divided into rival gangs, a **fransman** (Afrikaans) or **Frenchman** is an outsider, one who has no gang affiliations. The image is of 'French' as being generically foreign or alien. Three centuries back, among Britain's nicknames for the pillory was the **Norway neckcloth**; pillories, made of two hinged planks of wood, with holes cut for securing the prisoner's hands and head, were often constructed from Norway fir. **Welsh parsley** refers to a 'hempen halter', i.e. the hangman's noose, while in Germany **schwedische Gardinen**: 'Swedish curtains' or 'blinds' are prison bars made of Swedish iron. Metalwork, albeit at a distance, underpins one of the 18th century's most lurid synonyms for judicial hanging: to **dance at Beilby's ball (and let the sheriff pay the piper)**. As Francis Grose put it in 1796 'who Mr Beilby was, or why that ceremony was so called, remains with the quadrature of the circle, the discovery of the philosopher's stone and divers other desiderate as yet undiscovered', but there exist a number of suggestions. The most obvious is that *Beilby* was a well-known sheriff; a second is that *beilby* is a mispronunciation of *Old Bailey*, the court in which so many villains were sentenced to death. The third, and that espoused by the ever-inventive slang expert Eric

Partridge, is that **beilby** refers to the *bilbo*, a long iron bar, furnished with sliding shackles to confine the ankles of prisoners, and a lock by which to fix one end of the bar to the floor or ground. *Bilbo* comes from the Spanish town of Bilbao, where these fetters were invented. Bilbao was well known for its sword-making and *bilbow blades* were already rated as being outstanding in the 17th century. By 1700 the sword had been transferred to its user, and a bilbo was another word for bully (in its thuggish rather than schoolyard meaning) or swash-buckler.

The grimly named **Scotch easement** was also a pillory, while the **Scotch boot** was an instrument of torture by which the legs were crushed. Germany's **spanischer Stiefel**: a 'Spanish boot', fulfilled the same excruciating function. A **Spanish faggot**, reminiscent of the blazing wooden faggots on which so many heretics had been burnt to death in the name of piety, was the sun; a **Spanish windlass** is a strait-jacket. A **Scotch verdict** was less painful: based on the verdict of 'not proven', encountered only in the Scottish legal system, it refers to any inconclusive judgment or pronouncement, legal or otherwise. Still sustaining the world of torture **Russian law**, at least *c*.1640, represented a punishment of one hundred blows on the bare shin. Russia's **kosacker**: a cossack, was however more usually encountered outside prison than in. It meant a policeman, often a mounted one, and was a slang use of the name of the Cossacks, a pugnacious Turkish people, long under Russian rule and renowned for their horsemanship and enthusiastic anti-semitism. The word comes from the Turkish *quzzaq*: an adventurer or guerilla. **Cosquerie**: 'Cossackry', from France, translates as a sudden intrusion of rowdies, resulting in pillage. One phrase, the Yiddish **kozak hanigzl**: 'the robbed Cossak'; is full of grim irony. Meaning figuratively to make a ludicrous situation even more absurd, it gives the image of a Cossack, even as he sets about his unfortunate victim, swearing that he himself has been robbed – thus presumably justifying the pillage that follows.

Boys Fighting

VIOLENT PEOPLE

THERE IS something distinctly redolent of pots vs. kettles about this particular segment of the racist vocabulary. After all, the virtual violence that lurks within any of these words and phrases is hardly conducive in itself to an especially peaceful world. But a little hypocrisy never hindered the progress of a good piece of abuse, whatever its target, and why should racism, a world bereft of self-knowledge (albeit filled with self-pity) prove an exception?

The Wild Irishman

The Irishman, declares the English saying, **is never at peace except when he is fighting**. A good solid stereotype of the most predictable sort, but one that has, admittedly produced a good few pertinent terms, not least of which is the self-ordained nickname of the football team of America's Catholic (and thus distinctly American-Irish) Notre Dame college: 'the fighting Irish'.

Before moving onto the people, one can consider a pair of terms describing a rough, rowdy, violent party. **Barney** comes from the proper name *Barnabus* and entered the slang vocabulary around 1850;

the contemporaneous **donnybrook**, meaning a fight, a riot, a noisy brawl or as a verb to hit or beat up, comes from Ireland's once notorious Donnybrook Fair at which such events were a regular feature. Another, kindred term is **shindy**, probably derived from the word *shinty*: a game, mainly played in Ireland, that resembles a rougher form of hockey. In this context it means a noise, a disturbance or a commotion, and gives the phrases **cut shindies** or **kick up a shindy**: to create a disturbance; perhaps as a precursor of the modern concept 'tough love', it can also mean a fancy or an affection for someone.

As far as the Irish themselves are concerned, **Irish** alone can mean ready to fight or easily angered (thus the Manx saying: 'Hit him again, he's Irish), and to **get one's Irish up** is to lose one's temper. **De wilde Ier**: the 'wild Irishman' is used in Holland to describe an hysterical child (similar to Britain's *young Turk*) and comes from the activities of the Irish troops during the Anglo–Dutch wars of the 18th century. In railway jargon, on the other hand, the **wild Irishman** was the Irish mail train running between London and Holyhead. Other 'Irish' combinations include the **Irish coat of arms**: one black eye, and an **Irish beauty**: two, especially as inflicted by a husband or boyfriend on a woman. Francis Grose describes the **Irish wedding** as a brawl 'where black eyes are given instead of favours'; thus one who has **danced at an Irish wedding** is showing off their black eyes, while to go to such a celebration is to get the same marks of battle. An **Irish hoist** (*c.*1800) is a kick to the backside (or a clumsy, painful fall), while **Irish confetti** means bricks, particularly as thrown during the urban riots which were frequent in mid-19th-century New York. An **Irish theatre** is a military guardroom (from the number of Irish troopers 'playing up' inside), and an **Irish wake** is any boisterous occasion, and not neccesarily a wake.

A miscellany of allied terms prove, if nothing else, that the Irish are not the world's only fighters. The late-17th to early 20th-century **African** (like Irish, Dutch and Indian) means anger, while America's **jig cut** (from jigaboo) refers to the one-time frequency of knife-fighting among African Americans. The image is sustained in the mid-19th century **mean as a nigger** (*mean* here is the US use, meaning ill-tempered and potentially violent rather than England's parsimonious), and in the verb to **let off a little nigger**: to act in a wild spontaneous way (the reference is to the supposed instability of Black Americans). America also offers **wild as an Arab**, the early 19th century's **Indian hunting**: a fight between two men (neither of whom need be a Native American), and to **get one's Indian up**: to 'go on the warpath' or to get wrought up. What Britain calls a **Chinese burn** (squeezing and twisting the wrist – a popular school age torture) is known as an **Indian burn** in the US. Other American terms include **catch a Yankee** (*c.* 1810), meaning to take a beating; **hatchet-thrower**, used bizarrely of Puerto Ricans (given the clichés, the 'red Indians' would surely be a more logical target), and the **Mexican stand-off** which offers three meanings. The best-known is any situation in which neither party is willing to back down from a stated position but simultaneously neither party has a superior edge; the result is that both parties give in and walk off. The others characterize that situation in a game of poker when no player is willing to open the betting, and in railway jargon, a head-on collision between two trains (otherwise known as a *cornfield meet*).

Outside the US one finds Germany's **balkanische Zustande**: 'Balkan conditions', otherwise known as continual disorder, a reference that if it once seemed anachronistic – as the cold war raged – seems all too pertinent now. Greece uses **Boulgaros**: a 'Bulgarian' to mean cruel and violent, while America goes next door for the phrase **fight like a Turk**: to fight savagely.

Hooligan Nights

Like cheats and liars, thugs and bullyboys occupy no particular national enclave. Most countries can boast some kind of terminology. Thus Scotland's **Glasgow kiss** or **Gorbals kiss** (from the old slum tenement area of the city), which means a head-butt, a term less repellent than its southern peer, the **Chelsea smile**. This grimace, named for the more violent supporters of Chelsea Football Club, is achieved when the victim's face has been slashed from each corner of the mouth up to the ear. The resulting scars create the so-called 'smile'. The **Dutch rub** (otherwise known as a *noogie* or *dry shave*) is somewhat less terrifying: a schoolboy game, it involves rubbing the victim's skull with one's knuckles – painful, but not disfiguring.

Less active, but equally denunciatory, is the Swedish blanket condemnation of **en wild kroat**: a wild Croat, a concept echoed in
Austria's **Krowot**, a Croat, but used colloquially to mean a reckless
adventurer or a ne'er-do-well. Spain's term **breimante**: a 'Brabanter',
means a thug (a memory no doubt of the religious wars of earlier
centuries). Germany is especially well catered for: the Dutch **Feling**:
a 'Westphalian' is a synonym for roughneck and the phrase **zoo lomp
als een mof** criticized someone as being 'rough as a German'. Russia's
nemak means a German boor and the Poles, never over-complimen-
tary towards Germany, have **Niemczura**: a German lout, and **twardy
Niemiec**: the harsh German. **Un polonais**, in France, is both a
drunkard and a bouncer in a brothel, available, as Barrère puts it, 'to
intefere when any disturbance take place among the clientele and the
ladies of the place', and the Dutch word **pool**, a Pole, is used to mean
anyone considered rough and uncivilized. **Aller** or **passer à Rome**, in
French cant, means to get a beating.

Greek, which has elsewhere been synonymous with the Irish, is here
another word for Russians, specifically Cossacks, in the Yiddish term
yovn, which in Hebrew means Greek, but in Yiddish has become a
rough (Russian) soldier. Thus the phrase **Er is falln vi a yovn in
sukke**, literally 'he broke into the tabernacle like a soldier', meaning he
smashed up a peaceful place. The Poles are less circumspect: **Ha-
jdamak**,a reference to a specific Cossack tribe, means a looter. Like the
Cossacks, the Scythians come originally from Central Europe (in their
case a large part of European and Asiatic Russia) and in common with
other such tribes, Vandals and Goths, have been termed the epitome of
barbarity. Both French and English use **Scythian** to mean a coarse and
ruthless person from beyond civilization. Meanwhile Hungary used
orult spanyol: a 'mad Spaniard' to describe any unruly person, while
Schweizerhieb, in German a 'Swiss stroke', means a heavy blow.

The Turks, dealt with elsewhere (see *National Names*), are generally
pictured as a cruel, vicious nation. The Greeks, their enemies for
centuries, use **Tourkos**: 'Turkish' to mean impudent, rough and fierce.
But geographical proximity is by no means vital for such attacks. In
18th-century England, **Turk** meant a bully or a hardhearted person
and was widely seen as the ideal name for a vicious dog. **Turkish**

treatment was cruel treatment, parallelling the French phrase **traiter quelqu'un de Turc à Maure**: 'to treat one as a Turk would a Moor', meaning to abuse one frightfully; France also has **Turc**, an adjectival form that is rendered as harsh, predatory and unyielding. What were condemned as the 'Turkish atrocities' of the 1890s created the English phrase the **unspeakable Turk**, used widely in Britain and America. A far earlier phrase, and one used by Shakespeare, is **turn Turk**, meaning to change completely for the worse. One last Turk-related term is **Bashi-bazouk**, defined as a hooligan or cruel lout, it refers to one of the mercenary soldiers or irregular troops of the Turkish army; 'notorious for their lawlessness, plundering, and savage brutality' (*OED*).

Hooligan itself, usually defined as a 'a young ruffian', has some claim to a race-based origin. A slang term that had entered standard English by the 1920s, hooligan has a number of rival etymologies. It first appeared in print via a variety of daily newspaper police-court reports in the summer of 1898. To quote the *OED*, 'Several accounts of the rise of the word, purporting to be based on first-hand evidence, attribute it to a misunderstanding or perversion of Hooley or Hooley's gang [as suggested by Ware], but no positive confirmation of this has been discovered. The name Hooligan figured in a music-hall song of the eighteen-nineties, which described the doings of a rowdy Irish family, and a comic Irish character of the name appeared in a series of adventures in Funny Folks.' All this is largely born out by Clarence Rook's *Hooligan Nights* (1899), a story set in the rougher areas of the East End of London, which suggests that there was an actual Patrick Hooligan 'who walked to and fro among his fellow men, robbing them and occasionally bashing them.' An earlier citation notes T.G. Rodwell's farce *More Blunders Than One*, performed in 1824 and featuring a drunken ne'er-do-well Irish valet called Larry Hoolagan; this in turn is presumably a corruption of the standard Irish name *hUallachn* or *Houlihan*. Generally seen as an Anglo-Irish coinage, with use in Britain and America, the term also cropped up in Russia, referring to those perpetrators of the Kishineff massacre of the Jews. The Russians, lacking the 'h' in their alphabet, pronounce the name **Khooligan**.

The supposed characteristics of Native Americans, in myth if not reality, have provided the bases for a pair of words taken from the names of their tribes. A **Mohock** or **Mohawk**, an 'aristocratic ruffian night-infesting London' at the start of the 18th century, comes from the Mohawks, who were formerly supposed to be cannibals. Once the most powerful of the Five Nations or Iroquois, they originally inhabited the neighbourhood of the Mohawk River, in what is now the State of New York. The **Apache**, not especially aristocratic, but equally and randomly violent, adopted the name of a tribe of Athapascan Indians found in New Mexico and Arizona. Flourishing at the end of the 19th century, they were to be found in Paris, where the term was translated as 'thug' or 'strong-arm man' and created the phrase **ruses d'apache**: 'Apache tricks' or savage cunning. White America, at least in Black eyes, has also come up with some synonyms of its own. Thus Blacks have called Whites **beaters**, **lynchers** (Mencken's definition of the Bible Belt [see p. 264] included a reference to the 'Lynching' belt too) and **shit-kickers** – all based on mutually violent confrontations.

A Sea Fight

WAR

THERE IS a very good argument for saying that war, under whatever euphemistic guises, is the leitmotif of this whole book; that every slur, every stereotype, every nationalistic and racist assumption is no more than war without weapons and that the only wounds are those of words. Like sport, racist vilification accomplishes pretty much all that war requires, although, like sport again, less corpses are left on the battlefield. Words, especially these examples of racist and nationalist intolerance, can undoubtedly hurt and history has too many examples of propaganda wreaking its horrible effect. The words may only be the cause, but their effect is potentially lethal. Poeple are killed and maimed, imprisoned and tortured for what, after all, has begun as no more than language. It is not a power to be underestimated.

Like fighting and thuggery, the idea of creating a racial attack based on the fact that the other person goes to war seems somewhat short-sighted, but the words have emerged and must be noted. And while every country seems at one stage to have been involved in war, the language that such conflicts have created, while inevitably skewed by time and geography, does tend in one direction. As the boys' comics of the 1950s (and the xenophobic tabloids of today) underline: 'you can't trust the Germans.' Or, as one observer of the 1966 World Cup Final allegedly remarked, 'In the end it all comes down to the same thing: us against the Hun.'

'The Hun is at the Gate!'

'I am sorry for the losses you have suffered by the Goths and Vandals', wrote the American inventor and statesman Benjamin Franklin in 1779, and while he was referring to the depredations of Britain's troops in their fight to suppress American Independence, the background reference was a good deal older. Both **Goths** and **Vandals** were Germanic tribes who, between the 3rd and 5th centuries, moved out from their homelands to invade Western Europe. The climax of such invasions came in 455 when Genseric, the Vandal king, led his men to Rome, took it and sacked the city. The attack was of such savagery that the Romans coined the phrase **furor Teutonicus**: Teuton (or German) fury. The terms Goth, now largely confined to the description of a particularly gloomy form of post-punk music and its fans, and Vandal have, since the mid-17th century, both meant barbarian, one who cheerfully destroys anything beautiful, venerable, or worthy of preservation. Thirteen hundred years on, Franklin's condemnation could have been even more specific: the British army fought not alone, but with mercenary troops from the German state of Hesse, and **Hessian** became a synonym for a military or political hireling and a mercenary. The term persisted into the 19th century, when during the American Civil War it was used in the South as a term of loathing for the Union troops. Another form of Goth, the Ostrogoth or East Goth, is a name that serves, at least in France, to describe an uncouth or crude individual.

All of which, however deeply felt, was but a prelude to the flood of anti-German coinages that arose from two world wars. As well as Goths and Vandals, the **Huns**, under their leader Attila (nicknamed *Flagellum Dei*: the scourge of God) were among the tribes that stormed through Europe and hun, like those other names, joined the ranks of wanton destroyers and cultureless devastators, albeit somewhat later. Hun too became a term of abuse in the American Civil War, but it was not, however, until World War I that the word took on its modern meaning:

a bellicose, brutal, usually but not necessarily uniformed German. Seen as a pure negative by Germany's anglophone enemies, the image seems to have been cherished by the Germans themselves. It was coined, after all, not by some jingoistic Fleet Street propagandist, but by the German emperor, Wilhelm II or 'Kaiser Bill', who on 27 July 1900 addressed a battalion of German troops about to set sail from Bremerhaven to China to help suppress the Boxer Uprising, following the assassination that June of the German minister in Peking: 'No quarter will be given, no prisoners will be taken. Let all who fall into your hands be at your mercy. Just as the Huns a thousand years ago, under the leadership of Etzel [Attila] gained a reputation in virtue of which they still live in historical tradition, so may the name of Germany become known in such a manner in China that no Chinaman will ever again even dare to look askance at a German.' This was duly noted in *The Times*, but **hun** generally languished in England. In 1900 English interests were focussed not on China, but on South Africa, where the Boer War was still raging. The story of the so-called *Hunnenbriefe*: 'hun letters', sent from German soldiers to tell friends and relatives how assiduously they were pursuing their Emperor's orders, caused a minor stir, but that died – the main outrage was confined to August Bebel and similar socialist agitators. Only Rudyard Kipling, whose own jingoism would be cruelly curbed by the death of his beloved son at Loos, persisted with the name, as when in 1902 he wrote in *The Times,* which in 1898 had already carried 'The White Man's Burden' ('Your new-caught, sullen peoples | Half-devil and half child'), verses that included the lines 'With a cheated crew, to league anew | With the Goth and the shameless Hun!' All that changed in 1914. A month into the war Kipling was back, exhorting readers of the paper 'For all we have and are | For all our children's fate | Stand up and meet the war. | The Hun is at the gate!' and the term entered the language in earnest. One slightly anomalous use was to describe an RFC (later RAF) flying cadet: it referred to the way these gung-ho young officers wrote off an infinity of training machines before they gained their 'wings'. Otherwise it was Germany all the way. Combinations abounded: **Hun-folk, hun-hater, Hun-land, hun-eating** (violently anti-German), **hun-hunting** (RFC slang for chasing enemy planes or ground troops) and **hun-pinching** (rounding up Germans in their trenches in order to secure information). **Hunnish**, which had already been used in cultural terms, became another word for German, especially when coupled with child-bayoneting, nun-raping and kindred atrocities (fabled or otherwise). Especially foolish was **hun-pox**, which replaced chickenpox for the duration. A premonition (albeit reversed) of the World War II substitution of victory measles for German measles, it made less sense: did some *Kultur*-obsessed virus lurk amid the hitherto blameless farmyard fowls? Unsurprisingly the term was less in evidence between the wars, but it remained on tap, ready for a return to favour in 1939.

English was hardly World War I's sole language and French produced a word for German that held perhaps even greater loathing and which too would persist into the second round of hostilities. Like hun, **boche** predated 1914. Albert Barrère, writing with happy innocence in 1902, defines boche as 'rake, "rip", "molrower" [whoremonger] or "beard splitter". *Tête de* — , an expression applied to a dull-witted person. Literally wooden-head. Also *a German*.' The word is an abbreviation either of *caboche*: head, or from *Alboche*, a modification of *Allemand*: German. On either count, come World War II and the occupation of France by the Germans, the word was officially forbidden. Once more like hun, boche appeared in a variety of forms: **bochie**: a German; **bocherie**: German behaviour, i.e. atrocities; **bochisme**: German 'Kultur' whether of a militaristic (World War I) or Nazi (World War II) ideology; **bochisant**: collaborationist, and **bochiser**: to spy. America's **busher**, sometimes used for a German, might have come from boche, but it was more likely a wartime use of the slang term *bush*: rural, unsophisticated.

There have been a number of other wartime words describing Germany and its soldiers. At a time when White settlers were battling Native Americans, and they were seen as dangerous savages, the Germans were labelled the **Iroquois-of-Europe**. The Iroquois, leaders of the Five Nations who were based in southern Canada and upstate New York, were generally seen as one of the more bellicose tribes. **Gerry** or **jerry** is an abbreviation of German (sometimes itself abbreviated to **Ger**) and a homonym, fortuitously, of **jerry**, slang for a chamber-pot. The Polish use of **Bismarck**, named for Germany's 19th-century chancellor, for an outside privy, parallelled the equation. **Kamarad**, from the German for 'comrade', was usually used to placate a man on the verge of killing you. Thus the French **faire kamarad**: literally to 'make *kamarad*', in other words to give oneself up, from the cry of 'Kamerad!', when a German faced death. **Bucket-head** and **square-head** were supposedly based on the shape of the German helmet, although squarehead had certainly predated the war, and meant a dullard (similar to France's *tête de boche*) as early as 1903, while in the late-19th century it had played on the image of square, meaning uncomplicated, an honest person. As **Johnny Squarehead** it had also meant anyone of German extraction, including Swedes and Norwegians. **Roundhead**, in the late-19th century, also meant Scandinavian. **Goon** (especially as used by British and US prisoners of war to describe their guards) came from the cartoon character 'Alice the Goon', created by the artist E. C. Segar (1894-1938), in the 1920s. Civilian use of the word, which may have been derived from the older *gooney*: a booby or simpleton, defined it as a thug, typically a minor gangster or a strike-breaker. **Goon** has also been used, in America, to describe the citizens of the US Virgin Islands. It was the 'simpleton' use, however, that lay behind BBC radio's *Goon Show*, so popular in the 1950s.

The Nazi rule of Germany from 1933-45 introduced a new element. A German was known as a **Hitlander**, after his or her Führer Adolf, and Germany was known as **Naziland** or **Vaterland** (from 'Father-land', a term beloved of Nazi speechifying and propaganda). At the height of America's war fever German-Americans were also tarred with the 'Nazi' label. As Jews fled Germany's increasingly enthusiastic persecution of their faith, the term **refujew** emerged, describing such refugees; the Nazis themselves coined **Judenbude**: a 'Jew-hut' or 'Jew-den', to describe the huge crate in which Jews were allowed to pack their goods prior to emigration.

That Beats the Dutch

Britain and Holland were at war for much of the 18th century and the conflict naturally produced its effect on language. To **beat the Dutch**, which meant to do something outstanding, was transformed a century later into **that beats the Dutch** describing something that is otherwise barely credible; later still comes **sink the Dutch**, a general exclamation of distaste. During the American Civil War northern sympathisers, especially those from Missouri, were known as the **Dutch**, although this was almost definitely a case of mixing Dutch with *Deutsch* – Missouri had many German settlers. The 18th-century **Dutch caper** referred to a light privateering ship, while in World War II the Royal Navy **did a Dutch** when it ran a submarine aground on submerged rocks or a reef; such an accident had caused the well-documented loss of a Dutch submarine. A **Dutch rod**, once again confusing Germany and Holland, referred to a Luger pistol. The Dutch themselves had a pair of 17th-century terms, stemming from their fight with the Flemings, whose territories would become Belgium: **rotte Wale**, a 'rotten Walloon' and **Walenbeest**, a 'Walloon beast'. Belgium itself, characterized by the World War I propagandists as 'plucky little Belgium', was nicknamed the **cockpit of Europe,** from its geographical position between the often warring nations of France and Germany; and in World War I a foxhole was also known as a **Belgian pit**.

The Dirty Little Jap

If Germany has represented Britain's major enemy in the 20th century, then the Japanese take that role in America. **Jap**, the simple abbreviation, is the term of choice (the non-specific nature of abuse means that it can also refer to an African American). It was often extended as **dirty jap** (as in the World War II doggerel: 'We're gonna zap, zap, zap, | The dirty little Jap!). To **pull a Jap** means to ambush or to act in some other underhand manner, and the standard term **backstabber** was, for a while, translated as Japanese. **Tojo**, from the name of Hideki Tojo (1884-1948), the Japanese general and the embodiment in American eyes of Japanese militarism, was used generically to mean Japan and its soldiers. **Japland** and **Tojoland** inevitably, and unimaginatively, were Japan. During the Japanese occupation of Manchuria a collaborator was known in Chinese as **gou tĕi-ze**, literally 'dog's legs'. Other 'Asian' terms include **pékin**, the French army's term for a civilian, and which gives the phrase **être en pékin**: to be in 'civvies' – the equivalent of

England's *mufti*, a word that refers to the robes of an Islamic priest, which were seen as resembling the off-duty dressing gown, smoking cap and slippers, favoured by British officers. A **Bengal light**, in World War I, was an Indian soldier fighting in France, and punned on the name for a type of firework, while an **Indian warrior**, aside from meaning a lousewort in the Western US, has also meant a Saracen or Turk. Parthia, while usually associated with classical Greece, was in fact an Asian kingdom. The Parthian cavalry specialized in firing their arrows while turning backwards, when in real or pretended retreat, a manoeuvre that gave the term **Parthian shot** or **Parthian shaft**: having the last word, even when one has apparently accepted the other person's argument. The less well-known **Parthian war** is a retreat.

Spearchucker meets Jazzbo

Other than the British and each other, the Americans have also fought their own Native American population. Thus **bow and arrow** means a 'Red' Indian, and an **Indian haircut** refers to scalping, the Indian habit of taking scalps as war trophies. Indians retaliated with **long knife**, a reference to the White men's swords, and a term that has been more recently used by African Americans of Whites. The show-business **scalper** or a ticket tout, coined around 1870, comes from the same imagery. **Spearchucker**, an abusive term for Blacks, refers to the primitive weaponry of African tribesmen. A Black soldier, strictly segregated until after World War II was a **jazzbo**, a reference to his presumed affection for jazz, although the word was coined for the young White boys who in the 1920s had enjoyed this genre of music.

The Spanish Fury

For all that Spain was once a major imperial power, and that it, like the Dutch and French, has been one of England's national enemies, the country has generated nothing in the way of specifically 'military' abuse. Other than the **Spanish Fury**, a three-day massacre of the citizens of Antwerp by the Spaniards in 1576, all other terms, while sounding bellicose, are actually synonymous with plant-life. Thus a

Spanish soldier, in New Zealand, is spear grass; a **Spanish bayonet** is a stiff short-trunked plant similar to the Yucca, and a **Spanish dagger** (*Yucca gloriosa*) is its shorter cousin. All three are supposedly reminiscent of a Spanish sword.

Grim as a Swiss Guard

Resolutely neutral throughout this century, and indeed for several before, the Swiss, with their country in the very heart of feuding Europe, have not always stepped aside from conflict. Swiss mercenaries once appeared on every major battlefield and the German **Schweizer-degen**: 'Swiss sword' describes a weapon half way between a sword and a knife, used in combat at close quarters. The phrase **grim as a Swiss guard**, meaning stern-looking and immobile, refers not to the mercenaries, but to the modern Swiss Guard, found on ceremonial duty in the Vatican City. Given Switzerland's position, many miles from the nearest sea, the **Swiss navy** has come to mean something that does not exist, while **un Amiral suisse**: a Swiss Admiral, has been used in France to describe any naval officer, ostensibly a sailor, who never actually leaves his shore base.

The Swedish Drink

Given the propensity of nations to indulge in war, many others have managed to generate a few relevant words. A **Roman holiday** alludes to the shows in which prisoners of war were butchered by gladiators, wild beasts or other agents of entertaining death; today it means any occasion in which suffering and/or death provides others with an opportunity for amusement. The **Roman peace** or **pax Romana** was a peace that existed only as long as armed force was present to maintain it; the phrase provided the later **pax Britannica**, or British peace, which also meant an imposed, rather than a voluntary cessation of violence. The Swedes mock the Danes in their children's game **jutar skrämma**: 'to frighten the Jutes', while the Germans coined **Schwedentrunk**: 'a Swedish drink' as a reference to the story that during the Thirty Years' War (1618-48) would pour ditch water down the throats of their German prisoners and would then trample on their stomachs. **Old sweat**, meaning a veteran soldier, is thought to stem from the sweat of battle, but the British philologist Ernest Weekley has suggested, in *Xenophobia* (1932) that it too may have originated during the Thirty Years' War as the German **alter Schweele**: old Swede; its first appearance, *c*.1890 militates against the theory. The 19th-century heyday of the Austro-Hungarian empire gives **kaiserliche**: 'imperial', a term employed by the Swiss to mock the Austrians. The slur is on the doting admirers of the Austrian emperor, who was, at least in parody, barely able to speak without prefacing his remarks with 'The Imperial this...The Imperial that'. **Quisling**, meaning traitor, refers to the German catspaw Vidkun Quisling, who ran Norway for his Nazi masters in 1940. The end of World War I, when Italy expeditiously changed sides, abandoning Germany for the Allies, created the German term **Katzelmacher**. Finally the Cold War, that long period of super-power stand-off and war by proxy, usually fought in terms of rival linguistic orthodoxies, did produce the term **red-bait**: to use smear tactics or to accuse someone, quite unjustifiably, of being a communist or 'red'. **Redland** was Russia and **Red** itself, as a synonym for far left-wing and communistic, dates back to the revolutions of 1848 when France's revolutionaries established the short-lived 'Red Republic'.

I Spend all

MONEY

FAR FROM making the world go round, as romantics might suggest, it would appear that money, like so many other coveted commodities, brings it, if not to an actual halt, then to blows, at least metaphorical ones. It is hardly surprising. Other than for the dedicatedly self-denying, the possession of money denotes success, and like other covetable things, if others have it, then the all-too-human response to such a possession tends to be a jealous one.

Of course the 'culture of envy' is by no means an exclusively racial phenomenon. Fat-cat executives, lucky lottery winners, beneficiaries of wealthy parents – their 'good fortune' rarely meets with a round of generous applause. No-one, it seems, has much time for a winner. But once one mixes 'have-not' jealousy into existing racial hatreds the combination reaches inflammatory proportions. Nor are the racial groups stigmatised below exactly 'winners'. In the case of the Jews, at least, their involvement with money had largely been thrust upon them by circumstance and ideology. But others, equally adept at manipulating the folding stuff, find themselves similarly, if perhaps not so viciously, condemned.

Yiddish Renaissance, Dutch Reckoning

This is a book of stereotypes, and if there is one stereotype one cannot avoid, it is the equation of money and the Jew. Setting aside usury, which is considered below, the world of money and of commerce provides a vast arena for those who wish to typify the Jews as money-orientated. They are not alone in being allotted the role, but they are undeniably foremost.

To start with one of the best-known, and most unpleasant epithets, the word **kike** appears to spring from commercial roots. Although its etymology remains something of a mystery, and there is a reasonable case for suggesting that it comes from the Yiddish *kikel*: a circle, the mark used by some illiterate Jewish immigrants – rather than a cross – when signing papers at Ellis Island, New York (the immigrants' 'gateway to America'), others refer to the common 'Jewish' suffix *–ki* or *–ski*. The most likely origin may be that suggested by the word-collector and slang expert Peter Tamony. He opts for the German *kieken*: to peep and links it to Jewish American clothes manufacturers who 'peeped' at smarter European fashions and produced mass-market knockoffs, popular among their poorer customers.

America also offers **allrightnik**, a Yiddish term that describes one who has succeeded, one who has raized himself from immigrant poverty to material success; especially used of New York Jews, it gives **Allrightnik's Row**: Riverside Drive, once home to many successful Jews. Similarly Washington Heights, New York City was the **Jewish Alps**. (The *Swish Alps*, on the other hand, was a 1950s/60s name for the gay 'cruising' scene in the Hollywood Hills.) The obvious etymology is all-right, as in the phrase do all right for oneself, but in fact the term comes from the Yiddish *olraytnik*: an upstart, a parvenu. Such 'new money' does not, of course, pass unnoticed. **Jewish** or **Yiddish Renaissance** refers to any over-elaborate furniture in doubtful taste as does the upper-class English **Jewy Louis**, with its emphasis on fake if flashy Louis XV or XVI furniture. The South African equivalent is **boer baroque**. Not Jewish, but definitely arriviste, is **rastaquouère**, a French term used around the 1920s for a South American *parvenu* (many of whom made their way to the South of France) rendering himself obnoxious by squandering his money ostentatiously. The term, defined as 'a dashing but untrustworthy foreigner' comes from the South American Spanish *rastacuero*: an upstart.

But if Jews see their material success in a reasonably, albeit ironically positive light, few others share their optimism. The terms come from many countries and from every era. The Afro-American term **slick-'em-plenty** refers to the unscrupulous trader, using his slick patter to gull the credulous. Beethoven, among others, referred to what he termed a **circumcized ducat**, i.e. a smaller amount than hitherto agreed on or expected. Late-19th-century London sneered at the **Judaic superbacy**: 'a Jew in all the glory of his best clothes' (Ware); Jews after all were more usually found in the context of rags, thus the term **Abraham**: the lowest level of clothes shop, usually selling second-hand goods. Cognate terms are **Jew joint** and **Abraham store**. In law an **Abraham suit** is a bogus or illegitimate lawsuit, brought simply for the purpose of extortion. The **Jewish** or **Yiddisher piano** and **Jewish typewriter** are both a cash register or till (the **Scotch organ** is synonymous), while the **Jewish** or **Jew flag** is a dollar bill. In US college slang a course in **Jewish engineering** is one in business administration and, in a similar construction, the British Army's **Jewish cavalry** is the quartermaster corps, whose duties feature not gallant charges but mundane, if vital supplies. A **Jew sheet** is an account, often imaginary, of money lent to friends, and London's Cockneys use **as thick as two Jews on a payday** as a synonym for intimacy.

Yet paradoxically, in that way that lays at the alien's door every extreme of conduct, so keen are we to condemn him on any ground, the Jews, with all their smartness, their money-grabbing and their avarice are simultaneously mean, cheap and impoverished. One can see one version of this dichotomy in the German terms **Judenmünze**: 'Jew-coin', a special tax paid for the crime of being born a Jew, and **Judenheller**: 'a Jew-farthing' and as such a worthless coin, giving the phrase 'not worth a Jewish farthing'. The taxing of Jews also gives **Jew's eye**, as in 'worth a Jew's eye': something valuable or desirable. The phrase refers to the medieval practice of extorting money from the Jewish community on pain of the threatened torture of its leaders; such torture may or may not have involved blinding. Another version suggests that every organ carried a price, and that the ultimate was the eye, which would be gouged out were a wealthy Jew not to disgorge his fortune. However a further etymology, the French *joaille*: a jewel, cannot be discounted. In a wider sphere one finds such terms as **Jewish airlines**: walking on foot; **Jew-bail**: insufficient bail (or a promise of bail, which is not paid when the criminal absconds); **Abrahams** or **Jewish sidewalls**: White rubber sidewalls glued on blackwall tyres to make a cut-rate imitation of the real (and once fashionable) thing. **Mexican sidewalls** are equally spurious. Still in an automobile world, **Jewish overdrive** (like **Mexican overdrive** and **Portagee overdrive**) is freewheeling down hills to save petrol, and a **Jew(ish) Packard**, a relatively expensive car, is a cheap Ford while the assonant **Jew Canoe** refers in America to a Cadillac and in the UK to a Jaguar (commonly stigmatized as a nouveau riche, and *de facto* Jewish mode of transport). A **Jewish ice cream sundae**, a relatively luxurious sweetmeat, is an ice cream cone. (A **Chinese Rolls Royce**, in a similar mode, is the cheapest sort of Ford.)

Non-English-speakers have their own versions of the prevailing image. The Croatian **čifutariti**, 'to Jew' means to act or speak in the Jewish manner and specifically to engage in petty trading; in Polish **szachrajstwo** (from the German *Schacher* and Aramaic-Hebrew *sakhar*: gain, profit) means petty dealing, Jewish manipulation or unethical or insubstantial trading; in Iceland a shrewd dealer or profiteer is **gy[th]ingur**: a Jew; Holland offers **Jodenkoop, Jodenhandel**: 'Jew-trading', i.e. petty manipulation, and in Greece **hebrajico pazari** or 'Jewish bazaar' is any place where one has to haggle. In Greek **philargyros**, literally 'money-lover' means a Jew. Even Jews themselves have their worries: **Yiddishe bizness**, in Yiddish, refers to any misunderstanding with a fellow-Jew, often due to one party's failure to adhere strictly to an agreement. In Italian the phrase **trattar peggio d'un giudeo** means 'to treat one worse than a Jew', i.e. to deal ruthlessly, but perhaps most damning of all is the West Indian use of **jew**, plain and simple. It means any rich person, presumably White but with no actual religious overtones; other that is, than the all-encompassing stereotype. Another West Indian phrase, a **jew and a crown** is an obsolete form of the more general *joe and a crown*, based on the *joe* (from *Johannes*), a gold coin worth 22 Dutch guilders used in Guyana until the late 19th century. It means very expensive.

To round off the Jews' involvement with money and trading come a number of terms identifying Jews with intinerant peddlers. **Smous**, in Dutch (and Afrikaans), means variously (and paradoxically) a poor Jew and a profiteer; **mouchey** (possibly from Moses) means variously a sponger, an idler and a beggar. It is linked to the slang term *mooch* or *mouch around*, and to *mooch off*: to sponge. **Shonk** and its extension **shonnocker** (from the Yiddish *shonnicker*) both mean a Jewish peddler and in Demark and Norway **Schakterjüde**: 'a Jew-hawker', is a Jewish street vendor. In Texas a **blackpedlar** is another term for Jew.

The Jews themselves have a pair of words that fit in this section. Undesirable or stale goods, which a shopkeeper or peddler spurns, are **bovel skhoireh**: 'Babylon (or Babel) goods', while **baytzimer, betzemer** or **batesomer**, all meaning eggs (from the Hebrew *bezim*) was used by late 19th century New York Jews to refer to the Irish. Whether this comes from the vague similarity between the German *eier*: eggs and the word Ireland, or whether it hides some veiled reference to Irish sexuality, since *baitsim* is American Yiddish slang for testicles, is unknown. One variety of peddler, America's **banana-pedlar**, is not Jewish: he's an Italian.

As in other contexts, after the Jews, the Dutch, although one should note, as ever, that Dutch, at least in American coinages, can often mean German, on the basis of the frequent confusion of *Dutch* and *deutsch*. Thus **to dutch** is to ruin a business or someone's health or social standing or, in gambling usage, to bet in such a way as to bankrupt a casino; other gamblers' terms include a **dutch book**: a book in which bets are noted down, and **dutching plays**: betting on more than one horse in a single race. A **Dutch lottery** is a game of chance in which the prizes are arranged according to series and classes, the values increasing accordingly. A **Dutch bargain**, sometimes known as a *wet bargain*, is any deal concluded over drinks, while the German **holländern** means to mismanage a business and thus **ausgeholländert**: to become ruined financially through poor management. The German phrases **in Holland sein**: 'to be in Holland' and **nach Holland reisen**: 'to tour Holland', both refer to a stay in a debtor's prison. France has a similar term: **faire un tour en Belgique** means literally to 'take a tour of Belgium' and colloquially to become bankrupt. The same thing goes for the synonymous **filer sur Belgique** and **filer à l'anglaise**, a pair of colloquialisms translated as 'to do a bunk'. All the references are to the apparently common practice of German or French bankrupts skipping across the nearby border into Holland or Belgium, thus attempting to avoid their creditors. Flanders, a synonym for Belgium, gives **faire Flandre**, literally 'to make Flanders' or become a bankrupt; **Flanders fortune**: a modest inheritance, and **Flanders reckoning**: the spending of money in a place other than where it was received.

Other than in business, where inevitably one will return to 'Jewish practice', money references cover a number of nationalities. Non-judgmental, but pertinent are Australia's twin terms: **currency** and **sterling**. The words evolved in the early 19th-century when currency (often **currency-lad** or **-lass**) was used of the children born in Australia, often to immigrant parents, and thus the first White 'native Australians'; sterling referred to those born in Britain who had made the trip 'down under'. **African dominoes** and **African golf** are both nicknames for the game of craps (an **African golf ball** on the other hand is a watermelon). **African dust** is gold; the reference presumably being to the gold-mines of South Africa, and the use of the slang term *dust*, long accepted as meaning money in its own right (and simultaneously rubbish, thus Dickens' 'Golden Dustman' Mr Boffin) must be seen as coincidental. A **nigger roll** is a roll of single dollar bills, especially when wrapped in a single large denomination bill (similar slang terms include a *Chicago bankroll*, a *Philadelphia bankroll* and a *California bankroll*), while a **nigger tip** is a poor one. The term *jitney*, originally a five-cent piece, gives **jit**, an item of small or insignificant value and in turn an Afro-American. **Kaffir**, originally an Arabic term for infidel and more recently a South African pejorative for a Black person, was used in the late-19th century to mean South African mine shares (that section of the London Stock Exchange that dealt in them was the **Kaffir Circus**); a similar construction is found in **the jungle** (c. 1900), the West African share market, **kangaroos**, West Australian mining shares, **mummies**, shorthand for Egyptian securities, and **Bulgarian atrocities**, properly Varna and Rutschuk Railway 3%

obligations, and a reference to the massacre in 1876 of Bulgaria's Christians by the Turks.

The Romans termed payment in cash **Greek credit**, while the French **vivre à la grecque**, to 'live like a Greek', means to live in grand style. **China**, in Portugal, can mean both the country and money while the image of the untrustworthy 'Chinaman' persists in America's **chinese deal**: a business transaction that never actually materializes. The French **chine**: China, refers to anything that once loaned, after much begging and many protestations of honesty, is in fact unlikely to be returned. **Chinees** or **Chinese duckets**, also American, are complimentary tickets to a theatrical or sporting event. An **Indiano**, in Spain, was one who had profited from investments in the (West) Indies or in South America. The West Indian term **chinee-royal**, meaning a half-caste mix between a Chinese person and a Black or Indian, is based on the *real*, a Spanish coin of minimal worth, which used figuratively implies the lowest of social status.

'After misfortune, the Irishman sees his profit.' Thus Ireland's own saying and the Irish, suffering as ever with the brand of stupidity, give such phrases as an **Irish dividend**: a tax assessment (which takes rather than gives money); an **Irish rise**: a cut in pay, and an **Irish promotion**: a demotion or even dismissal. A **Mexican promotion** or **Mexican raise** is similar, but here, although the money gets no better, the status of the job does. The **Irishman's pocket** may be large, but it's also empty, while in 19th-century London the **Irishman's harvest** was the orange season, when the indigent Irish could make a little money selling the briefly abundant fruit.

As for the rest, the nation-money mix spreads pretty evenly. A **Polak**: a Pole, which to the Czechs can mean variously a Polish horse, a Polish sausage and a 'Polish', i.e. north-west wind, can also mean a Polish shilling. For Germans to make a superficial, possibly inaccurate calculation is **im polnischen Bogen berechnen**: 'to compute on the Polish sheet' and, German again, a **polnischer Wechsel**: a 'Polish note' is a monthly note for a trifling sum owing among poor students. **Polnische Wirtschaft**: Polish management, (like **oesterreichische Wirtschaft**: Austrian management), is inefficient management. **Spanish** is ready money while, in the early days of Australia to **speak**

Spanish and, in Dutch, to **speak English** (and **Spreekt hij Engelsch?**: does he speak English, is he rich?) means to have ready money, a term that comes from the earliest Australian currency, the Spanish dollar, worth some five shillings sterling. The kreuzer, a low-value Czech coin was a **Svejcar**: 'a Swiss', and the phrase **no money no Swiss** – referring to the practice of hiring Swiss mercenary soldiers, who only offered their help once the contract had been agreed – is still in use. A similar image lies behind a couple of French phrases: **secours Lombardien** and **secours de Venise**, respectively 'Lombard' and 'Venetian help'. In both cases it means help that arrives too late to be of use and the implication is that such help would not be forthcoming from these merchant adventurers unless some form of profitable deal had already been struck.

Amerikanismus in German refers to a materialistic or commercial point of view, while **welsh**, as a verb, means to fail in carrying out an agreement or, especially, in paying one's debts. The **welsher** was the one so guilty. The term stems from the supposed untrustworthiness of the Welsh (perhaps derived from the use of *welsh* or *welch* as an alien or criminal language) and was long summed up in the 'nursery' rhyme 'Taffy was a Welshman | Taffy was a thief | Taffy came to my house | And stole a side of beef'. In France **Panama** meant a financial 'bubble', the artificial inflation of share prices, while in England a **Morocco man** was one who plied a trade in bogus lottery insurances. Like the 'Morocco leather', the buyers were 'skinned' by the fraudsters. **Morocco** was also used by Longfellow as gipsy slang for stripped naked, an allusion that also comes from Morocco leather, which began its life as goatskin (Longfellow was probably ignorant of the slang meanings of *leather*: the vagina or anus). And despite the prohibition of money-lending, the English were seen to specialize in it, given the terms in which English means money-lender. Thus the German **Engländer**, the Provençal **anglès** and the French **anglais**, all meaning 'an Englishman', i.e. a creditor; thus too the French phrase **avoir un tas d'anglais à mes trousses**: 'to have a bunch of creditors at my coat tails'. The assumption is that such creditors will not be paid. To a French cab-driver **anglais** means a rich fare, of whatever race.

Finally, in France, the whole concept of commerce is given a nice twist by the use of the phrase **faire son bisness**: to ply one's trade, a term that cynics should note also refers to street-walking.

'No Christian is an Vsurer'

Writing in 1551, the scholar and politician Thomas Wilson (?1525-81), stated (in *The Rule of Reason*), 'No Christian is an vsurer'. Given the expanding economy of Tudor England, his remark was hardly accurate, but as a figurative if not factual statement it served perfectly to sum up the position of the men who lend money and take interest for their pains. But if the usurer was not a Christian, then who was he? The answer, as any of Wilson's readers would have known without hesitation, was a Jew. Of all the stereotypes with which the Jews have been weighed down, none, surely, exceeds in its pious venom that of the role of moneylender or usurer. Based in the Latin *usus*: use, and thus to 'use' money (to make a profit), usury has always been reckoned amongst the greatest sins by Christian theologians. Its practice became grounds for excommunication and the Jews, who were in any case forbidden to involve themselves in any of the more mainstream trades, were conveniently positioned to be given this theologically burdensome but economically vital employment. Usury, and the usurer, basically defined as the lender of money at interest, have unsurprisingly garnered a poor image. 'To whom Þat [that] vsery ys lefe,' declares a writer in 1303, 'Gostely [ghostly, i.e. in his spirit, in his soul] he ys a Þefe [thief].' Nearly five centuries on, nothing had changed. Jeremy Bentham, defining the practice in 1787, stated 'I know of but two definitions that can possibly be given of usury: one is, the taking of a greater interest than the law allows... The other is the taking of a greater interest than it is usual for men to give and take.' And if the fictional Jew has two predominant images, then while one is Charles Dickens' Fagin, a repository of centuries of grim stereotyping (for whose creation Dickens would never really make amends), then the other is Shylock, created by Shakespeare in *The Merchant of Venice c.*1598.

The rights and wrongs of Shakespeare's portrait, let alone the background against which Shakespeare wrote, are too complex for inclusion here. It is interesting however that for all the anti-semitic mythology that runs with usury, the use of **Shylock** as a synonym for usury is a late-19th-century construct (other than what seems to be a nonce appearance in 1786). Thus established it moved into the 20th century, and Peter and Iona Opie reported in 1959, in their collection of schoolyard wit and wisdom, that among the names schoolchildren used for Jews were 'Yid, Shylock, or Hooknose'. Meanwhile the term had crossed the Atlantic, to be used by such slang-wise writers as Damon Runyon. A shylock or **shy** became the accepted term for a money-lender. His ethnicity was irrelevant. The American cant term **shyster,** a dispreputable lawyer, may have links to shylock, but may equally well come from *shicer*, itself based on the German *scheiss*: shit. A twist on the usual meaning came in the 1920s when, with a (subconscious) nudge at the old stereotypes, America was known in Britain as **Uncle Shylock** (a play too on *Uncle Sam*) thanks to her insistance on repayment of the debts incurred by Europe during World War I.

Given the reach of the Church, the image was hardly confined to Anglo-Saxon usage. In Italy **giudeo**: 'Jew', is a usurer, a hard-hearted person or an obstinate or incredulous individual; the synonymous **Juif,** in France, means both a money-lender and a hammer-head shark (a **Jew's balance**, in English, also describes the shark); in Provence **judiou** is a profiteer. Germany's **Judenspiess** or 'Jew-lance', a term common in anti-semitic literature, is translated as usury. Eastern Europe too offers its share: for the Croatians usury is **čifutaria**: 'the Jewish practice'; **lichwiarz**: a usurer, is shorthand for 'Jew' in Poland as are **likhoimets** and **rostovshtshik**, both properly translated as 'profiteer', in Russia. In Scandianvia a **jödepris**: 'Jewish price' is an exorbitant one. An **international banker** is a coded term in right-wing rhetoric for Jewish banker (a paid-up member, no doubt, of the 'international Zionist conspiracy'), a term that is related to that other demon figure, this time of the left, the **rootless cosmopolitan**.

Only two terms escape the cliché. One is the Dutch **lombaerden**: 'to Lombard' and thus, a reference to the bankers of Lombardy, to practise usury; thus the phrase **Daer gaet men in den Lombaerd** – there prices are sky-high. The other is France's **arabe**: an Arab, a slang term for a usurer.

WORK

THE RICH man in his castle, the poor man at his gate, intoned the Victorians, those devoted subscribers to the concept of 'knowing one's place'. Devotees of racial stereotyping too, they would doubtless have approved of the stern categorization it imposes. As in life, so in language, the slurs and pejoratives that run with work ensure that here too, everyone 'knows their place'. As far as work goes these places fall into two major categories, to paraphrase the subtitle to Henry Mayhew's *London Labour and the London Poor* (1857): those who must work (like it or not) and those who can, or more properly, cannot work.

Slav means Slave

Of all the terms that equate a given race or nation with work, especially heavy, barely tolerable work, then **Slav** is the most obvious. A Slav, first noted by the scholar John de Trevisa (1326-1412) in his translation of Higden's *Polychronicon* in 1387, is 'a person belonging by race to a large group of peoples inhabiting eastern Europe and comprising the Russians, Bulgarians, Serbo-Croats, Slovenes, Poles, Czechs, Slovaks, etc.' (*OED*). As the etymology makes clear, Slav comes from the same Latin root *sclavus* as does slave, and as historians note the two words were politically synonymous – at least in the Middle Ages, when the inhabitants of these countries were indeed little more than slaves. The parallels are further strengthened by the 8th- to 9th- century spelling: for a couple of centuries a Slav was literally a slave. For English-language purposes slave seems to pre-date Slav, but chronology notwithstanding, the synonymity cannot be avoided.

Il me Faut un Nègre

Given their initial introduction to the 'civilized West' as its slaves and servants, it is hardly surprising that Africans and African Americans bulk large in this department of the racist vocabulary. **Il me faut un nègre**, says the French: 'I need a nigger', or I need someone to do the donkey-work and **nègre** by itself means a drudge and factotum (as well as a ghost-writer or hack). Two centuries back and a **negrier** served both as a slave-trader and a slave-ship, while **negrerie**: 'Negro quarters' was the barracoon, the slave-pen.

Words underpinning the primary Black role as menial labourer abound. **Boy,** addressed to any Black, irrespective of age, confirmed the master-servant relationship from the mid-17th century onwards. **Massa,** the old slave pronunciation of master, kept the imagery going, although any 20th-century use is strictly ironic. **Work like a nigger** (euphemized as **work like a black**) was coined in America in the 1830s; the last *OED* citation is a century later, but the phrase, while culled perhaps from literary and polite use, has yet to vanish and the lexicographers are being over-discreet. A **niggerhoe** (1862) is a slave's hoe (and can also stand for the entire Southern states' economy); to **nigger in** is to fill in the details in a painting (the 'nigger' is not capable of the subtlety required actually to create the picture); **boat nigger**, still used blithely by yachtsmen, refers to the lowest ranked member of the crew. Logging, for whatever reason, is especially keen: **to nigger** or **nigger off** is to burn a large log in two by laying ignited branches across it (the image is of a lazy workman, too idle to use a saw); a **nigger engine** is a machine used in a sawmill to position logs (a dirty and difficult task formerly performed by Blacks), and **nigger holes** are made during the burning or **niggering** process. Not that these hard workers were deemed especially efficient. Land that was **niggered out** had been exhausted by a lack of fertilization (Black farmers were deemed too stupid to appreciate the need for such efforts), and anything **nigger-rigged** was characterized by second-rate, inferior workmanship. The same attitude generates **African** or **Afro engineering**: shoddy, second-rate work. Blacks fought back with **peckerwood mill** or **peckerwood sawmill**, a small, usually portable sawmill characterized by its slipshod equipment and operation. The use of peckerwood attributes this inferior workmanship to Whites. But that is a single term and White prejudice is far more powerful. After all, despite the efforts of the **nigger driver**, a harsh taskmaster, the one thing the Black worker really did well was rest. Thus **nigger day** or **nigger night** was Saturday, from the alleged habit of Blacks getting drunk on Saturday night; **nigger daytime** was also the night, the only respite offered slaves from their back-breaking labour. Such respite, however, was brief, and soon the workers would be summoned back by the **American devil**, not some form of Black Muslim anti-icon, but a piercing whistle, used by American factories to signal the start or finish of a shift.

The jobs themselves created more terms. **Cotton-picker** referred to the slaves' primary labour, in the cotton plantations of the South, while **laundry-queen** pointed up the task allotted many Black women. **Shine** (and occasionally **shiney**), which may also come from the sheen of sweat on a labourer's blue-black skin, possibly refers to work as a shoe-shine, a typically menial task handed out to the emancipated slaves of the late-19th century and beyond. (As used in the West Indies the term means one with a very dark, smooth complexion and has no derogatory overtones.) Shine gives the combinations **shine box** and **shine joint**, both 1940s/50s, and both referring to a nightclub featuring entertainment by Black jazz musicians; it may also be patronized by a primarily Black clientele. Synonymous terms include **boots** and **brown polish**. The 1920s saw **hoofer**, usually referring to a stage dancer (from the slang *hoof,* meaning foot) as a generic for American Blacks, many of whom were recruited into the chorus lines of the all-Black revues to which slumming Whites loved to flock. The circus coined **Zulu ticket** to mean a credit slip given to a Black who was employed as an extra. Proper names also referred to work. **John Henry**, the mythical hero of a popular 19th-century work song, was a hard-working Black man, tough and indomitable in the face of appalling challenges; **stepinfetchit** ('step and fetch it')was a slave or a subservient Black person, the effective equivalent of an Uncle Tom. The term was perpetuated in the stage name of Lincoln Perry (1892-1985) who specialized in playing stereotypical 'dumb nigger' roles for Hollywood; he supposedly chose the nickname from that of a winning racehorse.

If such figures as the story-telling **Uncle Remus** (see *Animals*) are an idealized version of the 'happy darky' then his female equivalent is the **mammy**, a figure who epitomizes everything White America demanded of its Black females. She was a servant, she loved her White master and mistress, and even more so her golden-haired charges, and she made no waves. As quoted by the Dutch sociologist Jan Pieterse, referring to the fictional Dinah, cook to the fictional *Bobbsey Twins*, whose adventures have delighted generations of young Americans, she was 'the ultimate stereotype of the Contented Slave, the Buxom Mammy and the superstitious, watermelon-eating, eye-rolling, thieving black'. By 1950 (the original Twins appeared in 1904) her role had been modified to 'a plump good-natured Negro woman', but Brown vs. Board of Education (the landmark Supreme Court decision which officially, if not actually, outlawed segregation) was still four years off, and anyone could read between the most sedulously liberal lines. Another classic mammy is of course Scarlett O'Hara's maid in *Gone with the Wind*. It was an irony fully appreciated by actress Hattie McDaniel that, in becoming in 1940 the first ever African American to win an Oscar for her role, she was playing this most clichéd of stereotypes But, as she noted to reporters, 'Why should I complain about making $7,000 a week playing a maid? If I didn't I'd be making $7 a week actually being one.'

Coolie Christmas

Coolie too may be ranked among those terms used to characterize Black workers, but its real origins lay in the East, where it had entered the English vocabulary in the late-16th century (Portuguese use was

even earlier). The term seems to come from a variety of Indian languages, and whether the first was from Urdu, Bengali, Tamil, Telugu,
Canarese or Malayalam, the term invariably meant one who hired
himself out for labour. Although the etymology seems to point to south
Indian Tamil, where *kuli* means 'hire, payment for occasional menial
work', and thus creates *kuli-karam*: 'hire-man', and *kuliyal*: 'hire-per-
son', the first actual mention of coolie comes not from the south but
from Gujerat, in the west. Here it seems to stem from the *Kuli* or *Koli*,
an aboriginal tribe, which by the 17th century was spelt Coolie and
whose dealings with the Portuguese seem to have brought the first ever
use of coolie, albeit spelt *coles*, in 1554. When first encountered, the
Kuli/Coolies seem to have made their living through robbery, but
gradually swapped such activities for those of farming and labouring
for the European invaders. By the 1630s coolie was used throughout
India to describe a local labourer and within a century, as explorations
moved ever Eastwards, the term had been extended to China. It was
adopted in South Africa (in English and as the Afrikaaner term *koelie*)
in the 1920s. John Camden Hotten notes a slang use *coolie*: a soldier [of
the Indian army] in 1873 and such combinations as a **coolie hat** and
coolie Christmas (the name given in Natal, South Africa to the
ceremonies of the Moharram – the first month of the Muslim year and
a Shi'ite festival devoted to the martyrs Hasan and Husain – observed
by Indian immigrants) emerged alongside the mainstream term. East
Indian indentured labourers in the West Indies have also been known
as coolies: today the term is considered sufficiently offensive for its
public use to have been banned in Guyana.

However ancient and sophisticated Chinese culture may be, the
identification of China with menial toil infused a number of expressions. France used **chineur**: a 'Chink', to mean a hard-worked labourer
or a worker who peddles his own wares; a **chineur de la haute**: a 'classy
Chink', is a has-been who attempts to offset his financial problems by
looking up his old connections and begging for help. In Russia **xódja**,
literally 'walking', refers to Chinese street vendors, a common sight in
Russian streets before the Revolution of 1917. Aside from labouring
and peddling, when it comes to the work actually performed, the old
stereotypes return. A **Chinese copy** or **Chinaman's copy** is a slav-

ishly exact copy, mistakes and all, and in TV or movie work a **Chinese dolly** describes the movement of a camera moving backwards on tracks that are slanted at an angle to the action. One of the odder words, and one that delights those who mock the problems Japan has with the pronunciation of 'l' and 'r' is **intoray**, a term used in the Japanese TV and movie industry for scaffolding. The word come from the D.W. Griffith movie *Intolerance* (1916), typified by its enormous sets and a plethora of technical tricks – all needing scaffolding.

Walking on their Hind Legs

If Black work is labouring work, then so too is Irish. Young Irish men have been coming across the sea to seek work in England since the early 19th century and the work they have been given tends to be as brick-layers, road-builders (and once rail and canal builders as well) and similar tasks that demand brawn not brain. The vocabulary does nothing to mitigate the clichés. Aside from **banjo** (see *Food*), that quintessential Irish implement the spade or shovel has been known variously as an **Irish fan**, an **Irish spoon** and an **Irish harp**. An **Irish toothpick** is a pickaxe (although it is also used, as is the **Irish tooth-ache**, to mean the erect penis). A wheelbarrow can be an **Irish buggy** or **Irish baby buggy** or **baby carriage**, an **Irish local** or an **Irish chariot**. (A **nigger local** is a freight train requiring a good deal of heavy loading and unloading.) As the popular American joke had it around 1900, the wheelbarrow is 'the world's greatest invention be-cause the Irish learned from using it how to walk on their hind legs'. An **Irish wedding** is the emptying of a cesspool, while an **Irishman's rest** is the climbing up a friend's ladder carrying a hodful of bricks. The French navy's phrase **prendre des ris à l'irlandaise**: 'to take in a reef in the Irish fashion' means to handle the sails recklessly, often slashing them to ribbons. As noted elsewhere, Irish immigrants have been known as **Turks** and the Turks proper contribute a couple of terms here: a **Turk's head** is a round broom with a long handle while the French **Turc**: 'a Turk' is either a jeweller's tool or a tinker's iron.

The Mexicans, the 'Irish' of south-western and western America, are saddled with much the same clichés as are their Hibernian peers.

Bracero, from the Spanish word for day-labourer can mean any Mexican, while a **Mexican dragline** can be a shovel. **Mexican threads** refer to a stripped bolt which has been forced into a bole to cut new threads, when the worker could not bothered to thread it properly, and a **Mexican sea bag** is a paper bag in which a poor sailor carries his belongings.

Scandihoovian Dynamite

Scandinavia too is branded as a muscle-bound area and **Norwegian steam**, from the stereotype of the burly Scandinavian sailor or farmer, is muscle power. A similar feel underlies **Scandihoovian dynamite**, a logger's term for snuff. Strength also backs up the **Swedish fiddle**: a cross-cut saw, although **Swede** is less flattering, meaning either a blunderer or a piece of clumsy work; uses that offset the strength of Scandinavian workers with their alleged lack of refinement.

Empire Made

While the workers of Africa and the East are generally characterized in terms of their musculature, and the degree to which it can be exploited, Europeans are gauged much more by their abilities, or more properly the lack of them.

It is not, as the terms show, that the Dutch are incompetent *per se*, but if stereotypes are anything to go by, they do seem rather careless. Thus in sailing slang a **Dutchman's anchor** is a basic requisite that has been left at home (from the possibly apocryphal Dutch skipper who claimed after suffering a shipwreck that while he had an excellent anchor, he had unfortunately left it at home). **Dutch pennants** are untidy ropes on board a ship. So too are **Irish pennants**, which cover not just ropes but anything out of place on a ship. The term was first recorded in Richard Henry Dana's *Two Years Before the Mast* (1840). In America a **Dutch rose** is the mark left when a carpenter has missed a nail head with his hammer and left an indentation in the wood. (A **Spanish worm** is a nail, so-called by carpenters when they strike one while sawing.) A **Dutch turn**, in journalism, is a story that continues in the next column beneath another story that has started at the top of the column and ended short of the bottom; the 'Dutch' story thus fills the gap. A **Dutch lead**, another piece of newspaper jargon, is a lead sentence or paragraph in a story that is in fact utter fantasy – which fact is explained later in the story – but works to create a spurious and immediate dramatic effect, and thereby lures the reader into the piece.

France, another source of lackadaisical work, gives America's **French land**: land that unaccountably fails to produce a crop, and **French leave**: absenting oneself from a job or duty without prior permission. In German **Franzose**: a 'Frenchman', is a monkey-wrench, while in Britain and America a **French screwdriver** is a hammer. The **Birmingham** and **Irish screwdrivers** are hammers too, and the Dutch phrase **dat is met den Engelschen schroevendraaier gedaan**: 'That was done with an English screwdriver' means that received rough treatment (with a hammer). The anomaly here is the **Jewish** or **Yiddish screwdriver**, a phrase cited in New York *c*.1939, and meaning hammer like the rest, but one which seems quite out of character, stereotyped or otherwise. Jews have many 'typical' activities: bashing things with a hammer, competently or otherwise, is not among them. France is also responsible for two critiques of the German workplace. **Aller en germanie**: 'to go to Germany', and **travailler pour le roi de Prusse**: 'to work for the King of Prussia'. The former means to doctor, to fix or to 'bodge up' a job (and probably has no national bearing, coming instead from the phrase *je remanie*: 'I reshape'), while the latter means to work hard and get nothing for it. **Poste à la cosaque**: 'a cossack-posting', means an insignificant and irregular job in the French army, referring to the chance of a less than desirable posting to Russia.

A botched job also lies behind Germany's **Indianerarbeit**: 'Indian work', meaning a childishly slow or badly performed job, although the 'Indians' here are South American rather than sub-continental or 'red'. This later group, the Native Americans, give **siwash outfit**, an unproductive, unenterprising ranch (for **siwash** see *Names*). Poles, at least in Germany, are also bracketed with the blunderers. **Auf polnisch beenden**: 'to finish in Polish manner' is to leave loose ends, the Bavarian dialect phrase **das konnt mir polisch vor** means 'that looks funny to me' and **polnischen Urlaub nehmen**: 'to take Polish leave' is to absent oneself from work without permission. In Carpathia **Blesch Arbet**: 'Rumanian work', means third-rate work. In Greece **blachos**: a Rumanian also means a herdsman. In English **made in Germany** was a euphemism for badly produced goods some time before World War I, and **Empire Made**, which for some ought perhaps to have signified something grander, was a sign that, for those who were searching for quality goods, could best be translated 'Keep off'.

Career Opportunities

For Italians and Jews, among others, it's not not the way they do it, but what in fact they do. Thus an Italian can be a **grape-stomper** (as sometimes can other Southern Europeans, all of whom have a viticulture) or an **organ-grinder** (from the organ-grinders – often plus monkeys – who appeared in the streets of 19th-century London and New York). A **Roman knight,** in America, is a fireman – from the elaborate uniforms sported by America's early fire departments – and in France a **romain**: 'a Roman', is member of a claque, a section of the audience who have been hired either to cheer or boo – irrespective of its actual quality – a given performance.

In Britain's Royal Navy **jewing** refers to tailoring, a traditional Jewish occupation, while a **jewing-bag** is a small bag in which sailors keep their sewing material. A **gypsy**, appropriating the name of another much-vilified group is a peddler who, like the gypsies, trades from door to door. A **Jews' poker**, however, is not Jewish, but a person who is (or more generally was) hired to light the fires and perform other tasks that on the Sabbath a religious Jew may not perform, since no 'work' may be performed on that day. The Yiddish term for this same person is *shabbos goy*: a Sabbath gentile. Middle Europe gives **Czech**, an American term meaning an unpopular superior employee, Hungary's **drotos totok**: 'a wire Slav' means a tinker and the German **Ratt-und-Mause-faller**: 'rat and mouse trappers', were Slovaks, because in North Germany they peddled these appliances.

Jobs also underpin a couple of Pacific terms. **Krani**, which in Papua New Guinea means an Indonesian, is actually a Malay word meaning clerk; while Australia's **digger** refers to the prospectors who searched for gold and precious stones in the Australian deserts. The term came into wider use via the two World Wars, when both Australian and New Zealand troops were known as diggers, a tribute to the nations' history. **Diggerland**, naturally, enjoyed a brief vogue meaning Australia.

I'd Sooner be in Mañanaland

Like the Irish-American **hoper**, eternally wishing he were a WASP, the Australian **sooner** lives in fantasyland: he'd rather do anything 'sooner' than work for a living. It's a common emotion, and terms equating racial groups with laziness play no favourites. To the French a **Flandrin**, an inhabitant of Flanders, is a sluggard and a lazybones (and **un grand Flandrin**: 'a big Fleming' is a lummox), while in South Africa **kaffir**, an all-purpose derogative for a Black person, means also a poor and unreliable worker. **Nigger-fishing**, in America, is unhurried, leisurely fishing for catfish or carp, a laid-back attitude to the sport that is doubtless anathema to America's White, tackle-obsessed sports fishermen. The idea of a Black – who ought to be working – hanging around the corner, bar-room or poolhall, listening to the music and chatting gives **hand-jiver** and **finger-popper**. **Niggeritis**, used in the Caribbean and thus by Black West Indians of themselves, also promotes the Black = lazy link, and refers to the urge to lie down and take a nap after a heavy meal. More condemnations include Germany's **Chineser**: a 'Chinaman', defined as an impractical, inefficient, or daydreaming fellow; Moravia's to-the-point **cech neplech**: a lazy Czech; and **Greek ease**, meaning laziness and probably linked to the lotus-eaters (from the classical Greek *lotophagoi*: one who eats lotuses). The original lotus-eaters were a people in Greek legend who lived on the fruit of the lotus, which was said to cause a dreamy forgetfulness in those who ate it. *Zingara*, the Spanish for gypsy, gives **zangano**: an idler, sponge or drone, and in New Zealand **Maori P.T.** (physical training) means taking it easy doing nothing.

Mexico, better known as **Mañanaland** (from the Spanish *mañana*: tomorrow – on which day everything, pressing or otherwise, will eventually be done) gives **never-sweat**, **sun-grinner** and **shuck**, all of which allude to the perceived laziness of Mexican workers. Portugal gives the **Portagee lift**: one who carries less than his share of a load, while the Italian term **carpio**: a wastrel, means a Spaniard. Hungary's **Amerikanzi**: to 'American', means to loaf on the job, and France's **faire un lit à l'anglaise**: 'to make the bed the English way', is to make a bed without taking the trouble to remove and air the covers. The **English disease**, coined in this context during the 1970s, means two things, each according to the speaker. The bosses see it as the workers' propensity to strike at the drop of a hat; the workers see it as the bosses' class-bound, snobbish inability or unwillingness to change.

Last of all come four terms, all dealing with time. English and American time, it is to be assumed, is a byword for punctuality. Not so these. **Portuguese time** and **Brazilian time** both imply lateness, as does **Jewish time**, which implies at least an hour late. Norway's **gjore av sigi svenske**: 'to make a Swede of yourself' is to be late. It can also mean to wriggle out of obligations, such as hotel rent, military service, and so on; in short it means 'give the slip.' The Swedes, understandably, see it as a strictly Norwegian practice.

Avoir les Suisses

The Swiss, no doubt fittingly for a nation so sedulously keen on neutrality, have very few mentions, even in the generally wide-ranging lexicon of racist contempt. However there is one area in which they do make a mark. That of the supposedly typical 'Swiss' job, the hotel porter. **Schweizer** in Denmark, **shveytsar** in Russia, **Suisse** in France (where **suisserie** is the porter's lodge), **suizo** in Spain, **švýcar** in Czechoslovakia (where it can also mean shepherd) all mean a lackey, a doorman and especially a hotel porter. Only in Germany, where **switzer** refers to a personal guard (a throwback to the Swiss mercenaries of old – though for that matter so in its way is the clichéd role of porter), is the mould broken. In France a**voir les suisses**: 'to have the Swisses', rubs in the role: it means to be in a state of great excitement, or more pointedly to suffer *delirium tremens*, apparently an occupational hazard among hall porters.

POLITICS

F OR THE majority of the world, while race is undoubtedly a part of politics, race as such is more likely to be subsumed beneath the bigger picture. Far from signalling the 'end of history', as was once foolishly and short-sightedly trumpeted, the removal of the Cold War from international agendas has in fact unleashed a whole world of vicious nationalisms, held in suspension for the preceding forty-plus years and all the more venomous for that. But the battles of rival nationalisms, while indisputably tied into race, and undoubtedly relying on racial stereotyping to underpin so much of their propaganda, have origins that transcend race as such. Religion, economics, access to natural resources and trading posts, even in such supposedly polarized areas as Northern Ireland, the former Yugoslavia or the Middle East, make for so much more complex a picture.

For race as politics and vice versa, one must turn to America, and in particular to the African American community. The justification for slavery, aside from the chance of vast profits that tend so regularly to obscure society's more humanitarian instincts, was based on the belief that Black equals inferior. Whatever the pseudo-scientific, social or religious addenda that might overlay the core proposition, this was racism, pure and simple. The attempt to challenge that situation underpins the Black political experience in America. It is a struggle that for its apparent successes in the 1960s, the era of civil rights, has proved in the harsher climate of the 1980s and beyond far from over. If anything, Black America has lost as much if not more than that optimistic era seemed to have gained. Nor, as today's sinister resurgence of 'racial science' (unashamedly racist theories long believed to have been 'exploded' as comprehensively as were the concrete results of those theories: the gas chambers of the Nazi death camps) proves, are the racists yet willing to abandon their position. Theirs is a grander vision, more garlanded with academic obfuscation, but the line between their so-called science and the mindless braying of the 'good ol' boy' is merely cosmetic; indeed, the latter might even gain credits for honesty.

That politics and race can mingle in other linguistic contexts is undeniable. Such terms as the German **untermensch**: 'subhuman', as used to describe those whom the Nazis saw fit to consign to those same gas chambers, are undeniably linked to race. Indeed, the administration of the Nazi world was riddled with a form of brutalized jargon that the German writer Victor Klemperer, hinting grimly at the plethora of acronyms that so entranced Hitler's myrmidons, has termed *LTI: Lingua Tertii Imperii* ('Language of the Third Reich'). And those *untermenschen*, at least those who were granted some postponement prior to their death, were also slaves. But these unfortunates, for all that they were ruthlessly worked to death by some of Germany's greatest (and still massively successful) industrial giants, cannot be equated with the world of Southern American slavery. Indeed, to equate the governance of Nazi Germany with anything remotely resembling political 'business as usual' would be to promote a view of the world that, the words and phrases gathered in these pages notwithstanding, would be unacceptably negative.

In America, on the other hand, slavery was indeed part and parcel of politics. President Lincoln has won immortality for freeing the slaves, but one should not overlook his declaration: 'If I could save the Union without freeing any slave I would do it, and if I could save it by freeing all the slaves I would do it; and if I could do it by freeing some and leaving others alone, I would also do that'. In the end, willy-nilly, he did free 'all the slaves' and in fairness one must add a second quote, uttered when on New Year's Day 1863, he signed the Emancipation Proclamation: 'I never, in my life felt more certain that I was doing right, than I do in signing this paper'.

Aside from the simple term **slave**, African Americans might be termed **contraband** or **intelligent contraband**, a pair of terms that stemmed from a Federal proclamation issued at the onset of the Civil War, stating that any slaves owned by Confederates – known as **rebs** or **Johnny -rebs** to the North, but romantically as 'the chiv' or 'chivalry' to themselves – were 'contraband of war'. Once freed the former slaves gained new names, among them **free-jacks**, a term that abbreviated as **jack** would mean any Black man, **free-issue** and, perhaps most interestingly a **free man of color** (sometimes abbreviated to **F.M.C.**) which prefigures by more than a century the modern term 'person of color'. Those who hurried to move north were known as **exodusters**, a parallel with the Jewish exodus from a much earlier era of slavery.

In the world of slang, that alternative take on 'establishment', respectable language, black can mean White, positive negative and good bad. Nowhere more so than in the last category, where such terms as **bad boy**, **bad nigger** and **bad-ass nigger** all carry two opposed meanings. There is the literal one, as used by Whites, who found the appearance of an aggressive, tough Black man who rejected the constraints and humiliation of the role they or their agents had selected for him, quite unpalatable, even frightening; and that used by his fellows, who conferred on 'bad' the meaning that persists today: in a word, 'good'. Although the good-bad-good construction has existed since the 16th century's *rum*, which began as a cant term meaning good, but was downgraded by a respectable world that took it as read that what was good to a criminal or gypsy – the primary users of cant – must *de facto* be bad by the standards of the 'establishment' world, there can be little doubt that this espousal of the style by the Black world vastly encouraged and extended its use. The same social if not the same linguistic reverse, can be found in **cut-throat** and **hardhead**, terms that are found outside America, meaning simply a villain, but in certain contexts within the US can be seen as congratulatory. And just as the meaning of 'bad' is subject to the person who is using it, so too have a number of the terms, coined by African Americans in celebration of their own identity, been used negatively by their White opponents. An early example was the christening of those late-19th-century Southerners who fought for Black rights as **Black Republicans**, but the majority of these terms come from the 1960s, the era first of Civil Rights and subsequently of Black Power (the political movement created by the Black leaders Stokely Carmichael and H. Rap Brown around 1966). Thus the word **rights** itself was sometimes turned into 'riots', by those who refused to see, with Martin Luther King, that for African Americans, such outpourings, however destructive, were indeed 'the voices of the unheard'. (Blacks preferred the terms 'Black Power dance' and referred to themselves as 'Black 360 degrees' and 'all-original' – this latter a possible source for today's rap terms *O.G.* or *original gangsta* – while preaching revolution was 'blowing Black'). But the usual form of mockery came in nothing more subtle than sarcasm and sneers. Terms like **blood** or **bleed** (a fellow-Black) and **brother** (especially as **the brothers**, a generic for all Black men) could be rendered empty boasts with the right, White tone of voice.

It is however what one might term the downside of the revolution, the accommodation with White life and standards, that brings the majority of opprobrious terms, used by Blacks to other Blacks. Of all these the best-known must be **Uncle Tom**, and its derivatives, such as plain **Tom**, **Mr Tom**, **Mr Thomas** and **Dr. Thomas**. The term has created a number of derivatives, including the 1990s' take on **Uncle Tom**: a tattle-tale, who only befriends his fellows (typically at work) to inform against them later; **tom-a-lee** (1940s/60s): a Black so subservient that he might have served under the arch-Confederate general Robert E. Lee, and **Tom Slick** (1950s/70s): a Black police informer (as is a **pig brother**, using the slang equation of *pig* and policeman). Verb combinations include **tom** itself, used verbally as a synonym for grovelling; **play the tom**, to act in a toadying manner around Whites; **tom-and-try** (1960s/70s): to advance oneself professionally by conforming to White stereotypes of Blackness, and **tom out** (1950s/70s): to inform against one's fellow Blacks. All of which terms come from a single source: the anti-slavery classic *Uncle Tom's Cabin*, by Harriet

Beecher Stowe (1811-96) and published in Boston on March 20, 1852.

Melodramatic and grossly sentimental, *Uncle Tom* concentrates on the suffering endemic to slavery. Pious old Uncle Tom, the idealized contented slave, is sold by his well-intentioned if feckless Kentucky owner Mr Shelby, who needs the money to pay his debts. His first owner is the sensitive, idealistic Augustine St Clair, and in his house Tom becomes the favourite of St Clair's daughter, the saintly little Eva. Such happiness proves shortlived: both Eva and St Clair die and this time Tom is sold to Simon Legree, role-model for generations of brutal plantation owners. In the end Legree beats the hapless Tom to death. A parallel plot recounts the escape to freedom of another of Mr Shelby' slaves, Eliza, who with her infant daughter crosses the frozen lakes to Canada. The book ends with a paean to religiosity, with a mass exodus of the survivors to Africa where, Black and White, they begin a new life as missionaries. Mrs Stowe, the daughter of one pastor and the wife of another, had taken her story from the real-life memoir of a slave, Josiah Henson, who had escaped to Canada. Later, with the book a world-wide success, she created a more suitable myth for its inception: 'God wrote it,' she revealed, 'I merely wrote his dictation.' Either way, it was a massively influential book: the first printing, of 5,000 copies, sold out in week. It topped the million in just sixteen months. That said, its suffocating religiosity, which unsurprisingly endeared Mrs Stowe to Queen Victoria when the two women met in 1859, makes the novel more of a tract than a story. It has also meant that the name of 'Uncle Tom' himself, once the embodiment of goodness and, ironically, an inspiration for those who supported Black aspirations, came by the mid-20th century to represent for the militant descendants of those same slaves, the epitome of cavilling collaboration with the oppressor.

Nor is tom the only description of Blacks who are considered overly friendly to Whites. **Sam**, from the song 'Old Black Sam', means just the same, although there may be a further nudge in the direction of **Uncle Sam**, the embodiment of White America, as well as another 'uncle'. A **processed mind** denotes one who prefers a White perspective on life; the term comes from a *process*: a method of straightening one's kinky hair. **Black fay**, with its use of ofay (see *Colour)* mixes one colour with the other, while **an apple in the White folks' yard** is a

Southern term that refers to a Black person who is very well thought of by Whites. The **faded boogie** (i.e. a Black who has 'lost his colour') apes Whites and loses his own ethnicity; the **handkerchief head** or **hankie-head** (an Arab in other contexts) is a female tom, the headscarf tied at her neck the emblem of her subservience to White stereotyping. The mammy incarnate, Aunt Jemima, she of the now-dead fast-food chain, is her personification. (*Jemima*, without qualification, can mean in slang the female genitals). The **shuffle** is a Black man deliberately playing dumb and acting out the White man's stereotyped view of his race; the shuffling walk, along with a shiny smile and natural rhythm are major parts of this image. A piece of rather contrived Harlem slang, from the 1940s, has **bouncy on one's deuce of benders,** i.e. bobbing up and down and in other words bowing and scraping. Finally the adjective **seddity** describes this kow-towing process; no concrete etymology has been established, but it would appear to come from the standard English word *absurdity*. **Hincty**, which may come from *honky* but otherwise defies etymologists, means the same thing. The verb to **show one's colour** means to act in a stereotyped 'Negro' way; to behave in the way Whites expect Blacks to do; the phrase is an ironic reversal of the more usual *show one's colours*: to declare one's own standpoint, to act proudly despite any opposition. The term **okey-dokey** is another play on a standard term, meaning White standards and values, it presumably refers not to the variation on OK, but to the White Okies, whose Depression era poverty drove them west in search of a better life and possibly to *Joe Doakes*: generic slang for a White man. In American slang a *White-on-White* is a White Cadillac with White interior finish and White upholstery; thus **White-on-White-in-White** is a Black person who seeks the supposed status of association with White people, especially through a White girlfriend and a White Cadillac; the opposite, at least in automobile terms, is logically *black-on-black*: an all-black Cadillac. South Africa's mixed race 'coloureds' decry those among them who **try for White**.

One group of names play with foods to create the Black/White mix. The classic term Oreo, is the brand-name of a popular American biscuit or cookie that is composed of two disc-shaped chocolate wafers separated by sugar cream filling and is thus 'Black on the outside but White within'; in this context it refers to one whose opinions, attitudes, lifestyle and goals are all taken from White society and standards. The same goes for England's equivalent, the **bounty bar**, while America adds **fudgsicle**, although this ice-cream bar is in fact all-chocolate; the reference presumably is to the equation, irrespective of colour, of frozen food with ice and snow, and thus Whiteness. Nor are such terms limited to these Black wannabes. Native Americans characterize their fellows who yearn for assimilation as **apples**: red on the outside but White under the skin or, punningly, as **Uncle Tomahawks**. **Tonto** is a synonym, drawn on the 1950s television programme The Lone Ranger in which Tonto (played by Jay Silverheels) played the masked man's 'Red Indian' sidekick, best-remembered for his cod-Indian interjections, notably the phrase 'Kemo sabay' with which he addressed the Ranger. **Banana** (yellow on the outside and White inside) fulfils the same function for the Chinese. Mexicans have turned the avuncular images and the food into a single phrase, **Tio Taco** ('Uncle Taco') which describes any Mexican who is considered insufficiently nationalistic by his peers. The Hispanic equivalent is a **coconut**, while in Nazi Germany a **beefsteak Nazi** was 'brown' (the Nazi colour) on the outside but 'red' (that of Communism) inside.

More than a century after its formal destruction, the nomenclature of slavery returns in house nigger or **H.N.**, a term that recalls the division in slavery times between house and field slaves. The former, used as servants and thus relatively pampered compared with those who worked in the plantation fields, are seen in the 20th century as comfortable, middle-class figures, often employed by an otherwise White organization as their 'token' Black or **showcase nigger**. The **field nigger**, on the contrary, is the street-smart Black, working class, probably alienated from any form of mainstream society, and the very image of the 'Black underclass' so regularly pontificated upon. Extended to **big house nigger**, the former can also mean a proud, even arrogant Black person, although to what extent this pride is based upon the reflected glory of the White 'massa' is unknown. Paradoxically, while in the US 'field' denotes rough and poor, in the West Indies it can mean quite the opposite. As defined by the Caribbean lexicographer Richard Allsopp it is 'a Black person who shows shameless deference to Whites'. Unless this is a mistake, it quite overturns the normal hierarchy of the slave system.

Finally there is a phrase as redolent as any of the whole psychology of the European imperialist mindset. Writing in *The Times* in 1898, Rudyard Kipling coined the phrase **White man's burden** is his eponymous poem. It called upon America, a country that Kipling recognized as moving, whatever its pious evasions might aver, into the heart of the imperial status quo, subsequent to its war with Spain over Cuban independence and the conquest of the Philippines that followed. The White man, by whom Kipling without the slightest irony meant the civilized world, had a duty to care for subject people of other races in its colonial possessions. The idea that the 'White' culture might have a downside, that the antipathy the subject peoples felt might be engendered not by ungratefulness but by the genuine desire to be rid of these unwanted, arrogant 'guardians', was beyond Kipling's perception. It would be unfair to rewrite late-19th-century history with the perceptions of today, and Angus Wilson has suggested (in *The Strange Ride of Rudyard Kipling*, 1977) that Kipling's possibly excessive outpourings represented his very real fears of foreign 'non-White' anarchy. But even if the White man's burden was indeed a duty (and not as it has often been misinterpreted, the 'fluttered folk and wild' themselves), and Kipling saw only drudgery and rarely delight in imperial rule, the concepts he proposes and the stereotypes he defends make this a piece of unrivalled racism, a luxuriously appointed display-case of every prejudice that underpinned the imperial era. Nor was it Kipling's sole poem of the type. In 1902 he published 'The Song of the White Man', in which he hymned 'the road that the White men tread | When they go to clean a land' and noted 'the faith that the White Men hold | When they build their homes afar | "Freedom for ourselves and freedom for our sons | And failing freedom, War" '.

Fortune-teller.

LUCK

THE DEVIL'S children have the Devil's luck, say the English, and if the resentment of what appears to be others' good fortune is one of our less charming, but more understandable, characteristics as humans, it is hardly suprising that it finds a place in the armoury of racial antagonisms. Bad enough that these wretched 'others' should exist; that they should enjoy the benefits of good fortune as well – it simply isn't be be borne.

Perhaps it is their association with slantedness and 'not-quite-straightness' that has the Chinese linked with luck, usually with the implication that it has come unfairly. Whatever the reason a **Chinaman's** or **Chinese chance** is no chance at all, or at best a very slim chance; the phrase comes from the mid-19th-century California Gold Rush when the Chinese immigrants, denied the opportunity to file proper, potentially lucrative claims, were reduced to working mines that had been tried and long-since abandoned as useless. On US campuses a **Chinese B** (1950s) is a grade higher than a student's actual performance justifies; it is awarded from some form of affirmative action – at that time often aimed at otherwise disadvantaged Chinese students. The 'slanted' image can be seen in various sporting terms: baseball's **chinese blow** and **chinese homer,** the first a lucky hit, the second a home run that barely clears the outfield wall, and is thus seen as lucky; cricket, another bat-and-ball game, gives a **Chinese cut**, a shot that sends the ball in a direction quite other than that which was initially intended (although the Chinese imagery is quite suitable – given the 'slanted' stereotype – a **Surrey cut** or **Harrow cut** can mean just the same thing, now with a implication of ill-deserved luck rather than slantedness). America's **Chinese national anthem** refers derisively to an explosion, typically that of a weapon, that is far enough away for the speaker to find it amusing rather than frightening. The Australian phrase **I must have killed a Chinaman** is a widely used way of explaining away one's sudden spate of bad luck.

Apart from China, these terms are widely spread. Holland's **per arabier**: 'by an Arab' means through an irony of fate or, in student slang, by a fluke. **Nigger luck**, in America, describes any piece of good luck (and one should remember the American habit, now singularly unacceptable, of rubbing a Black child's nappy hair for luck), while a **White man's chance**, deliberately contrasted with the Chinaman's chance, means a good chance, as naturally deserved by a superior race. **Irish luck**, or more commonly the **luck of the Irish**, also means good fortune, with the proviso that it can often be meant ironically, and implies a degree of unfairness. A **Scotch prize**, in naval use, is a capture made more by luck than judgement, and **Scotch seamanship** indicates a degree of naval prowess marked by sheer luck rather than intelligence. The French phrase **avoir une chose d'agraco**: 'to get something from a Greek', means to get a windfall or to have unexpected luck, while Italy's **aver preso il turco pei baffi**: 'to have seized the Turk by his whiskers' is to have had special luck in some venture.

GEOGRAPHY

Out of the Way

T HAT SOMEWHERE is so far out of the way, so back-of-beyond, so utterly insignificant as to render it and its inhabitants virtually non-existant is always a surefire means of insult. It may be as much socially as racially based, but the images blur. The best-known of what might be termed 'non-places' is **Timbuktu**, in reality a perfectly solid place, with upwards of 20,000 citizens, albeit sited in Mali, in the Sahara. Once a prosperous commercial and cultural centre it was founded by the Tuareg in the 11th century and by the 14th was a major meeting place for nomads crossing the desert. Its gold trade was widely known. It remained a centre of Muslim learning until the 16th century but after it was sacked by the Moroccans in 1593 it never recovered. The French made it part of their empire in 1893.

Timbuktu is unquestionably real, but there are many other such places, real and otherwise. **Ginny** or **Guinea Gall** is an Afro-American coinage, based on Guinea, the African state from which so many slaves had come. Other American terms include **B. Luther Hatchett,**

Diddy-Wah-Diddy, Zar, Regular Hell and **West Hell**. Australia has **Nar Nar Goon** (from the real-life *Nar Nar Goon*, a small town south-east of Melbourne) and **Oodnagalahbi** (from *Ooodna(datta)*: a small town in Western Australia and the slang term *galah*, meaning a fool). Back in America, **Hoboken**, a perfectly well-known town in New Jersey, birthplace indeed of Frank Sinatra, has been condemned to this notional outer darkness, the reason being perhaps that the word *hobo*, meaning tramp, is contained in its name (which is in fact of Native American origin). Other American 'nowheres' include **East Jesus**, **Hog Island, Hog Town** and **Hog Waller**. Similarly **Dog Town** makes the roster, as do **Dog Holler, Dog Ridge, Dogtail Corners** and **Dogtrot Hollow**; the *locus classicus*, albeit fictional, is *Dogpatch* the home of the cartoon character 'L'il Abner'.

The Wrong Side of the Tracks

From invisible towns to neighbourhoods, usually with an ethnic slant. **Black Bottom**, otherwise a dance of the 'Roaring 20s', is the African American side of town, as is **Black Town, Dark Town** (as in the 'Darktown Strutters' of musical fame), **Niggertown** (as cited by Whites), **Jig Town, Ginger Town** and the **Black Belt. Egypt**, which means just the same, is at least a variation on the theme. The same construction goes for a variety of races. Thus one finds **Bean Town** (Mexicans), **Dutch Town** (Germans) and **Wop Town** (Italians) as well as **Jew Town**. This last (which remains the name of the old Jewish Quarter of Cochin, the spice-trading centre of South India, once populated by Jews) has a number of synonyms, most of which involve some form of play on the name of an actual town. They include **Yidney** (Sydney, Australia), **Jew York, Jew Nersey** (New Jersey), and **Jew Norker**. Both a **Bronx Indian** and **Brooklyn Indian** are Jews. A **Nuyorican, Newyorican** or **Neorican** is a New York-dwelling Puerto Rican. **Cork** (or **Cork Hill** or **Corktown**) and **Dublin**, both cities in the republic of Ireland, are synonymous with the Irish part of town. A fictional Irish town, **Balahack, Ballyhack** or **Ballywack** is used to euphemize hell. Thus the phrases **all to ballyhack**: in a terrible state (literally 'all to hell') and **go to ballyhack**. The word comes from the

Irish *baile*, meaning town and *heck*, another, softer version of hell. **Hell** itself, in the form of **hell's bottom, hell's hollow, hell's kitchen** or **hell's point** (tough place) means the dangerous part of town.

Boghoppers and Wetbacks

Physical geography – hills, mountains, swamps and the like – provide their own small lexicon. Moving through a swamp or bog, jumping carefully from one tuft of reasonably solid grass to the next was known in Ireland as bog-trotting. The word, if not the activity, moved with the Irish immigrants and in both Britain and America the Irish were christened **bog-trotters** from the mid-18th century on. Allied terms included **bogger, boglander, bog-hopper** and **bog-rat, peat-cutter** and **turf-cutter** (both from the use of peat to provide heat in Ireland's peasant cottages) and the phrase **down the banks**, denoting failure. The phrase comes from the steep banks found in peat bogs, those who fell off them rolled down into the deep, peaty water. A **swamp-yankee** began life meaning a rustic New England peasant or farmer, but was later generalized to mean any old-stock New Englander not of the upper classes. In Papua New Guinea **doti wara** meaning 'dirty water', as well as menstrual blood, applies to a native of the Sepik province. The river Sepik runs brown. The American term **wetback**, for an illegal Mexican immigrant, refers to the Rio Grande, running for many miles along the border dividing Mexico from the US. Immigrants chance their luck by swimming across the river, thus getting their backs, and everything else wet; most are promptly caught and sent home. Many try again, equally fruitlessly.

Mountains form the basis of several terms for the Appalachians, the poorest of America's poor Whites. Their nicknames include **mountie, mountaineer, mountain-boomer** (*boomer* in this case meaning a tramp) and **mountain-hoosier** (from *hoosier*: a peasant). Mountains also underpin the Danish phrase **islandske lover**, a phrase that literally means 'Iceland lions', and as such is synonymous with snakes in Ireland or mountains in Holland, i.e. the non-existant. A **moffen-zon**: a 'German sun' (or **poepenzon**: a 'poop' sun) is for the Dutch a sun which fools the onlooker: it shines but is immediately followed by a downpour. The **land of the rising sun**, beloved of cliché-mongers everywhere, is of course Japan. Gypsies, in England, are **bush-coves** (from the bushes in which they lurk and the slang term *cove*: a man), while in America **son of the forest** is a somewhat romantic image of a Native American. Another term, **vanishing american**, is more to the point. Distance, rather than vegetation gives the phrases **like a Welsh mile**: tedious and overly drawn-out and the German **schweizer Meile**: a short mile. **Spanish waves** are large and formidable billows, the reference is possibly to the destruction of the Spanish Armada, wrecked on the Scottish and Irish coasts as it fled its defeat in the Channel. **Čina**: China, in Czech, means rough weather, while an **Indian summer** (1778), a supposedly neutral term, may well come from the alleged duplicity of Indians, i.e. summer seems to be over and then it pops up again. Germany's **St Simon Jud**: 'St Simon the Jew' is October 28, a day that, like England's St Swithin's Day (which, if it is wet, is traditionally the precursor of 40 more days of sodden weather) is supposed to be cold and dreary, and as such ominous. As the rhyming proverb has it 'St. Simon the Jew brings the winter before it's due'.

England's capital London gives **London ivy**, either the smoke of London, which 'clings' to buildings and blackens them or to that thick London fog, also known as a **London particular**, both of which vanished with the passing of the Clean Air Act of the early 1950s, although not before the Russians coined the term **tumnnyj albión**: foggy Albion. Finally there is pure compass-work. In America, where regionalism is still fiercely contested, simple direction is sufficient to give cause for resentment. Thus **southron** (a term that orginally meant the English as opposed to the Scottish), a **southerner**, in northern, abolitionist use; a **northerner**, the southern term for those who live north of the Mason-Dixon Line (America's north-south divide) and thus were opponents during the Civil War, and both **easterner** and **down-easterner**: a New Englander. Direction also backs up a pair of Australian terms. **Head over turkey** means Australia, on the basis of the country being at the 'bottom of the world' and a **Mexican** is anyone from 'south of the border', thus a Victorian seen from New South Wales or a New South Walter or Victorian viewed from Queensland.

This Land is Your Land

Although the combination of a racial nickname and the suffix –*land* has been covered in a variety of sections, thus covering **Paddyland, Hunland, Japland, Hulaland** and so on, there remain a few others of the type still unaccounted for. **Aussieland** is Australia, **Yodelland** or **Yodelania** is Switzlerand, giving **yodeller** and **yodellander** as Swiss, and **Jazzland** means America. This was very much a media creation. Jazz hardly travelled with the Pilgrim Fathers: it arrived in America, as a music and as a word in the late-19th century, taking root among the Black population of New Oreleans. It came, or at least the music seems to have done, from Africa, and at best guess so too did the word, linking this Black music to the African West Coast, whence many slaves were imported; in America it meant 'hurry up' and was used as such in Creole dialect to name the fast, syncopated music that had emerged in New Orleans. Today jazz is generally associated with a musical style, which definition it gained in the 1920s: it had first appeared in New York in 1915, pioneered by Freddie Keppard's Creole Band; few registered the show, far more acknowledged a second arrival, in 1917, played by Nick LaRocca's Original Dixieland Jazz Band at the smart Reisenweber's Restaurant. From there on jazz primarily meant music. Nonetheless there were those, both Black and White, who acknowledged the background. As *Etude* magazine put it in 1924, 'If the truth were known about the origin of the word "Jazz" it would never be mentioned in polite society', and three years later America's *Journal of Abnormal & Social Psychology* declared that 'the word jazz...used both as a verb and as a noun to denote the sex act...has long been common vulgarity among Negroes in the South'.

Minor Features

Names, both national and personal, have been dealt with elsewhere, but this section deals with what might be termed geographical names; towns, cities and the like. Thus for Czechs **Polsko**, usually Poland, can also mean flatlands, from the featureless Polish landscape, rolling east to Russia. A **kramer**, otherwise spelt **krajner**, **greiner**, **griner** or even

grinder, refers to Kranjsko, a district in Slovenia from which many early immigrants came. Thus in Germany a **kramer** is a Slovene immigrant. Austrian dialect has **Jauk**, a wind that comes from the south of Carinthia and which, since it is a modification of the word *Jauche* (meaning suds or ditch-water) is intended to insult the Slovenes to whom it refers. The German **kaschubsch**: Kashubian (referring to an area of Pomerania) means out of order, malfunctioning or fitting badly.

Votjaka, a city in the Udmurtskaja ASSR, is used to categorize all the national minorities in what was once northern USSR, while **samody**, from the Finnish *Sameaena*: 'Lapland', covers those in the far north, West Siberia and the northern Russian coastal areas. Lapland also offers the phrase **as tedious as a Lapland day**, meaning extremely long and based on the long northern summers, when night barely falls. **Galician**, properly meaning a native of Galicia, set in East Poland and West Russia, was used in America and Canada as a less than complimentary description of any Central European immigrant. A Yiddish equivalent, **Galizianer**, used by Russian or Lithuanian Jews of their Polish peers, condemns anyone seen as fawning or overly subservient to their Christian neighbours. **Arkies** and **Okies** are both poor American farmers, from respectively Arkansas and Oklahoma; both were forced from their land during the Depression, and as recounted in such books as John Steinbeck's *Grapes of Wrath* (1939), made their painful way west to seek some form of employment in California. **Nashville**, usually seen as the capital of country and western music, is used by African Americans as a synonym for any unsophisticated, suburban, middle-American town or person.

SELECTED BIBLIOGRAPHY

Rather than offer a bibliography, which would cover a great many sources, few of which have been used to a major extent, I have chosen to list those books upon which I have drawn most consistently. As may be imagined, these are mainly dictionaries. Other works, when pertinent, are listed in the text.

Barrère, Albert. *Argot & Slang.* (London, 1902)

Brewer's *Dictionary of Phrase and Fable.* (London, 1994)

B.E. Gent. *A New Dictionary of the Terms ancient and modern of the Canting Crew...* (London, *c.*1690)

Farmer, John & Henley, W.E. *Slang and Its Analogues.* (7 vols. London, 1890)

Grose, Captain Francis. *A Classical Dictionary of the Vulgar Tongue.* (London,1785)

Hotten, John Camden. *The Slang Dictionary.* (London, 1857)

Maledicta: The International Journal of Verbal Aggression (1977-)

Mencken, H.L. *The American Language.* (rev. edn. New York 1936, 1945, 1948)

Partridge, Eric. *Dictionary of Slang and Unconventional English.* (8th edn. ed. Paul Beale London, 1984)

Roback, Abraham. *A Dictionary of International Slurs.* (New York, 1944)

Rosten, Leo. *Hooray for Yiddish!* (London, 1983)

Ware, J. Redding. *Passing English of the Victorian Era.* (London, 1909)

Wentworth, Harold, and Flexner, Stuart Berg. *Dictionary of American Slang.* (2nd Supplemental ed. New York, 1975)

Yule, Henry & Burnell, A.C. *'Hobson-Jobson'. A Glossary of Colloquial Anglo-Indian Words and Phrases* (London, 1886)

INDEX

gin-masher 203
Ginny 37
Ginny Gall 346
gin-shepherd 203
gin-stealer 203
ginzo 37
gip 139
gippo 162
gippy 162
gippy tummy 253
giudeaccio 100
giudeo 324
giudesco 100
give a Chinaman a music
lesson 89
gjore av sigi svenske 335
Glasgow kiss 302
Glasgow magistrate 149
glimpse 45
gluchorniemcy 287
glupi swabi 286
go ape 228
go back to Africa 203
go Borneo 175
go-ghetto 268
God's image cut in ebony
28, 275
Godamland 65
goddam 65
Godless country 275
go-ghetto 268
going to Egypt 188
Goldberg 52
golden ghetto 272
golden girl 47
gombay 28
gone coon 225
goo-goo 66, 111
goober-grabber 160
Good ol' boy 48
gook 66
goolie 195
goon 310
gooney 289
gooney-gal 289
goose 236
Gorbals kiss 302
go the whole coon 225
Goths 307
go to ballyhack 347
go to Mexico 175

go to the Bahamas 296
go turkey 273
Goulash 149
Gourock ham 149
gourouni 231
gou ti-ze 311
goy 274
goyishe kop 274
goyisher mazzl 274
Grèce 295
graesk Bjoning 221
gran Turco 163
grand Flandrin 334
grand Turk 133
grape-stomper 333
grass-skirt 221
gray 46
gray-cat 46
gray-dude 46
gray-nayga 45
gray-skin 46
grease-boy 162
grease-gut 162
greaseball 162
greaser 162
grechesco 98
grecheskaya kukhin-
isterskaya 166
Grecian 83
Grecian accent 70
Grecian bender 221, 250
greckosj 163
grecoteu 98
greek 63, 152, 193, 215
Greek back 250
Greek bottom 215
Greek credit 321
Greek cry 141
Greek culture 215
Greekdom 99
Greek ease 334
Greek fashion 215
Greek fire 181
Greek hash-house 166
Greek love 215
Greek mother 99
Greek puzzle 79
Greeks 83
Greek side 215
Greek trust 143
Greek way 212, 215

green 41
greenhorn 246
green nigger 41
greiner 350
Greta 118
Gretchen 118
Grey 45, 46
grey-bo 45
grey-boy 46
grey-broad 46
grey-owl 45
grey puss 45
grill 166
grim as a Swiss guard
313
grinder 351
griner 350
gringo 82
gris pik 162
grit-sucker 169
grubość niemiecka 167
Guddas 131
Gudde 131
guessers 67
gu-gu 66
guin 37
guinal 100
guinaliser 100
guinea 36
guinea football 37
Guinea Gall 346
guinea red 180
guinea-negro 36
guino 100
guinzo 37
gulley-digger 279
gully-jumper 49
gunjie 50
guppy-gobbler 148
gwei lo 80, 275
gyp 139
gyp artist 139
gyp flat 139
gyp joint 139
gyp moll 139
gyp racket 139
gypoo 162
gypper 139
gyppery 139
gyppo 139
gypsy 139, 333

INDEX